CW01024123

EXTRALEGAL GROUPS IN POST-CONFLICT LIBERIA

Extralegal Groups in Post-Conflict Liberia

How Trade Makes the State

CHRISTINE CHENG

OXFORD
UNIVERSITY PRESS

Great Clarendon Street, Oxford, OX2 6DP,
United Kingdom

Oxford University Press is a department of the University of Oxford.
It furthers the University's objective of excellence in research, scholarship,
and education by publishing worldwide. Oxford is a registered trade mark of
Oxford University Press in the UK and in certain other countries

First Edition published in 2018

Impression: 2

Published in the United States of America by Oxford University Press
198 Madison Avenue, New York, NY 10016, United States of America

British Library Cataloguing in Publication Data

Data available

Library of Congress Control Number: 2017963787

ISBN 978–0–19–967334–6

Printed and bound by
CPI Group (UK) Ltd, Croydon, CR0 4YY

To 媽媽 and 爸爸, for all of your love, and your sacrifices.

Acknowledgments

Writing this book has been a labor of love, and there are many, many people who have helped bring it into existence.

To My Friends in Africa

First, I owe a deep debt to my West African and ex-pat friends and colleagues. I arrived in Monrovia in 2005, uncertain about whether elections would bring violence back to the country. Thankfully, I developed an incredible support network of people who housed me, fed me, shared their thoughts about the country with me, and transported me around Monrovia and deep into the Liberian bush. I will never be able to repay them for their individual kindnesses; I can only promise to pay it forward to others.

From my time in Liberia, Sierra Leone and Côte d'Ivoire, I would like to thank Ashley Barr, Aine Bhreathnagh, Nathaniel Barnes, Johnson Bohr, Cholo Brooks, Raul Carrera, Matt Chessen, Cara Chester, Tyler Christie, Sophia Craig, Varfee Dorley, Derek Frank, Christopher Gabelle, Benoît Gauthier, Ibrahim Idris, Daniel Johnson, Emmanuel Jones, Kathryn Joseph, Taziff Koroma, Eliane Kraft, Erin McCandless, Boima Metzger, Bino Mohammed, John Morlu, Muchiri Murenga, Gloria Ntegeye, Chipo Nyambuya, Lietenant-General Chikadibia Obiakor, Sadie O'Mahoney, Paavani Reddy, Henry Reed, Philip Samways, Sophia Swithern, Byron Tarr, Simon Taylor, Victor Tweh, Alice Vahanian, Jerome Verdier, Dave and Audrey Waines, Patrick Wandobusi, Esther Wisseh, and Mohamed Yahya. Thanks also go to Brett Bruen and Sheka Mansaray for being fantastic hosts in Abidjan and Freetown respectively. It was a wonderful coincidence to reconnect with both of them in West Africa.

In Liberia, Wayne Bleier, Alfred Brownell, Francis Colee, Gabriel Frailich, Beth Eggleston, Margaret Hall, Kay Schweidinger, and Evariste Sibomana were generous friends. They provided me with great conversations, an instant social life, and constant encouragement. When I had nowhere to stay, they found me housing; when I had no internet connection, they gave me their passwords; when I was worried about being evacuated from the country, they provided reassurance. Having friends like these made everything possible—I appreciate their support and the support of their organizations (IOM, UNMIL, Oxfam, MERLIN, Christian Children's Fund, Save the Children UK, and UNDP).

In the fall of 2003, I also spent a formative period conducting independent research on gangs and post-conflict violence in South Africa, laying the groundwork for my extralegal groups work. I was hosted by Greg Mills and Elizabeth Sidiropoulos at the South African Institute for International Affairs (SAIIA) at the University of the Witswatersrand and also by Wilfred Scharf at the Institute of Criminology at the University of Cape Town. I want to thank all three of them for giving me an institutional home and for taking a chance on someone who had zero research experience and didn't really know what she was doing.

To My Academic Colleagues

Back home, I have benefited from membership in six vibrant intellectual communities which helped shape the direction of the project. I am profoundly grateful to: Princeton's Woodrow Wilson School, Oxford's Nuffield College, Yale's Order, Conflict, and Violence Program, Global Affairs Canada, Oxford's Exeter College, and King's College London's Department of War Studies. In each of these institutions, I have found inspiring mentors who have shaped the kind of scholar I am today. For their encouragement and advice, I would like to thank Mats Berdal, Richard Caplan, Chris Dandeker, Diego Gambetta, James Gow, Andy Hurrell, Ned Lebow, Neil MacFarlane, Funmi Olonisakin, Sarah Percy, Margit Tavits, Jennifer Welsh, Ngaire Woods, and Dominik Zaum.

Before I began my doctoral studies, I was mentored by some extraordinary individuals. They gave me the most valuable thing they had: their time. At different points in my career, all of them have offered me wise counsel. Among these generous souls are Rick Barton, David Black, Lois Claxton, John English, Bob Hutchings, and David Johnston.

My Oxford DPhil supervisor, Dave Anderson, gave me complete freedom to take the project in whatever direction I wanted, right from the start. Our conversations together always redoubled my excitement about the work, and spurred a frenzy of new ideas. I owe Dave a great intellectual debt, for helping me figure out what I wanted to do, and then pushing me to pragmatically "get on with it." I couldn't have asked for a more inspiring mentor.

Many others have also taken the time to substantively engage with this project over the years. I want to express my appreciation to Séverine Autesserre, Gina Bateson, Nancy Bermeo, Johanna Boersch-Supan, Michael Bratton, Tereza Capelos, Richard Caplan, Christopher Clapham, Anna Dimitrijevics, Diego Gambetta, Andrea Garaiova, Tim Glawion, Carolyn Haggis, Macartan Humphreys, Andrew Hurrell, Matt Kocher, Zachariah Mampilly, Harris Mylonas, Kieran Mitton, Joe Scott, Ricardo Soares de Oliveira, Ruben Reike, and Oisin Tansey. At different stages, each of them provided extensive comments and helped me work through my ideas—and this project is all the richer for their contributions. My Ph.D. student Alison Brettle provided many hours of research support by jumpstarting the redrafting process with me, and then pored over draft chapters with me. Our long conversations about war and statebuilding helped solidify my arguments in the final chapter, and I am extremely grateful for her assistance.

At King's, I feel fortunate to have found so many colleagues who I consider to be true friends. For bringing joy to the Strand and making me laugh, I want to thank Charles Alao, Birthe Anders, Mats Berdal, Rebekka Friedman, Dylan Hendrickson, Jana Krause, Kieran Mitton, Funmi Olonisakin, Domitilla Sagramoso, Oisin Tansey, Sarah von Billerbeck, and Barney Walsh. I also want to thank my superb MA students in my Conflict, Security, and Development seminars and my State Failure and Statebuilding classes. This book is all the richer because of our challenging discussions together.

I am also grateful to three great heads of department—Mervyn King, Theo Farrell, and Mike Rainsborough—who protected me from REF pressures and allowed me to write the book that I wanted to write, rather than the book that had to be written to meet REF timing. In today's academic pressure cooker, it is rare for a scholar in the British social sciences to have the luxury of time to rethink and refine her ideas—this would not have been possible if Mervyn, Theo, and Mike had not made the space for me to do so.

I am fortunate to have received funding for this project. I would like to thank the Social Science and Humanities Council of Canada (SSHRC), the Overseas Research Scheme (ORS), Global Affairs Canada, Exeter College, and the Department of War Studies at King's College London for their institutional support. For scholarships, fieldwork support, and conference funding, I would like to thank Nuffield College, the Norman Chester Fund, the British Federation of Women Graduates (BFWG), the Canadian Centennial Scholarship Fund, and the Oxford Research Network on Government in Africa (OReNGA).

For having the patience of saints, I want to thank Olivia Wells and Dominic Byatt at Oxford University Press.

To My Friends and Family

I will always be indebted to my brilliant friend Bindiya Patel for encouraging me to pursue this project all those years ago, when it was still a pie-in-the-sky idea. I am also grateful to my dear friends, Tereza Capelos, Veronica Chau, Jeff Colgan, Colin Provost, Mony Singh, Robin Spano, and Shirley Yee, for cheering me on to the finish line and for being their lovely, kind selves.

This project would have been impossible without the steadfast support of my extended family. Balancing an academic career and raising a child "takes a village," as they say. I'm grateful to my brother Vincent and my sister-in-law Sohanya who are always there when I need them. And I am forever indebted to my in-laws, Joe and Diane Scott. They have supported me in small and big ways, from cooking dinners to helping us move house to sharing their life wisdom. They are masters of kindness and compassion and I consider myself unbelievably lucky to have them in my life and to be part of the Scott family.

Completing this research has entailed sacrifices, and my husband Dave and my son Miles have borne the brunt of these sacrifices. Like many a working parent before me, I have given up family time to complete this book. Miles has always replied, "It's ok mummy, I understand." I want to thank his seven-, eight-, and nine-year old selves for saying these words, for cutting me some slack, and most of all, for reminding me of what is really important in life: sword battles, Harry Potter, chocolate buttons, knock-knock jokes, and the like.

In the background, through all of my adventures and travails, has been my husband Dave. I could not ask for a more supportive and loving partner in life. He has been my most enthusiastic cheerleader, my best friend, and an extraordinary dad. Academia has not always been a smooth ride, and he willingly traipsed across continents for me, as I uprooted our family life with five moves across three countries—and a baby in tow, no less. He has seen me through so many ups and downs, and kept me grounded throughout. I have no words to fully express my love and gratitude.

My final words go to my trail-blazing parents, who have taught me so many important life lessons and ways of seeing the world. So much of what I learned about dealing with people and empathizing with them was learned by watching my parents run their businesses. I wouldn't be half the person I am today without their love and support. From fly-in childcare to bottomless bowls of bone broth to tending our overgrown garden to fussing over my health via Skype—they have done so much to support me in my quest to write this book. I feel extremely fortunate that I've been able to rely on their unconditional love, and it is to them that I dedicate this book.

Contents

List of Figures

List of Tables

List of Abbreviations

ACS	American Colonization Society
AFC	Afrikanische Frucht Companie
AFL	Armed Forces of Liberia
BOPC	Butaw Oil Palm Company
CAP	Consolidated Appeals Process
CPA	Comprehensive Peace Agreement
DDR	Disarmament, Demobilization, and Reintegration
DDRR	Disarmament, Demobilization, Rehabilitation, and Reintegration
ECOWAS	Economic Community of West African States
ECOMIL	ECOWAS Mission in Liberia
ECOMOG	ECOWAS Monitoring Group
ECWC	Ex-combatants Welfare Committee
FDA	Forest Development Authority
FOB	Freight on Board
GoL	Government of Liberia
GRP	Guthrie Rubber Plantation
GSA	General Services Administration
IGNU	Interim Government of National Unity
IMF	International Monetary Fund
INPFL	Independent National Patriotic Front of Liberia
ITA	International Transitional Administration
LDF	Lofa Defense Force
LFDC	Liberian Forest Development Company
LFF	Liberian Frontier Force
LNP	Liberia National Police
LPC	Liberia Peace Council
LUDF	Liberia United Defense Force
LURD	Liberians United for Reconciliation and Democracy
MODEL	Movement for Democracy in Liberia
NGO	Nongovernmental Organization
NPA	National Port Authority
NPFL	National Patriotic Front of Liberia

NPRAG	National Patriotic Reconstruction Assembly Government
NTGL	National Transitional Government of Liberia
NTLA	National Transitional Legislative Assembly
NVRP	National Veteran Rehabilitation Project
ODP	Open Door Policy
OTC	Oriental Timber Company
PRC	People's Redemption Council
PTG	Post-Traumatic Growth
PTSD	Post-Traumatic Stress Disorder
RPAL	Rubber Planters Association of Liberia
RTC	Royal Timber Company
RUF	Revolutionary United Front
SCSL	Special Court of Sierra Leone
SRP	Sinoe Rubber Plantation
SRSG	Special Representative of the Secretary-General
TRC	Truth and Reconciliation Commission
TSR	Technically Specified Rubber
ULIMO	United Liberation Movement for Democracy
ULIMO-J	United Liberation Movement for Democracy-Johnson
ULIMO-K	United Liberation Movement for Democracy-Kromah
UNEP	UN Environment Programme
UNJMAC	United Nations Joint Mission Analysis Cell
UNMIL	United Nations Mission in Liberia
USAID	United States Agency for International Development
WRC	Wedjah Rubber Corporation

Introduction

"When *you* got a problem, I bet you call the police, right?" Michael said. "Well, we call the Kings. I call T-Bone because I don't have anyone else to call."

Michael Johnson, a resident in Black Kings' territory[1]
in Sudhir Venkatesh's *Gang Leader For A Day*

"The resumption of activity at [diamond] speculator sites near BOPC had been anticipated and inevitable, given the difficulties of policing the area. The potential consequences remain the same—hostile friction with locals, lawlessness, possible exploitation by warlord types and a recurrence of a plague—associated humanitarian crisis."

Briefing by UN Joint Military Analysis Centre (UNJMAC),
Sept 9, 2005[2]

On a swelteringly hot day in October 2005, I flew out to the southeastern reaches of Liberia. The morning sun was high in the sky as we headed toward an area that had been designated a national security risk. While the ink was still drying on the 2003 Comprehensive Peace Agreement, rumors of alluvial diamond deposits on Butaw Oil Palm Company plantation (BOPC) land had begun to circulate and local residents began to hunt for diamonds. A large ex-combatant population had been mining diamonds there just as the country's resource-fueled civil war had concluded. By 2005, thousands upon thousands had swarmed to the area. The BOPC plantation became one of several "hotspots" around the country that was to be controlled by ex-combatants.

The UNJMAC quote above summarizes a story that feels familiar to the region: in neighboring Sierra Leone, the Revolutionary United Front (RUF) had financed its rebellion through diamond mining, and in Liberia itself, rebel-leader-turned-president Charles Taylor had bought the RUF's diamonds and used the profits to fund his own military activities in Liberia. Not surprisingly then, there was considerable concern that BOPC diamonds would be used by one faction or another to finance a return to civil war. By 2005, even though

---

[1] Sudhir Alladi Venkatesh (2008).   [2] UN Joint Mission Analysis Cell (2005m).

Liberia's civil war had officially ended two years earlier, it was still not clear that the peace would hold. And yet, things really did seem different this time. After many attempts to end the fighting, the international community had finally chosen to invest deeply in Liberia's peace and there was a dogged determination to see it through. In this light, the ex-combatants at BOPC were viewed as peace spoilers, threatening to upend everything that had been achieved.

This concentration of diamond miners appeared threatening—many had migrated to BOPC hoping to strike it rich in the local diamond fields, and among them were many ex-combatants. This looked like the same toxic mix of ingredients which had fuelled the civil war in neighboring Sierra Leone: diamonds and rebels. Indeed, helping the transitional government to restore "proper administration of natural resources" was an essential part of the original mandate of the UN Mission in Liberia (UNMIL).[3] It was unsurprising, then, that UNMIL and Liberia's transitional government had labeled the situation a national security threat. A parade of government officials and peacekeepers alike had issued numerous warnings to stop the illegal mining in the area—to no avail. The mining continued.

Part of the problem was the location of the mining area. Travelling to this remote corner of Sinoe County was challenging. There were few roads that led to this isolated region, and the ones that did exist were unpaved. In the lead up to the BOPC visit, just about everyone I had spoken to—ex-patriates and Liberians alike—had gone out of their way to warn me that the area was dangerous, all the more so because it was "so deep in the bush." My perceptions of BOPC had also been colored by the newspaper articles referring to the local "Wild West" mentality that had taken hold. No NGOs—domestic or international—had been willing to set up programs in the area. In Monrovia, I searched for drivers who would be willing to make the twelve- to twenty–hour drive out to Sinoe County, and then accompany me on the additional eight-hour hike that led from the roadside into the gateway village of Shampe, but I could not find any who were willing to do more than drop me off at the roadside path that led to the camp.

In the end, I got to BOPC by hitching a ride on an old Ukrainian helicopter with a group of UN peacekeepers and Liberian government advisors. On the helicopter ride to BOPC, the UNMIL officers and government advisors dis-cussed the hostile reception they were expecting. Even though no one thought that the situation would become violent, two dozen Ethiopian peacekeepers had been assigned to accompany us and would arrive in advance to secure the area—just in case. I felt torn about this: arriving with two dozen armed soldiers with weapons at the ready was not going to create the kind of atmosphere that would allow for an open conversation with members of the local community. On the other hand, going out to BOPC unaccompanied seemed foolhardy (as well as logistically difficult) given the many warnings that had been issued.

---

[3] UN Security Council (2003a).

Further, the National Transitional Government of Liberia (NTGL) and UNMIL could not agree on how to best deal with this group and others like it. Besides repeatedly asking the group to leave, little action had been taken. This lack of agreement on how to proceed, a genuine and well-founded fear of violence and instability, and a variety of other factors meant that the area had largely been left to its own devices from 2003 through 2005, during the transitional government's tenure. The uncertainty about the future of the BOPC land only heightened the feeling of instability in the diamond-mining area.

So it was that I found myself on a rickety old helicopter, accompanying a group of senior UNMIL and Liberian NTGL government advisors who were jointly responsible for closing down these diamond mines. Their long-term goal was to assert central governmental control over the BOPC mines and the local leaders of the group. The purpose of the trip that day was to reiterate the government's official stance and to try, once more, to convince the miners to leave the area. Needless to say, outsiders were not popular, and no one on the helicopter expected this to be a successful visit.

* * *

Heading out from the Spriggs Payne airport in downtown Monrovia, we hugged the coast all the way out to the hinterland, with the Atlantic Ocean on one side, and endless stretches of bright green canopy on the other. When we landed in the middle of Sinoe County, I braced myself because I was not quite sure what to expect.

Upon our arrival, I was surprised to find that the gateway village of Shampe was bustling. Imported beer was being carried in on the backs of porters; a local brothel and a makeshift cinema were both open for business notwithstanding the early hour. Despite being located in one of the most remote corners of the country, the variety of goods available in the Shampe market area was comparable to the selection of goods that was available in much bigger cities like Buchanan, which was directly connected by paved road to Monrovia. There was a liveliness to the area that I had not anticipated.

By this point in my fieldwork, I had flown or driven through many different Liberian towns and villages, and it was plain to see that BOPC was home to a thriving commercial district—it was prospering in a way that most other parts of the country were not at the time. It was difficult to imagine why any resident would willingly give up this commercial success considering how poorly the rest of the countryside was faring.

All of us could sense that this area was enjoying a local economic boom, even though it had also clearly suffered during the war. In the air was bustle and movement—it felt as if the community was bouncing back. Resilient, was perhaps the word I was searching for. But it was not resilient in the way that policymakers and academics typically spoke of "resilience." There were no anointed "good" actors leading the way: no women's groups, no religious organizations, and no local NGOs. In truth, what I observed sat completely at odds with what I had been primed to expect.

On the one hand, diamond mining had been banned by the government, and there were international sanctions in place preventing the export of rough diamonds from Liberia—the vibrant market of Shampe had extralegal foundations. On the other hand, the marketplace was also a triumph of liberal market principles—the village in front of me was prospering. This was certainly resilience, but it did not come in the form that I had expected.

There were other surprises too: given what I had been told about local security conditions, I had expected to immediately sense fear, hostility, and insecurity upon our arrival. I had gradually come to trust my own instincts in smelling out fear or anger—literally.[4] But this was not the case at BOPC. I was watched carefully, but otherwise I was able to wander around on my own without feeling threatened. I sensed as much curiosity as hostility in people's body language. The peacekeepers were also present, but their stance was relaxed, with weapons at their sides. Shampe felt more like a vibrant place of commerce than a national security hotspot.

Despite being an outsider, I had also expected that it would be easy to detect signs of the coercive regime that dominated the lives of the miners and the local community. My working assumption was that these groups were dangerous and that those who lived and worked in the community would openly acknowledge this—because international peacebuilders and statebuilders from outside of BOPC had taken this as given. International officials and senior government representatives were equally fluent in their public denunciations of these groups—irrespective of their own personal views on the matter.

The rhetoric from Monrovia was that these groups were "bad" because they were operating in defiance of state authority and in defiance of the UN and the rest of the international community. Members of the public were wary of bringing back "war business" which implied violence, danger, and criminality. This was compounded by the fact that extralegal groups were constituted from the coercive power of ex-combatants, who had all been tarred by the same "bad" brush because of the horrific wartime atrocities that had been committed by all sides. In short, these groups—because of their ex-combatant members—were viewed with trepidation. Like most people, I was frightened too. I viewed these groups as harmful for consolidating peace, harmful for statebuilding, and harmful for Liberia's future prospects.

Yet, upon our arrival, the community-vs-rulers dynamic that I had expected to see was not readily apparent. What I detected instead was something more subtle: there was a coercive tension that colored people's answers to my questions (later confirmed through observation and in discussions). Nevertheless,

---

[4] On being able to smell fear, see Jasper H. B. de Groot, Gün R. Semin and Monique A. M. Smeets (2014).

there was also a clear sense of unity supporting the mining activities. By this point, it was becoming increasingly difficult to reconcile the official reports of insecurity and anarchy with the bustling commercial centre in front of me. *What was I observing and how did it come about? Who was in control?*

After fourteen years of on-and-off civil war, it felt remarkable that the people in front of me had rebuilt themselves a flourishing economy in such a short time. Yet there we were, all of us outsiders, insisting that it be shut down. It did not matter whether we represented the UN or Monrovia-based officials, we were threatening their livelihoods in pursuit of a well-intentioned, but misguided policy.[5]

Among the ex-fighters, many had been through the disarmament and demobilization process, and had even been officially "reintegrated" into the citizenry. Yet their day-to-day existence was suspended in a space somewhere between fighter and civilian. Surprisingly, ex-combatants from all of the major fighting factions were represented on the BOPC plantation, along with nearby residents and economic migrants from countries as far away as Tunisia and Libya. People who had been trying to kill each other not so long ago were now working and socializing in the same community.

Here, our respective narratives clashed: Was this a territorial enclave controlled by violent ex-combatants who were preparing themselves to return to war, or was it a thriving, informally run local business venture? Or was it both? Would shutting down Liberia's natural resource sectors actually prevent a return to war, or would this move simply push trading networks underground, making them harder to trace, and more likely to fund a new fighting faction?

In the months and years following, I re-examined the stories that had been constructed to explain BOPC and other resource enclaves like it. I asked myself: Was this environment consistent with the idea of a "security threat"? I began to question and rethink what these groups were and how I perceived their motivations.[6]

As I began to re-evaluate my prior assumptions, I realized that extralegal groups were important not only as a window into post-conflict transitions, but also that my reading of these groups was filtered through a distinctly Western lens. Initially, this perspective had led me to interpret events and actions in a way that confirmed my existing beliefs—these groups threatened the peace process and needed to be destroyed or they would wind up criminalizing the

---

[5] UN Security Council export sanctions against rough diamonds from Liberia had been instituted to prevent the Revolutionary United Front (RUF) in neighboring Sierra Leone from selling their diamonds to Charles Taylor and smuggling them out through Monrovia. The aim was to end Sierra Leone's civil war by cutting off the RUF's major source of funding. By 2005, the Sierra Leone war was long over—but the sanctions against the export of rough diamonds from Liberia remained in place, even though diamonds mined in Liberia were of considerably lower quality and value, and played a marginal role in funding Liberia's civil war.

[6] Over the past decade, a series of conversations gently nudged me in this direction. Thanks to William Beinart, Nancy Bermeo, Christopher Clapham, Andrew Hurrell, and Adrienne LeBas.

state over time.[7] But the reality on the ground was far more complex—there was much more nuance and variation to these groups and their activities than I had expected. Over time, I came to re-evaluate my own ideas of what constituted "statebuilding" and indeed, to question whether key governance functions had to be performed by the state at all.

How we react—how *I* reacted—to extralegal groups is telling. In this sense, extralegal groups serve as a useful Rorschach test:[8] our values and understandings of politics, states, and modes of governance are projected on to these groups in revealing ways.[9] While understanding the groups themselves is important for post-conflict transitions, it also became clear as the project progressed that understanding the range of *stakeholder reactions* to extralegal groups was just as vital.

There was no doubt that the BOPC group and others of its kind were critical to sustaining peace: after the war ended, they were regularly denounced on the front pages of Monrovia's newspapers as national security threats. These extralegal groups sat on the fulcrum of the war–peace seesaw; depending on which way they chose to shift their weight, the country would either remain at peace or be thrown back into war.

Yet it was too facile to say that they were "bad," or for that matter, that they were "good." It was not even clear *what* they were exactly because they did not fit neatly into any existing category of actors. Rather, extralegal groups represented forms of control that married coercion and managerialism, layered on top of local informal sociopolitical practices. What were these groups and how should we understand them?

∗   ∗   ∗

On the surface, one obvious goal of the post-conflict period is to minimize the probability of returning to war. However, key stakeholders often have clashing philosophies about how to best achieve this objective. For some, this means maximizing livelihood opportunities to ensure economic stability, while for others, nothing short of destroying the social networks of ex-combatants will do,[10] and for others still, the priority lies in destroying all local caches of small arms.

To make sense of these competing perspectives, empathy is essential.[11] On the one hand, this study examines the individual and group-based incentives

---

[7] For a full discussion of how this project evolved over time, see the final chapter to this book on Research Design Scaffolding.

[8] A Rorschach test is a widely used psychological assessment tool. Subjects are asked to interpret and discuss a series of ten inkblots. Their responses are used to diagnose personality disorders and mental health problems.

[9] For a complexity theory perspective, see Yaneer Bar-Yam and Jeff Schechtman (2016).

[10] On rethinking reintegration, see Stina Torjesen (2013) and separately, Richard Bowd and Alpaslan Özerdem (2013).

[11] This study's multi-perspective approach to post-conflict transitions was partly inspired by David Simon's TV show *The Wire*. See Helena Sheehan and Sheamus Sweeney 2009. In the same

of ex-combatants[12] who join extralegal groups. The theoretical framework shows how the emergence of extralegal groups is a product of livelihood and survival strategies constrained by the political economy of war and its aftermath. Borrowing terminology from Jonathan Goodhand, extralegal groups offer simultaneous glimpses into the combat economy, the shadow economy, and the coping economy.[13]

On the other hand, this study also analyzes the practical responses to extralegal groups that are open to the government and to international actors, taking into account the powerful social and political forces that constrain their decision-making. Each and every stakeholder must contend with its own individual goals, incentives, and constraints. Disaggregating states, rebel groups, and international organizations even further into individual and institutional-level units reveals deeper clashes between key actors as well as internal inconsistencies within organizations.

Closely examining the causal chain of decision-making in these ways adds depth to analyses of monolithic institutions like "the state," "the UN," "the international community," "ex-combatants," and "local populations." This study reveals contradictions and inconsistencies: even as donor governments (primarily from Organisation for Economic Co-operation (OECD) countries) purport to build peace and improve the capacity of the Liberian state, national economic interests of the same donor states may be simultaneously subverting this agenda. Similarly, where peacekeeping missions promise to protect the lives of civilians, the reality is that troop-contributing countries have little incentive to risk the lives of their own soldiers to protect citizens of the host country. And when political elites of post-conflict countries sign international pledges against corruption, they remain mindful of the social necessity of rewarding loyal patrons during their time in office. It is very difficult to reduce these dynamics to an ethic of "do no harm," never mind the greater aspiration of "doing good."

Because extralegal groups interact with every element of the post-conflict "ecosystem," from UN peacekeepers to local business leaders to ministerial regulators, their interactions provide unique insight into postwar statebuilding. If we can understand why people join extralegal groups, what these groups do, and what conditions facilitate their existence, then this creates a space for more creative, effective, and perhaps even radical statebuilding policies.

---

way that *The Wire* tackles the urban political economy of drugs and poverty by layering and interrogating the perspectives of key institutions (police, gangs, media, unions, schools, government), this study probes the war-to-peace dynamic by occasionally stepping into the shoes of ex-combatants, local residents, Liberian government officials, and UNMIL peacekeepers.

[12] The term combatant refers to a person who actively took part in the hostilities. It includes former fighters from all parties to the conflict. I do not use combatant in the legal sense, as defined by the International Committee of the Red Cross. See International Committee of the Red Cross (1949).

[13] Jonathan Goodhand (2004), p. 60.

WHAT IS AN EXTRALEGAL GROUP?

An extralegal group is a set of individuals with a proven capacity for violence, working outside the law primarily for profit, and providing governance functions to sustain its business interests. To relate extralegal groups to more familiar ideas, we can think of them as profit-driven nonstate armed groups or even as informal business entities backed with coercive force. They provide contract enforcement, but they exist outside the state; they trade, but their goods are prohibited; they provide a degree of local order, but they are also the greatest source of insecurity.

Their emphasis on profits rather than politics distinguishes them from warlords and rebel groups. Their willingness and capacity to use violence is key to their success; they succeed in precarious environments precisely because they attract individuals who are inclined to use force. But their violent capabilities are not what makes them interesting—rather it is their willingness to provide key governance functions that distinguishes them from related actors. *Extralegal groups' desire for profits creates the need for a stable trading environment, motivating them to provide basic governance functions, which, over time, form the kernel of the state.*

This "extralegality" underscores their nebulous status in an environment where the rule of law is deeply contested and enforced in an arbitrary manner. Even if laws exist on paper, they remain meaningless unless someone is willing to enforce them. In post-conflict environments like Liberia's, enforcement is inconsistent at best, and non-existent at worst. Consequently, it is extralegal groups and other informal authorities who de facto determine what is "legal" and what is "illegal"; they set the rules and enforce them. In these ways, they blur the lines between the formal and informal; the licit and illicit.

The existence of extralegal groups is not in itself new. Throughout history, a variety of armed nonstate actors have banded together to seek profits. Yet existing theories on related phenomena such as criminal gangs,[14] rebel rulers,[15] sobels,[16] nonstate armed groups,[17] mafias,[18] informal business networks,[19] big men in patronage systems,[20] militias-in-waiting, warlords,[21] stationary bandits,[22] and organized crime groups do not wholly capture what I observed in post-conflict Liberia, despite some commonalities. Each of these other framings highlights different characteristics. The particular frame that a

---

[14] R. T. Naylor (2001); P. Andreas (2004).
[15] Zachariah C. Mampilly (2011b); Jennifer Keister and Branislav Slantchev (2014); Ana Arjona, Nelson Kasfir and Zachariah Mampilly (2015).
[16] David Keen (1998); David Keen (2005).   [17] Annette Idler (2012).
[18] Diego Gambetta (1993); Federico Varese (2001).   [19] K. Meagher (2010).
[20] Anders Themnér (2012); Mats Utas (2012).
[21] William Reno (1998); Keith Stanski (2009); Kimberly Zisk Marten (2012).
[22] Mancur Olson (2000).

scholar chooses for studying a phenomenon like extralegal groups affects how one perceives and interprets the locale, the people, the country, the region, and even the continent. One challenge with adopting an existing frame is the conceptual baggage that it comes attached with. Existing terms stress particular features and evoke a set of assumptions about the group which add confusion or require constant clarification and active caveating. By creating a new term like "extralegal groups," the intent is to start with a blank slate, without assumptions or preconceived notions about who these people are, what they do, and whether or not we approve of their behavior.

Typically, the groups that I described earlier bring to mind images of bloodthirsty gun-toting bandits, ruthless organized crime gangs,[23] and calculating mafia dons.[24] Colloquially, these concepts invoke negative associations about how individuals organize themselves in the absence of state authority, but in an ahistorical way, without accounting for the powerful influence of social and political history.[25] With the term extralegal groups, I offer a unifying logic for thinking about what these groups have in common, how they evolved, and what they actually do—beyond simply suggesting that they are "bad" for the state and for statebuilding.[26]

At the same time, I do not want to mislead. These are not governments-in-waiting as articulated in the rebel governance literature.[27] While this study shares an interest with the creation of political and economic order at the local level,[28] extralegal groups do not promote explicit political projects. Extralegal groups are not seeking to take over the state (or to secede from the state); political governance is not their primary goal.

Without romanticizing these groups, I argue that extralegal groups are not necessarily more harmful than existing predatory states, cartel-mafias, ruling militias, criminal gangs, or exploitative multinational companies that also serve as quasi-rulers in other contexts. Demonizing them in the post-conflict context prevents us from fully understanding their varied roles in the war-to-peace transition process. Without taking the time to understand what they are and what would replace them, flawed assumptions are made about the state-making process. In some respects, the particular form that extralegal

[23] Sudhir Alladi Venkatesh (2008); Alice Goffman (2015).
[24] Charles Tilly (1985) provocatively argued that the state formation process has parallels with organized crime.
[25] On how communities in Afghanistan provide public goods in the absence of a strong central government, see Jennifer Brick Murtazashvili (2010).
[26] Other works that have challenged conventional wisdom on disarmed rebel groups and warlords include William Reno (2008); Jonathan Goodhand (2011); Mats Utas (2013); Laura Freeman (2015).
[27] Zachariah Mampilly 2011a; Jennifer Keister and Branislav Slantchev 2014; Ana Arjona, Nelson Kasfir and Zachariah Mampilly 2015; Jennifer Keister 2015; R. Huang 2016; N.H. Lidow 2016.
[28] Paul Staniland (2012).

groups take in Liberia may be more responsive to local concerns than the state-sanctioned alternative, and it may be possible in some circumstances for their interests to be made to align with those of the local communities they control.

THE RESEARCH QUESTIONS, AND SOME ANSWERS

Having observed this phenomenon in Liberia that defied categorization, my goal was to make sense of these groups:

> I. *How do extralegal groups emerge, develop, and become locally entrenched after the end of civil war?*

As I began to develop a theory of extralegal groups (discussed fully in Chapter 2), I realized that such a framework would be conceptually useful for breaking down "statebuilding" and "state formation" into a series of micro-processes. Extralegal groups serve as conceptual halfway houses, occupying an institutional space between the state of nature and full statehood. As the study progressed, I came to realize that my analysis of extralegal groups reflected my own deeply held biases and assumptions about states and statebuilding. Although I could not see this when I began the project, I was deeply biased in favor of states as fundamental institutions of social and political organization. Capable state institutions were my silver bullet of choice.

My time in West Africa, and especially in Liberia, shattered my illusions of what state capacity would be able to achieve. I was forced to confront the fact that states are often ineffective at providing security and stability, and at leading local economic development—especially after war. I knew this, and yet I was stubbornly wedded to the primacy of the state. International peace-building and statebuilding actors often adhere to the fiction of state integrity even when they know it to be false. Recognizing this bias has important consequences for policymaking. The ways in which different audiences choose to "read" and interpret extralegal groups can tell us important things about statebuilding policies, how donor countries and the UN choose to "make" states, and how states are *actually* made. Together, these realizations led to a second research question for this book:

> II. *What purpose do extralegal groups serve?*

While extralegal groups clearly had coercive capacity, it was also apparent that they were not simply ruling through fear—some of them had local legitimacy. As an outsider, this seemed puzzling because the public narrative about these groups emphasized how dangerous they were, and the threat that they posed to local communities and the peace process. So how did this legitimacy come about? The key to this puzzle lay in their ability to provide basic governance functions, and the commercial environment that they facilitated. Initially, this was difficult to appreciate because it required setting aside my own state-centric view of the world to recognize that armed nonstate actors could contribute to statebuilding in unexpected ways.[29]

While the state can play a valuable organizing role, its limitations are significant in a post-conflict environment. Government officials of established, secure states may find this harder to imagine, but the provision of public goods need not be led by state-approved actors. The predatory nature of some states and historical abuses of citizens in the name of the state means that "the state" is not always more trusted or more able to look after the interests of local populations than say, an extralegal group.

THE SPECTRUM OF EXTRALEGAL GROUPS—FROM NASCENT TO FULLY DEVELOPED

This book focuses on *nascent* extralegal groups—entities that are in the early stages and are attempting to create a stable commercial environment by providing key governance functions. Some of these nascent groups survive, though many do not. While this book only examines the nascent versions of extralegal groups, it is worth bearing in mind that they also exist at other stages of development. Returning to the definition of extralegal groups, what is distinctive about them is the fact that they provide governance functions—as a *by-product* of the stable business environment they require.

For example, more developed extralegal groups take the form of neighborhood gangs in cities like Chicago, Los Angeles, Port-au-Prince, and London; slumlord mafias in Mumbai; and favela gangs in Rio de Janeiro and São Paolo. All of these entities provide certain kinds of local governance functions for a specific territory. Similarly, pirate gangs maintain local control in a manner that is consistent with the logic of extralegal groups even though their locus of operations is sea-based. Indonesian pirate bosses in the Strait of Malacca, Nigerian pirates in the Gulf of Guinea, and Somali pirates in the Gulf of Aden—all of these have operated with impunity and exercised social control over their respective ports.

I opened this book with a quote from Michael Johnson, a resident of Robert Taylor housing project in Chicago, and a local mechanic. The sociologist Sudhir

---

[29] On governance by nonstate armed groups, see Diego Gambetta (1993); Federico Varese (2001); Vadim Volkov (2002); Kimberly Z. Marten (2006); Sudhir Alladi Venkatesh (2008); Regina Bateson (2011); Zachariah C. Mampilly (2011b); Annette Idler (2012); Sasha Jesperson (2014); Ana Arjona, Nelson Kasfir and Zachariah Mampilly (2015).

Venkatesh describes how Johnson's area was ruled by a Chicago gang, the Black Kings, who provided all sorts of governance functions, from community security to dispute resolution to sports tournaments. The Black Kings were the police, judge, and local mayor all wrapped up in one entity. They decided who was allowed to reside in the buildings, who could or could not open a business, what local "taxes" would be, and what kinds of behaviors were or were not permitted. The quote illustrates the degree to which residents from the South Side of Chicago, Cité Soleil in Haiti, or the Indian city of Govandi are ruled by extralegal groups. If asked who they would turn to in order to resolve an important local dispute, many would name their local gang leader ahead of their appointed or elected political representatives. While these gangs have become deeply embedded within the local social fabric, they do not overtly threaten the state's authority, nor do all of them have the capacity to do so. Although the groups may be well-financed and well-organized, the central state remains demonstrably more powerful in these particular cases.

However, the most developed extralegal groups are just as powerful or more powerful *as compared to the nation-state that hosts them*. In this category, we can include the Sicilian mafia, the Russian mafia, the Urabeños in northern Colombia, and the most powerful drug cartels in Mexico,[30] Honduras, and Guatemala. These extralegal groups have moved beyond local entrenchment and have graduated to capturing and criminalizing the state.[31] These entities have demonstrated that they are capable of threatening state authority and are able to operate with complete impunity.

Why Are Extralegal Groups Important?

They still pose a threat—they are all formed into youth groups which are organized along military lines… They have no jobs, no economic future, few skills and are angry. Even for those who have been trained, the economy is so bad, there's nothing to do with the skills they have. They're just looking around for another war.

Military intelligence source interviewed by Human Rights Watch[32]

Returning to the BOPC area, extralegal groups there and elsewhere in Liberia posed a very real and immediate threat to the peacebuilding process. People remained fearful and nervous about them, worrying not only about their influence over the local economy, but also about the extent to which members would behave with impunity inside their communities. The Human

---

[30] On the rise of Mexico's drug cartels, see Ioan Grillo (2011); Tom Wainwright (2016).
[31] Jean-Francois Bayart, Stephen Ellis and Beatrice Hibou (1999); J. Hellman, G. Jones, D. Kaufmann and M. Schankerman (2000).
[32] Corinne Dufka (2005), Section VII.

Rights Watch quote reflects this concern, its sentiment shared throughout the region in Sierra Leone, Côte d'Ivoire, Guinea, and Liberia—all countries which struggled and continue to struggle with young men and women who came of age with weapons in their hands.

The situation at BOPC illustrates the precariousness of Liberia's peace agreement and how ex-combatants were seen to be injecting fear and instability into the transition discourse. It was widely accepted that these groups had the capacity to take violent action and that it would be easy to do so given that the government was fragile and politically unstable. At the same time, extralegal groups also provided key governance functions in the short run, which in turn facilitated employment opportunities for some of the most hardened ex-combatants, as well as creating markets. Indeed, some extralegal groups viewed themselves as quasi-legitimate civil society actors providing an important regulatory function for local entrepreneurs and businesses.[33] Without these groups, these areas would not have been stable enough for a commercial environment to thrive. For better *and* for worse, these groups altered the calculus of state security in the short term.

Following this trajectory, extralegal groups pose a different set of problems as they prosper in the medium term. Once an extralegal group begins to tax in an organized manner, it has a strong incentive to keep doing so. Given the weakness of the state, local authorities are particularly vulnerable to being corrupted by an extralegal group. Consequently, the framework suggests that a corruption equilibrium will take hold at the local level. Extralegal groups bribe to maintain control and local officials have little incentive or capacity to defy these groups. This is authoritarian statebuilding in the making.

Some of these groups will successfully build up an independent power base and in the process of doing so, they will successfully compromise key political, judicial, and security institutions in undetectable ways. In practice, this means a statebuilding trajectory that is stable but corrupt. Unless the central government chooses to take an active interest in dismantling them, extralegal groups are likely to prevail at the local level, affecting the nature, quality, and viability of the post-conflict political and economic order. This is a concern not only for the local populations and governments of post-conflict countries but also for the international community. For those who are invested in strengthening the state, extralegal groups pose a medium-term challenge as well as a short-term one.

Yet it is equally important to recognize the role of extralegal groups in the long-term statebuilding trajectory. If we view them through a macro-historical lens, it becomes apparent that the nascent versions of these groups only exist for a sliver of time in the long march toward full-fledged statehood. Nevertheless, they play an important socialization role, and are critical to state learning.

---

[33] Management Systems International (2004); Bruce Baker (2005); William Reno (2008).

THE EXTRALEGAL GROUPS FRAMEWORK

To understand how extralegal groups emerge and develop, we need to put ourselves in the shoes of ex-combatants. We need to understand their motivations. *As an ex-combatant in a poorly governed post-conflict society, with few employable skills, what is the best strategy for survival?* For leaders of the group, how does this strategy change over time? For civilians, what factors affect local support for the extralegal group? If we consider ex-combatants to be rational actors, we can see that their choices are constrained. These constraints shape their behavior such that the emergence of extralegal groups logically follows.

I approached these questions by creating a theoretical framework of ex-combatant behavior. There are three stages to the framework: emergence, development, and entrenchment. The core of the framework is based on a rational choice model that is motivated by an individual's material incentives.

Emergence: After war, there is an abundance of low-skilled unemployed youth—civilians as well as ex-combatants—who seek employment. Limited skills means that they are all drawn to the same localities and end up vying for the same economic opportunities, namely those with low barriers to entry. Social ties and conflict capital may also draw them to these areas. Consequently, competition in these areas is fierce, leading to a greater probability of conflict between individuals (mostly young men) as they compete for jobs, local permissions, land, clients, contracts, women, and supplies. Where the state is weak, and legal and regulatory frameworks are lacking, there arises a need for dispute resolution and credible, third-party contract enforcement in order to create a stable business environment. What emerges to meet this need is an extralegal group, backed by credible, coercive force.

Development: The extralegal group can now "tax" within its domain. Ex-commanders are able to grow relatively wealthy and provide jobs for their foot soldiers, allowing once-powerful leaders to retain their "Big Man" status. Tax collection also strengthens the group by developing its organizational capacity. If the group operates on a medium-term or long-term timeframe, it may initiate revenue-enhancing public services over time. Such services ease community tensions while also building local loyalties.

Entrenchment: Once an extralegal group has developed organizational strength, it will seek to consolidate local control. It will do this by bribing, and if necessary, threatening local authorities. Once cooperation has been secured, the group will have established a local power base that could pose a security threat to regional or central authorities. This is ever more likely if the group has successfully aligned its economic interests with those of the local population. Further, the group creates an equilibrium of entrenched corruption by continuously bribing local officials who, in turn, help it to retain control of the area. At the most advanced stages of entrenchment, state capture or state criminalization are possible.

Despite the model's rational choice grounding, it is clear that human rationality does not begin and end with an economic cost–benefit analysis. Utility can also be derived from nonmaterial factors such as social relationships, maintaining group status, and feeling secure.[34] I share Aaron Wildavsky's approach to rational choice, recognizing that rationality requires contextualization in order for it to make sense:

> The choices contemplated in rational choice theory are not (and cannot be) discrete choices. Choices are also choices of friends. Every choice is not only intended to be decision rational, it must also be culturally rational. Which is to say that the objective in the specific instance must also support the way of life (or culture) in which the individual is embedded. Why "must"? Because if the choice is culturally irrational, there are penalties to pay.[35]

In this spirit of contextualization, chapters on Liberia's history and its civil war help flesh out the background against which individuals make social and economic choices in the postwar environment, while chapters on rubber, diamonds, and timber provide sector- and place-specific context.[36]

About the Framework

A theoretical framework is useful for highlighting similar processes occurring within a single post-conflict country, or across a variety of country cases. Where governance is poor and polities are unstable, the framework offers a basis for comparing the core trajectory across groups, and across countries. In the chapters on rubber, diamonds, and timber, the sector-level analysis allows for a comparison of groups within sectors, while the cross-sectoral analysis in Chapter 1 provides a snapshot of these groups across the country's economy.

Each of the three stages of the framework highlights a different dynamic. Understanding the emergence of extralegal groups tells us about how politics and governance develop in stateless societies,[37] about spaces that are considered "ungoverned"[38] or "failed,"[39] and about the types of choices that

---

[34] In theory, it is possible to derive conversion rates between material and nonmaterial forms of utility that would allow for an individual cost–benefit calculation, but preferences are specific to individuals so standard conversion rates could not be set. Further, preferences may change over time. Finally, even if such a calculation were possible, humans are not always rational decision-makers. For example, see Daniel Kahneman and Amos Tversky (1979) and the field of behavioral economics.

[35] Aaron Wildavsky (1994), p. 154.

[36] M. Bøås (2014) makes this point about the importance of social and political context quite powerfully in his book on conflict economies in "borderland" areas.

[37] Mancur Olson (2000); James C. Scott (2009).

[38] Anne L. Clunan and Harold A. Trinkunas (2010).

[39] Gerland B. Helman and Stephen R. Ratner (1992); Jean-Germain Gros (1996); Jeffrey I. Herbst (1997); Jack A. Goldstone, Ted Robert Gurr, Barbara Harff, Marc A. Levy, et al. (2000).

ex-combatants face once war ends.[40] The development stage is key to analyzing post-conflict outcomes because it explains the group's internal dynamic, namely, how it grows and strengthens itself.[41] Finally, entrenchment speaks to the group's relationship to the wider society, and how a corruption equilibrium is established.

Understanding these dynamics has implications for how the state and the international community should respond to extralegal groups, and they also tell us why some of these groups fall apart of their own accord. The full theoretical framework and its underlying logic are discussed in detail in Chapter 2.

Findings from Liberia

The findings from Liberia show support for the theoretical framework. First, there is confirmation that individuals gravitated to natural resource areas with the lowest barriers to entry and that more extralegal groups developed in these sectors of the economy.[42] It is telling that extralegal groups developed where they did and the way they did—these outcomes followed a pattern and were, to some extent, predictable. Second, even though not all of the groups emerged directly out of the need for dispute resolution and contract enforcement, these needs did play a critical role in the early stages of group emergence. Third, as expected, all of the extralegal groups built up taxation capacity and they became more organized and unified over time. While this study focuses on the extralegal groups that survived, it should also be noted that some of these groups simply fizzled out due to internal disputes or poor leadership. Fourth, several extralegal groups were successful in entrenching their economic interests at the local level, and had penetrated the political class—as predicted. Finally, I show that some of these extralegal groups served as de facto local authorities even though they were not formally recognized by the state. They maintained a basic level of local order but were also able to ignite episodes of collective violence as needed. The empirical findings from Liberia emphasize the dual nature of extralegal groups—their ability to contribute to statebuilding as well as their ability to undermine it.

---

[40] M. Humphreys and J. M. Weinstein (2007); Sarah Zukerman-Daly (2009).

[41] For an intriguing parallel discussion on the protection-driven motivations of Somali business support for Islamist groups, see Aisha Ahmad (2015).

[42] The permeability of borders plays an important role; if there are opportunities across the border that also have low barriers to entry, then extralegal groups could also emerge there. Ideally, this study should have been conducted at a regional level (Liberia, Sierra Leone, Guinea, Côte d'Ivoire). However, this would have introduced additional complexity given different cultural and political conditions.

THE ARGUMENT

Through the process of analyzing extralegal groups, this book makes two intertwining arguments about contemporary statebuilding, where statebuilding is understood as the process of establishing impersonal institutions that provide public goods and distribute them fairly across the citizenry. *First, in providing governance goods, extralegal groups become unintentional statebuilders and contribute to state learning.* Driven by business opportunities, extralegal groups provide core governance functions that are constitutive of the state. This leads to *my second argument: it is trade, rather than war, that drives contemporary statebuilding.* As wars of conquest became anomalous, it has been trade and commerce that have motivated the provision of fundamental governance goods in modern-day state-making.

Extralegal Groups Are Statebuilders and Contribute to State Learning

What makes extralegal groups distinctive is that they provide governance functions—but not because they want to govern. Governance is the by-product of creating the commercial environment. These functions include contract enforcement, dispute resolution, and regulation[43]—and they are backed up by coercive force (as discussed in Chapter 2). In a nascent economy, these basic governance functions are essential precursors to impartial justice. Further, the coercive force that supports these basic governance functions also underpins the foundation for physical security.

While these governance functions are initially provided as club goods (for those who pay) aimed only at facilitating trade and commerce, over time, they are made publicly available and offered to the entire community. In this way, extralegal groups are statebuilders—they move society closer toward the public provision of impartial justice and physical security. They build up the state despite the fact that they are not deliberately seeking political rule. Statebuilding is happening in direct and visible ways—as with dispute resolution, contract enforcement, and regulation—but it is also manifesting itself in hidden but equally vital functions. Extralegal groups:

(1) remove the right of individuals to judge and enforce their own disputes;
(2) consolidate coercive authority at the local level; and
(3) socialize communities into being governed.

---

[43] In a nascent economy, there is substantial overlap between these three functions, so I have grouped them together. I often use contract enforcement or dispute resolution as a shorthand for this collection of functions.

Although extralegal groups do not set out to deliberately create the kernel of the state, in providing these governance functions, they move society *away* from the state of nature, shifting people away from *self*-enforcement of societal norms toward *third-party* enforcement of these norms. This shift establishes (or re-establishes) the authority of the state.

What does this study of extralegal groups tell us then, about "ungoverned spaces" and territories that are not under the direct control of central authorities? I argue that even in spaces that are not firmly under the rule of states, *political authority can still develop as a by-product of the commercial environment*. The need for a stable environment for commerce, rather than an impetus for political rule itself, can spur the provision of local governance. In situations of contested or uncertain governance (like war), extralegal groups can shift individuals away from punishing wrongdoing on one's own (vigilante justice) by providing third-party enforcement and judgment in places where the state has not penetrated.[44]

Over time, a state develops a *repertoire of responses*. In the same way that humans develop heuristics and categories to speed up our decision-making processes,[45] states learn to do the same when they respond to violence, distribute wealth, pay for their public goods, and punish their lawbreakers. As states adapt and evolve in response, so does the state–society relationship.

The World Bank's seminal 2011 World Development Report refers to this push–pull cycle of statebuilding in similar terms:[46]

> [The] risk of conflict and violence in any society (national or regional) is the combination of the exposure to internal and external stresses and the strength of the "immune system," or the social capability for coping with stress embodied in legitimate institutions.

The survival of the state depends on creating a resilient system. Consider how the body's immune system fights off a virus: it first tests different strategies and deploys the most successful one, then it produces extra antibodies as an insurance mechanism to prevent a future infection of the same virus. In the same way, a state builds resilience by developing the capacity to absorb and respond to challenges like extralegal groups. From a purely statist perspective, individual states react to extralegal groups by testing a variety of strategies, from co-opting to confronting. The lessons from these experiments—failed and successful—are absorbed into a country's institutional memory and its political culture.

In the long term, extralegal groups should be understood as *one of many microprocesses of statebuilding* that link the "state of the past" with the "state of

---

[44] On the difficulties faced by the state in attempting to take back justice provision from nonstate providers (such as the paramilitaries in Northern Ireland), see Heather Hamill (2011).

[45] Daniel Kahneman, Paul Slovic and Amos Tversky (1982).

[46] World Bank (2011), p. 7.

the future." Their existence informs and shapes a state's trajectory; they are part of the state evolution process. In the longue durée, extralegal groups can be viewed as part of *histoire événementielle*.[47] Along with their relationships, institutions, patterns of interaction, and conflict capital, this is part of how a state learns to be a state.

Trade Makes the Contemporary State

Because wars of conquest are no longer considered acceptable or legitimate, the process of making states has had to evolve. Whereas European state formation is broadly understood as the product of wars of conquest,[48] war no longer plays the same role in the twenty-first century. Instead, I argue that contemporary statebuilding is driven by trade and commerce.[49] Trade requires a stable commercial environment that is underpinned by two core governance functions: physical security and consistent contract enforcement (as a subset of impartial justice). When extralegal groups provide these two core governance functions, they help legitimize both the concept of the state and the state itself. Over time, they socialize the population into accepting the organizing authority of the state. In this way, trade makes the contemporary state.

Given the history of European state formation,[50] politics scholars in the West have privileged the warfighting path over explanations from other disciplines that treat state formation as part of a broader discourse on the evolution of social complexity.[51] Bureaucratic capacity in various forms—financial, organizational, security, territorial—is broadly accepted as the result of warfighting and militarization.[52] In the words of Charles Tilly, "war made the state, and the state made war." By this logic, it was war that simultaneously drove taxation, nationalism, and bureaucratization to reinforce one another in a specific historical context so as to create the nation-state. State formation has been a continuous process of consolidating power and territory—until the

---

[47] The history of events, or episodic history. See Fernand Braudel (1958).

[48] Charles Tilly (1992).

[49] On trade and state formation, see Douglass C. North and Robert P. Thomas (1973); Douglass Cecil North (1990); Avner Greif (2006).

[50] For a nuanced, insightful discussion of European state formation processes and their impact on regime type, see Hendrik Spruyt (2011).

[51] For example, archeologists view law and order in early civilizations as the product of a balancing act between the lower classes, the upper classes, and the gods, with religion and spirituality playing fundamental roles. See Bruce G. Trigger (2003). In contrast, anthropologists have generally characterized the earliest states as despotic and large, though scholars like Norman Yoffee have contested these claims, turning to urbanization and processes of agricultural production for explanations of early state emergence. See Norman Yoffee (2005).

[52] But see Joseph R. Strayer (1965) who argues that administrative development preceded major military advances.

point when it was no longer acceptable to fight wars of conquest. Since that time, virtually all land on earth has been claimed by a state,[53] and national borders have stabilized. But even though borders have been demarcated, the state institutions within them have developed to differing extents. Today's drivers of statebuilding are necessarily different from what they used to be.

Centuries ago, it was kings, queens, and feudal lords who were the most common providers of physical security. As they conquered their way across the European continent, they became the most viable and efficient providers of protection from foreign invaders.[54] Today, it is no longer acceptable (nor possible) to build up the state through conquest and domination.[55] Instead, I posit that the motivation for providing these core governance functions is *commercially* driven—especially out in the hinterland where central authorities have little motivation to build state capacity.

Trade and commerce—not war—are responsible for nurturing the kernel of the state. Where there is a notional state, but no meaningful state presence, foundational statebuilding processes are propelled forward by the lure of commercial opportunities. *To fully flourish though, trade requires a safe and predictable environment.* Safety and predictability can be translated into two practical needs: physical security and contract enforcement. Ideal conditions require that the environment be physically secure, and buyers and sellers need a mechanism for sorting out their commercial disagreements. Where the physical environment is not secure or the arbitrating authority is contested, friction is added to each transaction, and sometimes, trade can come to a grinding halt. Hence, both of these conditions must be in place for commerce to thrive, and someone or some authority must maintain these conditions. I show how extralegal groups are best positioned to play this role after war.

DEFINITIONS

Defining the State and Statebuilding

The earliest versions of states offered only an indirect form of rule.[56] They exerted authority over vast areas but rulers did not seek to directly rule over the population, nor to change their ways of life.[57] The nature of society would remain untouched despite having control change hands. As early states gave

---

[53] Josh Lew (2014).   [54] Charles Tilly (1985).   [55] Hendrik Spruyt (2005).

[56] Archeology, anthropology, history, and sociology are seeing a greater integration of sources and methods in studying complex societies and early state formation. On African civilizations, see Susan Keech McIntosh (1999); Graham Connah (2001); Graham Connah (2012); D. W. Phillipson (2012).

[57] Ernest Gellner (1983).

way to modern states, rulers sought to create direct ties to the individual by asserting control over local authorities, and by forging a common identity.[58] The concept of the modern state also became associated with the notion of ruling over specific territory within defined borders. As societies became larger and more complex, we have continued to re-evaluate and reformulate the criteria for statehood.

In this tradition, I define the contemporary state as a political community with two essential elements: "a monopoly of the legitimate use of physical force within a given territory"[59] and reliable access to impartial justice for its citizens.[60] In practice, these two elements translate into (1) physical security, and (2) contract enforcement and/or dispute resolution, in order to form the kernel of the state.

Following Weber, there is a broad consensus on the necessity for the state to monopolize the legitimate use of force. Indeed for some, this is *the* defining element of statehood. The second element, which I also deem to be essential to the contemporary state, speaks to the legitimacy of the state. Legitimacy is derived from the citizenry, and its best proxy is the state's ability to offer impartial justice and rule of law to their populations in an accessible manner. However, it is also important to highlight that this element does not speak to the *content* of laws and judicial norms, only that they be applied impartially. This second element is also silent on what bodies can legitimately provide justice, creating room for Western-style courts and arbitration mechanisms, as well as other kinds of mechanisms like Sharia or Beth Din courts.

From this definition, a successful contemporary state provides to all citizens equal and reliable access to essential governance goods (physical security, impartial justice) and distributes these goods fairly through impersonal institutions. While there is certain to be a debate around what is deemed "essential" and "fair," and how strictly "all" should be interpreted, this version of state success offers the possibility of operationalization without being over-prescriptive about the content of the state. It takes its starting point to be equality between citizens, but makes no further normative claims.

The concept of statebuilding follows directly: *to establish impersonal institutions to provide public goods and distribute these fairly across the citizenry.* The emphasis here is on the quality of post-conflict life for the "average" person. I evaluate statebuilding impact in relation to the broader public interest[61] and its effects on "regular" people (as opposed to elites). Accordingly, instead of calling for the wholesale replication of the Western Weberian state— and measuring success or failure by that standard—I am interested in how statebuilding provides tangible public goods and services that are accessible to

---

[58] Benedict Anderson (1983).
[59] Max Weber (1919). See also Thomas Hobbes (1651).   [60] John Locke (1690).
[61] On the broader public interest and how to create it, see John Ralston Saul (1995).

the population on a day-to-day basis.[62] This definition of statebuilding is separate from state-making, which I consider to be a long-term evolutionary process that is inclusive of the initial formation of the state as well as its subsequent struggles for survival. State-making is a continuous process replete with stops and starts, sudden bouts of progress and consolidation, as well as existential crises and periods of major decline.

The first point about statebuilding is that it is actor-neutral: it is not rooted in the actions of external actors, and it need not be carried out by the state. The World Bank's pathbreaking 2011 World Development Report acknowledges that nonstate actors can and should have a role to play in securing peace.[63] Setting aside preconceptions of who can or cannot be a statebuilder, extralegal groups take on a different light if we evaluate their ability to provide governance functions at the local level rather than focusing on them as national security threats. Consider that in some states, the military can be as much of a national security threat as any nonstate armed group. This bottom-up perspective contrasts sharply with the top-down ways in which the international community typically approaches post-conflict statebuilding.[64] Prioritizing the local level instead of the national level leads to very different policies.

This links to another crucial policy implication: statebuilding, as I have defined it, is not merely a technical problem that requires a centralized technical fix. International efforts to build competently resourced, top-down state institutions will not, by themselves, achieve the desired outcomes despite spending vast sums. Over the past decade, the mantra of the international community has been: "If we can just get the national institutions right, then political stability and economic development will follow." While national institutions are an important part of any stable post-conflict resolution, the evidence from Liberia suggests:

(1) Building impartial *local* institutions is just as important, if not more so, than building *national* institutions;

(2) *Informal* institutions matter as much as *formal* institutions; and

(3) Institutions must be perceived as legitimate by local political networks.

The first two points speak to the creation of *impersonal* institutions. This is a long, difficult process requiring continuous review and constant vigilance. Even the most capable states with the highest levels of citizen legitimacy have not wholly succeeded in creating institutions that are completely impersonal,

---

[62] For a discussion of statebuilding definitions, see HPCR International (2007).

[63] This speaks to the role of informal justice across varied country contexts including Kenya, Guatemala, Lebanon, Japan, and East Timor. See World Bank (2011), p. 155–6.

[64] Attempts by the U.S. and the U.K. to rebuild and reshape the state in Afghanistan (post-2001) and Iraq (post-2003) typify such a top-down approach. Some of the lessons that were learned were later incorporated into the UK Government's Approach to Stabilisation, see UK Stabilisation Unit (2014).

so expecting impersonal institutions in weaker, more precarious places is unrealistic. This problem is especially pronounced in Africa, where the personalization of politics has been a long-running theme.[65] In particular, the Development and Entrenchment stages of the extralegal groups framework reveals how a corruption equilibrium develops where personalization is strong and institutions are weak. Organizational and financial strength allow an extralegal group to convert their success into lasting forms of local "legal" and "executive" power. Studying these groups opens up the black box of personalized politics and makes explicit the logic by which the exploitation of people and resources for private benefit end up being gradually institutionalized into the state system.

The third point speaks to fair distribution. Fairness is implicitly understood in the *public* part of public goods; however, "fair" means different things to different people, and each society must decide for itself how "fair" should be realized. Coming to a societal agreement on fair distribution poses an enormous challenge for even the wealthiest of states, and remains subject to constant revision.[66]

In practice, it is impossible to reach this ideal standard of the state in one giant leap. What should be recognized as "progress" is movement toward this goal through a series of incremental steps that move roughly in the direction of public goods provision, impersonal institutions, and fair distribution. This is how the actions and functions of extralegal groups should be framed.

The quality of peace also speaks to the trade-offs that are inherent in dealing with extralegal groups in the aftermath of war. *In the post-conflict window, institutions and institutional practices are malleable and influential networks of political and economic actors are being configured and reconfigured.* The problem is that "buying off" certain groups and actors for the sake of short-term peace and stability can lay the foundation for future grievances and also set a nationwide tone of might makes right—with moral hazard implications.

So how should bold, reform-minded government leaders and international actors balance short-term needs for security and political stability while minimizing the possibility of entrenched corruption, authoritarian peacebuilding, and state capture? Ultimately, there is no set answer—that would be too easy—but rather, there is usually a spectrum of viable responses that depend on the constellation of actors, resources, political will, and levels of local cooperation. What is deemed appropriate depends on the domestic political situation at a given point, the dynamics of the local and regional political economy, and how these factors interact with the incentives of key international actors.

[65] Jean-François Bayart (1993); Michael Bratton and Nicolas van de Walle (1994); Bruce Berman (1998); Patrick Chabal and Jean-Pascal Daloz (1999); Robert H. Bates (2008); Daron Acemoglu and James A. Robinson (2012). For a narrative account, see Chinua Achebe 1958.
[66] For example, see John Rawls (1971) and the debates that have arisen after the publication of *Capital* by Thomas Piketty (2013).

Defining "Post-Conflict"

How do societies shift from being *at war* to being *at peace*? What does it mean to be "post-conflict"? In discussions of post-conflict countries, the distinction between war and peace is not always clear. Visually, we imagine the transition from war to peace as a step function, with a singular and distinct increase in violence and killing when war "begins" and a sudden finish to that violence when war "ends."

Yet the reality of how wars begin and end is usually more ambiguous. There is not necessarily a declaration of war to marks its start, nor a peace agreement to mark its finish. The shift from "peace" to "war" and back again is more likely to resemble a jagged trend line replete with peaks and troughs of violence. Under these conditions, how do we identify when war ends and peace begins?

In considering what it means to be post-conflict, there is an assumption that the end of war also brings an end to violence by all armed groups and an assumed renewal of trust in government—as if it should be as simple as

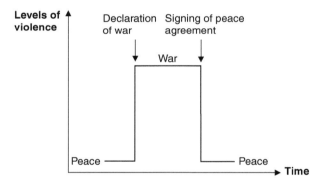

Fig. 0.1. Violence in war as a step function

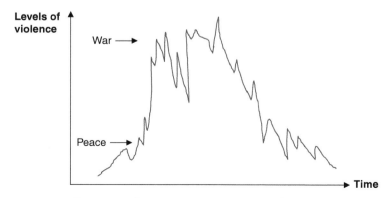

Fig. 0.2. Violence in war as a noisy step function

flicking on a light switch. But this study of extralegal groups shows that being "post-conflict"—a period which is typically marked by the signing of a peace agreement or a ceasefire—does not necessarily mean that violence ends or that insecurity ceases to exist. For the citizens of post-conflict countries, this is obvious, yet the policies of external actors typically fail to fully acknowledge the implications of this point. Many states exist for long periods in a status that is akin to "no peace, no war."[67]

In this study, I use the terms "post-conflict" and "postwar" to refer to the period after war where a recognizable peace has consolidated. This terminology acknowledges that civil war violence cannot be turned on and off so easily, and only with hindsight is it possible to distinguish between a lull in the fighting and a marked shift toward peace. Clearly, the signing of a peace agreement does not create peace in itself. The shift from war to peace must be understood as a whole-of-society process.

The notion of a post-conflict transition denotes gradual movement along the war-to-peace continuum—but it may take generations or centuries to make a permanent move from one side of the continuum to the other. Liberia is a case in point. Twelve separate peace processes were undertaken[68] and sixteen separate ceasefire or peace agreements were signed[69] and then subsequently torn up before the Accra Comprehensive Peace Agreement (CPA) of August 18, 2003 was finally upheld. Despite the fact that Liberia was declared to be "post-conflict" many a time, the ceasefire and the subsequent transition from war to peace required numerous attempts. Successive failures made it even more difficult for mediators to achieve an agreement that would hold.[70]

THEMES OF THE BOOK

The "Good" State

If you are able to access and read this book, you were probably raised in a stable, peaceful society where there is generally a shared belief in the goodness of

---

[67] Paul Richards (2004).

[68] The ECOWAS Peace Plan; Banjul I, II, III, & IV; Bamako; Lomé; Monrovia; Yamoussoukro I, II, III, & IV; Geneva; Cotonou; Akosombo; Accra Clarification; Abuja I & II, Accra Ceasefire. Many of these processes failed to produce a peace agreement. See George Klay Jr Kieh (2011); UN Mediation Support Unit (2015).

[69] Banjul I, II, III, & IV; Lomé; Yamoussoukro I, II, III, & IV; Geneva; Cotonou; Akosombo; Accra Clarification; Abuja I & II; Accra Ceasefire. See U.S. Agency for International Development (2003); Dorina Akosua Oduraa Bekoe (2008); George Klay Jr Kieh (2011); UN Mediation Support Unit (2015).

[70] Nita Yawanarajah (2014).

the state. But where does that belief come from? And how does this belief affect the policy prescriptions for states that are transitioning from war to peace?

There are two linked problems here that affect how we approach statebuilding: one concerns the state's ability to provide governance goods, and the other relates to how international actors judge a state's ability to provide and distribute these goods. First, there is significant subnational variation in how individual citizens relate to the state. The state may have a strong presence in some areas, but none in others; it may protect some communities and ethnic groups while deliberately preying on others; it may be strong in some sectors (e.g., defense) but weak in others (e.g., social welfare). Elites will also experience the state differently than the rest of the population—this is not unique to post-conflict settings. For example, elites are more likely to have full access to political, economic, and legal rights than the rest of the population—this elite experience of the state creates an illusion, albeit a mistaken one, of what would be possible *if only the state worked the way it was supposed to*. Well-meaning elites—domestic and international—can fall prey to this trap.

These dormant expectations of a fully functioning state feed into the second problem of how international actors conceive of the state and what they think it should be. There is a tendency to compare *existing* forms of extralegal governance to *idealized* forms of state governance. Rather than comparing extralegal governance to a more realistic counterfactual of clientelist state control, international statebuilders fund and support policies that favor the replication of Western Weberian state institutions even though these are usually unsuitable and patently unrealistic in the short term. The problem is that acknowledging and supporting illiberal forms of governance and authoritarian peacebuilding poses domestic political difficulties for Western donors and opens them up to charges of hypocrisy and corruption.

Digging deeper, a core problem is that most rich-world citizens begin with the assumption that the state is and *should* be the sole legitimate provider of security[71] and political authority; all other providers are illegitimate by definition. Moving beyond this assumption to evaluate the basis of the state's claim to this authority lays bare another layer of assumptions about state behavior. International policymakers, politicians, and researchers who write about the "state" conceive of it in benevolent terms in part because they represent the machinery of the state system. They *are* the state. Not only do they rely on the state system for their livelihoods and their social identity, but many also *believe in* the system itself—or have never thought to question it. Given that their own formative experiences with their home governments have been positive and beneficial—it is possible to imagine how things *could* work, if only the right systems were put in place. For those brought up in rich-world

---

[71] There are exceptions. For example, the *Michigan Militia* in the U.S.

countries, the default setting for the state is benevolent rather than malevolent, protective rather than predatory.

This view of the state as being inherently "good" is problematic: the first implication of such a framing is that anything that is nonstate is considered "bad." For example, this quote from an International Crisis Group report captures how international actors (mostly Western) perceived ex-combatants[72] at the time:

> The internationals saw the ex-combatants as greedy and dangerous, ready to threaten violence to coerce as much money from the [Disarmament, Demobilization, and Reintegration] DDR operation as possible. Many ex-combatants were happy to play the role, considering that the internationals wanted only to buy them as cheaply as possible and leave before the failure to address the conflict's root causes became evident through new fighting.[73]

My own experiences with international policymakers and Western scholars suggest that such dichotomous views are pervasive—for example, the formal economy and the informal economy are often simplistically juxtaposed in just such a manner, with the "good" tax-paying economy on one side and the "bad" gray and black markets on the other.[74] Also consider that in the West, those who fight on behalf of the state are venerated as soldiers and patriots, and when they return home from war, become veterans and are treated with respect for their service.[75] In war-affected societies, governments and their militaries are generally accorded greater legitimacy by international actors— even where the state is shown to have committed a disproportionate share of wartime abuses and atrocities. On the other hand, we generally speak of those who fight against the state or outside of it as being rebels, militias, insurgents, terrorists, and traitors, no matter how just the cause may be. The way in which the term "ex-combatant" is used is very different than how the term "veteran" is used. It serves as a catch-all term for what these fighters once were, and typically carries with it the stigma of their nonstate status. By implication then, ex-combatants pose a threat to the state and must be demobilized by destroying their command-and-control structures—which also destroys their social networks.[76]

---

[72] While I use the term ex-combatant to refer to anyone who fought on any side in the civil war, others will use ex-combatant to refer only to nonstate fighters (rebels, militias, paramilitaries).

[73] International Crisis Group (2009), p. 33.

[74] For a rethinking of formal and informal markets and their related political economies, see John C. Yoder (2003) on Liberia and K. Meagher (2010) on Nigeria.

[75] See Alison Brettle (2017) on how the DDR literature (focused primarily on civil wars and fighters in developing countries) would benefit from the veterans literature in military sociology (focused primarily on soldiers returning home from war).

[76] There is increasing recognition of the positive socio-economic benefits of these networks. See Nat J. Colletta, Markus Kostner and Ingo Wiederhofer (1996); Nat J. Colletta and Michelle

The same kind of state favoritism also applies to local security: the local police are "good," but self-organized vigilante groups are "bad" even though both groups may be viewed by locals as effective, but exploitative.[77] Despite recognition that there cannot be a one-to-one mapping from a peaceful, developed country context to a post-conflict one, the default mental model of the benevolent state remains in place. And yet, most communities in conflict-affected areas have probably never experienced a benevolent state. Therefore, there is no reason to trust the state any more than say, an unsanctioned extralegal group made up of familiar wartime personalities. As the saying goes, better the devil you know.

Even while international actors might recognize that the state is predatory, external intervenors are overly optimistic about their ability to change the state's rapacious practices. There is a failure to recognize the stickiness of predatory institutions and the difficulty of changing an entire ecosystem of values, norms, and social relations.

The danger of having a "benevolent" default setting for the state is that international statebuilders who are familiar and comfortable with states will try to recreate a version of the state that they are familiar with, replete with bureaucracies and paperwork, even if it is ultimately ill-suited to post-conflict societies. This may be an unconscious goal, such that bureaucracy winds up being mistakenly equated with useful state capacity. A second worry is that in creating these so-called state institutions, international peacebuilders and statebuilders are misled into thinking that formal state institutions are the only ones with the power and authority to change the conditions on the ground.[78] This assumption is understandable but, ultimately, harmful. In this way, Western preconceptions of political, economic, and social order feed into and perpetuate the problems that external actors claim they want to fix.

There is a forgetful quality to this analysis—an underappreciation of how painful it was for subjects to become citizens in Western societies, and how hard it was for them to gradually invest their trust in the state.[79] Eventually, it may be possible to create more trustworthy institutions, even in places where people do not currently trust the state. Perhaps, in the future, technical innovations such as the block chain will be able to induce trust.[80] But until

---

Cullen (2000); William Reno (2010); Hugo de Vries and Nikkie Wiegink (2011); Abigail Hardgrove (2012); Anders Themnér (2014); Mats Utas, Anders Themnér and Emy Lindberg (2014); Johanna Söderström (2015). On formal and informal reintegration in particular, see Abigail Hardgrove (2012) and Alison Brettle (2014).

[77] K. Meagher (2007). Also note the overlap in functionality between community policing groups, self-defense patrols, local militias, private security groups, and vigilantes.

[78] G. Helmke and S. Levitsky (2004); Dipali Mukhopadhyay (2009); Christine Cheng (2012).

[79] This trust has not been fully vested in some cases, as with the Michigan Militia in the U.S., clinging to their second amendment rights to organize an armed militia.

[80] Mike Gault (2015).

that technology or another like it becomes widely adopted, third-party institutions like extralegal groups, mafias, banks, courts, hawala, regulators, and governments will be used to backstop transactions, contracts, and disputes.

When outside actors render judgment, they are likely to be comparing extralegal groups to an ideal type Weberian bureaucracy—if only these groups would dissolve, then the state could do its job and *real development* could begin. This is naïve. Instead, attempts to evaluate extralegal groups ought to be more nuanced—the peacebuilder's desire to categorize actors as either "goodies" or "baddies" is unhelpful when the postwar landscape shuns such oversimplifications. Scratch beneath the surface and it will be difficult to find any actor who is wholly "good" or wholly "bad."[81]

While many of us share built-in assumptions about the benefits that come with statehood and the dangers that are associated with nonstate actors, these preconceptions should be temporarily set aside. Rather than automatically casting the state or the UN or members of the "international community" as *good* actors and extralegal groups as *bad* actors, the framework sets aside these normative assumptions and examines the actual behaviors, actions, and outcomes of extralegal groups.[82]

Alternative Governance

If it was possible to ask every person on this planet, "Who or what institution provides order where you live?", how would people respond? While there would be variation in these answers, many people in the world, perhaps even most people, would cite governmental authority and the power of the state. Yet some significant proportion of the world's population would *not* name their government, despite the fact that almost every individual on this planet lives within the territorial boundaries of a recognized nation-state. In fact, as Thomas Risse argues, the limited role of the state is more common than we think, and importantly, this kind of "limited statehood" is not a transitory condition that developing countries can modernize their way out of.[83]

---

[81] The long history of sexual abuse and exploitation of women and children by UN peacekeepers provides a useful rejoinder. For theory and discussion, see Kelly Neudorfer (2015). On abuses by the UN Operation in Mozambique (ONUMOZ), see E. Schade (1995). On abuses in West Africa, see UNHCR and Save the Children UK (2002). On abuses by the UN Organization Stabilization Mission in the Democratic Republic of the Congo (MONUC/MONUSCO), see K. Holt and S. Hughes (2004); G. Caplan (2012).

[82] On the dangers of romanticizing local and informal systems, see Roger MacGinty (2011); Kate Meagher (2012); Jesse C. Ribot, Arun Agrawal and Anne M. Larson (2015).

[83] T. Risse (2011). See also the interdisciplinary research of the Governance in Areas of Limited Statehood (SFB700) project, which imaginatively re-examines the parameters of the state.

To illustrate, up to 80 percent of the population in fragile states relies on nonstate actors for access to justice and security.[84] The Afghan militias in Helmand province serve as a case in point. The journalist Ben Anderson describes his visit to the area:

> With the Afghan National Security Forces woefully undertrained and under-equipped to protect its citizens against the Taliban, local militias... are still also heavily involved in the fighting. For instance, when two young fighters I met in Marjah—one just 12 years old and the other 14—were kidnapped by the Taliban, their 53-year-old commander, who also happened to be their grandmother, was forced to kidnap several Taliban family members and organize a prisoner exchange for their release. At no point was the authorities' help offered or sought.[85]

Even in "peaceful" countries like El Salvador, criminal gangs like the Barrio 18 and the Mara Salvatruca (MS-13) exert authoritarian levels of control over vast swaths of the country with their 60,000 members. As Óscar Martínez notes:

> People from Bosques del Rio [a neighborhood in San Salvador] may not know the phone number of the nearest police station, but they definitely know what gang member is the palabrero (shot caller) of their neighborhood. To survive one must understand who is boss.[86]

By asking one question—Who governs you?—it becomes possible to divide the world's population into two categories: state-governed and alternatively governed. While studies of governance under nation-state rule abound, studies of alternative governance systems are less common.[87] If we were to separate out the "alternatively governed" answers into further categories, these would include traditional institutions (e.g., tribal chiefs, clan chiefs, village elders), religious institutions (e.g., imams, rabbis, zos), rebel and insurgency groups[88] (e.g., the Sudan People's Liberation Army (SPLA) during the Sudanese civil war, Tamil Tigers during the Sri Lankan civil war, Hamas), paramilitaries,[89] and extralegal groups (mafias,[90] drug cartels, pirate gangs, informal security providers,[91] prison gangs in the US[92] and South Africa[93]) which provide governance

---

[84] Organisation for Economic Co-operation and Development (OECD) (2007).

[85] Ben Anderson (2015).   [86] Óscar Martínez (2016).

[87] While there are exceptions such as James C. Scott (2009), these studies are more common in anthropology and sociology. For example, see Sudhir Alladi Venkatesh (2008).

[88] For an exploration of rebel governance, see Zachariah C. Mampilly (2011b); Ana Arjona, Nelson Kasfir and Zachariah Mampilly (2015). For a warlord's perspective on governance, see William Reno (1998); Victoria Tin-bor Hui (2005); Kimberly Zisk Marten (2012); Dipali Mukhopadhyay (2014).

[89] As with Protestant and Catholic paramilitary groups in Northern Ireland. See Heather Hamill (2011).

[90] Diego Gambetta (1993); Federico Varese (2001); Vadim Volkov (2002).

[91] Ana Kantor and Mariam Persson (2010); Richard Reeve and Jackson Speare (2012).

[92] David Skarbek (2014).

[93] Heather Parker Lewis (2006); Marie Rosenkrantz Lindegaard and Sasha Gear (2014). For a narrative account of life in one of the Number gangs, see Jonny Steinberg (2005).

in order to facilitate commerce. The boundaries between these categories are fuzzy, and there is significant blurring and overlap across groups. For example, captured states,[94] shadow states,[95] and criminalized states[96] all occupy a conceptual space where formal and informal power intertwine.

Alternative systems of governance arise in a variety of circumstances. Sometimes they coexist with the state, as with the Jewish Beth Din courts or Islamic Sharia courts that are active in many Western democracies. Sometimes, individuals choose to leave their society behind and rebel against it, and day-to-day governance comes from the new organization that they have joined, as with the recruits of Islamic State who moved to Eastern Syria and Western Iraq or to Borno State in Nigeria. Sometimes, the central state has collapsed, but civil society organizations have moved to act as substitutes—with varying degrees of success.[97] During civil wars, militias and local political leaders can also offer political stability through elite bargains and informal arrangements,[98] while at other times, the state does not have a significant local presence and extralegal groups are able to stake out a space. Such arrangements can even offer a Pareto improvement for local populations in a situation of uncertain or contested authority by providing greater stability, particularly in facilitating commerce and trade.

Overlapping Spheres of Crime and Conflict

In the late 1990s and early 2000s, the political economy of war literature[99] emerged partly as a response to ethnic and identity-based conflicts, and partly as a response to the forces of globalization. This body of scholarship established an overlap in the worlds of crime and conflict with respect to actors and methods. Scholars such as Mary Kaldor, Carolyn Nordstrom, John Mueller, Peter Andreas, and Michael Pugh pointed out that militia members and criminals were one and the same.[100] There were examples of organized crime groups actively fighting in wars and controlling wartime smuggling networks; soldiers and rebels alike were shown to behave like criminals, putting profits ahead of military victory. On the ground, crime and war overlapped, as the

---

[94] J. Hellman, G. Jones, D. Kaufmann and M. Schankerman (2000).
[95] William Reno (1995).
[96] Jean-Francois Bayart, Stephen Ellis and Beatrice Hibou (1999).
[97] Laura Seay (2009).   [98] Paul Staniland (2012).
[99] Early inspiration for this project came out of the political economy of war literature, including Paul Collier and Anke Hoeffler (1998); David Keen (1998); William Reno (1998); Mary Kaldor (1999); Mats R. Berdal and David Malone (2000); Mark R. Duffield (2001); Philippe Le Billon (2001a).
[100] Mary Kaldor (1999); John E. Mueller (2003); Peter Andreas (2004); Carolyn Nordstrom (2004); Michael Pugh (2004).

casualty rates of "criminal conflicts" hit the tens of thousands, spurred on by a thriving Latin American drug trade.

This confluence of crime and conflict has intensified. As processes of globalization have forced efficiencies into manufacturing supply chains in every sector of the economy, it has become easier than ever for the worlds of crime and conflict to cooperate and expand into new regions.[101] Supply can now meet demand more quickly, cheaply, and with less scrutiny than ever before, and criminal networks and parties to armed conflict have developed ever more opportunities to collaborate.

Whether an activity is labeled as "crime" or "conflict" depends on understanding the motivations of the offending group in relation to state and society.[102] Crudely stated, we categorize criminal activities as profit-based and conflict activities as rooted in ideology or grievance. This takes us back to the false dichotomy of the greed vs. grievance debate.[103] Setting up an either/or situation cannot account for activities where criminals are recruited into armed conflict or where organized crime leaders make strategic alliances with militias, rebel groups, terrorists, and governments for financial *and* ideological reasons.[104]

The crime vs. conflict distinction also rests on the application and enforcement of the law. In weak states, this is problematic because the justice system can be captured and manipulated. Without impartial rule of law, what is or is not considered criminal can depend solely on *who committed the act* and *who is doing the enforcing* rather than the legality of the act itself.[105] When the law becomes another tool of those in power, the boundaries separating legal, illegal, and extralegal grow blurred.

Wartime smuggling and trading networks are rooted in human relationships and social identities. Relationships between criminals, smugglers, terrorists, rebels, and militias are maintained for personal, as well as economic reasons. Identities are layered and malleable,[106] and can change over time as smugglers become powerful business leaders, and generals become ministers.

---

[101] See Michael Miklaucic and Jacqueline Brewer (2013). On the global narcotics markets, see Julia Buxton (2006). On the recruitment of criminals into the ranks of Islamic State, see Anthony Faiola and Souad Mekhennet (2015).

[102] For example, see Charles Tilly (1985) and Diego Gambetta (1993). See also Christina Steenkamp's (2009: Chapter 1) incisive discussion of this quandary.

[103] Originally, see Paul Collier and Anke Hoeffler (1998); Mats R. Berdal and David Malone (2000). For critiques of this framing, see Karen Ballentine and Jake Sherman (2003); Laurie Nathan (2005); Christopher Cramer (2006).

[104] For example, on Afghanistan's heroin trade, see Jonathan Goodhand (2011); on the Revolutionary Armed Forces of Colombia's (FARC's) involvement in narcotrafficking, see Helen Murphy and Luis Jaime Acosta (2013); on kidnapping, smuggling, and arbitrage of legal goods by Malian Islamist terrorist groups AQIM (Al Qaeda in the Islamic Maghreb) and MUJAO (*Mouvement pour l'unicité et le jihad en Afrique de l'Ouest*), see Wolfram Lacher (2012).

[105] This problem is not exclusive to weak states. Even in the U.S. judicial system, there are vast disparities in the treatment of blacks and whites under the law. See Dylan Matthews (2013).

[106] On social identity theory, see Henri Tajfel (1981); Blake E. Ashforth and Fred Mael (1989).

In this way, criminal legacies of war should not be read as a pure expression of market supply and demand for illicit goods—as characterized by economists. Instead, it is more useful to think of these relationships as a function of conflict capital, a concept which is discussed in greater detail in Chapter 1. These relationships and "industry knowledge" are key ingredients in the creation of extralegal groups.

Extralegal groups can exist before, during, and after conflict. The worlds of crime and conflict intertwine and bleed into one another,[107] and extralegal groups are most likely to be found where these two worlds overlap. Yet extralegal groups (and specific forms of these groups like organized crime gangs) are relatively understudied by politics scholars.[108] Depending on who is asked, extralegal groups may also be labeled as criminals, as rebels, as "rogues" (thieves), or as a combination of all of the above. Further, the nature of these groups can also change over time—for better or for worse. In the worst case, these groups can perpetuate an atmosphere of fear and violence, embedding themselves into the environment in such a way so as to create (or reinstate) an equilibrium that favors corruption and private interests. They can shut out the public interest and threaten state survival. While policymakers and politicians should be alert to this danger, the functions of extralegal groups can also be presented quite differently: these groups *also* provide key governance functions and contribute to statebuilding in invisible ways. As I will show, Somali pirates, Mexican cartels, and Liberian ex-combatant groups also enforce contracts, resolve local disputes, and maintain local order for commercial purposes.

While this study argues that the end of war creates conditions that are particularly ripe for the emergence of extralegal groups, they are by no means exclusive to post-conflict situations. They operate successfully in rich and poor countries, under free and oppressive regimes, and even in countries where the rule of law is regarded as highly effective—as with the Japanese Yakuza or the gangs of East Los Angeles. Normally, we think of gangs, militias, and rebel groups as being vastly different because of their form, their function, their ideology (or lack thereof), and the different cultural contexts in which they are rooted. Yet despite their differences, these entities share some vital organizational features and tactics:

- willingness and capability to use violence strategically;
- ability to maintain local legitimacy and authority (to varying degrees);
- self-contained regulatory mechanisms;
- capacity to undermine the state; and
- reliance on conflict capital.

[107] This is notable in the evolution of Islamic State. See Aymenn al-Tamimi (2015).
[108] But see Phil Williams (1994); Roy Godson (2003); P. Andreas (2004); Carolyn Nordstrom (2007); James Cockayne and Adam Lupel (2009); Sasha Jesperson (2013); Michael Miklaucic and Jacqueline Brewer (2013); John de Boer and Louise Bosetti (2015).

Analyzing how different kinds of extralegal groups form and develop provides a common framework for comparing functions of crime and conflict. This makes common dimensions more clear, and applies a shared vocabulary to their actions and decisions. To make the concept of extralegal groups more concrete, let us turn to examples from three different contexts: Somalia, Mexico, and Liberia. In each case, extralegal groups have taken differently dangerous forms, responding to the economic opportunities available as well as the political conditions of the time—yet they share structural similarities.

The first example is that of Somali pirates in the Gulf of Aden. At the peak of their operations, these pirate syndicates routinely hijacked large container ships, demanding multi-million dollar ransoms for the release of crew and cargo. From the late 1990s through to 2013, pirates were active up and down the entire Somali coastline.[109] Moreover, their hijacking and kidnapping activities spawned an entire cottage industry based on providing long-term care for hostages (catering, accommodation, security). Importantly, these groups successfully embedded themselves into local authority structures in several provinces of Somalia.[110]

The second example is of peacetime extralegal groups at their most powerful and organized: Mexico's narcotrafficking cartels. In 2009, these groups had assumed de facto control over 233 "zonas de impunidad" along the US–Mexico border. The drug trade operated openly in these zones of impunity; the cartels were the ones with real authority.[111] Not only do the cartels control these areas, but their power is so entrenched that some view them as a real threat to the integrity of the Mexican state.[112] The Calderón government's aggressive efforts in the late 2000s to diminish the power of the cartels unleashed waves of violence that has since resulted in tens of thousands of deaths—with many of the killings carried out brutally and publicly in order to make an example of those who dared to threaten a cartel's business interests.

While Somali pirates and Mexican drug cartels illustrate the potential threat posed by more mature and organized extralegal groups, this book turns to the Liberian context to show extralegal groups at their inception. For example, in Liberia's rubber sector, two large groups of armed ex-combatants each took over a major rubber plantation, and successfully controlled the rubber trade in their respective areas for several years—*after* the civil war had ended. Both the Guthrie Group and the Sinoe Group inspired deep-seated fears over local security conditions and even threatened a return to war. Residents described them as "rogues" and gangs.

---

[109] International Commercial Crime Services (2014).
[110] David Anderson (2009). See also an interesting discussion by Expedition (2008).
[111] Marc Lacey (2009); Ioan Grillo (2011); Tom Wainwright (2016).
[112] Sam Quinones (2009); Anja Shortland (2012); John Bailey (2014).

The UNMIL and the Liberian government did make several attempts (some of them serious), to dismantle these groups and reclaim the rubber plantations. Yet even though UNMIL had the military capability to wrest control of the rubber plantations, their attempts to reclaim these areas still failed on multiple occasions. Remarkably, these groups ruled over these areas despite the sizeable presence of UN peacekeepers in the country—at the time, Liberia had 13,000 blue helmets on the ground covering a population of only 3 million people. This was the highest concentration of peacekeepers in the world.

These three examples illustrate the blurring of "crime" and "conflict," and the different policy responses (police vs. military) and disciplinary approaches (criminology vs. politics) that are implicit in each of these terms. The extralegal groups framework acknowledges that the problem extends beyond police and military capacity, and that complex political economy dynamics are at work.

The Quality of Peace

> Organising an official ceremony cannot take us from here … If they want war we will give them the cause to have war.
>
> Ex-combatant Mark Wedo, from the Guthrie plantation[113]

It is common to think about peace as a binary state: a society is either at peace or at war. But in quantitative studies of armed conflict, "peace" is commonly operationalized as "not war."[114] This is because the way in which we determine whether a society is "at war" or "at peace" rests largely on one aggregate measure: battlefield violence. As long as no organized group is actively fighting to overthrow the state, then the transition from war to peace can be portrayed as a success. There is heavy emphasis on the national security dimension, but minimal attention is given to threats from someone like Mark Wedo (in the quote above) who affects the "everyday" quality of peace.[115] As long as there are relatively few battle-related deaths, then there is "peace."

When we think about what constitutes a "successful" war-to-peace transition, the most basic criterion is an absence of battlefield violence. Yet even with such a seemingly straightforward measure, "success" still comes in shades of gray. The focus on extralegal groups makes plain how large that gray area really is, and the crime–conflict overlap only reinforces his point. Within the borders of a state, there can be substantial variation in how provinces and cities experience peace, and also variation within individual communities as some groups are targeted while others are left alone. There is further variation

---

[113] Zoom Dosso (2006).   [114] But see the Global Peace Index.
[115] But see Seema Patel, Steven Ross, Frederick Barton and Karin von Hippel (2007); Oliver P. Richmond (2010); Roger MacGinty (2013); Pamina Firchow and Roger MacGinty (2014).

within households as some vulnerable family members are more likely to continue to experience violence at home (e.g., victims of domestic abuse). All of these variations coexist in countries that are technically post-conflict and "at peace."[116]

One problem with this war–peace binary is that a country's status becomes the defining criteria from which all other policies and judgments follow. A country's war–peace status has an anchoring effect, in the social psychology sense, on how we judge and categorize that country.[117] The less familiar we are with the country in question, the more powerful the anchor. As long as a state of "not war" prevails, the actual *quality* of that peace is immaterial from a statistical standpoint and a policy perspective—contrary to the experiences of the people who live there. When wartime violence (as proxied by battle-related deaths) drops below a certain threshold, then the data implies that "peace" has set in.[118] But a threshold approach leaves little room to reflect on what the quality of that peace looks like and feels like in a particular place, at a particular time. For example, the widely used Correlates of War dataset sets the civil war threshold at a minimum of 1000 annual battle-related deaths. Having such a high threshold implies that, say, 823 battle-related deaths for a given country–year pairing does *not* signify civil war, irrespective of any other abuses that may be occurring, including rape, amputations, and forced migration.[119] By this standard, a country is considered to be at "peace" despite these 823 deaths and despite whatever other abuses may be happening.

This discussion assumes, of course, that 823 was in fact the correct number of battle-related deaths for the country–year pairing in question. This in itself is likely to be a poor assumption, especially if these are African statistics. In a bold critique of where econometric analysis has fallen short, especially in African studies and international development, Morten Jerven argues:

> The literature has either neglected the issue of data quality and therefore accepted the data at face value or dismissed the data as unreliable and therefore irrelevant ...
>
> Numerical expressions of social, economic, and political phenomena are all, to various degrees, social, economic and political phenomena themselves. Seldom do these numbers provide the untainted, objective observation through which societies can be gauged, analyzed, and evaluated in the manner that much statistical analysis seems to presume.[120]

---

[116] These variations in how individuals and communities experience safety and security are not exclusive to post-conflict environments; they are also present in countries that have not been touched by war.

[117] Daniel Kahneman, Paul Slovic and Amos Tversky (1982).

[118] For two examples of peace duration analyses, see Michael W. Doyle and Nicholas Sambanis (2006); Virginia Page Fortna (2008).

[119] For a discussion of the problems associated with a threshold approach, see Paul Collier (2011), p. 92–3.

[120] Morten Jerven (2013), p. 111.

Statisticians refer to this problem of poor data as GIGO: "Garbage in, garbage out." Yet even if we set aside these enormous data problems, we still lack the context needed to understand whether 823 is more likely to represent "war" or "peace." Was there a precipitous drop in violence from tens of thousands of war casualties down to 823 that year? Or was this simply a lull in the fighting? Was fighting isolated to a particular part of the country where those 823 deaths occurred? Or did a new, separate conflict begin? Are other kinds of violence being perpetrated (amputations, rape, forced migration) even while battle-related deaths have fallen? Does an atmosphere of fear persist?

Adding to the problem of contextualizing armed conflict data is the fact that some portion of these deaths may not even be war-related. If we take Colombia as an example, the FARC, the National Liberation Army (ELN), and the paramilitaries have all had a hand in narcotrafficking—this means it is not always possible to neatly categorize drug trafficking (criminal) deaths from battle-related deaths (conflict). In spite of these uncertainties, quantification suggests precision; there is an aura of exactness and certainty that is projected on to peace itself, even though the reality on the ground would make a mockery of any claims to peace.

Approaching the transition to peace using only standard quantitative war/peace measures is problematic because these tend to obscure critical differences in levels of violence within a country. The data are silent on the process of becoming peaceful, and they do not speak to the quality of peace.

National peace does not imply local peace

While the absence of battlefield violence is a necessary condition for peace, such a narrow interpretation suggests a misleading uniformity to post-war "peace." This data point does not reflect how a post-conflict transition is actually experienced by individuals, communities, and regions. Rather than taking the temperature of peace by using the goings-on in the capital as the key indicator, or averaging out peace across the country, this study examines the quality of peace in selected localities, taking into account key episodes of collective violence. For example, it is possible to have "peace" at the national level even while armed conflict continues at the local level,[121] and more intimate violence pervades the community and the family. As is evident from Afghanistan,[122] the Democratic Republic of Congo, Myanmar,[123] Northern Ireland,[124] Guatemala,[125] Indonesia,[126] and Nigeria,[127] the quality of peace can vary tremendously across time and space. I use extralegal groups as a

---

[121] Séverine Autesserre (2008).   [122] Jonathan Goodhand (2011).
[123] Patrick Meehan (2011).   [124] Heather Hamill (2011).
[125] Regina Bateson (2011).   [126] Jana Krause (2013).
[127] Jana Krause (2017).

means of disaggregating post-conflict peace by exploring what "peace" looks like in specific places and how it is constituted under specific modes of control.[128]

However, when episodes of violence are aggregated at the country-level and on an annual basis, a nationwide decline in battle-related deaths (as the key proxy) gives a general impression that peace is building gradually and the assumption is that violence is evenly distributed, even if some pockets of the country never stopped fighting. The localized conflict dynamics of extralegal groups reveal how an entire national peace process can be held hostage using persistent threats to take the country back to war or to destabilize border areas. In a case like Liberia's, conflict is as much a function of local tensions and power struggles as it is a product of formal statebuilding processes at the national level. This link between microlevel and macrolevel conflict is important. For example, even though the threats and violence on the Guthrie rubber plantation were confined to a small area, these clashes could have reignited a broader civil war.

Aggregation can obscure the fact that particular groups or communities or regions may continue to be targeted, and as long as this does not result in too many battle-related deaths, it is possible to maintain the fiction of "peace." A general downward trend in battle-related deaths can deceive, just as a national narrative of "peaceful transition" can overshadow local conflicts. Given the inherent problems in gathering and validating battle deaths data, we need to be more circumspect about its use; it is most useful for outlining rough trends over time and for broad strokes comparison, but less appropriate for analyzing conflict dynamics and causal mechanisms.

This survey of extralegal groups reveals that beneath the surface, "peace" is not experienced uniformly across a postwar landscape; it has an uneven quality that all too often remains unacknowledged. Even for a "successful" post-conflict case like Liberia, key outcomes (peace, security, development, reconciliation) are actually much more uneven than national indicators suggest. Clearly, the quality of peace varies not only by geography, but also by ethnicity,[129] gender, religion, age, and other factors.

So what does it mean to be "at peace"? How does the conversation change when we ask not only whether a country is *at peace*, but also about the *quality of peace, and how regular citizens actually experience peace*? In a postwar environment, should peace be equated with negative peace, defined by Johan Galtung[130] as an absence of violence or war? Should peace have the aspirational characteristics of positive peace, offering a more utopian vision

---

[128] As our ability to gather real-time, geolocated wartime data improves, so too will our understanding of how violent conflict breaks out at the local level. With perfect information, both utopian and dystopian futures are possible. For an extended discussion, see Radiolab, Alex Goldmark and Manoush Zomorodi (2015).

[129] Ann Laudati (2011).   [130] Johan Galtung (1969).

for societal interaction, absent of structural violence?[131] Or should peace be evaluated by some other standard, grounded in local ideas of pragmatic coexistence[132] or reconciliation? Should the standards for post-conflict peace evolve as the peace itself matures?

This study does not directly examine how the average person experiences peace in their normal lives (as with a dismaying rise in violent crime rates or a heartening increase in the number of petty traders). Nevertheless, if we examine extralegal groups using Firchow and MacGinty's frame of "everyday peace," their activities take on new significance—in terms of their day-to-day impact on local employment, on local markets, and local security. Even as extralegal groups pose problems for everyday peace, they *also* contribute to the stability of that peace.

Consolidating peace

It is self-evident that the process by which peace is consolidated deeply affects the quality of that peace. Yet the statistical simplicity of indicators such as battle-related deaths implies a crisp delineation between war and peace—skipping over the difficult and unsteady transition process.[133] Even as war casualty figures drop precipitously from one year to the next, the bonds of war remain sticky, and societies need time to do two things: configure a new coexistence and reconstitute their institutions.

First, learning how to reconcile and coexist again requires transforming a society's stock of conflict capital into social capital—a process that I discuss in greater depth in Chapter 1. In part, studies of disarmament, demobilization, and reintegration (DDR),[134] security sector reform (SSR),[135] and transitional justice[136] speak broadly to the problem of destroying and converting conflict capital, and coping with its influence.

---

[131] David P. Barash and Charles Webel (2002), p. 8 (as quoted in Gregg Barak (2003), p. 319) offer an inspiring discussion of positive peace: The "ancient Greek concept of *eirenei* (English *irenic*) denotes harmony and justice as well as peace. Similarly, the Arabic *salaam* and the Hebrew *shalom* connote not only the absence of violence but also the presence of well-being, wholeness and harmony within oneself, a community, and among all nations and peoples. The Sanskrit word *shantyi* refers not only to peace but also to spiritual tranquility, an integration of outward and inward modes of being, just as the Chinese noun *ping* denotes harmony and the achievement of unity from diversity. In Russian, the word *mir* means peace, a village community, and the entire world."

[132] In Sierra Leone, Johanna Boersch-Supan (2009) finds that Sierra Leonean communities have carved out a peaceful coexistence with ex-combatants, but that there is also systematic discrimination of ex-combatants.

[133] Kevin Clements (2004).

[134] Nat J. Colletta, Markus Kostner and Ingo Wiederhofer (1996); Nat J. Colletta and Michelle Cullen (2000); Mats R. Berdal and David H. Ucko (2009); Jaremey McMullin (2013); Alison Brettle (2014); Walt Kilroy (2015).

[135] Monica Duffy Toft (2010a).

[136] Priscilla B. Hayner (2001); Jon Elster (2004); Leslie Vinjamuri and Jack Snyder (2004); R. Kerr and E. Mobekk (2007); Bronwyn Anne Leebaw (2008); Philip Clark (2010).

Second, on the institutional side, the vast statebuilding and peacebuilding literature confronts many of the problems of constructing and reconstructing postwar institutional arrangements. Scholars have tackled these complexities by examining critical factors such as local ownership and the legitimacy of the peacebuilding process;[137] respect for the rule of law;[138] power sharing and the management of peace "spoilers";[139] mitigating corruption;[140] the structure of peace agreements;[141] democratization and economic liberalization;[142] and the role of peacekeepers and third parties in maintaining peace.[143] Each of these determinants is examined separately in relation to the "success" of peacebuilding.[144] But in practice, all of these processes happen simultaneously and interact with one another in myriad ways, and it is possible that they will reinforce or counteract one another.

In this study, the ways in which states and international actors respond to extralegal groups illustrates how interdependent many of these processes are, and how fruitless it can be to try and affect change by only focusing on one dimension at a time *in isolation*. The entrenchment of extralegal groups makes this particularly clear: a coherent strategy on behalf of government interests would require simultaneous responses from the police, the judiciary, the military, the prisons, the legislature, and the executive. There cannot be any weak links in this chain of response.

Rethinking the Resource Curse

What can extralegal groups tell us about the resource curse? One strand of this extensive literature has focused extensively on whether and how certain types of natural resources contribute to the onset, duration, and termination of

---

[137] Dominik Zaum (2007); J. Whalan (2010); Timothy Donais (2012); Chuck Thiessen (2013); Sarah von Billerbeck (2015).

[138] T. Carothers (1998); Seth G. Jones, Jeremy Wilson, Andrew Rathmell and K. Jack Riley (2005).

[139] Stephen J. Stedman (1997); Ian S. Spears (2000); Denis M. Tull and Andreas Mehler (2005); Edward Newman and Oliver P. Richmond (2006); Nita Yawanarajah (2014).

[140] Philippe Le Billon (2003); Christine Cheng and Dominik Zaum (2011).

[141] Caroline Hartzell, Matthew Hoddie and Donald Rothchild (2001); Stephen J. Stedman, Donald S. Rothchild and Elizabeth M. Cousens (2002); Virginia Page Fortna (2004c); Michael Kerr (2011).

[142] Nancy Bermeo (2003); Oisín Tansey (2009); Richard Ponzio (2011).

[143] Robert Cooper and Mats Berdal (1993); Christopher Dandeker and James Gow (1997); Michael W. Doyle and Nicholas Sambanis (2000); Adekeye Adebajo (2002); Virginia P. Fortna (2004a); Virginia P. Fortna (2004b); Jane Boulden (2013), but see Monica Duffy Toft (2010b).

[144] A key exception to this is the security sector reform literature which takes a more holistic view of post-conflict security challenges. For example, see Dylan Hendrickson (1999); Mark Sedra (2006); Monica Duffy Toft (2010b).

civil wars[145] and international wars.[146] While this literature has produced long-running debates on the precise nature of the relationship between natural resources and war,[147] the emphasis has primarily been on how natural resources are used to finance armed conflict.[148]

Less attention has been paid to the secondary effects of this wartime economy.[149] For example, the question of how these same resources are exploited *after* war has received less attention even though it is clear that war economies do not just dissolve at war's end.[150]

Theoretically and empirically, this study contributes to the resource curse literature in two ways. First, extralegal groups demonstrate that one overlooked legacy of financing war through the exploitation of natural resources is that illicit trading networks and their supply chains survive and adapt after war.[151] Extralegal groups show that an important way in which the resource curse manifests itself is through wartime networks of natural resource exploitation. The contacts and knowledge base that are activated live on in the post-conflict transition, with the continued potential to influence the country's statebuilding trajectory.

Smuggling routes and conflict-related trade can sometimes be curbed if sanctions are enforced, but not always. And sanctions enforcement can be accompanied by undesirable side effects. Trade in natural resources—licit and illicit—will continue, supported by newly configured extralegal groups unless there is a concerted effort to stop them. Further, the networks that were once created to illegally move diamonds or oil or coltan around the world can also be used to move other precious cargo. This is conflict capital that is ready to be reactivated; it does not disintegrate after war simply because the battles have ended and there is "peace."

By the time war ends, the natural resources themselves may be secondary to the wartime smuggling networks that they have spawned and empowered. In this way, it is corruption that lies at the heart of the resource curse—not the resources themselves. Natural resources are merely an economic conduit for entrenching a set of "winners" who will make it their business to hold on to

---

[145] Paul Collier and Anke Hoeffler (1998); Philippe Le Billon (2001b); Michael L. Ross (2004a).

[146] Jeff Colgan (2013).

[147] On the importance of causal mechanisms, see Macartan Humphreys 2005.

[148] But see Jeremy M. Weinstein 2007.

[149] Important and notable exceptions include William Reno (1998); William Reno (2000); Michael Pugh, Neil Cooper and Jonathan Goodhand (2004); Christian Webersik (2005); Jeremy M. Weinstein (2007); Jonathan Goodhand (2011).

[150] Scholars have begun to tackle this subject. See the series on Post-conflict peacebuilding on natural resources: Päivi Lujala and Siri Aas Rustad (2011); David Jensen and Stephen Lonergan (2012); Carl Bruch, Carroll Muffett and Sandra Nichols (2015); Helen Young and Lisa Goldman (2015). See also Alexandra Gillies and Page Dykstra (2011).

[151] R. T. Naylor (2001); P. Andreas (2004).

political and economic power in a manner that is consistent with fulfilling the resource curse dynamics.[152]

Second, this study undercuts the structural determinism that pervades much of the resource curse literature. While individual scholars are careful about the probabilistic nature of the claims they make in their statistical analyses, when this body of studies is taken together as a whole, the subtleties of correlation and probability are lost. The curse is taken as read. Andrew Rossler points out that:

> various political and social variables mediate the relationship between natural resource wealth and development outcomes. But rather than acknowledge that *these variables are shaped by a range of historical and other factors* in each case, scholars have tended to see them as determined by the natural resource base [emphasis added].[153]

In this study of Liberia's natural resource sectors, particular individuals like Charles Taylor played critical roles that directly impacted the arc of extralegal group development and their failure. While the presence, geographical configuration, or particular characteristics of natural resources can shape and constrain choices, these should not be taken as predetermined.[154] The resource curse is *by no means inevitable*.[155] Human agency and socio-historical context are important to influencing the outcome. This study of extralegal groups shows the various ways in which the resource curse is likely to be fulfilled, but *also* confirms that there is scope to reject the determinism implied by such a "curse."

WHY READ THIS BOOK?

Through the lens of extralegal groups and Liberia's transition out of war, this book contributes to two related bodies of academic literature: (1) post-conflict transitions and (2) state failure and statebuilding. To the state failure and statebuilding debates, I show how the operations of extralegal groups and the role of extralegal governance undermines the argument that weak and failing states simply need "more stateness"—more institutions, more capacity, more competence. This study shows that a stronger state presence need not translate automatically into gains for the public good; the long-term entrenchment of extralegal groups directly calls into question this institution-building approach.

---

[152] Christine Cheng and Dominik Zaum (2015).   [153] Andrew Rossler (2006), p. 7.
[154] Abiodun Alao (2007); Macartan Humphreys, Jeffery D. Sachs and Joseph E. Stiglitz (2007).
[155] This point is made by the Extractive Industries Transparency Initiative (EITI), civil society's Publish What You Pay campaign, the Natural Resources Charter, the Revenue Watch Index, the Resource Governance Index, the transparency and accountability movement, as well as by organizations like Global Witness, Natural Resource Governance Institute, and Natural Resource Governance Institute (formerly Revenue Watch).

Strengthening the state is often viewed as a double-edged sword by the citizenry,[156] and current discussions of post-conflict statebuilding fail to acknowledge this point. Western scholars and policy practitioners should begin by rethinking the assumption that states are good, and that more stateness will automatically lead to more peace or more security. To be clear, this is not to say that strong states cannot provide peace and security, but rather that strong state institutions by themselves are insufficient for achieving these goals.

My second point of departure from current debates on post-conflict transitions is to de-emphasize what external actors can or should do—traditionally, an area of importance for Western scholars and policymakers—and to reorient the research agenda toward local politics, and its problematic interactions with international actors. Through a detailed analysis of local political economies, I demonstrate how political actors are compromised and how incentives are structured to encourage this. This book discusses how difficult it can be to find an "honest broker" among local actors, and why such a credible, idealized, neutral "local" actor cannot exist in an environment of armed conflict. This finding poses practical and theoretical challenges to the debates on local ownership and peacebuilding—and paves the way for a more meaningful operationalization of local ownership.

The third contribution that I offer to our collective analysis of post-conflict transitions is to show how local livelihoods—specifically the socio-economic ecosystem of ex-combatants—drive the post-conflict environment. More often than not, both the peacebuilding and statebuilding scholarship refer to the importance of local economic development and unemployment, but allude to these factors in an abstract way. I show concretely how a livelihoods calculus affects individuals' decisions to coalesce around extralegal groups, and how ex-combatants can remain economically bound to their former commanders, even after war ends.

To the failing and fragile states literature, this study shows how governance *actually* arises in what some term an "ungoverned space," where authority is contested. In doing so, I make the point that governance provision is unevenly distributed across a territory, and also that deep historical legacies of subjugation, abuse, and coercion at the local level find echoes in contemporary practices. In this way, I show how the socialization of authority and patterns of social rule become entrenched over time in the detailed examinations of each economic sector. The causal processes of state fragility are magnified and examined up close—with special emphasis on what I term the "weakest link problem" and the challenge of establishing trust in the state.

---

[156] The Kurds in Turkey are a case in point. In defining a new citizenship, ethnic minorities can choose to resist and subvert statebuilding attempts (Ceren Belge, 2011). A related point is made by Marta Iñiguez de Heredia (2012) about resistance to statebuilding in the Democratic Republic of Congo.

I bring to the state failure discussion a warning and a plea: a warning about the double-edged nature of state–society relations, and a plea for an empathetic approach to history as it is experienced and interpreted at the community level.

To explain state failure, existing arguments point to how predatory elites and extractive institutions induce state failure—we see this most clearly in the century of Americo-Congo rule over Liberia (discussed in Chapter 3). I present a variation of these arguments to explain why it is so difficult to emerge out of that vicious circle. I show that the problem is not simply one of extractive institutions per se, but the challenge of reforming several sets of institutions simultaneously. There is a "weakest link problem." Unless the police, military, courts, judges, lawyers, prisons, and politicians are all united in targeting local ruling elites—extralegal groups in this case—these powerful elites can easily subvert any attempts to curtail their power by targeting the weakest of these institutions with blackmail or a bribe. The problem of state fragility is not merely one of weak institutions that lack financial resources and know-how, but the challenge of simultaneous reform when *any single one of a state's critical functions can be captured and corrupted by private interests.*

The state failure literature and the policymakers who are influenced by it frequently make three flawed and simplistic assumptions: that states are "good," that strengthening state capacity always benefits citizens, and that citizens want to be ruled by strong states. These assumptions overlook how governments actually treat their own citizens and incorrectly extrapolate from Western processes of state-making.

By approaching the study of extralegal groups from the bottom up, I show how citizens experience and engage with statebuilding processes differently from the way that international actors think they do. *When viewed through the eyes of citizens in conflict-affected and fragile states, extralegal groups do not lose legitimacy because of their nonstate status.* Rather, they are evaluated based on their ability to deliver governance functions in comparison to state-sanctioned alternatives. To understand why groups that are viewed as undesirable can sometimes thrive under conditions of uncertainty and risk, it is important to accept the possibility that nonstate actors can seed state formation practices.

OVERVIEW OF THE BOOK

At its core, this book is about the complexities of post-conflict transitions—the starts and stops; the unevenness of experiences across space and time; the trepidation and the hope that accompanies an end to war. Extralegal groups provide an entrée to understanding how a society makes this shift from war to peace, from violent contestation to commerce.

The core of this book is divided into four parts. The first part (Chapters 1 and 2) explores the primary research question of how extralegal groups emerge by proposing an incentives-based framework to analyze the behavior of ex-combatants in the aftermath of civil war. Chapter 1 introduces two ideas that are useful for analyzing extralegal groups: conflict capital and time horizons. Conflict capital helps to explain the stickiness of wartime bonds, the ease with which extralegal groups can form, and the difficulty of dismantling them. Incorporating time horizons into statebuilding discussions is critical to understanding how the incentives of the state, of international actors, and of extralegal groups, are structured.

Chapter 2 provides an in-depth treatment of the extralegal groups framework. It sets out the initial conditions and discusses each of the three stages of emergence, development, and entrenchment and how a group transitions between them. The theoretical framework adopts a rational actor model and incorporates insights from the state formation and organized crime literatures. In this chapter, I argue that the key factor that determines whether an extralegal group engages in statebuilding depends on how far into the future the group believes it can control its enclave. The farther into the future it believes it can retain control, the greater the incentive to build institutions to provide public goods and to become, effectively, a "statebuilder."

Through an exploration of Liberia's political history, the second part of this book (Chapters 3 and 4) provides the social and historical context that is needed to fully understand how and why Liberia's extralegal groups developed the way they did and how these groups echo the country's long-term statebuilding processes. While extralegal groups form all over the world, their exact nature varies from place to place. Chapter 3 explores the troubled relationship between the settlers and Native Liberians and how this relationship prepared the ground for the emergence of extralegal groups. Chapter 4 then turns to the civil war, building on the social roots of the 1980 coup and the rebalancing of the Americo-Indigenous relationship. This discussion of the conflict focuses on the exploitation of resources and sheds light on the subsequent patterns and behaviors of the ex-combatants in the war economy.

The third part of this book (Chapters 5, 6, and 7) applies the extralegal groups framework to individual sectors of the Liberian economy (rubber, diamonds, timber). In each of these chapters, I provide basic information about the sector and then evaluate the framework using the extralegal group example for that sector. In Chapter 5, the evidence shows that the framework largely holds for the groups in the rubber industry, but that the findings reveal inconsistencies. In Chapter 6, evidence from the BOPC diamond-mining group largely, but not entirely, supports the theoretical framework. In Chapter 7, the extralegal groups framework is tested on the Nezoun Group in the artisanal logging sector, with the evidence suggesting that the framework holds for the development and entrenchment stages, but is mixed for the emergence stage. While the Nezoun Group formed during the final stages of the war, it was not until it took on local regulatory and dispute resolution functions that it became an extralegal group.

The fourth part of this book (Chapter 8) explores the secondary research question, linking the basic functions of these groups to the existence of the state. This chapter puts extralegal groups into historical perspective by exploring the foundations of the state and turning to Hobbes and Locke to examine Western expectations of statehood. I reflect more deeply on statebuilding theory and practice, and the *hidden functions* of extralegal groups. Ultimately, I conclude that contemporary statebuilding is driven by the need to trade. As such, extralegal groups need to be viewed not only as a problem "to be solved," but also as groups with long-term statebuilding utility. I draw some broad conclusions about extralegal groups based on Liberia's experiences, and also offer policy recommendations for post-conflict governments, local communities, and the international community.

In a final coda to this project, I reflect back on the entirety of the research project in Chapter 9 and argue for greater honesty in our approach to research design. This chapter reflects on the evolution of the research design of this project with the goal of opening up the black box of academic research.

I began this book by describing the puzzle that I confronted when I came to face-to-face with the BOPC group: instead of the violent criminal gang that I had expected, I encountered a vibrant market; instead of men with guns, I saw men with umbrellas and shovels; instead of locals and ex-combatants opposing each other, they appeared to be working together. By conceptualizing these groups purely as security threats, I missed seeing all of the other ways in which these groups impacted the transition from war to peace. Ultimately, I intend to share with you my own story about how the BOPC group and others like it gradually led me to question my own assumptions about states and statebuilding. Over the next eight chapters, I hope to take you on a condensed version of this journey, as I wrestled with the concept of extralegal groups, the role they play in statebuilding, and how they have slowly changed the assumptions that I hold about states.

Part I

Extralegal Groups

1

How to Study Extralegal Groups

In the fall of 2005, two years after Liberia's civil war had officially ended, the country appeared to be on a halting but stable track to recovery. On the surface, the transition from war to peace was proceeding smoothly. Yet a closer look revealed that across the country, groups of former fighters had taken over pockets of land and were illegally exploiting natural resources for personal profit. Some of these groups were terrorizing local populations, co-opting key local and national government figures, and even threatening to take the country back to war. Surprisingly, even with the support of the world's largest United Nations (UN) peacekeeping force at the time, Liberia's transitional government seemed powerless to stop these groups.

By late 2005, the Comprehensive Peace Agreement had been in force for two years, but Liberians still remained wary of these groups. They had good reason to be concerned: the country's brutal civil war had originally begun with only one hundred or so fighters, so the possibility of a small group of fighters renewing the war was very real in people's minds. An editorial from *The Analyst*,[1] a major newspaper in Liberia, captured the visceral fear inspired by two of the ex-combatant-led groups that had taken over the Guthrie and Sinoe rubber plantations:

> what will happen when the simmering discontent at Guthrie becomes open clashes . . . ? . . . Now, add that scenario to the situation in the Sinoe Rubber Plantation (SRP) in Sinoe County where one "General Satan" of the former MODEL rebel militias is holding out and bragging about his right over the plantation . . . we have a potentially explosive situation at hand in those plantations

At the time, Liberia's political stability was hanging by a thread and the influence of these two particular groups and others like it extended far and wide. Similar groups were illegally occupying and extracting natural resources in other enclave areas across the country. These included groups doing gold mining in Sapo National Park, pit sawing timber near the town of Nezoun, and diamond-mining on the Butaw Oil Palm Corporation (BOPC) plantation.

---

[1] *The Analyst* (2005).

While some of these extralegal groups disintegrated, others managed to control their enclaves for many years. The most successful groups flourished over time, cementing territorial control and operating in open defiance of the transitional government and the international community. Some of them threatened national and local security while simultaneously providing extralegal governance. They co-opted government authorities and embedded themselves within state institutions; they also built parallel structures of authority. Seen in a different light, these same groups created an economic space where young unskilled men could meaningfully participate in the economy when the peace was at its most delicate. Without the internal regulation and dispute resolution mechanisms that these groups provided, local commodity markets would probably have operated more erratically and more violently.

In this transitional period, the status of these groups was unclear. The government was in flux and ex-combatants were just barely kept in check by UN peacekeepers. Given the uncertainty of this environment, how can we study extralegal groups, and how do we make sense of them? This chapter answers these questions in four parts. The first section begins by defining extralegal groups in relation to conceptual cousins such as warlords and mafias. The next two sections introduce concepts that are helpful for tackling the study of extralegal groups: conflict capital and time horizons. The final section discusses the research design and methodology of this study.

SAME CAR, DIFFERENT DRIVER? WARLORDS, ORGANIZED CRIME, MAFIAS, BIG MEN

Scholars have long written about related concepts such as warlords, criminalized legacies,[2] rebels,[3] remnants of war,[4] political-criminal nexuses,[5] organized crime groups,[6] state capture,[7] shadow states,[8] big men,[9] and mafias.[10] But Africans realized long ago that these individuals are oftentimes one and the same. Liberians use the expression, "same car, different driver" to acknowledge that even though there are new faces in charge, the underlying power structures remain the same. So, are extralegal groups simply a matter of "same car, different driver"? Not quite. While there is overlap between concepts, each of these terms encapsulates a particular set of interactions or a mode of existence—rebels are juxtaposed in

[2] P. Andreas (2004).

[3] Ted Robert Gurr (1970); James C. Scott (1985).

[4] J. Mueller (2003).   [5] Roy Godson (2003).

[6] Thomas C. Schelling (1971). For a collection of organized crime definitions, see Klaus von Lampe's website on organized crime, Klaus von Lampe (2017).

[7] J. Hellman, G. Jones and D. Kaufmann (2000).   [8] William Reno (1995).

[9] Mats Utas (2012).   [10] Francesco Strazzari (2003).

a fight against the state; organized crime stresses hierarchy and lines of control in the name of illegal profit-making; state capture focuses on private sector interests manipulating the state. However, many of these terms are used interchangeably, which dilutes and distorts their individual meanings.

Despite the conceptual richness on offer, none of these ideas matched the phenomenon that I had observed in Liberia. Moreover, I could think of others (Congolese mining militias, Afghan opium militias, Iraqi kidnapping syndicates) at the intersection of war and crime that had been mislabelled because they eluded classification. Others still had been characterized as organized crime rings, mafias, rebel groups, and warlords, but these terms underemphasized the governance role of these groups.[11] (See Table 1.2) Rather than appropriate an existing term, it made more sense to define a new one. In doing so, the goal is to provide a reference point around which similar concepts can be compared and contrasted.

Extralegal groups is an umbrella term that encompasses varying degrees of organization. It is distinct from other criminal groups in its provision of governance. It includes groups that are disciplined, cohesive, and have strong institutional hierarchies (i.e., what we colloquially refer to as organized crime) as well as those that are nascent with weak and undisciplined organizational structures (Figure 1.1). This book is focused on *nascent* extralegal groups that begin with minimal capabilities. However, parts of the framework (development, entrenchment) are also theoretically useful for understanding the dynamics of well-established entities such as organized crime groups.

At their core, all extralegal groups possess the basic characteristics outlined in the definition: a set of individuals with a proven capacity for violence, working outside the law primarily for profit, and providing governance functions to sustain its profit-making activities. Here, governance is a by-product of creating a viable commercial environment—not an end in itself. These core attributes

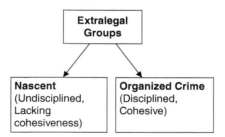

Fig. 1.1. Degree of organization

---

[11] A notable exception is the mafia literature: see Diego Gambetta (1993); Federico Varese (2001).

Table 1.1. Related concepts

	Extralegal Groups	Mafia	Organized Crime	Warlords	Big Men
Profit motivation	High	High	High	Variable	Variable
Political power motivation	Low	Low	Low	High	Variable
Uses mass violence as strategy	Rarely	Rarely	Sometimes	Often	Rarely
Degree of organization	Variable	High	Variable	Variable	Variable
Degree of territorial control	Variable	High	Variable	Variable	Low
Provides basic governance functions to the public	Always	Always	Sometimes	Sometimes	No

Table 1.2. Categories of extralegal groups

Extralegal Groups		Degree of Organization	
		High	Low
Public goods	**Governance and welfare**	Sicilian mafia,[12] Los Angeles Black Kings,[13] Mexican narcotraffickers, Brazil's favela gangs,[14] Colombia's Urabeños, El Salvador's Mara Salvatrucha (MS-13)[15]	Haitian street gangs[16]
	Governance only	Russian mafia, Bosnian cigarette smugglers, South African prison gangs[17]	Liberian ex-combatant-led resource-based groups (e.g., Guthrie Group, Nezoun Group), Congo's militia-led mining groups, South Africa's taxi associations[18]

provide a means of comparing the concept of extralegal groups with others (Table 1.1).

Extralegal groups are not limited to operating in specific industries or "services." While the focus of this study is on natural resources, the logic of the framework also applies to economies with a different mix of commodities and services. Moreover, this study is confined to extralegal groups in the post-conflict context, but the framework can also be applied to "peaceful" settings (Table 1.2).

---

[12] Diego Gambetta (1993).   [13] Sudhir Alladi Venkatesh (2008).

[14] Misha Glenny (2015).

[15] Óscar Martínez (2016); Oscar Martínez, Efren Lemus, Carlos Martínez and Deborah Sontag (2016).

[16] Michael Deibert (2015).   [17] Skye Forrester (2016).

[18] Jackie Dugard (2001); Christopher Glen Malgas (2003).

Aren't These Warlords?

The closest conceptual cousin to extralegal groups is warlords. Many scholars have written about warlords,[19] but the black and white simplicity that this term invokes poses challenges to a more nuanced view. It is difficult to use the term "warlord" in a way that recognizes their capacity to govern and the positive statebuilding externalities that their rule might offer. For example, the insightful work of Dipali Mukhopadhyay identifies the tensions of strongman governance and the political ecosystems that sustain them.[20]

But ultimately, the term "warlord" has been used as shorthand for "bad guy" or "actors that the UN and the West disapprove of." The term "warlord" has become a political tool: when governments and politicians seek to discredit someone in a conflict or post-conflict society, an easy way to do this is to apply the label of warlord. Over time, the warlord discourse—as conceived by William Reno[21] and later adopted by others—has been subject to "conceptual stretching."[22]

In Reno's seminal *Warlord Politics and African States*, he does not directly define the term warlord, but he does highlight specific characteristics of warlord politics: personal rule, a lack of public or collective interest, the outsourcing of key economic opportunities, and strong patronage networks.[23] The essence of Reno's argument is that globalization made warlord politics possible by offering a new type of symbiotic partnership between those who controlled weak states and foreign companies. He articulates a specific warlord dynamic:

> anxious rulers contract a wide array of economic roles to outsiders, in part to deny resources to internal rivals and to use outsiders' skills and connections to gather as much wealth as possible. Rulers then convert wealth into political resources, buying the loyalty of some and buying weapons to coerce others and thus gather more resources and so on.[24]

This dynamic remains important, but one key difference from extralegal groups is that warlords—as defined by Reno—are motivated by political power. In contrast, extralegal groups are driven by profit. This is not just a matter of semantics, but a fundamental difference that drives the group's behavior and its organizational dynamic. Reno's conception of "warlord" allows for mixed motives, but it subsumes economic activities under the pursuit of political power. Similarly, the concept of extralegal groups also embraces the ambiguity of mixed motives, but emphasizes the primacy of economic incentives. At the

---

[19] See, for example, John MacKinlay (2000); S. Skaperdas (2002); Paul Jackson (2003); Leonard Wantchekon (2004); Victoria Tin-bor Hui (2005); Kimberly Z. Marten (2006); K. Stanski (2009).

[20] Dipali Mukhopadhyay (2009); Dipali Mukhopadhyay (2014).

[21] William Reno (1998).   [22] G. Sartori (1970), p. 64.

[23] William Reno (1998), pp. 1–4.   [24] Ibid., p. 1.

Fig. 1.2. The profits and politics spectrum

risk of oversimplifying, it is possible to think of the motivations of warlords and extralegal groups as lying along a spectrum (Figure 1.2). Extralegal groups occupy the profit side of the spectrum while warlords and rebel groups occupy the political side of the spectrum.

Inferring motivation is a difficult, if not impossible, task. The same group of armed individuals will be driven by an array of personal, social, ideological, and material interests—most of these motivations will not be observable.

I use the motivations of leaders as a proxy for the group's intentions. This assumes that "political" employers like rebel leaders or warlords use the group to advance a political agenda, while "business" employers use the group to turn a profit. Of course, the reality is more complex: warlords and rebel leaders may also be motivated by personal profit, while business leaders might desire political power. Even those who are directly carrying out orders might not know what ends their actions ultimately serve.

Finally, it is important to note that warlords and extralegal groups can change and shift their position along the profits–politics spectrum. This is not a static classification. For example, rebel leaders in Charles Taylor's National Patriotic of Liberia (NPFL) shifted from the politics side of the spectrum at the start of the civil war to the profits side as the war progressed. It is also possible to shift the other way, from profits to politics. During the war in Yugoslavia, extralegal groups and organized crime groups who had been motivated by the economic opportunities of the war economy gradually became more politicized during the course of the conflict.[25]

CONFLICT CAPITAL

A key concept that underpins the extralegal groups framework is *conflict capital*. In previous work, I have referred to conflict capital as having the same social features as social capital, but created specifically as a result of war—it is a form of social capital[26] forged in the intense crucible of violent

---

[25] Mary Kaldor (1999); John E. Mueller (2004).

[26] In his 1831 study tour of the United States, Alexis de Tocqueville identifies the associational life that we now call "social capital." He speaks of the power of "associations that are formed in

conflict.[27] In its most recent incarnation, Putnam et al. refer to social capital as "features of social organization, such as trust, norms, and networks that can improve the efficiency of society by facilitating coordinated actions."[28]

Building on this notion of social capital, I posit that repeated exposure to violence during a period of war conditions a set of predictable responses in how a society deals with violence. Over time, these responses develop into behavioral heuristics.[29] Put simply, individuals, families, communities, and societies all develop habits for coping and responding to violence. The intensity of these shared experiences of violence creates "sticky" social bonds. For ex-combatants, these bonds are especially strong and will persist beyond the end of war.[30]

Conflict capital consists of the wartime social connections that allow for that violence to be committed more readily because there already exists a *repertoire of violence* from the war. For those who fought, standard operating procedures were developed for dealing with different types of victims, for interrogating prisoners of war, for saving wounded colleagues in the middle of a firefight, and for sharing loot.

Conflict capital is not a direct function of the availability of armaments in a society. While the availability of small arms can certainly multiply the efficiency and effectiveness of violence, violent threats can also easily be carried out with basic household implements. For example, the machetes that were used to slaughter Tutsis *en masse* during the Rwandan genocide were a common farming implement.

While there is conceptual overlap with the notion of "anti-social capital" in recognizing how socialization and indoctrination affect those who have been trained to kill, conflict capital does not focus solely on the destructive.[31] In the same way that professional militaries in strong states find ways to create celebrated group bonds around the shared task of fighting and killing the enemy, conflict capital also acknowledges the positive dimensions of high in-group trust. The importance of these bonds is now recognized as critical to the socio-economic reintegration of ex-combatants.[32]

Moreover, there is empirical data demonstrating that the violent experience of war can bring about positive personal psychological change in unexpected ways. This emerging literature on Post-Traumatic Growth

---

civil life and which have an object that is in no way political." See Alexis de Tocqueville (1835), p. 29.

[27] Christine Cheng (2012).

[28] Robert D. Putnam, Robert Leonardi and Raffaella Nanetti (1993), p. 167. For deeper theoretical roots to social capital, see also Pierre Bourdieu (1985); J. S. Coleman (1988); and Alejandro Portes (1998).

[29] Amos Tversky and Daniel Kahneman (1974).   [30] Jennifer M. Hazen (2005), pp. 3–7.

[31] For a thoughtful synthesis on the contradictory evidence on wartime trauma, see Jonah Schulhofer-Wohl and Nicholas Sambanis (2010), Section 2.4.

[32] For example, Hugo de Vries and Nikkie Wiegink (2011); Abigail Hardgrove (2012).

(PTG) has begun to overturn conventional ideas on how war affects social dynamics.[33] Speaking to this literature, conflict capital represents the black box of social processes that can also help explain the counterintuitive findings of the PTG literature.

While post-traumatic growth was originally coined to describe an *individual's* personal growth in response to a traumatic experience, I suggest that PTG also applies at the *community* level and the *national* level, as demonstrated by a number of recent studies. For example, Richard Traunmüller, David Born, and Markus Freitag demonstrate that societies which experienced more intense levels of violence experienced dramatically higher levels of social trust after war, all else equal.[34] Further, Steve Shewfelt's research found that ex-combatants have higher rates of political participation,[35] and even more surprisingly, Chris Blattman found that former fighters from northern Uganda—who had been recruited through abduction rather than conscription—were more likely to vote and assume positions of community leadership after the war.[36] Regina Bateson found related results showing that crime victims of all types—combatants and civilian, during war and peace—became more politically empowered and engaged more deeply in politics.[37] All of these PTG results are contrary to expectation.

Incorporating post-traumatic growth into the conflict capital framing provides a unifying way to understand how these counterintuitive effects underpin community-level transformation.

However, conflict capital not only resides in those who commit acts of violence but also among victims and witnesses, who have forged their own repertoires in response to the violence.[38] Beyond the specific networks of those who committed violent acts during war, conflict capital also refers to the changed ways in which people respond differently to violence—as individuals and collectively—as a result of wartime experiences. One potential implication is that those individuals and communities with larger stores of conflict capital are more likely to respond to conflict (armed or otherwise) by using violence themselves (as compared to those with lower levels of conflict capital) because *their threshold for the use of violence has been lowered during the course of the war.* They may also be *quicker* to use violence. Another potential implication is that being violent becomes more valued within a community. For example, Heather Hamill describes how young men in Northern Ireland are harshly punished by local paramilitaries for stealing cars and other delinquent behavior, yet rather than serve as a

---

[33] On PTG after war, see R. Rosner and S. Poswell (2006). On PTG, see Lawrence G. Calhoun and Richard G. Tedeschi (2006).

[34] Richard Traunmüller, David Born and Markus Freitag (2015).

[35] Steven D. Shewfelt (2009).   [36] C. Blattman (2009).

[37] Regina Bateson (2012).   [38] Christine Cheng (2013).

deterrent, these punishments are instead used as currency to signal toughness and establish power.[39]

With each new act of violence, individuals, families, and communities are forced to develop a response, a coping mechanism, a way to deal with specific kinds of tragedies. With each passing year that a war marches on, those repertoires of violence grow deeper and richer and more ingrained. The underlying hypothesis here is that the frequency and intensity of exposure to violence matters for individual and group behaviors.[40] Repertoires of violence grow in response to acts of sexual violence, to ethnic cleansing, to amputations, to political assassinations, and to innumerable mindless acts of destruction and cruelty and horror.

We know, for example, in a non-wartime environment, that children and youth who witness violence have "higher rates of posttraumatic stress disorder (PTSD), depression, distress, aggression, and externalizing behavior disturbances."[41] We also know from neurological research that cortisol, a stress hormone that is released, plays an important role in brain development. For children brought up in high-risk environments, high levels of cortisol change their brain structures so that they permanently live in a "fight-or-flight" mode. These children are so attuned to danger that they are unable to focus, and further, they are predisposed to use violence pre-emptively.[42] These are just two of many ways in which the legacies of war can make their presence felt— long after the guns have been silenced.

At the same time, conflict capital also grows in response to acts of extraordinary courage and kindness, to noble acts of sacrifice, to suffering that is shared together. Bøås and Dunn note that "War is a social drama over the distribution of ideas, identities, resources, and social positions, and it often forces the disadvantaged to design alternative survival strategies."[43] In being forced to create these strategies of survival under extreme duress, conflict capital is also generated, helping to explain some of the post-traumatic growth findings.

---

[39] Heather Hamill (2011).

[40] Economists have found that life outcomes in the U.S. of poor children could be substantially improved by the duration of their exposure to "good" neighborhoods vs. "bad" neighborhoods. See R. Chetty, N. Hendren and L.F. Katz (2015). A wartime environment may have similar "bad neighborhood" effects that are difficult to capture through existing data. Better longitudinal data, with data collection that begins immediately after the end of war would allow for more nuanced hypotheses to be tested more readily. See Christopher Blattman and Edward Miguel (2010).

[41] Stephen L. Buka, Theresa L. Stichick, Isolde Birdthistle and Felton J. Earls (2001).

[42] J.P. Shonkoff, A.S. Garner, The Committee on Psychosocial Aspects of Child and Family Health, Adoption and Dependent Care Committee on Early Childhood, Section on Developmental and Behavioral Pediatrics, B.S. Siegel, M.I. Dobbins, M.F. Earls, L. McGuinn, J. Pascoe and D.L. Wood (2012).

[43] M. Bøås and K. C. Dunn (2007), p. 5.

Conflict Capital as a Moral Resource

Like social capital, conflict capital can also be thought of as a social resource whose supply expands and deepens with use, and atrophies from lack of use.[44] Over the course of a war, a society's stock of conflict capital will accumulate; the longer and more intense the war, the greater the accumulation of conflict capital. After war, once the violence ends, the stock of conflict capital will decline, naturally and gradually. However, if ex-combatants and others continue to activate their conflict capital, the stock of conflict capital will not decline as quickly—with positive and negative consequences (Figure 1.3).

On the one hand, ex-combatants' social ties are important because former fighters may be alienated from their family and friends and rely on these networks for support.[45] When war ends, conflict capital acts as a buffer during the transition period. On the other hand, this also has potentially destructive results: the skills, contacts, and knowledge created through the experience of war could easily find other uses.[46] We see this in Liberia, where Mariam Persson describes how the conflict capital of ex-combatants and vigilantes was reactivated as prominent political candidates such as Winston Tubman mobilized security teams and Ellen Johnson Sirleaf wooed the ex-combatant

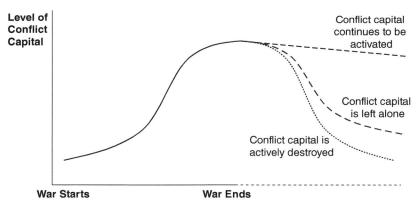

Fig. 1.3. Conflict capital

---

[44] A social resource is much like the moral resource concept defined by Albert Hirschman to categorize love, benevolence, and civic spirit. However, a social resource does not becomes scarce when it is excessively activated. See Albert Hirschman (1984), pp. 93–4.

[45] Abigail Hardgrove (2012); Alison Brettle (2014).

[46] Jean-Francois Bayart, Stephen Ellis and Beatrice Hibou (1999); Mary Kaldor (1999); R. T. Naylor (2001); J. Mueller (2003); P. Andreas (2004); Carolyn Nordstrom (2004); Omar Shahabudin McDoom (2014); E. Nussio and B. Oppenheim (2014). For an updated version of the criminalization of the state argument, see M. Naím (2012).

vote during the 2011 election.[47] Eight years after the war had officially ended, ex-combatants still represented "force, power, and status" and the latent conflict capital that was still embedded in these networks was easily activated.[48] The symbiotic relationship between politicians and fighters remained: ex-combatant networks are useful "for personal gains, mobilising votes, unofficially employing security providers or for other financial or political purposes," and for ex-combatants, these networks provide access to employment opportunities.[49]

Given that war economies tend to thrive on the illicit, another commonly expressed concern is that a criminalized war economy could transform into a criminalized peace economy (see p. 140–50).[50] As conditions of war create an environment where illicit activities are permitted or even encouraged, those who have a stake in this economy will attempt to sustain the war economy for as long as possible.[51]

At the end of war, a society's stock of conflict capital is likely to be at or near its peak: relationships between combatants will have had time to develop and strengthen, and people at all levels of society will have adapted their behaviors, networks, and relationships to reflect the circumstances of war—this provides the stickiness that is inherent in the concept. However, conflict capital rests on shared experiences and memories—its stock depends on human relationships which must be maintained and renewed through regular contact. When stocks of conflict capital are not activated, they decline. This gives conflict capital a natural half-life. Because it is a function of social relationships, a society's stock of conflict capital will gradually decay over time if left alone, as shown in Figure 1.3.

In theory, it may be possible for DDR programs to hasten this process, with demobilization efforts directed at breaking down conflict capital. Of course, there is no evidence to show that DDR works this efficiently, nor that actively destroying conflict capital provides a net benefit to post-conflict societies.

In the immediate aftermath of war, the stock of conflict capital is likely to remain high. The possibility of returning to war provides a strong incentive to keep wartime relationships and networks on standby in the event that fighting should break out again. However, after an early period of uncertainty, prospects for peace will improve and priorities will change—provided that conflict capital is not activated. At this point, levels of conflict capital should decline

---

[47] Mariam Persson (2012).   [48] Ibid.   [49] Ibid.

[50] Roy Godson (2003); P. Andreas (2004); J. Goodhand (2004); Jonathan Goodhand (2011); E. Nussio and B. Oppenheim (2014). On the Balkans, see Francesco Strazzari (2003); P. Andreas (2004); Michael Pugh and Boris Divjak (2011). On South Africa, see Sasha Gear (2002); Marie Smyth (2004). On Northern Ireland, see ibid.; Heather Hamill (2011). On Somalia, see Christian Webersik (2005).

[51] See David Keen (1997); David Keen (1998).

more rapidly as society begins to reallocate its resources and reorganize itself for a peacetime economy. This does not imply that the social networks that are an inherent part of conflict capital will necessarily dissolve—these may endure or strengthen—but the repertoires of violence that were once second nature will be replaced by new social practices.

Even still, conflict capital is a contingent idea: ex-combatants who have close connections to the state are less likely to want to return to war because they can leverage these connections to benefit from the peacetime economy. In contrast, ex-combatants who are not connected to the state are more likely to activate their conflict capital and remobilize.[52]

Alternatively, conflict capital can be activated to provide local regulation and contract enforcement, and in this way, it serves as a catalyst for the emergence of extralegal groups. This regeneration of conflict capital can delay or redirect the process of peace consolidation.

It is important to stress here that conflict capital is neither intrinsically good nor bad[53]—it simply represents a set of social processes and common understandings about how a society is likely to react to episodes of collective violence (based on past experience). In this way, it generates a common social script for how fighters, officials, and citizens are expected to behave given their collective experience of armed conflict. At the same time, conflict capital may also be activated by commanders to retain social control and "Big Man" status.[54] Maintaining these associations and regularly activating these networks also provide a means of connecting with former fighters and influencing their activities.

THE IMPORTANCE OF TIME HORIZONS FOR GOVERNANCE PROVISION

Governance sits at the core of the extralegal groups framework. Who provides it and under what circumstances? Here, it is helpful to turn to existing theories of governance emergence.[55] In Chapter 2, I examine Mancur Olson's model of

---

[52] Anders Themnér (2015).

[53] Mats Utas, Anders Themnér and Emy Lindberg (2014) make a similar point about ex-combatant networks more broadly.

[54] Danny Hoffman (2011); Anders Themnér (2012); Mats Utas (2012).

[55] The state formation literature offers many useful theories. For a political theory perspective, see Jean-Jacques Rousseau (1762); Friedrich Engels and Ernest Untermann (1884); Franz Oppenheimer (1922); Robert Nozick (1974). On modern state formation, see Douglass Cecil North (1990); Douglass C. North, John Joseph Wallis and Barry R. Weingast (2009); Daron Acemoglu and James A. Robinson (2012).

stationary banditry. In the abstract, it comes closest to describing extralegal group behavior.[56] Building on this model, it is possible to extrapolate how extralegal groups make strategic decisions. Yet, to appreciate why Olson's model does not lead to state formation in contemporary post-conflict contexts, it is critical to understand the role of time horizons.

Seen from the perspective of the group itself, time horizons strongly influence the behavior of extralegal groups after emergence. *Short-term* time horizons mean that extralegal groups will behave like roving bandits, looting opportunistically. In this scenario, an extralegal group will disintegrate since it will quickly run out of things to loot and the population will flee. Roving banditry becomes more and more difficult to sustain in practice.

Holding *long-term* time horizons means that extralegal groups will have to eventually face off against the state to retain territorial control because both parties recognize the state as the default owner of the land. With the potential for confrontation comes an existential threat to the extralegal group itself. With its future in doubt, it is not rational for the group to make long-term investments in the local economy.

However, *long-term* control leads to "stationary banditry" and the provision of basic public goods. This logic implies that there exist circumstances whereby an extralegal group is incentivized to provide certain public goods to enhance productivity, which in turn will benefit the "rulers" through increased tax revenues.[57] Hence, *creating institutions to provide basic public goods—in effect, statebuilding—can emerge out of rational, privately motivated incentives.* Put differently, public goods provision can still evolve in the absence of long-term time horizons and despite the fact that statebuilding itself is not the end goal. By adopting *medium-term time horizons*, extralegal groups can derive enough benefit from basic public goods that it becomes willing to bear the cost of provision for the broader community.

Building on Olson's theory and taking it to its logical conclusion, an extralegal group would eventually provide more and more public goods, and build accompanying institutions. Eventually, it would control an entity that looks and feels like a "state." In this optimistic scenario, the public interest would eventually prevail provided that the extralegal group remained confident about its ability to control the enclave over the long-term. Yet, therein lies a fundamental problem, as will be discussed with respect to long-term time horizons—it is not possible for an extralegal group to ever be fully certain about long-term control.

---

[56] Mancur Olson (1993); Mancur Olson (2000).
[57] Mancur Olson (2000), p. 18.

Evaluating Assets Using Present Value

A different way to think about the uncertainties of territorial control is to evaluate the present value of an extralegal group's assets. The present value is the price of an asset on a fixed day, taking into account future income streams, but discounted to reflect what that asset is worth at that moment.[58] For an extralegal group, the present value of the asset increases as the expected duration of control lengthens. As the expected duration of control shortens, the present value of the asset falls.

To explain present value in relation to this context, an example is helpful: if mining taxes for a plot of land are expected to yield U.S. $100 in a year's time, then an extralegal group that is confident of its control over the area will expect to generate $100 in a year's time.[59] Theoretically, it could sell this revenue stream to someone else. Of course, there is a risk that the income will not materialize in a year's time. There might be a mining disaster or commodity prices could drop. A theoretical buyer would need to price in the risk factors that would affect the income stream over the course of the following year.

If a theoretical buyer is reasonably certain that the extralegal group will retain local control and be able to generate $100 of anticipated revenue in the next year, then the buyer might offer say, $80 for that income stream at present. However, if the UN announces the next day that it plans to take over the mining area, then the present value might drop, down to say, $40. The value might drop further to $20 once deployment plans are announced, but then rise again to $30 if local politicians attempt to scuttle the UN's plans.

This crude cost–benefit analysis demonstrates how a group's time horizons can affect its behavior: the longer the group expects to control the area, the higher the present value of the asset, and the less likely it is that the group will loot. For example, when an extralegal group must decide whether and when to loot, we can imagine that the group is making a calculation much like this one.

Having introduced the concepts of conflict capital and time horizons—both of which run through the book and are critical to understanding the theoretical framework—the next section will speak to issues of research design and methodology.

RESEARCH DESIGN AND METHODOLOGY

This is a study of processes. To understand extralegal groups and how they function, it is important to examine how they evolved. How did they come

---

[58] Present value is typically used to price financial assets with a temporal element (such as bonds, treasury bills, mortgages, and annuities).
[59] U.S. dollars are the default currency in this book.

into being and why do they behave the way they do? The more time I spent in Liberia, the more I realized that I had to think about the world as if I were an ex-combatant: What choices would be available to me after war? What constraints would I face? What resources would I have to draw upon? What social pressures would I face? How would I be regarded by my community now that the war is over? How would I see myself and my relationship to society? By framing the answer to these questions as a set of incentives and constraints, the series of decisions made by ex-combatants and extralegal groups appear reasonable and rational. In this way, it becomes possible to imagine how the decision-making process might unfold for individuals and for the group. The choices of ex-combatants take on distinct pathways.

In methodological terms, I conceptualized this pattern of successive choices as an "ideal path."[60] This ideal path describes a set of specific events which are expected to occur in a particular order. Here, the ideal path sets out the emergence, development, and entrenchment of an extralegal group. I examine this ideal path more intimately through a sectoral analysis.

My analysis combines focused, structured comparison and process tracing to determine how extralegal groups developed.[61] I also use hypothesis tests to assess the theoretical framework at each stage. Hypothesis tests serve as signposts within the framework, while process tracing checks the order in which events occur.

Combining these methods provides a stress test of the framework, revealing where the framework holds up empirically and where it does not. By breaking down the process into stages, the dynamics of a post-conflict transition become more transparent, and the importance of timing and sequencing is emphasized. This allows for stronger claims to be made about causality since each specific stage is examined in detail, and in relation to the other stages (Table 1.3).[62]

Five hypotheses are presented here that correspond to the three stages of the framework. The first set of three concern the emergence of extralegal groups, the fourth hypothesis addresses their development, and the fifth one deals with their entrenchment. The unit of analysis is the extralegal group except in Hypothesis 1a where it is the natural resource sector.

---

[60] An ideal path is patterned after a Weberian "ideal type" emphasizing only the core characteristics of the phenomenon in question.

[61] Alexander L. George and Andrew Bennett (2005).

[62] There are as many ways to study extralegal groups as there are questions being posed about them. Alternative methodological approaches that tackle different dimensions of extralegal groups include: formal models of state–society relations in a repeated game; community surveys on local perceptions of these groups; an ethnography of the group's social and organizational dynamics; social network analysis of the membership and the surrounding community; field experiments to measure the effectiveness of specific state or UN interventions, etc.

Table 1.3. Guiding questions and hypotheses

EMERGENCE

Why do extralegal groups emerge in some sectors of the Liberian economy but not in others? How do they emerge?

Hypothesis 1a: Low barriers to entry increase the probability of extralegal groups developing in a given sector of the economy. (Meso-level)	Confirmed
Dependent variable: Number of extralegal groups in each sector	
Independent variable: Sector-specific barriers to entry (a combination of skills and capital)	
Hypothesis 1b: Extralegal groups are more likely to emerge in job sites with lower barriers to entry.	Confirmed
Dependent variable: Emergence of extralegal group	
Independent variable: Capital barriers to entry, skills barrier to entry	
Hypothesis 1c: Extralegal groups emerge where there is a demand for local dispute resolution and contract enforcement, and a supply of coercion specialists (e.g., unemployed ex-combatants). (Micro-level)	Mixed
Dependent variable: Emergence of extralegal group	
Independent variable: Voiced demands for local authority, ex-combatant population	

DEVELOPMENT
How do extralegal groups develop?

Hypothesis 2: Extralegal groups' organizational capacities and finances are strengthened through tax collection.	Confirmed
Dependent variable: Organizational capacity (number of agents, geographical coverage, organizational structure)	
Independent variables: Types of taxes, percentage of population taxed, tax revenues, growth of organization, defined tax collection procedures	

ENTRENCHMENT
How do extralegal groups become entrenched?

Hypothesis 3: Extralegal groups use their increased organizational and financial capacity to corrupt government authorities.	Confirmed
Dependent variable: Corruption in government authorities as proxied by delays in performing official requests that act against the group's interests (e.g., arrests, prohibitions, sanctions), campaign contributions to political candidates, change in number of local officials willing to publicly speak out against the group, bribes paid (not directly observable)	
Independent variables: Change in organizational and financial capacity (number of agents, geographical coverage, organizational structure, revenues collected, bribes paid)	

THE MICRO-LEVEL AND MESO-LEVEL

The empirical part of this study takes a two-level approach: the framework is applied at the extralegal group level and, briefly, at the sector level. This is done within the setting of a single-country case study: Liberia. At the micro-level, extralegal groups from three sectors were chosen for further analysis (timber, rubber, diamonds). These were selected on the basis of their economic importance.[63] For the meso-level analysis, all of Liberia's natural resource sectors were included, with the exception of fishing. These sectors— timber, rubber, iron ore, diamonds, and gold—constituted the most important sectors of the Liberian economy, and taken together, allow for a subnational comparison.

Focusing on a single-country case has a major disadvantage: the findings are less likely to be generalizable to other countries because it is difficult to determine whether Liberia's extralegal groups are representative of similar groupings in other country settings. However, using a within-case approach allows for country-level variables to be held constant, allowing for stronger local claims to be made about causality.[64] Also, single-country case studies provide a richer contextual background, allowing for causal mechanisms to be untangled and examined more carefully. This is difficult to achieve in large-N and cross-national studies.

A micro-level analysis makes it possible to evaluate the relative and combined effects of different individual-level incentives (material, social, security, psychological)—without prioritizing material incentives above all else. Instead, a micro-level approach recognizes the possibility that many different kinds of utility—not just the kinds that are easily measured—are taken into account when ex-combatants are evaluating what to do and where to go after war. Probing the micro-level reveals the multidimensionality of these decisions. In contrast, aggregating these factors into a single, national-level binary variable of war/peace encourages oversimplification and offers an illusion of certainty and precision. In this way, this project can also be seen as responding to a call by Jeremy Weinstein to "move beyond cross-country studies of civil war toward the investigation of the micropolitics of violence."[65]

Care must be taken to distinguish the core mechanisms that are driving forward the formation of extralegal groups in Liberia from its country-specific drivers. While the core of this book focuses on the empirics of specific extralegal groups in Liberia, the logic of the framework is also tested at the meso-level. Country-level characteristics remain the same while sectoral barriers

---

[63] Gold mining, which was not included in the study, is a relatively minor industry in Liberia. Iron ore was also excluded because no extralegal groups emerged in that sector—as predicted by the framework.

[64] Richard Snyder (2001).   [65] Jeremy M. Weinstein (2007), p. 339.

Table 1.4. Extralegal groups by sector

SECTOR	BARRIERS TO ENTRY (U.S. DOLLARS)	EMERGENCE OF EXTRALEGAL GROUPS IN EARLY POSTWAR YEARS (2003–8)
Rubber tapping	~$20 (equipment) + $30/month (supplies) + minimal skill	**Guthrie:** Flourished. Later targeted by the state and UNMIL. **Sinoe:** Flourished. Later targeted by the state and UNMIL. **Cavalla:** Existed briefly, then dissolved. **Cocopa:** Existed briefly, then dissolved.
Gold mining (Alluvial)[66]	~$20 + $30/month (supplies) + minimal skill	**BOPC:** Flourished. Later targeted by the state and UNMIL. **Gbapa:** Asserted, but not confirmed. **Lofa Bridge:** Asserted, but not confirmed.
Diamond mining (Alluvial)	~$20 + $30/month (supplies) + minimal skill	**Sapo:** Flourished. Later targeted by the state and UNMIL.
Pit sawing (Timber)	~$1600 + some skill	**Nezoun:** Flourished. Not targeted by the state and UNMIL.
Iron ore mining	Large capital investment + a variety of skills	None
Gold mining (Hard Rock)[67]	Large capital investment + a variety of skills	None
Diamond mining (Kimberlite)[68]	Large capital investment + a variety of skills	None

to entry vary.[69] The goal is to systematically collect information about the same variables across sectors.[70] Table 1.4 lists the barriers to entry for each sector, from the lowest barriers to entry (at the top) to the highest barriers to entry (at the bottom).

For Liberia's government (and governments of other post-conflict countries) and actors belonging to the international community, the micro-level and the meso-level of analysis can be used to identify potential sites of instability, and to

[66] Alluvial gold and diamond deposits are found in the gravel beds of rivers, oceans, and other bodies of water. They are usually mined artisanally, on an informal basis.

[67] Hard rock gold deposits are encased in rock and cannot be readily extracted.

[68] Kimberlite diamonds are encased in rock and cannot be readily extracted.

[69] This approach draws inspiration from the work of D. Michael Shafer (1994); Peter B. Evans (1995); Terry Lynn Karl (1997).

[70] Alexander George and Timothy McKeown (1984); Gary King, Robert O. Keohane and Sidney Verba (1994), p. 45.

target programs in communities where conflict capital could be harnessed to smooth the transition to peace rather than disrupt it.

Table 1.4 lists the extralegal groups that were known to have emerged in Liberia when the war ended in 2003, providing a comparison across sectors.[71] This includes nascent groups. No extralegal groups emerged in hard rock gold mining or kimberlite diamond mining. With alluvial diamond mining, both Gbapa and the Lofa Bridge area had been home to the trade for decades. However, insufficient time was spent in Gbapa and Lofa Bridge to confirm that these areas hosted extralegal groups.

The findings show that sectors with lower barriers to entry had more extralegal groups. This data is consistent with Hypothesis 1a: Lower barriers to entry increase the probability of extralegal groups developing in a given economic sector.

The data from Liberia suggest that the specific locations in which extralegal groups emerged was somewhat predictable. From a livelihoods perspective, this hypothesis makes it possible to narrow down the localities where extra-legal groups are most likely to form and to target different types of interventions (state, community, tribal, civil society, UN) in these areas. These interventions need not be militarized, but can encompass a range of activities from easing local tensions to providing alternative dispute resolution to formalizing the range of economic activities that have materialized. This finding is useful in an environment where financial resources are limited and peacebuilding actors—local and international—are unsure of where and how to direct their efforts.

THE IMPORTANCE OF POLITICS, PEOPLE, AND PLACE

The underlying logic of the framework outlined in Chapter 2 is based on individuals who make rational choices and maximize their "utility," though I have defined utility not only in material terms but also emotional and social terms.[72] However, it is clear that the logic of the "ideal path" only forms the backbone of our understanding. By wrapping a narrative around this ideal path, the theoretical framework provides a degree of order to our thinking.

---

[71] A small number of groups attempted to "emerge" but did not achieve the stability of an extralegal group.

[72] While a seminal body of research has shown that humans are not perfectly rational all the time under every circumstance, the approximation of rational behaviour is sufficient for this framework. For example, see the work done by Daniel Kahneman and Amos Tversky (1979) on prospect theory.

But an extralegal group still remains an abstract construct in the absence of specifics. Specific politics. Specific people. Specific places.

John Odell (2000) argues that:

> More comprehensive and more detailed contact with concrete instances of the events and behavior about which we wish to generalize helps sharpen distinctions. It stimulates fresh concepts, typologies, and hypotheses ... [T]he farther we move from direct observation of the people we wish to understand—say by using only proxy indicators that can be measured uniformly over many cases, or by importing models from other fields—the greater the risk of generating theory that turns out to be invalid for this domain.

In this book, the historical and empirical chapters flesh out the framework. They tell the story of Liberia in social, economic, and political terms—not only at the national level but also at a local level in the rubber, timber, and diamond sectors. By tackling the local and the specific, this book speaks to the central role of context in understanding civil war and its aftermath.

WHY LIBERIA?

From a research design perspective, there were several factors that made Liberia a "hard" case for the emergence of extralegal groups: it had the world's highest concentration of UN peacekeepers on a per capita basis;[73] the international community contributed substantial amounts of humanitarian and development aid; *and* it received significant political attention and international media coverage. Liberia is also a small country, with a population of just over 3 million people when the war ended. Its land mass is about the same as Pennsylvania's or half of the UK's.

Given the preventive factors in place—a robust and widespread international security presence over a relatively small area, the large amounts of aid money, and the prolonged period of international engagement—Liberia had many advantages that should have prevented the rise of extralegal groups. Yet rise they did. The implication is that if they can emerge and thrive despite such a large international presence and significant humanitarian aid investment, and despite an *explicit* UNMIL directive to help the government regain control over natural resource areas, then extralegal groups could gain a foothold in most post-conflict environments.[74] As a hard case, Liberia demonstrates the *limits of outside intervention in a fragile state.*

---

[73] In its early years, UNMIL was also the world's largest peacekeeping operation by troop count.

[74] See UN Security Council (2003a), 3(r), p. 4.

I also chose Liberia because I needed a country where peace had not fully consolidated in order to maximize the likelihood of witnessing extralegal group emergence in real time. A limited number of countries in the world experienced wars that ended in 2003 and 2004—Liberia was one of them.

Choosing to focus on a part of the world that had mostly been overlooked by scholars came with notable advantages and disadvantages.[75] For example, I anticipated that Liberians would be more receptive to researchers because the country was not yet research-fatigued. Thankfully, this was the case.[76] This expectation of greater accessibility to interviewees and information might seem counterintuitive given the violence that the country had experienced, but in fact, arriving in the country while the security situation was still unstable meant that there was *more* fluidity and openness. As one of the first researchers to arrive in Liberia after the civil war ended, I was warmly received by Liberians and expatriates alike. There were few gates and even fewer gatekeepers; arrangements were always flexible; and almost everyone was amenable to being interviewed. Not only were Liberians and expatriates willing to speak about the war, they were often *eager* to talk about it.

On the other hand, conducting research in an insecure environment meant that it was difficult to accurately assess risk. How safe am I? How safe are my interviewees? There were additional worries concerning mobility, fear, intimidation, and evacuation that needed to be managed.[77] In 2005, it was still difficult to access reliable real-time information about the security situation from outside the country.[78] There were virtually no scholars or practitioners available for consultation about what was happening "on the ground" in Liberia. The first wave of peacekeepers and NGO workers had arrived in the country, but internet access was limited, and making phone calls to Liberia was prohibitively expensive. Journalists were rare. Twitter did not exist and Facebook had not yet been opened up to the public. At the time, Liberia was a low-information environment.

---

[75] Liberia has also received little attention until recently because African politics scholars view the country as being too historically different from the rest of the continent. Further, Liberia is not important to any of the major powers; it is not a regional hegemon or security hub; it has no natural resource monopoly that is vital to the global economy; it does not have a terrorism problem; and the spillover effects of its civil war have been confined to West Africa.

[76] Countries and specific populations that are commonly studied can pose a challenge for data gathering, especially with respect to obtaining a representative sample. In-country intermediaries (local civil society leaders, expats, government officials) tend to provide introductions to the same individuals again and again leading to answers that are filtered, polished, and rehearsed.

[77] For example, in 2005, travel advisories from the U.K.'s Foreign and Commonwealth Office (FCO), the U.S. State Department, and Canada's Department of Foreign Affairs and International Trade (DFAIT) warned prospective visitors not to travel to Liberia under any circumstances because of potential election violence. Thankfully, violence did not occur on the scale that had been originally feared.

[78] I want to thank Ray Studer and Karin von Hippel for their help with assessing Liberia's security situation in 2005.

GATHERING DATA

The timeframe for this study focuses on the immediate five years after the war ends, from the summer of 2003 through 2008. Much of this material was gathered in 2005 and 2007 through observation and interviews conducted during six months of fieldwork in post-conflict Liberia. My first trip began in the summer of 2005, before the Liberian election, and lasted four months. I remained in the country during the post-election turmoil, when the political situation was still unstable. The second trip took place in the spring of 2007 and lasted two months.[79]

In addition to primary sources, I also made extensive use of secondary source materials including: academic books and articles, NGO reports, public and internal UN reports, statistics and reports from International Financial Institutions (IFIs) and other international organizations, Liberian and international court documents, U.S. and E.U. government reports, domestic government documents, and international and Liberian newspaper articles. Many of these documents were collected during fieldwork.

Interviews were key to this project. I conducted semi-structured interviews with over 150 people. Some people were interviewed multiples times. Most of these interviews took place in Liberia, but conversations also took place in Freetown, Abidjan, Washington, D.C., and New York. Interviewees included ex-combatants, alleged members of extralegal groups, UNMIL civilian staff, UNMIL peacekeepers, diplomats, World Bank and UN officials, international NGO workers, Liberian politicians and bureaucrats, local chiefs and elders, civil society leaders, local police officers, journalists, and business owners. In the decade since I first visited Liberia, I have also held hundreds more formal and informal conversations with doers and thinkers which have helped shape my views on transitioning from war to peace. Most of these interviews and conversations are not quoted directly in this book, but they deepened my understanding of Liberia, of civil war, of peacekeeping, of the "international community," of local perceptions, and the history of the Liberia and its neighbors in the Mano River region.

Fieldwork posed two distinct sets of challenges. The first set of challenges related to operating in a post-conflict environment and how the level of insecurity potentially affected the data, the way in which it was gathered, and how it was ultimately interpreted. The second set of challenges related to the sensitive nature of the research topic itself.

Conducting fieldwork in a post-conflict environment posed distinct practical difficulties: I needed secure accommodation and some type of security umbrella in case of evacuation. Previous fieldwork experiences suggested that

---

[79] For some personal reflections on fieldwork in Liberia, see my blog post, Christine Cheng (2010).

large international NGOs were the most willing and able to support an independent researcher in my position. So, I developed affiliations with several large international NGOs (Oxfam, International Organization for Migration, Save the Children, Merlin). There were clear benefits to having an institutional safety net in an insecure environment, but these affiliations also affected how I gathered and processed data. For example, mentioning my relationship with these NGOs changed how I was received by some of my interviewees: some interviewees opened up more while others became more careful about their choice of words.

The affiliation with the international NGO community also made me more sympathetic to the operations of international NGOs and UN staff. The senior leadership of these organizations mostly came from Western democracies while the vast majority of the operational staff were Liberian.[80] Interestingly, even though they came from a mixture of nationalities, the NGO and UN leadership shared a common set of ideas in terms of how Liberia should be "fixed." This core "peacebuilding language" tended to incorporate the tenets of the liberal peacebuilding project without question.[81] Some members of the expatriate community genuinely believed in these values; others were more skeptical but did not feel comfortable with openly questioning the peacebuilding and democracy orthodoxy.[82]

Because the international community was so small, and because of the uncertainty of the moment, there was a sense of solidarity among expatriates, especially those from the West. It is difficult to assess how this feeling of solidarity and loyalty to the expatriate group affected my judgment. Having been welcomed into this community, it was easy to sympathize with their perspective. Although I made a conscious effort to retain my research independence, it would be naïve to think that my NGO and expat affiliations had not shaped my views on extralegal groups.

Yet being in a post-conflict country also made it risky to travel independently around the country. Extralegal groups were based far from Monrovia. Often, the only way for an individual researcher to access these areas was to travel with UNMIL peacekeepers or international NGOs. I was often prejudged based on the logo that adorned the vehicle I arrived in, and in more remote areas, people made assumptions about my motives based on their previous interactions with foreigners. Knowing that some of my interviewees were wary of me made it difficult to assess the validity of the information they shared. Nevertheless, it would have been logistically impossible, and probably foolhardy, to visit these areas on my own.

---

[80] A typical organizational structure might have five or six expat staff and 100–50 Liberian staff reporting to them.

[81] For a discussion of the liberal peacebuilding project, see Roland Paris (2004, 2010). For a rejoinder, see D. Zaum (2012).

[82] For an in-depth examination of international peacebuilding "culture," see Séverine Autesserre (2014).

The nature of the research question posed further problems for data collection. While diamonds, timber, and rubber were not illicit goods in themselves, sanctions had made the export of diamonds illegal, and there were also local prohibitions on diamond mining, pit sawing, and rubber tapping. This posed specific challenges in conducting interviews.

First, the extralegal groups in question were operating outside the law, so participants were often reluctant to speak to outsiders about their economic activities. In some instances, people categorically denied any knowledge of rubber tapping or diamond mining or pit sawing—even when the evidence was in plain sight. This often made it difficult to ascertain an individual's level of involvement in the group. In other cases, program officers that I had trusted turned out to be hiding information to protect "friends" and "associates" inside and outside their organizations. For these reasons and others, greater weight was given to sources who had been monitoring and observing the groups on a regular basis and over a long period of time.

To some extent, it was possible to triangulate information by cross-checking with civil society experts, UNMIL staff, local residents, Liberian newspapers, and members of the Panel of Experts. But not always. In choosing to study extralegal groups, it was important to carefully consider not only *how* data was collected, but also the motivations of those who collected it, as well as the motivations of those who were willing to provide it. Proper triangulation of sources became all the more important for assessing the validity of the data itself, even though it was often difficult to establish the independence of sources given that rumor and hearsay were often treated as fact.

Since all data are not created equal, part of a scholar's work is to adjudicate between sources. Whose information is credible, and on which issues? This is usually a difficult question for outsiders to answer because the local web of connections and incentives is opaque. We try to assess other people's motivations, decisions, and behaviors—but we do so with the assumption that others think the way we do, when in fact, their social relations and cultural values are structured very differently. Hierarchy, family values, social obligations, reconciliation approaches, reciprocity norms, gender attitudes—all of these operate differently depending on the community, and these differences affect how we judge the credibility of our sources.

LIMITATIONS

I anticipate two substantive sets of objections to this study. First, the structure of the extralegal groups framework stresses the rationality of its actors: the leaders and members of extralegal groups. While my conception of utility is not limited to the material but also includes the social and the political, the logic that underpins the framework still emphasizes its material dimensions. Such a structural approach may be overly deterministic, neglecting the importance of agency. For example, the case of the Guthrie Group reveals the leadership role played by Ellen Johnson Sirleaf in ending the group's operations. The influence of individual political actors is potentially transformative, but this framework admittedly leaves limited scope for this type of agency.

Another criticism that I anticipate is that the results are not surprising enough. Why is it unusual that those who fought during the war then used their coercive power after the war ended? On the face of it, this criticism makes sense until we recall that the vast majority of Liberia's 100,000 official ex-combatants underwent the transition from fighter to civilian in a peaceful manner. Even if we accept that only half of these people were actual ex-combatants, only a small fraction of these former fighters (3000 to 6000) ended up leading, joining, or supporting an extralegal group. Clearly, fighting in the war does not in itself imply extralegal group membership after war, nor does it imply that ex-combatants will commit acts of violence. The peaceful path of reintegration for most ex-combatants suggests that the emergence of extralegal groups is not inevitable, and that episodes of collective violence were also not inevitable.

Having laid the conceptual groundwork for extralegal groups in this chapter, Chapter 2 will introduce the full theoretical framework.

2

Theoretical Framework

"when the state collapses, order and power (but not always legitimacy) fall down to local groups or are up for grabs. These ups and downs of power then vie with central attempts to reconstitute authority."

I. William Zartman, *Collapsed States*[1]

In 1995, Bill Zartman presciently wrote about collapsed states. In this quote, he captures the churn and disruption of the statebuilding process—the tug of war that takes place as the state crumbles and rebuilds itself anew. It is this process of churn and disruption that is the focus of this chapter. The order and power that are up for grabs is seized by extralegal groups: a set of individuals with a proven capacity for violence, working outside the law primarily for profit and providing governance functions to sustain its business interests. But what conditions the manner in which local groups seize power or constitute order? What are the parameters of this process? And what might this competition between local groups and central authorities look like if it could be characterized in generalizable terms?

This chapter provides a framework[2] for analyzing extralegal groups in a post-conflict context. It is divided into four sections which broadly correspond to the stages of the extralegal groups framework: post-conflict conditions, emergence, development, and entrenchment. While the first section examines general conditions of post-conflict states, the sections that follow are explored from the perspective of the groups themselves. I emphasize the rational nature of individual and group incentives. The first stage in particular speaks to the circumstances of ex-combatants, but it also has broader applicability to other insecure business environments where there is a demand for contract enforcement

[1] I. William Zartman (1995), p. 1.
[2] For comments and suggestions on the framework, I am grateful to David Anderson, Regina Bateson, Mats Berdal, William Beinart, Nancy Bermeo, Mayling Birney, Johanna Börsch-Supan, Michael Bratton, Richard Caplan, Christopher Clapham, Anna Dimitrijevics, Diego Gambetta, Carolyn Haggis, Macartan Humphreys, Andrew Hurrell, Matt Kocher, Adrienne Le Bas, Neil Macfarlane, Zachariah Mampilly, Harris Mylonas, Ricardo Soares de Oliveira, Ngaire Woods, and Dominik Zaum.

capabilities and an organized supply of specialists in coercion. Despite the distinct challenges posed by extralegal groups, I conclude at the close of the chapter that, on balance, they do as much good as harm for local statebuilding in the early postwar years but pose greater challenges for long-term statebuilding.

The theoretical framework can be summarized as a three-stage process: In the aftermath of war, ex-combatants seek employment. But most are unskilled and have little education; years of war have also destroyed the local economy. These factors severely restrict their prospects. Consequently, most ex-combatants end up looking for work in sectors of the economy with low barriers to entry. Most of them congregate in a few geographical locations where barriers to entry are relatively low as with industries like rubber tapping, alluvial mining, and timber.

Such large concentrations of ex-combatants in a few locations create difficulties with contract enforcement, dispute resolution, and internal regulation—all of which are necessary for trade to thrive. Extralegal groups, backed with the coercive power of ex-combatant leaders, emerge to meet this demand. In the development stage, leaders of the group choose to profitably engage in "taxation" and commodity brokers. The taxation process allows them to develop organizational and financial capacity. As they grow more powerful, extralegal groups learn to hold on to power by bribing local officials in the entrenchment stage. Over time, local officials are compromised by these patterns of corruption, and extralegal groups become embedded in the local political economy.

POST-CONFLICT CONDITIONS

Most post-conflict countries face four specific challenges: they have weak state capacity, they lack legitimacy, they have problems of trust, and their political stability is often reliant on an international security presence. Not all post-conflict countries face all of these challenges, but they are common to societies transitioning from war to peace. Three of these challenges—weak state capacity, a deficit of legitimacy, and problems of trust—contribute to the local demand for extralegal groups in the emergence stage. The fourth challenge—relying on outsiders to provide local and national security without the ability to control them—directly impacts the development and entrenchment of extralegal groups.

Weak State Capacity and the Potential of the Post-Conflict Moment

Weak state capacity means that the government is not providing the governance goods that are needed by the population. This creates an opening for another entity to step into this void.

First, post-conflict countries often lack the funds, the personnel, and the institutions to properly address the multitude of urgent challenges that they face.[3] At its most basic, this translates into an inability to provide security for large areas of territory that it theoretically governs, especially outside of the capital. For people living in these areas, this usually means that the government is unable to perform the most basic of state functions such as arresting criminals, enforcing basic property rights, adjudicating disputes, or regulating basic economic transactions.[4] In more peaceful times, chiefs, elders, or other local authorities like police officers might have performed these functions, but after conflict, these authority figures may have been killed, displaced, or they may have lost the respect or legitimacy needed to carry out these tasks.[5] For example, in Liberia, Kantor and Persson refer to the vigilante groups who arrest and try suspects. They describe these groups as being "the real gate-keepers to Liberia's justice system," arguing that the role of formal state institutions is overstated.[6] Consequently, where the relationship between the state and its citizens is characterized by mistrust, other actors can and will step in to meet that need for justice.[7]

Seen optimistically though, a post-conflict transition also presents the possibility of transformation—an opportunity to create a more fair and robust system of governance. Thus, there is pressure from the international community to build sustainable state institutions, a transparent political system, an impartial judiciary, a professional military, a responsive civil service, and a trustworthy police force.[8] These ideals originate from a problematic tabula rasa assumption[9] whereby postwar governments are critically measured against a standard of civilization[10] without an appreciation of what is realistically achievable on the ground, nor the risks that go hand-in-hand with a major transformation of the state.[11] In the wake of successive failed attempts at statebuilding in places like Afghanistan and Iraq, this blank slate assumption is

---

[3] This is not strictly a result of war, but war undoubtedly exacerbates this problem. According to a variety of measures, many post–civil war countries also qualify as failed or collapsed states. See Robert H. Jackson (1990); I. William Zartman (1995); Robert I. Rotberg (2004); Fund for Peace and Foreign Policy Magazine (2007).

[4] According to Boas and Utas, there are still no national institutions in Liberia: M. Bøås and M. Utas (2014).

[5] R. Reeve and J. Speare (2012) discuss the role of "informal security providers" as peace consolidates in Liberia. This concept provides another lens through which to understand the phenomenon that I refer to as extralegal groups.

[6] A. Kantor and M. Persson (2010).

[7] This particular dynamic explains the ascendance of a number of nonstate actors, some of which are viewed as terrorists: the Taliban in Afghanistan, the Islamic courts in Somalia, PAGAD in South Africa, and most recently, the Islamic State in Iraq and Syria.

[8] J. Dobbins, S. G. Jones, K. Crane and B. C. DeGrasse (2007); Ashraf Ghani and Clare Lockhart (2008).

[9] M. R. Duffield (2001); P. Englebert and D.M. Tull (2008).

[10] Roland Paris (2002).   [11] Dominik Zaum (2007).

not as prevalent or as deeply held as it once was. Nevertheless, there is still a normative streak that runs through Western sensibilities and shapes modern-day expectations of statehood.

The reality faced by most (but not all) post-conflict governments is a lack of capacity across sectors and at all levels; they cannot fund the basic necessities of the state. For example, it is not uncommon for governments to owe their employees years of back pay. In this type of environment, government employees will be more likely to seek other sources of income. They will have an incentive to abuse the authority with which they have been entrusted as government employees. Under these circumstances, even the most honest of civil servants cannot avoid accepting bribes without invoking the mistrust and anger of colleagues. For example, in Afghanistan, police officers must pay a substantial entry bribe worth several multiples of their official annual salary in order to be hired—this is because police officers are in a position to regularly extort payments based on their position.[12] Over time, officers are able to extort enough to profit from their role and repay the large debt they had to incur in order to pay the initial entry bribe to become a police officer. As will be discussed in the Entrenchment section of this chapter, this type of pattern creates institutional arrangements that weave corruption right into the fabric of the state.[13]

In a context like Liberia's, the weakness of the state poses an immense challenge. A 2006 review of the U.N.'s Rule of Law program reveals the depth of the postwar problem:

> In respect of the Local National Police (LNP) [sic], a severe lack of resources has meant that they have had to rely on the International Police Service (IPS) for basic operational tools like papers and books for the recording of incidents etc. Even in areas where vehicles have been provided...complainants sometimes have to provide fuel for the police to be able to deal with their cases. Most police stations are dilapidated with leaking roofs and insecure premises. The LNP operated in a policy vacuum for a long time and officers were not paid thereby leading to a corrupt culture within the organization....
>
> Most prison doors could be broken down just by prolonged shaking. The prisons lacked basic facilities as officers had not been paid for long periods... The judicial system was also extremely weak. The whole of Liberia has less than 200 qualified lawyers. Of 145 magistrates recently appointed only three are qualified lawyers. Judges/judicial and police received very low salaries if at all.[14]

The problem of state capacity was also painstakingly clear in my own observations. In several of the police stations I visited, the jail cell doors were made

---

[12] Lorenzo Delesgues and Yama Torabi (2010). Admission to Rio de Janiero's police academy works in a similar way.

[13] For example, see Boris Divjak and Michael Pugh (2008); Kelly M. Greenhill (2009); Jonathan Goodhand (2011).

[14] L. Botchwey (2006), p. 2.

of splintering plywood, and held in place by a rusty latch (if there was a latch at all). Those who had been arrested were led away voluntarily because the police could not afford handcuffs. Indeed, suspects had to arrange for relatives or friends to bring them food and water because jails did not provide any.

Another way of thinking about weak governmental capacity is that the functioning of the state relies more on personal relationships within the system, which makes for greater institutional malleability when the government changes. The post-conflict moment presents a rare opportunity to change the dynamics of local institutions by making them more *impersonal*.[15]

After the end of war, there exists a brief window of opportunity to reset relationships. It is during this post-conflict period that government institutions establish patterns of interaction with citizens, with businesses, with political groups, with civil society groups, and with the outside world that set the state's future course.[16] Because the social and political norms of society are in flux as individuals and organizations re-establish ways of working together again, it becomes possible to establish new norms. It is a moment in which states and societies can learn to change their habits and routines.[17]

As the state's institutional capacity increases during this period, the ways in which government chooses to interact with different groups within society become increasingly routinized. Gradually, this period of institutional flexibility gives way to settled forms of interaction. The post-conflict moment is a critical juncture where the state can lay the foundation for institutions that are transparent and impersonal, or it can choose institutions and habits that are opaque, personalized, and ad hoc. However, for extralegal groups, this period of government malleability also offers a unique chance to set the terms of that relationship *to their own advantage*, giving rise to longer term problems of entrenchment and corruption.

Do Citizens Feel Their States Have Political Legitimacy?

In post-conflict environments, it is common for citizens to feel that the government of the day and the state itself lack political legitimacy. In many cases, problems of legitimacy are likely to predate war—especially since many citizens will have had little interaction with government officials. Armed conflict further compromises the citizen–state relationship either because government cannot protect civilians during armed conflict, or because the military itself is

---

[15] For a compelling argument on why impersonality is fundamental to building a functional state, see pp. 12–33 in Bo Rothstein (2011). (Rothstein refers to impartiality rather than impersonality.)

[16] Christine Cheng (2012) and World Bank (2011), Part 2, Lessons from National and International Responses.

[17] Charles Duhigg (2012), Part 2, The Habits of Successful Organizations.

persecuting civilians. Especially for those who live in rural areas, the state is likely to be perceived as an abstract entity that resides in the capital but provides little or nothing in the way of public goods or local governance.

At worst, governments may have actively persecuted groups or individuals, stolen their land, forcibly conscripted their children, collaborated with colonial administrators, silenced their complaints with threats, demanded bribes, detained protestors, or even killed and tortured those who dared speak against them. In many countries, the legacies of colonialism and the co-optation of various local elites has compounded the problem of trust in government.[18] Consequently, some proportion of citizens will only know the state in its most predatory form. This problem of domestic political legitimacy opens up a space for nonstate actors.[19] This cynical and wary view of the state contrasts sharply with the views of the international community which views a strong state as a prerequisite to achieving political order and stability.

Particularly in a post-conflict environment, segments of the citizenry will have good reason to be suspicious of the state because generations of interactions have shown that agents of the state cannot be trusted. For example, where one might notify the police after a robbery, police are found to be in cahoots with the thieves; where one might seek justice in the courts, bribes are demanded to ensure a favorable outcome; where students expect schools to be safe, teachers demand sexual favors in exchange for good grades. When these are the conditions through which a citizen forms its relationship with the state, it is not surprising that so many view the state as exploitative.

In short, civil war is often preceded by other deeply embedded problems of poor governance that have gradually eroded the people's trust in the state. This problem of state legitimacy lingers: the net effect is that the state will have a tougher time convincing people that *this* time, government officials *really are* looking out for the population's interests. The end of war does not automatically dispel these past failures of government and governance, *nor does it wipe out people's memories of abuse.* The state must still earn its legitimacy from its citizens, rather than expecting it to automatically materialize as part of a post-conflict peace dividend. For an extralegal group, this lack of state legitimacy provides an opening for the provision of local order in an unstable environment.

This leads to the question of how it is possible to objectively assess local political legitimacy. Who gets to represent the interests of the local population? And who gets to decide which views are representative and which are not? What

---

[18] On cooperation between local elites and repressive colonial administrators, see for example, Mahmood Mamdani (1996).

[19] Governments themselves can invite nonstate actors to fill this void (e.g., International NGO Médecins Sans Frontières provides local healthcare in many conflict and post-conflict environments).

does this look like in practice for local communities? Building on Beetham's conceptions of legitimacy,[20] as well as recent discussions by Whalan,[21] von Billerbeck,[22] and Zaum,[23] on the political legitimacy of peacekeeping and peacebuilding operations, and incorporating earlier work by Jackson on the legitimating role of the international community,[24] it is possible to separate out five types of legitimacy:

(1) Source legitimacy: derived from the position held. E.g., Clan chiefs.

(2) Charismatic legitimacy: linked directly to the personality of the leader.

(3) Process/Input legitimacy: derived from the procedure or method. Also referred to as input legitimacy. E.g., Meaningful local consultations should enhance legitimacy.

(4) Output legitimacy: derived from the success or failure of the action.

(5) International legitimacy: derived from external recognition.

In thinking about these five separate sources of legitimacy, it is important to consider how political legitimacy in Western/OECD countries operates differently from non-Western/non-OECD countries. Source, charismatic, process, output, and international legitimacy may be weighted very differently. For example, in Western societies, a crucial component of legitimacy is process-based, and it can be difficult to separate out political legitimacy from the democratic process given the substantive overlap in several dimensions of both concepts.[25] In non-Western societies, other forms of political legitimacy may hold more weight, and community-based sources of legitimacy could trump central-government sources of legitimacy.[26]

Given these differences, scholars of international politics and international policymakers should be cognizant of the limitations of the state paradigm before overriding local views on how that legitimacy should be constituted. This is especially important in light of Rothstein's compelling argument that it is output legitimacy that matters most:[27] "To be blunt, while what happens on the input side usually has little consequence for the immediate welfare of the individual citizen, what the state does or does not do on the output side may be life threatening."[28] This is to say that, despite an extralegal group's lack of process-based or international legitimacy, *such a group may be seen as locally legitimate because of the outputs (order, conflict resolution, regulation) that it*

---

[20] David Beetham (1990).
[21] Jeni Whalan (2013). Note that Whalan builds on David Beetham (1990) and Daniel Bodansky (1999).
[22] Sarah von Billerbeck (2017).   [23] Domink Zaum (2013).
[24] Robert H. Jackson (1990).   [25] Bo Rothstein (2011), pp. 25–6.
[26] Sukanya Podder (2013).   [27] Bo Rothstein (2011), pp. 80–97.
[28] Ibid., p. 92.

delivers. All else equal, the central state's lack of domestic political legitimacy will make it easier for an extralegal group to control a given area.

Providers of Trust

There is a general expectation in the literature that civil war destroys a country's social fabric, breaking the bonds of everyday trust.[29] Importantly, it is social trust (also known as generalized trust)[30] that forms the bedrock of the modern economy in facilitating all kinds of transactions that would not otherwise take place.[31] In a post-conflict society, this kind of social trust—the trust one would extend to strangers[32]—declines markedly.[33]

An extension of the trust problem is that there is not only low trust between citizens, but there is also low trust in government institutions such as the police, the courts, the prisons, and the legislature.[34] Whether this lack of trust in the state predates armed conflict or not, it nonetheless poses a huge challenge to post-conflict statebuilding. In developed countries, these state institutions form the foundation of the social contract between citizens and the state, for example, in providing a backstop in the enforcement of economic contracts. Where third-party enforcement is lacking, cheating is rampant.[35] In the absence of third-party enforcement institutions, markets can be distorted.

Writing on the Sicilian mafia, Gambetta shows how the mafia maintains a regulatory system which facilitates and polices transactions (both legitimate and illegitimate) for parties who find it difficult to trust one another.[36]

---

[29] See Margaret Levi (1998), p. 78: "Trust has three parts: A trusts B to do X. The act of trust is the knowledge or belief that the trusted will have an incentive to do what she engages to do...trust is a form of encapsulated interest. A trusts B because she presumes it is in B's interest to act in a way consistent with A's interest. Further, trust is relational. The initial grant of trust depends on one person's evaluation that another will be trustworthy. Its maintenance requires confirmation of that trustworthiness, or else trust will be withdrawn."

[30] This is usually measured using the survey question: "Generally speaking, would you say that most people can be trusted or that you can't be too careful in dealing with people?".

[31] For an extended discussion of these ideas, see Martin Raiser (1998); Paul J. Zak and Stephen Knack (2001).

[32] There is a vast literature on social trust in psychology, sociology, anthropology, politics, and economics. For example, see J. Berg, J. Dickhaut and K. McCabe (1995) and B. King-Casas, D. Tomlin, C. Anen, C. F. Camerer, et al. (2005). See also the discussion of trust in Robert D. Putnam, Robert Leonardi and Raffaella Nanetti (1993).

[33] J. Widner (2004); Kati Schindler (2011); World Bank (2011), Ch. 4 Restoring confidence, Moving away from the brink.

[34] On the importance of trust in government, see for example, A. H. Miller (1974) and M. Levi and L. Stoker (2000).

[35] For example, this failure of the state to provide trust in China's export manufacturing market has allowed Chinese factory owners and agents to successfully exploit contracts with foreigners, inevitably resulting in long-term quality fade. See Paul Midler (2009).

[36] Diego Gambetta (1993).

If one party to a transaction reneges, it knows that it will have to face the mafia's consequences. To make money, the mafia charges an "insurance" fee for using the system. The mafia provides a much-needed service by acting as a guarantor: it facilitates transactions that otherwise would not have occurred. Drawing on this idea of third-party enforcement to facilitate economic transactions, it will be argued that extralegal groups fill a similar void in an environment where there is a trust deficit, and where the government cannot play this role because of its own lack of capacity and legitimacy.

Reliance on Peacekeepers and External Security Providers

The fourth challenge of postwar environments is that a reliance on international peacekeepers and external security providers has become the norm in post-conflict situations. Usually led by the UN, peace operations not only deal with security, but also play a de facto role in governing at the national level. By providing security guarantees, the presence of peacekeepers substantially lowers the risk of a return to war.[37]

Provided that peacekeepers are welcome, the perception on the ground is that the larger and more extensive the international presence, the more stable the situation will be and the more likely that peace will endure after peacekeepers leave.[38] For example, the substantial long-term presence of international transitional administrations (ITAs) established in Bosnia, Kosovo, and East Timor signalled to potential peace spoilers that waiting out the UN would not be a viable strategy.[39] Further, the presence of international peacekeepers indicates to civilians that the international community is willing to invest significant energy and resources into peace, which in turn boosts local confidence, enticing civilians and members of extralegal groups to make economic investments for the future.

With respect to how peacekeepers impact the strategies of extralegal groups, such a presence will influence how long a group believes it can govern the area before its control will be contested. A large and committed peacekeeping presence in the country suggests that, at some point, control over territory will

---

[37] B. F. Walter (1999); M. W. Doyle and N. Sambanis (2000); V. P. Fortna (2004a). There are other potential causal mechanisms that could explain the effectiveness of peacekeepers. For a discussion of these mechanisms in the context of interstate war, see V. P. Fortna (2004b).

[38] The degree to which the international or regional community is committed to a country's post-conflict recovery varies widely. Amongst peace operations, some peacekeeping missions receive authorization for higher troop levels and more extensive operations than others. Where more extensive intervention is required, the U.N. or regional organizations may enter into shared sovereignty agreements or even assume executive political authority to establish an international transitional administration.

[39] For an informative discussion of ITAs, see Richard D. Caplan (2005). See also Simon Chesterman (2004); Oisín Tansey (2009).

be contested by the state and backed up by peacekeeping force. The specific locations outside the capital where peacekeeping units set up will also have direct effects on extralegal groups' decisions.

EMERGENCE OF EXTRALEGAL GROUPS

The emergence of extralegal groups evolves out of the supply and demand for basic local governance functions—in the form of dispute resolution, regulation, and contract enforcement—functions that are critical to a trading environment.[40] On the supply side, most of the population, including a significant number of ex-combatants (typically unskilled), will be unemployed and looking for work after war. Thus, economic activities with the lowest barriers to entry will be the only viable options for them[41]—this results in an influx of people to specific sectors of the economy and specific geographic areas where these employment opportunities are concentrated.

Ex-combatants will be drawn to industries where they can find work most easily—where barriers to entry are lowest. Being specialists in violence, they will have a distinct competitive advantage in an insecure environment. Civilians from the wider population will also be drawn into these economic opportunities, though the presence of former fighters is likely to intimidate noncombatants and consequently limit the kinds of people who would be willing to join.

In Liberia and other resource-rich countries, low barriers to entry is closely linked to lootability—the ease with which a resource can be extracted. Hence, this type of employment migration will be concentrated in lootable areas.[42] Philippe Le Billon has made this argument with greater specificity, arguing that geographical constraints and physical attributes affect how war is conducted, specifically with respect to point versus diffuse sources, and the location of these resources in relation to the capital city.[43] Le Billon asserts

---

[40] This occurs in a range of country contexts including Sicily (Diego Gambetta (1993)), Russia (Federico Varese (2001); Vadim Volkov (2002)), and China (Kolin Chin and Roy Godson (2006)).

[41] Given the limited scope of employment options, some individuals capitalize on their expertise in violence by joining private security firms, or local militias, while others return to the battlefield in neighboring countries. Others still will take advantage of local opportunities in organized crime. E.g., piracy in Somalia, professional smuggling in the Balkans, or drug trafficking and kidnapping in Colombia and Nigeria.

[42] William Reno (1998); Michael L. Ross (2004b); Päivi Lujala, Nils P. Gleditsch and Elisabeth Gilmore (2005); Richard Snyder and Ravi Bhavnani (2005); Richard Snyder (2006); and Jeremy M. Weinstein (2007) have all constructed models that link resource lootability to the nature, duration, and termination of armed conflict.

[43] Philippe Le Billon (2001a, 2001b).

that point resources tend to be harder for extralegal groups to capture because government can control them with limited resources.

On the other hand, diffuse resources tend to be more difficult for governments to control. This means lower barriers to entry. Similarly, resources that are positioned close to the capital have higher barriers to entry since the government has easier access to these areas. All else equal, remote areas have lower barriers to entry because governments are less likely to be able to exert control. In practice, Liberia's ex-combatants congregated predictably in locations with low barriers to entry—such as mining enclaves, rubber plantations, and logging areas, most of which were far from Monrovia. In other countries, without easily extractable resources, low-skilled ex-combatants are also likely to end up competing against each other, but in different sectors because the economic opportunity structures will be different.[44]

With such a sudden influx of individuals with "conflict capital" being drawn toward the same locations and the same employment opportunities, problems of competition arise. There is competition for the best extraction sites, jobs, access to supply routes, land, female companionship, etc. In addition, terms of trade may be violated, agreements are difficult to enforce and there is the threat that competitors, suppliers, and workers will steal or cheat. When these disputes occur within a "firm," there is clear jurisdiction for a boss or sponsor to decide on the matter. But when these disputes arise across "firms," there can be unrest. The commercial environment becomes unpredictable. Consequently, where the state is weak or failing, as in post-conflict situations, there is a clear need for some form of credible, internal regulation. The physical environment and the commercial realm both need to be stable. Put simply, there is a need for governance and local order—not for its own sake, but in order for the business environment to operate with predictability.[45]

Extralegal Groups as Regulators

The end result is that those with violent capabilities and conflict capital will mobilize to meet this demand for local regulation. This *need for a stable environment for commerce, rather than a direct desire to create political rule,* leads to the provision of local governance. Violence is managed and permitted, but only certain types of violence that do not disrupt business. In this way, local order can be established—but not by the state.[46] *It is nonstate actors that*

---

[44] Like Richard Snyder and Ravi Bhavnani (2005), this framework supports the claim that it is the *mix* of lootable and non-lootable resources that matter, and not the presence of lootable resources alone.

[45] Matthew Lange (2005).

[46] For insights on local order during war, see Paul Staniland (2012).

fulfill the need for basic governance functions. This is governance without government.[47]

These circumstances are not unique to Liberia or to post-conflict situations. Where there is trade, there will always be someone who emerges to ensure a predictable environment if the state cannot be relied upon. Depending on the context, the providers will vary in form. In some cases, they may be Big Men[48] who have influence by virtue of their personality or their moral authority; in other cases, they may be prison gang leaders,[49] mafia types,[50] rebel leaders,[51] or drug barons who wield coercive capacity. What is interesting about these various groups is that they have formed, at least in part, to facilitate commerce—*not because they wanted to govern* per se. *They provide extralegal governance.*

In post-conflict countries, perhaps the greatest challenge is that "regulators" would need to be powerful enough to command the respect of the ex-combatants who are working in these locales. Postwar governments typically do not have this capacity or may be unwilling to commit precious resources, especially if these areas are far from the capital, unless the groups pose an existential security threat. Instead, when such disputes become violent, the conflicts are likely to be regarded as "local," and then, dismissed as unimportant.[52]

In the early stages, the core extralegal group can vary in size from a dozen people up to a hundred. A sizable proportion of group members (though not necessarily all) are ex-combatants. Most will be loyal to a particular commander or leader. The leader may be an ex-commander, but this need not be the case provided s/he is known to control or have ready access to coercive capabilities.

An extralegal group need not start out as a consciously formed organization; the informal nature of the affiliation means that in the early stages of emergence, it can be difficult to identify its members. Membership is varied and can extend far and wide to encompass community leaders, government officials, or even co-opted UN peacekeepers. At the heart of the leadership structure is coercive authority—typically wielded by an ex-combatant leader. Individual members will also have different levels of commitment to the group. In this study, active support for the group can occasionally be measured via participation in a demonstration, a protest, or a violent collective event—this provides an approximate measure of group cohesion and overall support.

Among the groups themselves, there may be several that arise to control and regulate an area. Rival groups may compete with each other to become the

---

[47] In conflict-affected areas, see William Reno (1998); Ken Menkhaus (2007); A. L. Clunan and H. A. Trinkunas (2010); Zachariah Cherian Mampilly (2011); Ann Laudati (2013); A. Idler and J. Forrest (2015). In mafia and organized crime environments, see Diego Gambetta (1993); Federico Varese (2001); Peter Hill (2003). In gang areas, see J. M. Hazen and D. Rodgers (2014).

[48] Mats Utas (2012).   [49] David Skarbek (2014).

[50] Federico Varese (2001); Marina Tzvetkova (2010).

[51] William Reno (1998); Zachariah Cherian Mampilly (2011).

[52] S. Autesserre (2008).

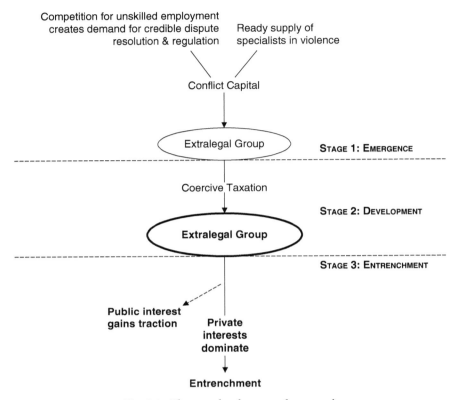

Fig. 2.1. The extralegal groups framework

local regulator. Sometimes, the weaker group will cede to the stronger one, or they may negotiate a merger, or fight each other for control. Where there are multiple groups competing for dominance in a locale, the size of the group serves as a reasonable proxy for the group's initial organizational strength, the quality of its leadership, and its financial resources. Conflict capital helps to bind the groups together (Figure 2.1).

Short-Term and Long-Term Time Horizons Are Not Viable

Ex-combatants can always choose to loot, moving from community to community, so that each encounter takes place with a new population. Mancur Olson characterizes this behavior as roving banditry,[53] a series of one-shot deals as the bandits move from place to place, with the goal of maximizing

---

[53] Mancur Olson (2000).

their gains at each successive location. Indeed, roving bandit behavior is common as rebel group factions and militias move through wartime landscapes. But this is not how extralegal groups behave. They do not hold short-term time horizons; constant looting would undermine their ability to resolve disputes and regulate.

There is only one situation in which an extralegal group will choose to loot: when the present value of its assets drops so low that it makes rational sense to ransack the asset itself. This might occur, for example, if the extralegal group is set to cede territory to the government or to a rival group, and it decides to flee. However, the decision to loot can only be made once. After this, the asset base is destroyed and so too is the group's *raison d'être*. In theory, looting signals the demise of the group.

Yet even though extralegal groups do not behave like roving bandits, neither do they behave like Olson's stationary bandits. This is unsurprising given that Olson's state formation model was not designed to account for a modern twist: extralegal groups occupy lands that are recognized as belonging to the state. The groups can no longer "claim" that land for themselves through conquest, so they have no chance of developing an "encompassing interest." Long ago, this possibility of seizing and ruling over an area once would have provided an incentive for bandits to develop long-term time horizons. A monopoly over the area would have theoretically created an incentive to lower the "theft rate"—the proportion of lootable wealth that is "taxed" or stolen—which, in turn, should have incentivized more production. By extension, greater production leads to greater overall revenues for the ex-combatant group. An encompassing interest in the area would also have created an incentive to provide public goods in order to make society more productive. But this is not possible. Conquest has become normatively unacceptable, and the immutability of international borders since the 1960s testifies to this.[54] Without the possibility of seizing permanent control of an area, extralegal groups will not adopt long-term time horizons.

Medium-Term Time Horizons

"Though the autocrat's encompassing interest implies that he will use some of the resources he controls to provide public goods that increase the productivity of his domain, he does this only to maximize the absolute amount of his net extraction from society."

Mancur Olson, *Power and Prosperity*[55]

---

[54] For a discussion of exceptions, see Stuart Elden (2006).
[55] Mancur Olson (2000), p. 14.

If extralegal groups cannot hope to rule over their areas in the long run, then they will adopt medium-term time horizons. They do not loot and flee but instead engage in repeated interactions with the community by providing basic governance functions. However, as Olson reminds us, the goal is to maximize net extraction, so governance provision is limited to functions that provide *immediate* gains in productivity, which, in turn, lead to immediate increases in tax revenues. There is no outlay for public goods which improve tax revenues far into the future. Territorial control is too uncertain to justify this type of long-term investment. Extralegal groups, if we take them as rational, understand that their authority will eventually be contested by either a rival group and/or the state. Future territorial contestation is certain—this necessarily limits investment in the future.

An extralegal group faces two kinds of rivals. First, it can be usurped by another armed group. Refining his model, Olson noted: "Autocrats often lose their jobs . . . But each autocrat is most often succeeded by another stationary or roving bandit."[56] The second rival is the government, which will eventually try to regain authority over the territory. The question is when will this occur, and how forcefully? Even if the extralegal group negotiates successfully with the government in retaining control over the enclave, governments can always renege on any deal that is made. No extralegal group can guard against this possibility. With the uncertainty of a territorial takeover hanging in the air, an extralegal group will not hold long-term time horizons, nor underwrite governance provision that does not produce immediate tangible benefits.

Extralegal groups cannot hold short-term time horizons, but neither does it make sense for them to hold long-term time horizons given the inevitability of territorial contestation. Instead, an extralegal group holds medium-term time horizons from a few months to a few years, with an acute awareness that even though territorial control is momentarily assured, the long-term prospects remain uncertain (Table 2.1).

Table 2.1. Extralegal groups respond to time horizons

Anticipated Period of Control	Extralegal Group Response
Short-term	Loot
Medium-term	Provide public goods that immediately increase tax revenues
	If takeover is imminent, shift to short-term time horizons and loot
Long-term	Co-opt local and state institutions to prolong period of control
	Provide public goods that increase tax revenues in the short-term and the long-term

---

[56] Ibid., p. 29.

DEVELOPMENT

When extralegal groups initially emerge, they are usually confined to a small area and represent a very low-level threat to the state and to national security. Since their goals are economic and not political, they are unlikely to directly target the state. The objective for members is primarily to accumulate wealth, and in the case of leaders, to also retain their status as "Big Men" by redistributing wealth and employment to their "boys" (women are a rarity). The aim is not to seize political control per se.[57] To achieve this goal, they need a minimal level of governance provision. The aim is to create predictability in the business environment. Practically, this translates into ensuring a level of security that allows for trade to occur and also providing a simple way to resolve disputes. Yet the groups are well aware that they are in a race against time: the ever-present risk of territorial takeover means that they have no incentive to engage in long-term statebuilding activities.

Nonetheless, these groups succeed in growing stronger. How?

"Taxation" and Public Goods

The answer is taxation. In *Coercion, Capital, and European States*, Charles Tilly argued that bureaucracy—and by extension, state formation—was an unintentional by-product of creating systems of resource extraction. Building on this idea, I argue that it is taxation that allows extralegal groups to develop not just their financial capacity but also their organizational capacity.[58] An extralegal group begins by collecting an "occasional tax" for its services (security, dispute resolution, contract enforcement). Regularizing this process strengthens the extralegal group organizationally and financially, and is a fundamental part of the statebuilding process.[59]

With this newfound capacity, the group can, in theory, extend its basic organizational capacity to effectively govern the local area. At a minimum, the money that is collected is used to support the membership of the extralegal group. This is how the group grows its power base. By providing a predictable environment with credible, internal regulation and a degree of local order, an extralegal group begins to behave like a de facto local ruler.

[57] Conceptually, extralegal groups view politics as a means of achieving wealth, whereas warlords view wealth as a means for controlling politics.

[58] See Charles Tilly (1992). Tilly claims that "extraction and struggle over the means of war created the central organizational structures of states..." It was this process of systematic extraction that *unintentionally* created treasuries, supply services, mechanisms for conscription, tax bureaus, etc. In other words, it was taxation in support of war that led to the development of state institutions.

[59] Deborah Brautigam, Odd-Helge Fjeldstad and Mick Moore (2008).

If we think about statebuilding in functional terms—devoid of any associated ideological or political agenda—it is plain to see that learning to tax is an organizational imperative for longer term control. This applies not only to Liberia but also to other country contexts such as the territory controlled by Mexico's infamous Zetas; provinces and territories in Afghanistan that are effectively ruled by warlords;[60] the mafia areas in Japan, Italy, and Russia; and even Islamic State, which has succeeded in part because of its ability to bring a degree of order and justice to a war zone—however brutal and misogynistic.[61] At the same time, providing order is itself a public good. Although Olson's quote refers to the selfish motivations that lead to the establishment of order, the *ability to provide* local order confers a legitimacy all its own.

Because overt violence is bad for business, extralegal groups employ it sparingly in their activities; consequently, they are also less likely to attract attention from the police and other security forces. The government will be busy with other priorities. Even if government officials or international actors recognize that extralegal groups are taking root, they still will not have the resources, the political will, or the mandate to do anything about it.

Given the weakness of government institutions, an extralegal group has the potential to create a power structure that rivals that of the state. Governments of post–civil war countries should become increasingly concerned as the group spends less of its time on direct extraction and shifts its focus toward administration, governance, and taxation.

In the next stage, I outline how extralegal group entrenchment occurs, and discuss the limited ways in which public (rather than private) interest can gain traction.

ENTRENCHMENT

Understanding incentives is crucial: What kinds of incentives can be created to turn the warlord into a statesman or the black-marketeer into a legitimate businessman?... [P]rofiteers will continue to invest in short-term, low-risk activities until there is a state that can provide a secure and predictable environment for legitimate commerce.

Jonathan Goodhand[62]

In order for an extralegal group to secure a longer tenure over its resource enclave, it needs to convert its current authority into future control. The most effective strategy for doing so is to cement its first-mover advantage by

---

[60] Paul Jackson (2003); Dipali Mukhopadhyay (2014).
[61] Tim Arango (2015), Ben Hubbard (2015).
[62] Jonathan Goodhand (2004), p. 82.

co-opting state institutions. In economic parlance, this is a version of regulatory capture, whereby the regulators that have been assigned to protect the public interest instead end up advancing the interests of those they are supposed to regulate.[63] Entrenchment describes a similar process but is accompanied by the threat of coercion, implicit or explicit.

An extralegal group uses the wealth that it accumulates through taxation (backed up with a violent threat, if necessary) to bribe and coerce the necessary politicians, judicial officials, police officers, and local authorities that are needed to maintain operations. Persistent political uncertainty means that frequent bribes are required to maintain the status quo. As a result, the extralegal group ends up building (or reinforcing) a system of entrenched corruption.

A functioning state could confront an extralegal group through the executive, the police, the military, the judiciary, or some combination of these institutions. However, eliminating these groups would require that all of these key government institutions present a united front. All of them would need to become corruption-proof *simultaneously*. These institutions—the executive, the judiciary, the police, and the military—would need to support and enforce one another's decisions at the highest levels of leadership and they would need to do so *for an extended period in a coordinated manner* to successfully rebuff the entrenched power of an extralegal group.

Weak and fragile states face a number of challenges: they typically lack competent staff and financial resources; their civil servants may be corrupt; and their political systems may be too weak to handle an open confrontation with local or national power brokers. Where civil servants are competent and ethical, taking a stand against corruption invites trouble from colleagues and superiors.[64] And even if one arm of the government functions as it is expected to and remains corruption-free, there is no guarantee that all the other parts of the system will also be working. In exceptional cases, UN peacekeepers may be willing to assist the government with domestic matters, but the UN is generally reluctant to interfere in the nitty gritty of local politics.[65] As a result, achieving a coordinated government response to extralegal groups across domestic and international agencies is unlikely.

The ideal response to extralegal groups as envisioned by donors and UNMIL requires: the executive to actively monitor the situation; the police to have the capacity and resources to investigate crimes; the prison officials to ensure that arrested or incarcerated suspects do not escape; the judiciary to competently hear the case; and the military to provide on-site support in case the situation got out of hand. Each arm of government would also need to coordinate their actions with others.

---

[63] J. Hellman, G. Jones and D. Kaufmann (2000).   [64] Shaazka Beyerle (2014).
[65] Severine Autesserre (2010).

However, to retain control of its enclave, the extralegal group would only need to focus on breaking *one* of these links. This is the *weakest link problem*: if one politician tries to stop the group, a more senior politician could be bribed to quash that initiative; if a police officer tries to arrest the group's leaders, another police officer or prison guard could be bribed into releasing them; if a judge is asked to hear the case, she could be bribed to offer a favorable outcome; if a military officer is asked to take action, other officers could be bribed into isolating and marginalizing this person. Consequently, it becomes extremely difficult to break out of this *corruption equilibrium* because all the tools of state power are vulnerable to bribery. *As long as individuals believe that someone else in the chain will break, they see no point in resisting.* Even if they do not personally accept any bribes, someone else in the system will and the extralegal group will get its way eventually.

Entrenchment and Corruption

> "The war is finished and they are taking control of everything again, the politics and businesses. They are throwing us out of this place to take it for themselves, not for the government. There are big hands involved in this, this is unfinished war business, just them taking this place."
>
> Twenty-four-year-old ex-combatant, Guthrie plantation[66]

Such a corruption equilibrium, where extralegal groups undermine state institutions through systematic bribery and coercion, poses a short-term security threat and a long-term threat to local and national statebuilding. In the short-term, an extralegal group has the capacity for violence and can destabilize the state and disrupt the peace, especially if the government threatens to reclaim the area that it controls.

In the long-term, this corruption dynamic threatens the public interest in two ways. First, public authority structures, be they local or national, are captured by private interests.[67] The quote that opens this section comes from an ex-combatant of the Liberians United for Reconciliation and Democracy (LURD) rebel group on the Guthrie plantation who alludes directly to this problem. Second, additional harm is done to the state's reputation in the eyes of its citizens: if state authorities can be easily and systematically bought off, this signals to the public that the state cannot be trusted. Often, such behavior reaffirms a deep-seated cynicism toward state institutions.[68]

If an extralegal group succeeds in maintaining control of the area by establishing channels of corruption, then it will grow stronger and wealthier

---

[66] Landmine Action UK (2006), p. 19.
[67] J. Hellman, G. Jones and D. Kaufmann (2000).   [68] John Bailey (2014), Ch 1.

over time. This in turn will make the group even more difficult to shut down if the government decides to try. The framework lays out a plausible causal pathway for how the entrenchment of such a group could gradually lead to a criminalized state.

For those who are concerned with building a strong, credible state, entrenchment is the most critical of the three stages in the extralegal group framework. The effects of entrenchment are particularly potent during the post-conflict period because it offers a rare window of institutional malleability. Patterns of corruption that are set up during this period are likely to endure. While the Emergence and Development stages are difficult to disrupt, the problem of private interests grows in severity during Entrenchment. Each part of the state system that is designed to tackle extralegal group activities can easily wind up *protecting* them because individuals in the system have been co-opted. Once various governmental levers have been compromised by corruption, any attempt to change fixed patterns of corrupt behavior will become doubly difficult. For example, John Bailey describes the influence and power of Mexico's drug cartels:

> Since the 1980s, some of the organizations had acquired enough money and political savvy to corrupt numerous local governments, several state governments, and key federal agencies…By the early 2000s, the strongest DTOs [drug trafficking organizations] had amassed enough manpower, weaponry, mobility, and leadership to confront and intimidate local and state police forces, mainly in drug producing areas and along the principal smuggling corridors in Mexico's northern states.[69]

In the long run, a trajectory of entrenchment can eventually lead to "the criminalization of the state."[70] According to Bayart et al., this describes a situation in which criminal practices are considered so routine that they are woven into the fabric of the state itself. Examples of such an outcome include the mafia enclave of Sicily, the above-mentioned "zones of impunity" in Mexico,[71] and the militarized mining camps in the Democratic Republic of the Congo (DRC).[72] The danger, of course, is that extralegal groups threaten security, and broadly subvert the public interest.

The extreme version of this scenario has already happened with Mexico's drug cartels. The cartels are not interested in taking over the state per se, but neither will they stand for government interference in their business. When President Felipe Calderón dared to take them on and threatened their livelihood, these groups directly fought the state: by posting a hit list of seventeen

---

[69] Ibid., p. 1.
[70] Jean-François Bayart, Stephen Ellis and Béatrice Hibou (1999). Similar in concept, M. Naím (2012) refers to these as mafia states.
[71] See Marc Lacey (2009); John Bailey (2014).
[72] See N. Garrett, S. Sergiou and K. Vlassenroot (2009).

police officers in Ciudad Juárez and killing half of them in four months; by murdering three of the top officers in the Federal Preventive Police; by lobbing grenades into the middle of a public celebration in the heart of the president's home state of Michoacán; by murdering the family of a soldier who had been killed while targeting a cartel boss; by assassinating US consulate employees, ever more police officers, a gubernatorial candidate, and at least eleven mayors.[73]

From Entrenchment to an Impersonal Sphere

The extralegal group framework privileges structure over agency—in effect, the framework suggests that private interests are likely to prevail over public interests. Yet it is also clear that public interests *can* prevail and that it is possible to create an impersonal sphere; the question is how this comes about.

According to Olson, the emergence of stationary bandits implies that there will be statebuilding, and that democracy will logically follow. While I agree with Olson that *rational, privately motivated incentives can lead to statebuilding*, we diverge in how far this explanation is able to take us along the statebuilding path.[74] Even if an extralegal group could be certain of long-term control, they will only provide public goods up to the point that direct material benefits can be realized. Beyond this point, both stationary bandits and extralegal groups have little incentive to redistribute their profits or to reinvest significantly in public goods. Instead, they will tax as heavily as possible, provide minimal public goods, and pocket the rents. Hence, public goods for local populations beyond a basic level would still entail a struggle. Olson skips over this struggle.

Statebuilding should not be assumed, nor should it be expected to progress as a matter of course. The formation, development, and entrenchment of extralegal groups is not a linear, unidirectional process. Instead, after a basic level of trade-driven governance, *statebuilding is better understood as a tug of war between rulers and the ruled*—or in this case, the leaders of extralegal groups and local populations.

Having discussed what extralegal groups are and how they develop, the question of how these groups are perceived depend critically on how different actors and populations view the state itself. I will take it in turns to consider a national, state-centric response before revisiting extralegal groups through a livelihood lens.

---

[73] John Bailey (2014), pp. 2–3.

[74] Olson lists a set of conditions that lead to democracy: the imposition of democracy from the outside; internal dispersion of power without a clear winner; when mini-autocracies aren't possible because power is geographically interwoven; no outside invaders.

The State's Response to Extralegal Groups

In the long run, if entrenchment is taking place, Zartman suggests that sooner or later, the national government will be forced to respond to the extralegal group. It has three choices: confront, co-opt, or ignore. These options are briefly summarized in Table 2.2.

One possibility is for the government to *confront* the extralegal group, break it up, and reassume control over the area. Since the government has the

Table 2.2. Government responds to extralegal group

Government Options	State vs. Extralegal Group Capacity --------- Extralegal Group ———— State
Confront • Will only occur when the government believes it can defeat the extralegal group • Extralegal group will try to circumvent any external intervention or confrontation	
Co-opt • Convert the group's time horizon from medium-term to long-term • Most likely to occur when the extralegal group poses a significant threat to state stability • Too risky to confront • But how can the extralegal group trust the government to keep its word?	
Ignore • Extralegal group is most likely to be ignored if the government does not view it as a serious threat; • However, if the government ignores the group, the group's capacity could surpass the critical level; • The group may fail of its own accord.	

advantage of deciding when to act, there should be no confrontation unless the government is confident that it will prevail.[75] When the state has the advantage, we can expect it to opt for this strategy. While the government is preparing for confrontation, it is reasonable to expect an extralegal group to use the resources at its disposal to undermine any such intervention.

A second possibility is for the government to *co-opt* the group. This is most likely to happen when the government and the extralegal group have roughly the same organizational and financial capacity. In this case, the national government will try to shift the group's time horizons from medium-term to long-term. To do so, the state can offer a deal that gives the extralegal group better long-term financial security and a degree of legitimacy in exchange for giving up its autonomy. This would create the conditions for "joint extraction" or a public–private partnership.[76] Theoretically, joint extraction should engender a long-term interest in the area which in turn should eventually lead to the extralegal group providing productivity-enhancing public goods.

Nonetheless, there are problems with co-optation: there is no guarantee that one side will not renege if it could benefit from doing so—how can government convince an extralegal group that its offer is credible? Additionally, a public–private partnership will strengthen an extralegal group's local hold on power; legitimizing the actions of the extralegal group may also encourage potential extralegal groups to grow in strength. In theory, co-optation implies an initially clear separation between formal and informal channels of power, yet in practice, the distinction between formal and informal power—and those who hold it—is often indistinguishable.

Finally, if the government is confident that it is stronger than the extralegal group, then it can choose to *ignore* the group since it is not perceived as a threat to the central government. However, if the government chooses to ignore, then the group has an opportunity to build up its financial resources and organizational capacity, and attempt to secure its hold over the area. Over time, the group's influence will deepen, and for government, the cost of confrontation will rise.

A Race for Capacity

A different way of thinking about the interaction between an extralegal group and the central state authority can thus be interpreted as a race between the government and extralegal groups to build organizational, financial, and political

---

[75] The government should favor this strategy since, if left alone, the extralegal group could viably develop an independent economic base and eventually pose a political threat. See Catherine Boone (2003).

[76] Richard Snyder (2006).

capacity at the national and local levels. The extralegal group does not necessarily need to be stronger or more powerful than the state—it only needs to develop enough capacity to pose a significant threat to the state. On the other hand, the state must be able to definitively defeat the group, or else it loses legitimacy in the eyes of its citizens. The asymmetry of this dynamic is important.

Up to this point, the response to the rise of extralegal groups is considered from the viewpoint of the state. It has been assumed that it is desirable for the state and its government to prevail, and that the integrity of the state is the crux of a stable peace. The next section questions this core assumption by shifting the focus to the functions performed by extralegal groups. On balance, do they do more harm than good?

THE FUNCTIONS OF EXTRALEGAL GROUPS

This chapter has focused on introducing the extralegal groups framework in three stages: emergence, development, and entrenchment. But it is important to consider not just how these groups developed, but also *what functions they serve*. Seen through the eyes of states, extralegal groups are simply usurpers to government power. But that is too simplistic a view once we consider that governments themselves are often just as predatory.

Rather than judging extralegal groups as "good" or "bad" actors based on their ability to conform with present-day Western norms, it is more useful to consider what functions these groups are performing in order to assess their potential to impact short-term and long-term statebuilding processes.[77] In the short run, extralegal groups serve four important sets of functions. Bearing in mind that war severely disrupts normal patterns of societal interaction:

(i) Extralegal groups provide dispute resolution and regulation in governance-poor environments.[78] This governance backstop facilitates local order which in turn stimulates the local economy and provides participants with an economic stake in peace;

(ii) Extralegal groups stabilize communities by providing local employment, especially to ex-combatants. In this way, they help fulfil the peace dividend promise that so many commanders made to their fighters during the war;

(iii) Extralegal groups create a social support network for ex-combatants which helps them retain a sense of identity and self-reliance while providing a sense of community belonging.

[77] David Keen (1998).   [78] This function is discussed on pp. 83–6.

(iv) Extralegal groups facilitate society's shift away from the state of nature (self-enforcement of societal norms) and back toward third-party enforcement of societal norms.

Dispute Resolution and Regulation

In a functioning and peaceful state, it is the government that facilitates these economic transactions and serves as a regulator of last resort. But what happens when the state is not able to regulate or resolve disputes, if only because its presence does not extend into remote areas? What if local, informal leaders (like chiefs) who used to provide this kind of conflict resolution have since lost their power and legitimacy? In this situation, those who require dispute resolution or contract enforcement are likely to turn to informal actors and networks established during war because of their coercive power.[79] In some cases, this could mean resurrecting elements of command and control structures of former fighting factions,[80] in other cases, it might mean activating a wartime smuggling network or a sanctions-busting cartel. Ex-combatants are in the best position to meet this need given their comparative advantage in the use of violence.

Employment for Ex-Combatants and Local Populations

Despite the obvious difficulties posed by the emergence of extralegal groups within natural resource sectors, the other employment opportunities available to ex-combatants are potentially more harmful and disruptive to a fragile peace. This is not to imply that extralegal groups are a force for good. However, they do perform a useful economic function by keeping ex-combatants employed (directly and indirectly) through a tumultuous transitional period. Arguably, this prevents a worse outcome from occurring despite the downstream difficulties with corruption (see Entrenchment discussion).

Given the dire economic situation in a place like Liberia, most people have no choice except to find some form of paid work, no matter how vulnerable they are to exploitation or how poorly paid the job might be. Data from Liberia's most comprehensive survey (2010) of its labor force in decades reveal high rates of vulnerable employment[81] (78 percent) and informal employment

---

[79] Carolyn Nordstrom (2004); Dipali Mukhopadhyay (2009); Christine Cheng (2012).

[80] Hugo de Vries and Nikkie Wiegink (2011); Anders Themnér (2012).

[81] This was only the second Labor Force Survey that Liberia had ever conducted. In this context, the unemployment rate is not as useful a measure as vulnerable employment and informal employment. Vulnerable employment includes those who are self-employed and those who work

(68 percent).[82] Although the proportion of the population that is employed seems high, these figures mask sweeping economic desperation that lingered for years after the war ended in 2003. Like everyone else, ex-combatants had to find their own way of surviving these harsh economic circumstances. Indeed, the UN's own internal audit of the UNMIL DDRR program revealed that 88 percent of the 160 interviewees remained unemployed approximately two years after the war had ended.[83]

The failure of Disarmament, Demobilization, and Reintegration (DDR) programs to bring former fighters back into the civilian fold is unsurprising. Alejandro Eder, Colombia's former High Commissioner for Reintegration, notes that a short DDR process of eighteen to twenty-four months is insufficient, and that successful reintegration typically requires *seven years*. This sits in contrast to a typical UN DDR cycle which lasts from six to twelve months.

While a proportion of ex-fighters opt for work in the informal sector, these types of semi-licit jobs pay poorly. Instead, they can opt to make use of their high levels of conflict capital in other ways—by fighting in neighboring wars, by joining criminal gangs, engaging in petty crime, or by agitating for a return to war. The end of war does not necessarily mean an end to violence,[84] and conflict capital can be put to other destructive uses.[85]

Unsurprisingly then, former fighters will seek out whatever job opportunities they can, leading them to converge in areas with low barriers to entry. This kind of employment provides an alternative economic path, providing a much-needed release valve for those who are uneducated and poorly skilled. Given that many ex-combatants were told by their faction's political leaders and commanders that they would "be taken care of" when the war ended, employment of any sort helped to absorb the disappointment of these unfulfilled promises.

In theory, this ex-combatant security gap should be filled by DDR processes. For ex-combatants, the basics of DDR are simple:

> The ex-combatants have simpler definitions: disarmament means bringing "peace back to Liberia by giving up guns" and demobilization is "changing our minds from bad things," "changing our behavior from all wicked ways," "sending us back to school to fit in the society," and "to benefit from a trade I'm going to learn."
>
> UNMIL Audit of DDRR, January 2006[86]

And yet the expectations placed on reintegrating swaths of former fighters are unrealistic given the time and resources that are typically allocated. The programs

---

for the family but are unpaid. Liberia Institute of Statistics and Geoinformation Services and Liberia Ministry of Labour (2011), xiii.

[82] Ibid., xiii.   [83] Via Wikileaks. Juanita Villarosa and Lianett Diaz (2006).
[84] Robert Muggah (2005).
[85] For Sierra Leone and Liberia, see Corinne Dufka (2005), Section VII.
[86] Juanita Villarosa and Lianett Diaz (2006), p. 6.

themselves rarely last for more than a year and seldom achieve their ambitious aims.[87] Even in the most successful DDR implementations where former fighters enter DDR in a timely fashion and progress through a training program that provides them with useful skills, it remains extremely difficult for ex-combatants to find a steady job and be socially accepted back into society.[88] This problem is compounded because DDR itself is normally *not* a smooth process,[89] and ex-combatants can face severe delays between different stages of the process, or they can end up enrolling in ill-conceived mass training programs that produce an oversupply of certain skill sets (e.g., car mechanics, soap makers, IT specialists, tailors, carpenters) that cannot be absorbed by the local labor market.[90]

In contrast, extralegal groups were creating resource enclaves that offered a do-it-yourself version of a DDR program, all the while removing the most combustible individuals far away from the capital. Leaders of the fighting factions from within the transitional government saw a direct interest in letting the extralegal groups operate despite their own vociferous public condemnations. For the country's political elite, which now had a vested interest in maintaining peace, extralegal groups served a practical purpose. They were halfway houses for potential "peace spoilers."

When compared with what these individuals might otherwise be doing if they were not working in these enclaves, the sorts of illicit commercial activities undertaken by extralegal groups (mining, logging, rubber tapping) in a place like Liberia should actually be viewed as a net positive for peace, stability, and development. For transitioning societies, extralegal governance provides the stability needed so that individuals (including ex-combatants) have an economic stake in peace. Without such economic opportunities, a volatile situation like Liberia's could have easily seen a return to war.

A Social Support Network

When war ends, there is a period of precariousness because the political leadership is in flux, and it is not clear whether or not peace will hold. At this moment, ex-combatants may be as vested in war as they are in peace. The end of

---

[87] Reflecting on the DDR process in Liberia, see Kathleen M. Jennings (2007).

[88] World Bank (2011). On Liberia, see Wolf-Christian Paes (2005), p. 258.

[89] For a detailed discussion of the "unwieldy and fragmented" structure (p. 4), the lack of proper evaluation (p. 6), the inefficiency of operations (p. 11), and general problems with UNMIL's DDRR program in Liberia, see the leaked report authored by Juanita Villarosa and Lianett Diaz (2006).

[90] Corinne Dufka (2005), Section VII. Difficulties with DDR processes have been critiqued by a number of researchers, from weapons recovery all the way to severe funding shortfalls from international donors. For example, see M. Knight and A. Ozerdem (2004); Kimberly Theidon (2007); Mats R. Berdal and David H. Ucko (2009); Jaremey R. McMullin (2013). For an overview of DDR research, see Robert Muggah (2010).

war brings a fall in status and power, and a reshaping of their identities;[91] communities stand ready to condemn them; and former fighters may face charges of war crimes. This is the moment where commanders and foot soldiers need employment and social support precisely because they are vulnerable to rearming and the political situation is volatile. This is complicated by the fact that those who have fought may suffer from mental health problems. For example, Alejandro Eder from Colombia notes that 90 percent of those who left the FARC suffer from psychological problems, most commonly post-traumatic stress disorder (PTSD). While second generation DDR programs have begun to address this issue by incorporating more psycho-social support,[92] psychological counselling is still viewed as more of an extra than a core DDR component.

During this uncertain transitional period, extralegal groups not only facilitate an alternative to DDR programs, but they also allow former fighters to retain a sense of identity and self-reliance. Extralegal groups provide a social support network for ex-combatants at a time when fighting factions are being disbanded and fighters are unsure about their future prospects. Given that many ex-combatants do not retain close ties with family and friends,[93] and others have had these relationships forcibly severed,[94] an ex-combatant's closest relationships may well be with fellow fighters. These relationships—which are core to conflict capital—are resilient. Attempts to destroy them (as with DDR efforts to demobilize) are unrealistic and may actually harm prospects for reintegration.[95]

Socially and economically, extralegal groups act as a safety valve for airing the grievances and dissatisfaction felt by those ex-combatants who felt that they never received the rewards they were promised.

Depersonalizing Dispute Resolution

Moving beyond short-term statebuilding, extralegal groups also play a role in larger historical statebuilding processes. In post-conflict environments where local order is contested, local recognition of an extralegal group marks an important shift away from punishing wrongdoings on one's own (vigilante justice) toward allowing a third party to perform this function. The importance of this shift has not been fully recognized even though *moving*

---

[91] See the comments of Mark Duttwiller, the Legal Analyst for the Transitional Justice Unit of the Organization of American States' Mission to Support the Peace Process in Angelika Albaladejo (2015).

[92] Erin McCandless (2010). Includes many case study examples of DDR innovation.

[93] Macartan Humphreys and Jeremy Weinstein 2004; Abigail Hardgrove (2012).

[94] C. Blattman (2009); Kieran Mitton (2015).

[95] Hugo de Vries and Nikkie Wiegink (2011).

from self-enforcement to third-party enforcement is a critical step in state formation. This entails having a third party that can provide dispute resolution, whose authority is locally recognized, and can shift a community away from Hobbes' "state of nature." Starting from this narrowly defined version of anarchy, extralegal groups mark the beginning of delegated governance: individuals must once again place their trust in someone else to resolve disputes and mete out justice.

When war ends, individuals may be accustomed to meting out their own punishment for transgressions. Moving back toward a commonly recognized authority for dispute resolution—as it was before war—could prove challenging. Yet having a third-party provide this dispute resolution function—however biased it may be—is still the first step in depersonalizing this process. Depersonalization of dispute resolution creates a space for regulations to be applied impartially, which gradually leads to the creation of an impersonal sphere and, eventually, to the concept of public interest. In short, depersonalization of dispute resolution is the first step toward establishing rule of law.

CONCLUSION

This chapter has examined how extralegal groups can play a critical role in a post-conflict transition. It introduces a theoretical framework to make sense of the socio-economic dynamics of the postwar years. The extralegal groups framework lays out a causal logic for how ex-combatants seeking employment can transform into extralegal groups in response to local opportunity structures. The framework shows how and why these groups become enmeshed in webs of local corruption over time. In subsequent chapters, I apply this framework to the rubber tapping, diamond mining, and logging sectors.

There is no doubt that some extralegal groups pose a security threat and that continued activation of conflict capital also facilitates a remobilization of fighters, should any of the faction leaders desire a return to war. Yet, if we examine extralegal groups purely from a security standpoint, we miss out on the role that they play in the political economy of transition. Taking these dimensions into account, extralegal groups do more good than harm in the short run. They serve as a stabilizing force by filling a governance gap and enabling a commercial environment; they provide employment—directly and indirectly—at a critical moment when ex-combatants have no other sources of income; they provide a social support network at a time when the futures of ex-combatants are uncertain.

To fully appreciate the influence of extralegal groups, it is important to consider the counterfactual—what would have happened without extralegal groups? Even if the state itself attempted to meet the governance gap or decided to cede this authority by selling concession rights to private commercial interests, it is not clear that the possibilities would improve the lives of regular people or benefit the public interest. These alternatives could easily lead to state predation[96] or to situations of violent contested authority—factors that typically contribute to the outbreak of war in the first place.

For long-term statebuilding, the verdict on extralegal groups is not as clear. By re-establishing a norm of third-party dispute resolution and providing an alternative to vigilantism, extralegal groups help to depersonalize dispute resolution—the first step toward creating order and establishing rule of law. Yet extralegal groups also have the capacity to exploit their position while providing only the most basic public goods—here, it is difficult to see why an autocrat would give up its right to rule without being forced out. Further, the entrenchment of these groups over time means that they become more and more powerful, which gives local communities less leverage to push back. The longer the group stays in power, the less likely it is that public interests will prevail.

This chapter challenges traditional notions of state-led statebuilding and who gets to do the thing that scholars and policymakers label "statebuilding." Despite an implicit emphasis on *state-led* statebuilding in the peace operations literature, it is important to note that states, and weak states in particular, are not always in the strongest position to form robust local institutions or to provide local public goods. Fundamentally, "difficult" actors like extralegal groups have no place in the Western liberal version of statebuilding.The following chapters will provide a more nuanced look at these groups, at times concluding that nonstate entities may be better placed to provide governance than the state itself. Extralegal groups may pose a security threat and undermine central government authority, but on the ground, nonstate interests—legitimate or extralegal—may be better placed to provide the basic governance goods that are needed to revive local communities.

[96] On the logic of predatory states, see Robert H. Bates (2008); Daron Acemoglu and James A. Robinson (2012).

Part II

How Context Matters

3

History and Society

Nestled on the coast of West Africa, Liberia is perhaps best known as a colony established by freed slaves from the United States. Yet this narrative of universal freedom, so widely accepted in the West, is steeped in controversy and obscures a troubled and tumultuous history. Historian James Ciment has even argued that its very foundation is factually wrong.[1] Unpacking Liberia's creation myth is critical to understanding the nature of Liberia's extralegal groups. While the theoretical framework is important for analyzing these groups on an abstract level, this chapter will flesh out the social and historical context to shed light on the particular forms that these groups have taken in the Liberia.

The theoretical framework tells a rational actor story that collectively results in the emergence of extralegal groups: these groups form as a result of many people making individually rational decisions. At the same time, this study also recognizes the importance of local, national, and regional context. History matters. Politics matters. Social and economic institutions matter. They mold the people that pick up guns and go to war as well as those who protest in the streets against it. However, the ways in which these factors affect behavior are context dependent and specific to individuals or groups. This chapter and the next provide a deeper sense of how important context really is—by demonstrating that extralegal groups can also be read as a phenomenon with deep historical roots.

In this chapter, the focus is on the interplay between Liberia's history and its state–society relations. While providing a broad sociopolitical sketch of the country's evolution, the chapter highlights four key ideas: distrust of the central state, the use of violence and coercion to control outsiders, Firestone's role as a model enclave economy, and the liberalization of the trade in commodities. Although these factors are not necessary conditions for the formation of extralegal groups per se, evidence from the empirical chapters that follow will nonetheless show that they influenced the character of

---

[1] Ciment asserts that not a single one of the original Settlers who arrived in 1820 had ever been a slave. See James Ciment (2013).

these groups. I will show how these ideas came to reverberate many decades later, influencing extralegal group formation and development.

The first of the four sections examines the founding of the Liberian state and the relationship between Americo-Liberians (Americos) and their indigenous counterparts. It considers how the country's vast inequalities gradually developed and were systematically institutionalized through state structures, and why, as a consequence, many native Liberians continue to regard the country's central authorities with distrust. The second section explores how the Americos (and later, the Congos) came to control the country, the specific means they used to take power, and how the practice of coercive taxation that was developed during this period was later echoed in the practices of extralegal groups. The third section is about the important economic and political role that Firestone has played in Liberia, especially in providing a model of an enclave economy for extralegal groups to aspire to. The fourth section discusses the impact of Liberia's Open Door policy and how this liberal trade policy linked the country to the international economy, setting up an environment which would allow rebel groups, and later, extralegal groups, to thrive.

THE CONGO–NATIVE CLEAVAGE

Since the first group of freed American slaves set foot in West Africa in 1820, the relationship between the "Founding" Settlers (henceforth Settlers) and the original inhabitants of the area has been an antagonistic one. Yet despite these early hostilities, Liberia went on to experience long periods of stable central government and significant economic success—in sharp contrast to other states on the continent. In 1978, Christopher Clapham remarked that "the most salient features of the Liberian experience over the last twenty or thirty years have been political stability and economic growth."[2] In fact, through much of the twentieth century, Liberia had fared better than most African countries according to standard social and economic measures. The country seemed to offer a promising future given its wealth of natural resources, its ability to attract large amounts of foreign direct investment, and its modern universities and hospitals. As late as the 1970s, it was still viewed as a model of African modernity and bureaucratic competence. But even at that point, anyone who scratched beneath the surface of society could see that the country's success and prosperity were not being shared equally. One group in particular, the descendants of the original group of Settlers, were reaping enormous benefits, while those who were part of the native population lived in

---

[2] Christopher Clapham (1978).

deep poverty. Social, economic, and political tensions were so palpable that confrontation seemed all but inevitable. The cord that had bound Liberian society together was about to snap—the elites lost control during the 1979 Rice Riots. The façade of invincible authority was shattered. Through the 1980s, 1990s, and the early 2000s, the country was turned upside down, first by a military dictatorship and then by a brutal civil war.

The Settlers Cannot Be Trusted

If there is a single defining narrative about Liberia, it is that it was founded by freed American slaves in 1821. What is less well known about its founding is that the original Settlers and the indigenous Liberian communities that originally occupied the area shared an antagonistic relationship from their earliest encounters. This need to forge a separate community is reflected in the fact that the Settlers later referred to themselves as Americo-Liberians (Americos).[3] They set themselves apart—socially, politically, and culturally. They saw themselves as civilized, in contrast to the indigenous tribes who surrounded them.[4] Later, they also incorporated into the Americo community other Africans who had been rescued from intercepted slave ships. Since many of the original returned slave ships originated from the Congo river basin,[5] African "recaptives" who were rescued and sent to Liberia were called informally referred to as "Congos."[6] Over time, the Congo population was integrated into the Americos.[7] As Jesse Congrue notes, over time, being "Congo" came to signify someone "who is a 'civilized' person or lives like a civilized person";[8] being "Congo" was understood as a positive way of accruing status.[9] (For the most part, Americos and Congos are collectively referred to as Congos in this book.)

Despite various rivalries and differences among local tribes and ethnic groups, the dominant cleavage has been between the Congos and the native Liberians (the local inhabitants who lived there prior to the Settlers' arrival). This section will explore this cleavage and show how, over time, native Liberians' attitude towards the state evolved towards one of distrust of central authority.

---

[3] "Americos" are treated as a distinct ethnic group, before their subsequent integration with the Congo "recaptives."

[4] Timothy D. Nevin (2011), p. 279.   [5] Now Congo-Brazzaville.

[6] Timothy D. Nevin (2011), p. 279.

[7] As the number of Congos grew, the groups blended together, and together, they became colloquially known as Congos. Initially, Americos and Congos made up a very small proportion of the Liberian population (less than 1 percent). Even today, only about 5 percent of Liberia's population is descended from this group.

[8] Jesse N. Mongrue (2011), p. 18.   [9] Charles Johnson, as cited in ibid., p. 18.

This wariness towards the state can be traced all the way back to the nineteenth century and the first encounters between the Settlers and local populations. As a country, Liberia was "founded" by the aptly named American Colonization Society (ACS).[10] With a vision of an African territory for freed slaves in mind, the ACS undertook several trips to Africa in the early 1800s. The goal was to establish a permanent colony of ex-slaves on the Western coast of the continent. During this period, a succession of ACS maritime missions arrived in West Africa and attempted to purchase land from various chiefs up and down the coast. These attempts were repeatedly rebuffed.

In 1821, frustrated by its past failures in securing a deal, the ACS representative Dr Eli Ayres decided to bring along Navy officers from the U.S.S. Alligator. When negotiations dragged on, American Lieutenant Robert Stockton and his accompanying soldiers pulled out their pistols and aimed them at the head of King Long Peter, the local chief of the Dey people. Faced with the barrel of a gun, King Peter had little choice but to "sell" this tract of ancestral land to the ACS. In exchange, the chiefs received an assortment of muskets, gunpowder, iron bars and pots, nails, rum, pipes and tobacco, cutlery, clothing, beads, mirrors, and other odds and ends worth about $300.[11] This 130 square mile plot of land known locally as Dukor (now a shantytown on the edge of Monrovia) would later become the Republic of Liberia.

However, soon after the deal was struck, it became apparent that the Dey and Bassa chiefs did not fully understand that they had permanently signed away their rights to Dukor.[12] When the colonists later tried to land their boats and claim their property, the Dey people threatened them with swords and guns. A temporary peace was reached, but it did not last long. In the end, the dispute between the indigenous West African tribes and the ACS colonists was settled in blood. Various local tribes banded together to attack the new colony, but the Settlers were expecting an attack and had spent months preparing for it. The battle was bloody, but it did not last long. The Settlers won an overwhelming victory and established their right to stay on the land that the ACS had negotiated for them.

With hindsight, it seems obvious that the violent manner in which the country was founded—from the negotiation of the original Dukor agreement to the brutal defeat of the local tribes—poisoned relations between the Settlers and indigenous West Africans from the outset. This air of hostility set the tone for Congo–Native relations for the next 150 years.

---

[10] The ACS is formally known as The Society for the Colonization of Free People of Color of America.

[11] J. Gus Liebenow (1987), p. 19; Helene Cooper (2008), p. 36.

[12] Charles Spurgeon Johnson (1987), p. 44.

Congo Dominance through the State

Over time, Americo-Liberians (and the Congo population they later integrated) came to dominate every aspect of politics and business in the country. Their leadership in society seemed unassailable. They controlled key governmental posts through the True Whig Party and occupied the top tiers of the social strata for most of the country's history.[13] They were the professors, doctors, judges, lawyers, politicians, entrepreneurs, army officers, bureaucrats, and landlords. In spite of their minority status, they constituted an impenetrable elite with an iron grip on power.

Part and parcel of their domination over the country was their incredible wealth: remarkably, 4 percent of Liberia's population held 60 percent of its wealth.[14] Congos were powerful and native Liberians were marginalized; Congos were rich and native Liberians were poor; Congos set the rules and native Liberians obeyed. There was little room to reflect on how this social order came into being or how it was sustained. In her memoir of growing up as a Congo in Liberia, writer Helen Cooper expresses how naturally she assumed her status in society:

> It never occurred to me at that time that all across Liberia, native Liberians were getting more and more upset about the things I took for granted; things that, for me, were as normal as the crow of the rooster in the morning. This was life in Liberia, and who questioned daily life?[15]

Nowhere was this domination more clear than in Liberian state institutions. Not only did Congos hold every position of political power, they also enacted laws that purposely excluded native Liberians from the polity. While indigenous Liberians may not have trusted the Settlers when they first arrived, the Congos themselves were also disdainful of native Liberians. They saw themselves as separate, pious, and deserving of a higher status.

Congo contempt for native Liberians was reflected in Liberia's founding state documents, from the Declaration of Independence to the Constitution. The Dey, Bassa, Kru and others were labeled "aborigines" rather than "Negroes" and excluded from the state under a constitutional clause that limited citizenship to "none but persons of Negro descent..." On this basis, they were also excluded from owning property and consequently, from voting and participating in the new Liberian political order.[16] Given the circumstances of Liberia's founding and the animosity they generated, the exclusions were not surprising. But existing historical accounts that foreshadow the civil war tend to focus on how the Congo class ruled over native Liberians, without considering whether the local

---

[13] Merran Fraenkel (1964).   [14] Adekeye Adebajo (2002).
[15] Helene Cooper (2008), p. 72.   [16] John-Peter Pham (2004), p. 20.

tribes themselves would have wanted to integrate at the time.[17] Instead, the assumption is one of exclusion rather than one of mutual dislike and distrust.[18]

The original Settlers from America shared a very strong bond. Not only did they all have roots in American slavery, but they had survived a hard journey across the Atlantic which had killed many of their kin. This was followed by a violent battle between the Settlers and local indigenous groups. Given that only two decades had passed since the two groups had gone to war, inviting local indigenous groups to join the Liberian polity at its founding would have been a difficult proposition. The Settlers were not militarily strong enough to securely welcome the local tribes into the fold, and these relationships were tenuous at best. Further, such a move would have required a more imaginative and inclusive vision of the future.

For their part, it is not clear that native Liberians *would have wanted to join* the Americos in their new political project, even if they had been invited to do so. Nor did local indigenous groups want the Settlers to join their own polities. Native Liberians had their own separate structures of political governance. Further, at the time that the Settlers founded Liberia, local indigenous tribes had several clear advantages. The territory they controlled surrounded that of the Settlers; native populations far exceeded the Settler population; and the local indigenous groups had a far better understanding of the local geography and how to survive in it. Given these conditions, it would not have made sense for native Liberians to take a subservient role in an upstart and alien social system.

Of course, the term "native" Liberian is itself an artificial construct. Research on Liberia often refers to the West African people as "indigenous" or "native" Liberians, effectively treating them as one homogenous and cohesive group. Yet there are important differences between the sixteen government-recognized ethnic groups that make up modern-day Liberia. However, for the purposes of this discussion, history has bound them together by their otherness, as defined in relation to the Settler class.

It is difficult to deny the stark contrast between the country's founding principles and the de facto political reality that developed. Based on Liberia's Declaration of Independence, it is clear that the Settlers had explicitly established Liberia as an *antidote to racial discrimination* (1847). Yet despite the lofty political ideals espoused in its founding document, *Liberia's Settler class systematically replicated a discriminatory political and economic order much like the one that the freed slaves themselves had fled from in the United States.* The only difference was that this time, those who had once been slaves were now in charge.

---

[17] For example, Mark Huband (1998); Heneryatta Ballah (2003); John-Peter Pham (2004).

[18] See Jesse N. Mongrue (2011), Ch 3 for a discussion of local power dynamics that preceded the arrival of the Settlers.

Historian Fred van der Kraaij described it as a system of apartheid. He lists exactly how the state had politically oppressed native Liberians:

> the disputed acquisition of tribal lands by the Monrovia-based Government, the forcible annexation of tribal lands and communities, the imposition of allegedly unjustified and discriminatory taxes, retaliatory expeditions of Government forces to revolting tribal people, the exclusion of indigenous people from public offices and, until [1907] from citizenship . . . [there were] . . . different laws for the coastal counties where virtually all Americo-Liberians lived and the Hinterland . . . which was inhabited by tribal Liberians (1983: V).

Congos thrived socially, economically, and politically. Power shifted, and eventually, they became the dominant polity. It was not until 1946, almost one hundred years after the country's founding, that Liberians of indigenous descent were finally allowed to vote, and then they were only permitted to do so if they owned a hut and had paid taxes on it.

If there was any doubt about the systematic oppression of native Liberians, one need only turn to the 1956 Code of Laws governing land tenure. Under these regulations, tribal lands were considered "public lands" and only when a tribe was considered "sufficiently advanced in civilization" would it be able to petition the government for family ownership.[19] At the same time, Congos were offered the opportunity to acquire massive estates in the interior at annual rental rates of fifty cents an acre (about U.S. $4.44 in 2016). The premise for these discounted rates (along with tax breaks and numerous other financial incentives) was that Congos would offer a "civilizing" presence to the interior.[20] This practice was particularly humiliating for indigenous groups because land ownership was often tied to cultural and spiritual traditions. Ancestral lands were never meant to be bought and sold.

For native Liberians, the State had gradually become synonymous with Congo rule. Consequently, attitudes towards the central government and towards Congos were difficult to disentangle. Not only were Congos not to be trusted, but the state was tainted by association. Thus, given the manner in which native Liberians had been treated in the past by the central authorities, their distrust of the state and of statebuilding practices more generally was not surprising. In repeated interactions with central authorities since the country's founding, native Liberians had been cast out socially, economically, and politically. They had been consistently treated like second-class citizens in a territory that their ancestors had inhabited for several millennia.[21]

Interviews in the BOPC diamond mining town of Shampe give voice to the strength of this sentiment to this day. When the local clan chief was asked

---

[19] Government of Liberia (1957), p. 272.   [20] John-Peter Pham (2004), p. 63.
[21] D. Elwood Dunn (1995), xxi, states that archeological work and oral history accounts show that predecessors to the Kissi and Gola lived along the coast and in the tropical rainforest for several millennia before the arrival of the Settlers.

about political authority, he was adamant that foreigners had only ever come to exploit local resources, and that central authorities should stay away because no benefits had ever come from government.[22] On a continent scarred by the legacy of colonialism, native Liberians' attitudes of state distrust are echoed throughout Africa.[23]

The key legacy of this social cleavage—and the history that undergirds it—is that native Liberians remain deeply cynical about the state and its representatives. There is broad suspicion of central authority and attempts at state-led statebuilding—for good reason.[24] Suspicion and skepticism remain despite the overthrow of the Congo political regime in 1980, the shift to electoral democracy, and heavy UN oversight over the statebuilding process. The country's more recent experiences with corruption scandals has merely reinforced the view that state officials only act in their own interests.[25]

Overall, the Congo–Native cleavage has impacted the trajectory of extralegal groups in two ways. First, it helps explain why locals chose not to turn to government authorities when they initially needed a regulatory mechanism to facilitate trade and commerce. Indeed, given their past experiences, it seems more likely that they would have done their best to avoid calling the attention of central authorities. This distrust of the state extends beyond the Congo elite. Second, this general suspicion of central statebuilding also helps contextualize the challenge faced by Monrovia-based politicians and officials in their attempts to co-opt extralegal groups (made up of native Liberians) during the entrenchment stage.

In short, this distrust of central statebuilding effectively means that in a post-conflict setting, local populations are less likely to turn to central authorities or state institutions for security and governance. *Consequently, when it came to contract enforcement and dispute resolution, local solutions would have been favored over centralized state authority.* Further, a history of mistreatment by central state authorities made it difficult to co-opt extralegal groups as they became more entrenched later on. Not surprisingly, the Liberian state's long history of exploitation and enslavement has made it difficult for native Liberians (who made up the extralegal groups) to trust the promises made by central authorities.

---

[22] Clan Chief (2005).   [23] Mahmood Mamdani (1996).

[24] Tangentially, John C. Yoder (2003) finds that Liberians' values are predisposed to favor order, stability, and hierarchy.

[25] For example, the 2005 European Commission audit (originally established to investigate corruption during the Taylor years) confirmed the international community's worst fears: corruption within the National Transitional Government of Liberia was so pervasive that it had the potential to politically destabilize the country. The results of the EC audit were considered so explosive and potentially destabilizing that they were originally withheld from the public. See European Commission Official (2005); Renata Dwan and Laura Bailey (2006). A follow-up audit conducted by ECOWAS was similarly damning. Again, the results of this investigation were so alarming that they also were not released to the public.

PACIFYING THE INTERIOR

As Americo-Liberians set about statebuilding in the late 1800s and early 1900s, they had to devise a way to project their power into the interior of the country where native Liberians resided.[26] These efforts eventually resulted in two key policies: the establishment of indirect rule and the creation of the Liberian Frontier Force (LFF). The effective impact of these two policies was a system of coercive taxation. In turn, this led to an extension of Americo political influence, an expansion of their organizational capacity, and increased revenues for state coffers. Decades later, the legacy of these policies is visible in the practices of extralegal groups. This section discusses how coercive taxation originally developed as a policy of the Liberian state.

Originally, Separate Polities

When Liberia was first established in the 1800s, native Liberians were not concerned that they had been excluded from the political order of their neighbors, the Settlers. In the same way that the Settlers were not about to include the local population in their social and political structures, local tribes were not about to include the Settlers in theirs. Indigenous groups already had their own systems of authority and governance, and while some of the local chiefs might have been forced to cede land to the new arrivals, they still maintained dominance in the area and completely controlled the interior of the country, away from Monrovia and the coast.

Among the regions and tribes, there were a variety of governance arrangements, with the most common one being chieftaincy.[27] In these regions, chiefs were in charge of adjudicating disputes, conducting trade, collecting taxes, assigning land, and arranging marriages. There was no need to belong to the formal political order of the newly arrived Americos—it did not offer native Liberians anything that they did not already have, and would have redirected revenues away from their tribes and towards the Settlers. However, once the Settlers began to physically expand their colony, their dominance in the area became difficult to ignore. The Settlers-turned-Americos fought a succession of wars, but at every turn, there was the risk of another uprising, as well as continual threats from British neighbors to the West and French neighbors to the East and North. By the late 1800s, internal and external pressures forced Americo political leaders to begin a process of consolidating the state.

---

[26] On African state formation and patterns of local rule, see Mahmood Mamdani (1996); Jeffrey Ira Herbst (2000); Catherine Boone (2003).

[27] Svend Holsoe (1974).

Even by the early 1900s, authorities had yet to establish a meaningful presence in the interior—in spite of the fact that the government was under enormous pressure to do so from their French and British neighbors. President Barclay and his Cabinet were required to create a robust bureaucratic system and a well-defended border in order to secure their sovereignty, but they did not have the funds to carry out their vision.[28] The tax base in Monrovia was small and imposing heavy taxes on their constituents was not an option—any politician who attempted this would have been voted out of power. Barclay needed another solution.

Indirect Rule and the LFF

To reconcile their ambitions for expanding the state into the hinterland with the country's financial reality, President Barclay decided to do two things. In 1904, he borrowed the concept of indirect rule from the British and applied it to the Liberian interior, presenting it as the Barclay Plan. Then in 1908, he established a permanent Liberian military: the Liberian Frontier Force (LFF).[29]

These two changes gave Monrovia the ability to assert a limited degree of authority in the interior. However, these changes also fundamentally changed the nature of the Congo–Native relationship and the political governance of Liberia.

Following the British model, indirect rule was administered by district commissioners who were directly appointed by the president. Commissioners and paramount chiefs shared responsibility for the district; commissioners worked with chiefs who were charged with maintaining order within their own tribe.[30] District commissioners were responsible for hearing appeals from traditional courts (presided by chiefs) and they maintained control over education, health, agriculture, and commerce in their areas. Provided there was no conflict with the central authority, the district commissioners upheld the power of the local chiefs. To do this, each district had a unit of the LFF at their disposal to enforce the decisions of the commissioner. In the words of Charles Tilly, "those who apply substantial force to their fellows get compliance."[31]

---

[28] Timothy D. Nevin (2011), pp. 280–1.
[29] Immediately, Barclay was forced to hand over control of the LFF to the British, along with Liberia's rubber concessions, and customs duties as collateral for a $100,000 loan that the government had been forced to take out to stave off an economic crisis. The first head of the LFF was a British military officer, Major MacKay Cadell, who was later succeeded by an American army officer, Major Charles Young. See ibid., and Fred P.M. van der Kraaij (1983), pp. 12–46.
[30] For an interesting discussion on the evolution of "tribes" in Liberia, see Stephen Ellis (1999), pp. 31–43.
[31] Charles Tilly (1992), p. 70.

LFF units were infamous for their brutality and survived by "taxing" residents in their assigned district.[32] They often behaved like bandits, leaving a trail of destruction in their wake—though this was to be expected given that the officer corps of Americos and the enlisted indigenous soldiers conceived of warfare very differently.[33]

This new governance configuration marked a substantial change in the distribution of power among local authorities. Initially, paramount chiefs were elected by clan chiefs, but had to be approved by the president. The credibility of paramount chiefs as community leaders became further compromised in 1914 when President Daniel Howard changed the system and eliminated the election process so that these positions were directly appointed by the president. Bit by bit, the political legitimacy of chiefs was eroded as they "came to be seen as representatives of the regime among their people rather than their people's representative to the national authorities."[34] Yet their lack of political legitimacy did not erase the fact that the new chieftaincies were extremely powerful.

Whereas chiefs had traditionally been subjected to checks and balances by secret religious institutions like the Poro and Sande societies,[35] the new institution of the paramount chieftaincy created by the central government was all-powerful. The Americos had succeeded in politically marginalizing the Poro and the Sande by establishing the Liberian Frontier Force. The Americos had transformed the position of chief into something akin to a feudal lord.

Given such easy access to unchecked power, the ruling families of each ethnic group were easily co-opted by the central authority. It was impossible to circumvent the Americo rulers because there was always someone willing to collaborate with them. As historian Carl Burrowes noted:

> The alliance between executive branch officials and local traditional rulers was mutually beneficial. On the one hand, chiefs delivered soldiers and voters en bloc to urban leaders. [...] National leaders in turn provided their rural allies with the resources needed to overcome local challenges.[36]

For their part, chiefs were responsible for general welfare, resolving local disputes (for a fee) and encouraging agriculture. Their judicial authority initially covered domestic disputes, though by 1958, this had expanded to encompass debt and damages cases.[37] In this way, dispute resolution and local contract enforcement had fallen under the purview of local chiefs. Initially, the chiefs were independent of the state and their legitimacy had local roots. But later, under indirect rule, chiefs were co-opted by the state.

---

[32] See R. C. F. Maugham (1920), pp. 87–8 and Stephen Ellis (1999), p. 209.
[33] Timothy D. Nevin (2011).   [34] John-Peter Pham (2004), p. 60.
[35] Stephen Ellis (1999), p. 204.   [36] Carl P. Burrowes (1995), p. 119.
[37] For a detailed description of the tribal justice system (*circa* 1958), see Merran Fraenkel (1964).

Critically, chiefs were also in charge of local tax collection, conscripting labor for public works projects, and providing the district commissioners with a regular quota of supplies. Chiefs received nominal salaries, but were extremely well-positioned to exploit the land and services under their control.[38] For this reason, there was also a lot of competition to become a paramount chief. Because they were personally entitled to 10 percent of the taxes they collected, some paramount chiefs earned as much as $8000 annually in the 1950s—a salary greater than that of many government officials, and a fortune by local standards.[39] Similarly, district commissioners also had the opportunity to take advantage of their office by re-selling excess supplies owed to them, exacting bribes, or selling forced labor on a commission basis. Those who dared to defy the chief or the district commissioner would be subjected to the brutality of the LFF. This system of indirect rule remained in place until 1963. Decades later, we find extralegal groups fulfilling similar dispute resolution functions, and leveraging their abilities to coercively tax.

As Charles Tilly, Victoria Hui, and scholars of nineteenth- and early twentieth-century colonial states have already shown, violent taxation is not unique to Liberia.[40] Nonetheless, it is empirically significant that this mode of violent tax collection, as introduced via the Barclay Plan and the LFF, is replicated decades later by Charles Taylor and other fighting factions (including peacekeepers from the Economic Community of West African States Monitoring Group, ECOMOG) during the civil war. Almost a century later, extralegal groups are shown to employ these same practices. While the establishment of extralegal groups may not have been intentionally modelled on a system of indirect rule, there are undeniable similarities with the type of coercive taxation that was practiced during the Barclay era.

In an analogous example, Eric Uslaner shows that generalized trust can be transmitted through generations.[41] His research empirically demonstrates that "people whose grandparents came to the United States from countries that have high levels of trust . . . tend to have higher levels of generalized trust." Similarly, research by Alesina, Giuliano and Nunn (2010) compared societies that traditionally used the hoe with those that traditionally used the plough. The authors found that generations later, there were significant differences in the behavior and treatment of women in hoe vs. plough societies. The authors hypothesized that this was because hoes required less upper body strength than ploughs, allowing women to work alongside men in the fields. Alesina et al. believe that this history of agricultural participation had a lasting effect on women, resulting in surprising gender differences many generations later.

---

[38] Christopher Clapham (1978).   [39] Henry B. Cole (1956), p. 117.
[40] Ibid.; Merran Fraenkel (1964); Charles Tilly (1992); Carl P. Burrowes (1995); Victoria Tin-bor Hui (2005).
[41] E. M. Uslaner (2008).

Both of these examples demonstrate how the legacies of social patterns, interactions, and attitudes from centuries past have long-lasting effects and can be passed on to future generations. Given such a deep tradition of indirect rule and violent taxation in Liberia, it should not be surprising to see these practices echoed in the behaviors of modern-day extralegal groups.

FIRESTONE: A MODEL FOR EXTRALEGAL GROUPS

The arrival of Firestone in 1926 is one of the most important events in Liberian history. The company had a major impact on the country, transforming domestic politics, reconfiguring its economy, reshaping its border policies, rejuvenating its finances, and fundamentally altering its relationship with the United States. This section will briefly describe the conditions under which Firestone originally came to Liberia, the ways in which it operated, and how the country was transformed by its operations. Drawing from these historical roots, this section will demonstrate how Firestone served as a quasi–role model for extralegal groups.[42]

The Arrival of Firestone

In 1926, the Firestone Rubber and Tire Company was America's largest producer of rubber tires in a rapidly expanding American automobile market. But Firestone had a problem: the price of natural rubber had spiked in recent years. This was largely due to the implementation of the 1922 Stevenson plan which limited rubber exports from Great Britain's Asian colonies and effectively allowed the British to set the world price for rubber. At the time, the U.S. controlled a scant 3 percent of world rubber production, but consumed 75 percent of the world's rubber output at the time, primarily due to a growing appetite for cars. These were the economic circumstances that led Harvey Firestone to turn to Liberia. With its perfect tropical climate and a plantation of rubber trees that was mature enough to immediately begin production, Firestone decided to make a large, long-term investment in Liberia.

On the Liberian side, the political and financial situation was desperate. In 1912, the government had almost gone bankrupt and had to turn to the U.S. for a bailout. The U.S. Senate refused to help forcing President Daniel Howard to borrow U.S. $1.7 million[43] from private lenders. To secure the loan,

---

[42] J. Munive (2011) makes a related argument about the importance of the rubber sector in mobilizing fighters before the civil war.

[43] Equivalent to $43 million in 2017 inflation-adjusted dollars. Note, however, that purchasing power parity may not be the best way to represent the magnitude of this loan in relation to the local economy.

the government was required to sign over its customs revenues to outside powers. To make matters worse, Liberian government leaders were worried about territorial encroachment by the French from the East and by the British from the West. By this point, Liberia was considering desperate measures— Firestone's plan offered the best hope of dealing with the country's financial problems and obtaining the American government's support for securing its borders. Since the Liberian government had no leverage in negotiations, Firestone—with the support of the U.S. government—was able to dictate the terms of the deal.

In their richly detailed chronicles of Firestone's involvement in Liberia, Phillip Johnson,[44] Carl Burrowes,[45] and Fred van der Kraaij[46] each describe the company's massive investment and the extortionate terms it was able to secure at a time of desperate need. Not surprisingly, the agreements stirred up a great deal of controversy within Liberia. Under the terms of the first of three contracts, the Barclay plantation (with its existing rubber trees) was leased to Firestone for $1 per acre in the first year and an annual rent of $6,000 for the plantation for subsequent years. The second contract granted the company the right to lease one million acres for ninety-nine years at the rate of five cents per year for each acre developed in the first six years.[47] In return, the government was permitted to impose a 2.5 percent rubber export tax.

Native Liberians were furious: Americo politicians had signed over rights to native land that they only had nominal control over and they were doing so at fire sale prices. On top of that, the government had been forced to accept the $5 million "Clause K" loan to pay off foreign creditors and to fund state services. For the next forty years, foreign officials were appointed to manage the country's expenditures as well as its military affairs and native popula- tion.[48] In a letter to his son Elmer dated October 11, 1925, Harvey Firestone noted that the "banker's loan" was "made through our State Department, which gives us full control over Liberia, that is, all their finances . . . So you can see we are well protected from a Government standpoint on going into Liberia."[49] The Firestone agreements effectively placed control of the country in the hands of company executives.[50] The terms of the 1926 Firestone accords were so one-sided that even today, they still provoke an outraged response from Liberians.[51]

---

[44] Phillip James Johnson (2004).   [45] Carl P. Burrowes (2005).
[46] Fred P.M. van der Kraaij (1983), especially Chapter 3.   [47] Ibid.
[48] Carl P. Burrowes (2005).
[49] Raymond Leslie Buell (1928b), pp. 823, 837–8.
    [50] Leif Wenar 2008 argues that investment agreements like this are illegal because dictators cannot sell a country's resources given that it is not possible to obtain the people's consent to do so.
    [51] Mauritz A. Hallgren (1933), and Phillip James Johnson (2004), p. 103.

Reconfiguring Power

The Firestone deal altered the Liberian social, political, and economic land-scape in several fundamental ways. Chief among these was the reconfiguration of economic power in the country. Before the arrival of Firestone, Americo-Liberians were long on political ambitions but short on economic clout. In the short-term, the money from the Clause K loan brought with it unwelcome scrutiny into the country's financial affairs. But in the years that followed, especially as the investment turned profitable, revenues from Firestone's land rents and rubber taxes provided the Americo elite with a reliable source of funds *without any corresponding intrusion into domestic politics.* The country was transformed from a subsistence economy into one that was dominated by rubber exports. This served as a dry run for what William Reno describes as the strategy of the shadow state: when those in power parcel off the country's resources to external agents and collect rents that allow them to sustain personal networks of influence.[52]

Using the Firestone money, Americo politicians built up a patronage machine used to reward loyal chiefs and punish those who refused to cooper-ate. In this way, the entry of Firestone upped the stakes of membership into the Liberian polity. The presidential patronage system became embedded into national politics: jobs, contracts, scholarships, and personal favors were viewed as state resources that could be doled out however the president wished. This patrimonial system was also replicated at the regional level, with local politicians maintaining their own client networks and rewarding their own followers with jobs, contracts, and personal favors.[53] Later, Charles Taylor practiced a similar kind of resource politics, using taxes collected from natural resource concessions to sustain his supporters and pay for war.

Thus, with the arrival of Firestone in the 1920s, Liberia lost all claim to being a "rational legal" state in the Weberian sense; instead, it became a place that existed so that those who ran it could extract resources from it for their own benefit.

Geopolitically, the Firestone deal also offered a substantial advantage to the ruling Americo elite: it aligned American economic interests with Liberia's security interests. Suddenly, the United States had a reason to protect the country's sovereignty. With the American automobile industry at stake, Liberia took on strategic value. Crucially, the Americans informally agreed to hold the French at bay on the country's eastern border in exchange for signing off on the Firestone deal. For the first time in a long time, Liberia's leaders did not have to worry about French expansion from the East.[54]

---

[52] William Reno (1995).   [53] Christopher Clapham (1978).
[54] Phillip James Johnson (2004).

The Exploitation of Native Labor

There was still more controversy embedded in the fine print of the Firestone deal: it committed the government to procuring labor for Firestone's operations. In an area like Nimba County, this proved to be less of a problem, but in most parts of the country, Firestone's workers were forcibly recruited.[55] Without some form of forced labor, it would have been impossible for the government to meet the company's initial demand of 350,000 workers. Even by 1930, only 18,000 workers had been found.

Given the size of the country, it would have been implausible that the Firestone leadership and the Americo politicians did not know that coercive recruitment was taking place. The fact that financial incentives had to be provided to procure labor would have made this amply clear. As outlined by Johnson:

> Through the Labor Bureau, Liberia would supply two thousand workers from each of its five counties in return for payment from Firestone of one cent to the government, one half cent to chiefs, and one half cent to paramount chiefs for each day of work performed under the arrangement... Before long, the government shifted control of labor recruitment from the Labor Bureau to the district commissioners, who demanded a fee of one half cent per day for each worker supplied to Firestone.[56]

Based on this agreement, government officials, paramount chiefs, and district commissioners all profited handsomely. For those who still needed to be convinced, there was the hut tax payment.

The hut tax itself only applied to those who lived in the interior—in other words, it was only imposed on native Liberians. In addition to its discriminatory nature, there was the practical problem of payment: most of rural Liberia grew what was needed and bartered for the rest. Money was rare in this subsistence economy. As such, it was very difficult to pay this tax without hiring oneself out as a laborer. Ellis has argued that the hut tax was actually created to monetize the economy, and to indirectly provide cheap labor to foreign companies like Firestone.[57]

For those who still did not submit willingly, the chiefs and commissioners had the Liberian Frontier Force at their disposal for conscripting workers. Americo politicians and the paramount chiefs were no strangers to forced labor. For all of their rhetoric condemning slavery, many Americo-Liberian politicians had no qualms about conscripting native Kru and Grebo people for "public works" projects through the Liberian Frontier Force. Native Liberians were routinely forced to do everything from road construction to serving as

---

[55] Raymond Leslie Buell (1928a); James Riddell (1979); Phillip James Johnson (2004).
[56] Phillip James Johnson (2004), pp. 137–8.   [57] Stephen Ellis (1999), p. 46.

public porters for visitors to the area.[58] Those who refused to work were harshly and cruelly punished.[59] Forced labor was even legally recognized by the government:

> Compulsory labor recruitment for government service, perfectly legal under Liberian law, required tribal citizens to be away from their villages for a few months each year. District commissioners, however ... subjected natives to much longer periods of service and required them to supply their own tools and food. Native chiefs who failed to turn over enough workers could expect fines, beatings, and other forms of intimidation.[60]

In effect, several decades worth of Firestone tires were manufactured for American cars under slave labor conditions.[61] The effects of these slave-like practices would echo down the generations.

The degree to which these practices were commonplace was only revealed after an international League of Nations investigation. In addition to the problem of forced labor within Liberia, the report revealed that native Liberians were also being sold into contract labor abroad to work on the cocoa plantations of the Spanish island of Fernando Pó.[62] The details of the 1931 League of Nations report shamed Liberia's leaders and shook the country to its core—but not enough.

On the one hand, Congos saw their country as a haven free from racial persecution; on the other, Liberian government officials and their native collaborators were systematically profiting from the enslavement and forced labor of their indigenous neighbors.[63] It was not until the 1960s that the practice of forced labor truly ended in Liberia.[64]

Firestone as Role Model

Despite its regularly flouting of the law, Firestone would not qualify as an extralegal group according to the terms that I defined in the Introduction because it operated with state consent and its operations existed within the boundaries of the law *at the time*. The company's policy of coercing labor,

---

[58] Graham Greene (1936), John-Peter Pham (2004), p. 61.
[59] Charles Spurgeon Johnson (1987), pp. 196–7; and Martin Ford (1992), p. 2.
[60] Phillip James Johnson (2004), p. 132.
[61] On natural resources and our moral complicity in the rule of dictators, see Leif Wenar (2016).
[62] I. K. Sundiata (1974, 1996).
[63] International Commission of Inquiry into the Existence of Slavery and Forced Labor in the Republic of Liberia 1931.
[64] Unfortunately, working conditions on rubber plantations are still abysmal. Recently, a lawsuit has been launched against Firestone alleging modern-day slavery and the systematic use of child labor. International Labor Rights Fund (2005).

however abhorrent it seems today, was consistent with Liberian law at the time and sanctioned by the state. Nonetheless, it is notable that during the civil war, coercive labor practices were employed by armed actors in the rubber, diamond, and timber industries. After the war, we continued to see echoes of these practices on the Guthrie rubber plantation, Firestone's closest neighbor. These practices can be treated as a precursor to the country's more recent incarnations of extralegal groups.

Presently, Firestone continues to control territory for profit in the form of its rubber plantations. It also continues to exploit local labor (though it does so within the limits of the law). Through its Plant Protection Department, which also serves as a local quasi-police force, the company uses violence to maintain its control over the plantation. Further, it provides internal dispute resolution by housing its own court. Yet despite the evolution in the company's operations over the years, and civil society's attempts to prevent Firestone from escaping the boundaries of Liberian law, many still believe that the company operates with a large measure of impunity. Simply put: it is commonly perceived that Firestone operates as a law unto itself.

While many Liberians view Firestone's early activities as the epitome of "extralegal," the company's long and secure tenure in the country has also encouraged the provision of public goods. In addition to basic governance functions such as providing security and resolving local disputes, it has also built up an impressive infrastructure presence through its construction of schools, roads, workers' housing, and hospitals. In several areas, the presence of Firestone has penetrated far deeper into the lives of Liberians than the state itself.

These contrasting aspects of Firestone's operations suggest that the present-day leaders of Liberia's extralegal groups may have originally been trying to (consciously or unconsciously) replicate the Firestone enclave model. In the case study chapters examining individual extralegal groups, it will become more apparent that some extralegal groups wanted a commercial fiefdom like Firestone's—especially those groups in the rubber sector.

THE OPEN DOOR POLICY

Before the arrival of Firestone in 1926, Liberia had been completely closed off to foreign investors. This policy changed once Edwin Barclay became president in 1930. Early in his tenure, he instituted the Open Door Policy (ODP). The policy was based on the premise that the country had neither the ability nor the capital to develop itself, so it needed the help of foreigners to achieve its potential. An Open Door Policy would welcome foreign investors by providing them with incentives to invest in the country.

The Open Door Policy got off to a slow start during Barclay's tenure, but it fully took off during the presidency of William Tubman (1944–71). During his presidency, Tubman provided a very generous operating environment for foreign corporations by offering tax holidays, exemptions from import and export duties, special tax rates for selected investors, and tax deductions on items that should not have been tax deductible.[65] With these incentives, Liberia transformed itself into a hotbed of international investment opportunity.

On paper, Tubman looked like an economic genius. Liberia had the fastest growing economy in the world through the 1950s; new construction created roads, railroads, airfields, and ports for the transportation of natural resources. Schools and hospitals followed. Over the course of the first twenty-five years of the Open Door Policy, foreigners invested U.S. $1 billion in Liberia.[66]

While the lasting benefits of the ODP for the Liberian people have been widely debated,[67] there is no denying that the role of foreign investment fundamentally changed how Liberia's economy worked. Even after the arrival of Firestone, much of the country still relied on subsistence farming. But after instituting ODP, Liberia became a supplier of raw materials to world markets. Investment in the rubber sector, in iron ore mining, in logging, and to a lesser extent in gold and diamond mining, began during this period as a result of foreign investment liberalization. In this way, ODP laid the foundation for the subsequent extraction of natural resources.

The ODP is particularly relevant to the analysis of extralegal groups because it demonstrated that natural resources could be profitably monetized without diluting the power of the Congo elite. It offered proof-of-concept for an untested model. The key was to create a link between the Liberian economy and international markets, as both Reno[68] and Ellis[69] demonstrated. Domestically, the ODP established a ready market for various types of natural resources including iron ore, rubber, and timber. In practical terms, it was because of the ODP that transportation links were built, providing a means for these resources to travel from the hinterland to international buyers. *The Open Door Policy linked Liberia to global supply chains long before globalization hit the rest of the world.* Liberia was well ahead of the curve when it came to foreign direct investment. On the international side, the policy gave Liberia a global business profile. It familiarized companies, traders, and importers with what Liberia had to offer in the way of raw materials and established it as a business-friendly environment. In this way, the ODP laid the groundwork for the financing of rebel groups, and later, for extralegal groups, half a century later.

---

[65] Fred P.M. van der Kraaij (1983), xvii.

[66] Adjusting for inflation, using 1957 dollars (midpoint between 1944 and 1969), this investment is roughly equivalent to U.S. $8.5 billion in 2016 dollars.

[67] Lawrence A. Marinelli (1964); R. E. Miller and P. R. Carter (1972); T. H. Bonaparte (1979); Fred P.M. van der Kraaij (1983).

[68] William Reno (1995b); William Reno (1997).   [69] Stephen Ellis (1999).

CONCLUSION

This chapter has provided a brief historical overview of Liberia's history and society, focusing on the historical moments, relationships, actors, and institutions that are relevant to understanding and analyzing extralegal groups. It focused on four key themes: the Congo–Native cleavage, the "pacification" of the interior through coercive taxation, the arrival of Firestone, and the Open Door Policy.

It began by demonstrating how the Congos' systematic oppression of native Liberians *through state mechanisms* had engendered a strong sense of distrust towards central authorities among native Liberians. This skeptical attitude meant that locals were unlikely to turn to the state for contract enforcement or dispute resolution, creating fertile conditions for extralegal groups to emerge. An additional consequence of this hostility towards the state is that the government would have found it difficult to co-opt extralegal groups (who were predominantly native Liberians) because native leaders and communities could not trust the state.

Second, this chapter examined the specific policies that the Congos adopted in their efforts to control and manipulate the native population. It pointed out that the practices of extralegal groups resembled those of local chiefs in the provision of dispute resolution services, and in the coercive taxation used against the native population. Third, it argued that Firestone has served as a model for Liberia's extralegal groups: a permanent resource enclave that could be controlled independently of the state. The fourth and final section makes the case that the liberalization of foreign investment through the Open Door Policy was responsible for reorienting the economy from subsistence farming towards the extraction of raw materials. By providing this critical link to the international economy, the Open Door Policy laid the economic foundations for rebel groups and extralegal groups to thrive many decades later. Having covered key aspects of Liberia's political history, Chapter 4 will focus on Liberia's civil war, and the aspects of the conflict that directly impacted on the formation of extralegal groups.

4

Civil War

By all accounts, the Liberian civil war was brutal and devastating. It destroyed Liberia's wealth, its institutions, and its infrastructure. Its government was deemed illegitimate; its most educated citizens were driven out of the country. By the time the fighting ended in the summer of 2003, 100,000 people had been killed, and many thousands more had been maimed, wounded, raped, or sexually assaulted. At least 1 million people had been displaced out of a prewar population of 3 million. (See Appendix for a detailed discussion of these figures.) The civil war had completely destroyed the country that had once been the envy of Africa.

Building on Liberia's social and political inheritance, this chapter places the Liberian civil war in historical context and shows how conflict dynamics affected the development of extralegal groups. It examines the period of political instability leading up to the war (1979–89) and the post-conflict transition period that followed it (post-2003), as well as the war itself (1989–2003). The aim is to show the continuities as well as the disruptions in state–society relations. Extralegal groups do not spring up from nowhere; they arise partly in response to the environment which gave birth to them. Understanding the war economy and the incentives and patterns of interaction embedded within it is critical to the commodity chapters that follow (Rubber, Diamonds, Timber).

While this discussion draws deeply on the work of other scholars who have written about Liberia's civil war, the emphasis is not on the battles that were fought, the military tactics that were employed, or the atrocities that were committed.[1] Rather, the intention is to understand how the practices and

---

[1] For a historical approach to the civil war, see Colin M. Waugh (2011), A. Sawyer (1992); Jeremy I. Levitt (2005). For a discussion of regional dynamics, see Adekeye Adebajo (2002); M. Bøås (2003); A. Sawyer (2004). For a political economy perspective, see William Reno (1995); William Reno (1998); Stephen Ellis (1999). For a discussion of post-conflict elections, see D. Harris (1999); Terrence Lyons (1999); D. Harris (2006); Mary Moran (2006). For a discussion of youth and the civil war, see Danny Hoffman (2011), Abigail Hardgrove (2012). For a quantitative approach to conflict events, see H. Hegre, G. Ostby and C. Raleigh (2009); Rob Blair, Chris Blattman and Alexandra Hartman (2012). For a field perspective, see James Brabazon and Jonathan Stack (2004).

interactions that were specific to Liberia's war impacted the emergence of extralegal groups. Core to this understanding is the idea that war leaves behind a legacy of conflict capital, and this legacy of relationships, interactions, and social expectations persists long after war ends.

The chapter is divided into four sections, each one pertaining to extralegal groups in different ways. Building on the earlier discussion of state distrust, the first section examines the collapse of the Americo-Liberian regime and the weakening of state and local authority. This decline of the ruling class created a space for other forms of authority to emerge. The second section focuses on how the exploitation of the country's natural resources helped build social and commercial networks of resource exploitation. It also speaks to how Charles Taylor and other faction leaders developed a thriving war economy and how these wartime practices prepared the ground for the extralegal groups that would later follow. The third section delves into the strategic alliances that formed during the civil war and considers how they impacted the membership of extralegal groups in the postwar period. The final section discusses how the war ended and the country's gradual transition toward peace.

THE STATE DISINTEGRATES

Since the founding of the Liberian state, the dominant cleavage that has defined the country's politics has placed Congos on one side of the divide and native Liberians on the other side. While the descendants of the original settlers prospered financially and socially, the rest of the country has long lived in poverty. (See Chapter 3.)

Tensions had been mounting for decades. By the 1970s, Native Liberian leaders were fighting for political reform and a greater share of power. The situation came to a head in early 1979 when President William Tolbert increased the price of a bag of imported rice from $22 to $30. Thousands of native protestors demonstrated peacefully against the increase but the government panicked and cracked down violently, leading to the country's infamous Rice Riots. In this moment, it became clear that the Tolbert government had lost its grip over the indigenous population. The veneer of Congo invincibility was crumbling. The Rice Riots presaged the violence that followed.

In the end, it was a group of seventeen low-ranking army soldiers that destroyed the regime. They led a coup d'état on April 12th, 1980. Under the cover of darkness, the soldiers took control of the Executive Mansion. President Tolbert was gruesomely disembowelled and 26 other staff members in the president's home were also killed. The group of soldiers, led by Sergeant Thomas Quiwonkpa, established the People's Redemption Council (PRC) and placed Liberia under military rule. Samuel Doe, one of the soldiers who participated in the coup, and a childhood friend of Quiwonkpa, was named head of state and co-chair of the PRC. The newest leader of Liberia was twenty-eight years old, semi-literate, and was taking night classes to obtain his high school diploma.

On the streets of Monrovia, indigenous Liberians responded to Tolbert's execution with jubilation. Spontaneous parties erupted to celebrate the end of the Congo era; people got dressed up and danced in the street. For most of the population, Tolbert's demise signalled the end of an era of corrupt repression. Someone from outside the Americo-Liberian oligarchy was finally in charge, and people expected that liberation would bring with it broad economic and political reforms.[2] They were to be deeply disappointed.

In the following weeks, the PRC jailed and harassed former members of the government. Thirteen of the most prominent government officials in the Tolbert administration were summarily tried, convicted of corruption, and then publicly executed at Barclay beach. At the execution, hundreds of indigenous Liberians celebrated their newfound power as one cabinet minister after another was shot. The crowd chorused: "Who born soldier? Country woman! Who born minister? Congo woman!"

Congos who had the means to leave the country soon fled and took their assets with them: they knew that they were vulnerable targets under the new PRC. The country lay in turmoil as drunken soldiers from the Armed Forces of Liberia (AFL) took the opportunity to loot from Congo mansions while others raped the women.[3] It was a sloppy and brutal foreshadowing of the new regime's penchant for violent tactics. The "book people" had been removed from their posts to be replaced by young soldiers, many of them uneducated and inexperienced. Thrust suddenly into positions of power, they revelled in the excesses that they felt were part of the job. Seemingly overnight, those who had been on the margins of the polity became the new regime's central players.

It did not take long before the brutality of Doe's PRC became apparent. Despite his "country" roots, he proved to be just as corrupt and nepotistic as those who had ruled before him. Under Doe, the personalization of the presidency took an extreme form. Just as the Congos had favored their own with political appointments and government contracts, Doe bestowed special privileges to his fellow Krahn kinfolk, surrounding himself with a political and military buffer of co-ethnic loyalists. Compared with Doe's excesses, Congo patronage now seemed restrained.

Citizens had hoped that the overthrow of the Congo class would lead to economic and political reforms and a new era of emancipation. Instead, Doe's rule substantially exacerbated ethnic tensions and heightened distrust of

[2] M. A. Sesay (1996).   [3] Helene Cooper (2008).

government. For non-Krahn native Liberians, it did not seem to matter who was in power—Congo or Native—the state and its institutions could not be trusted.

This disintegration at the national level had serious implications for local authorities who took their remit from the central government. In Liberia's villages, the political class that had once been dominated by Congo supporters now looked vulnerable. This crumbling of the state is important because it opened up a space for other forms of local authority. In effect, the 1980 coup marked the beginning of a long period of state weakening. It is this weakening that eventually allowed rebel groups, and then later, extralegal groups, to emerge. Over the course of the next twenty-odd years, the central government would steadily lose its influence over the interior—including its management of natural resources.

NATURAL RESOURCES

The role of natural resources in civil wars, especially Africa's civil wars, has been deeply explored by scholars over the past two decades. In the late 1990s and early 2000s, the first generation of studies on conflict and resources usefully provided an alternative political economy of war lens for understanding civil wars, helping to broaden debates that had framed war as a problem of ethnic hatred or culture clash.[4]

Pioneering studies using statistical methods on cross-national datasets explored whether the presence of natural resources promoted the onset of armed conflict[5] or lengthened the duration of civil war.[6] Complementing the quantitative work, early qualitative studies probed how the war economy fueled the fighting,[7] sometimes focusing on the role of specific resources in country cases.[8] As researchers began to probe deeper, a demand for more refined data and more nuanced approaches developed, with a concomitant improvement in our understanding of the interactions between resources and civil wars.[9]

---

[4] Samuel Huntington (1993); Robert D. Kaplan (1993); Robert Kaplan (1994).

[5] Paul Collier and Anke Hoeffler (1998); James D. Fearon and David D. Laitin (2003); Michael L. Ross (2004b).

[6] Paul Collier, Anke Hoeffler and Mats Soderbom (2004); Havard Hegre (2004).

[7] David Keen (1994); Mats R. Berdal and David Malone (2000); Philippe Le Billon (2001b); Karen Ballentine and Jake Sherman (2003); Ian Bannon and Paul Collier (2003).

[8] William Reno (1997); Ian Smilie, Lansana Gberie and Ralph Hazelton (2000); Philippe Le Billon (2001a); Stephen Jackson (2002).

[9] Michael L. Ross (2004a); Macartan Humphreys (2005); Päivi Lujala, Nils P. Gleditsch and Elisabeth Gilmore (2005); Jeremy M. Weinstein (2007); Philippe Le Billon (2008); Oeindrilla Dube and Juan Vargas (2013); Christine Cheng and Dominik Zaum (2016); Leif Wenar (2016).

Yet the management of these same resources *after* war has received much less attention from scholars and external policymakers.[10] Once war is declared over, the natural resource problem shifts from being a security problem to a problem of domestic politics, which tends to attract less international attention. Those less familiar with the context of post-conflict transitions might be forgiven for thinking that an end to war should lead to the dissolution of the networks that were established to finance that war. Yet this would be the exception rather than the rule—there are clear continuities between civil war economies and postwar economies. To properly understand the postwar economy—and by extension, extralegal groups—it is important to recognize that its structure has been deeply shaped by the civil war economy.

The role of natural resource has been particularly prominent in Liberia's civil war. Evidence abounds concerning how timber, rubber, and diamond revenues were used to finance the various factions who took part in the war.[11] Although this study focuses on the *post*-conflict environment, this section will briefly consider the legacy of the war economy and the ways in which it has facilitated the emergence of extralegal groups—directly and indirectly.

Rule by the Gun

Despite the PRC's early promises of economic and social reform, Samuel Doe's regime became more and more repressive as time wore on. When the civil war began on December 24, 1989, the invasion was conducted by a group of roughly one hundred National Patriotic Front of Liberia (NPFL) rebels who entered Nimba County from the Côte d'Ivoire border.[12] After the initial surge across the border, the early group of NPFL rebels joined up with a contingent of seven hundred Burkinabé fighters provided by Blaise Compaoré along with a medley of revolutionary freedom fighters from across West Africa.[13] In nearby Burkina Faso, Compaoré had just ousted Thomas Sankara with the help of Charles Taylor and members of the nascent NPFL.[14] Now it was time for Compaoré to repay the favor.

The arrival of the NPFL was largely welcomed by the Gios and the Manos who had been subjected to waves of violence and abuse during Doe's presidency. Gradually, Taylor built up his militia as he battled through Nimba County, gathering new recruits. Building on local anger and taking advantage

---

[10] The most notable exception is the multi-volume series on peacebuilding and managing natural resources, see Carl Bruch, David Jensen, Mikiyasu Nakayama and Jon Unruh (2011).

[11] William Reno (1995); Philippa Atkinson (1997); Mark Huband (1998); Global Witness (2002); Silas Siakor (2002); Truth and Reconciliation Commission of Liberia (2009).

[12] The estimated number of fighters ranged from ninety-six to 167, with Charles Taylor claiming a force of 105 "trained commandos," as cited in Stephen Ellis (1999), p. 75.

[13] Adekeye Adebajo (2002).   [14] See Stephen Ellis (1999), p. 69.

of his Gio roots, Taylor claimed that people wanted to fight Doe. In an interview with Bill Berkeley, Taylor said, "As the NPFL came in, we didn't even have to act. People came to us and said, 'Give me a gun. How can I kill the man who killed my mother?'"[15]

Responding to the NPFL's attacks, Doe unleashed an even more vicious wave of civilian killings targeted at Gios and Manos. The country's simmering ethnic tensions—between the Krahns and Mandingos on the one hand and the Gios and Manos on the other—had finally spilled over into war. With the violence becoming more intense and many in Nimba County hungry for revenge against Doe, the NPFL grew even more undisciplined as Taylor invited soldiers to pay themselves by looting the areas that they had taken control of.

The success of the NPFL as a rebel group marked a significant change in the control over coercive force in Liberia. Up to that point, violence had been wielded almost exclusively by the state and its agents.[16] Previously, any group that had attempted to violently confront the government had been quickly and harshly put down. Even in the period following the 1980 coup, Doe and the PRC had moved quickly to take over the state and secure its monopoly on violence. Despite the chaos of this period, state authority survived this transition intact. But the collapse of the Americo regime marked the end of a long period of political stability.

The violence unleashed by the NPFL, and the counterattacks by Doe's illicit death squads undermined the state's monopoly on violence, legitimate or otherwise. Coercive force was now being exerted by anyone willing to carry a gun. State weakness provided the space for other forms of local authority to emerge, including rebel groups, and later on, extralegal groups.

Charles Taylor's come-one-come-all recruitment efforts in Nimba County fundamentally shaped the way in which the war was fought. Interestingly, the NPFL's early battlefield successes masked the substantial internal divisions and logistical setbacks they faced at the time.[17] As the fighting intensified, these divisions became harder to hide. The discipline and training that had been exhibited by some of the more professionalized elements of the NPFL (such as Prince Johnson's faction) gradually gave way to arbitrary brutality as the rebel group attracted a significant population of untrained and undisciplined fighters. As the NPFL expanded, it became possible to kill someone with little or no recourse. During his trial in the Special Court for Sierra Leone, even

---

[15] Bill Berkeley (2001), p. 49.

[16] There were other types of violence taking place (domestic violence, criminal violence), but these did not pose an existentialist threat to the government.

[17] For a riveting account of how Charles Taylor consolidated his power over his rivals (especially Elmer Johnson, Prince Johnson, Cooper Teah, and Jackson Doe) in the early days of the NPFL, see Stephen Ellis (1999) Chapter 2.

Taylor acknowledged this problem: "Without training they had become NPFL and were going after other people."[18]

Within months of the initial invasion, the country was awash in weapons and normal constraints on the use of force had been lifted. Taylor himself admitted that in retrospect, the situation was "out of control."[19] As the NPFL rampaged through the country, power structures in rural areas also changed: those who had guns, knew how to use them, and could defend themselves against others became the new de facto leaders. Local authority structures that had been ruled by elders[20] begun to crumble in the aftermath of the 1980 coup; these were left shattered by the onset of war.[21] Acts of brutal violence were committed by both sides with remarkable ease. The battle scenes were gruesome, with rapes, beheadings, burnings, and cannibalism forming part of the everyday landscape of war.[22]

The heinous forms of torture and violence, the utter disregard for human life, and the way in which killing had been turned into a spectacle made the civil war especially difficult to comprehend, for outsiders and Liberians alike. Acts of extreme violence were no longer exceptional, and fighters and civilians alike inevitably became desensitized to it. Atrocities became commonplace. International reporting of Liberia's war consistently portrayed it as primitive and barbaric.[23]

In these violent conditions, the nature of social relationships transformed, creating a fresh stockpile of conflict capital. People were forced to adapt to the conditions of war: farmers became fighters; mothers became prostitutes; children became cooks and porters. Survival networks formed, vengeance was sworn, and new patterns of interactions developed, reflecting a fundamental reordering of power structures within Liberian society. Acts of violence, fear, and mistrust were woven into the fabric of day-to-day survival: individuals were killed because they belonged to an opposing ethnic group; parents might respond to a knock at the door by hiding their children. As the

---

[18] Charles Taylor (2009a), p. 24869.   [19] Ibid., p. 24870.

[20] On the renegotiated social contract between generations in the wake of Sierra Leone's civil war, see Johanna Boersch-Supan (2012).

[21] See Paul Richards 1996 on the motivations of the young men who joined the RUF in Sierra Leone.

[22] Horrific depictions of violence were recounted during the Truth and Reconciliation Commission of Liberia 2009 and also during the trial of Charles Taylor by the Special Court of Sierra Leone 2009. The author is also in possession of a collection of civil war photos depicting scenes of atrocious acts of violence.

[23] Since this time, our understanding of atrocities committed in civil war has evolved to consider strategic reasons for violent acts (Jeremy M. Weinstein (2007); Alexander B. Downes (2008)). For a sophisticated analysis that explores the social psychology dynamics of systemic brutality in Sierra Leon's civil war, see Kieran Mitton (2015). See also Paul Richards' seminal study of the RUF (1996). In Uganda's conflict with the Lord's Resistance Army, see Anthony Vinci (2005).

war persisted, these patterns of interactions deepened over time, building up stores of conflict capital.

Importantly for the emergence of extralegal groups, there was a marked shift in how disputes were resolved. The new conditions meant that violence (or the threat of violence) was more likely to be used to settle disputes that had once been peacefully (though not always fairly) settled by chiefs, elders, and other local officials.

In his interviews with foreign businessmen who had conducted business in the bush during the war, Stephen Ellis remarked that they "recalled almost nostalgically how they could sort out problems by going straight to the local NPFL army commander or military police commander."[24] The new Liberia was ruled by the gun. Moving away from this mode of conflict resolution would later prove difficult, even after the war ended. This was one way in which the war had permanently changed the social and political landscape.

The Exploitation of Natural Resources in War

By August 1990, the country had been at war for eight unrelenting months. Samuel Doe was clinging to the presidency while Charles Taylor and his NPFL rebels controlled most of the country's territory. Doe had barricaded himself in the Executive Mansion with his remaining bodyguards, unwilling to leave the security of the grounds. When he finally left the Mansion grounds for a visit to ECOMOG headquarters (ECOWAS' peacekeeping mission), he was kidnapped, tortured, and then killed by Prince Johnson[25] and the Independent National Patriotic Front of Liberia (INPFL), a splinter faction of the NPFL.[26]

In the aftermath of Doe's death, intense fighting ensued between the NPFL, the INPFL, the armed forces, and ECOMOG peacekeeping forces. By the time the situation stabilized in November 1990, ECOMOG had gained control of Monrovia while the NPFL rebels effectively held the rest of Liberia. Yet without the capital city, Charles Taylor found himself shut out of the presidency that he felt was his by right. Unwilling to lay down his arms, Taylor set up a competing regime based out of Gbarnga: the National Patriotic Reconstruction Assembly Government (NPRAG). The NPRAG controlled the rest of the country, an administrative entity that came to be known as 'Greater Liberia'.

---

[24] Stephen Ellis (1999), p. 91.

[25] Footage of Doe's torture and execution was publicly circulated and widely viewed. It can be accessed on YouTube.com.

[26] There has been extensive speculation around Doe's capture and the extent to which ECOMOG, Nigerian peacekeepers, and the U.S. government had a hand in his death. See Stephen Ellis (1999), Introduction.

However, without full access to the trappings of the official Liberian state, Taylor had to find other ways to generate income. He opted to exploit the countryside's resources, proving that he could raise revenues like a sovereign. Extralegal groups would later learn from this operational model.

In testimony to the U.S. House of Representatives, America's former Ambassador to Liberia, William Twaddell, estimated that Taylor was earning at least U.S. $75 million by "taxing" various natural resource exports.[27] In the early 1990s, these exports included diamonds ($300 million/year, almost entirely from Sierra Leone), timber ($53 million/year), rubber ($27 million/year); iron ore ($41 million/year) and gold ($1 million/year). The trade in natural resources (diamonds, timber, rubber, etc.) was also one of the ways in which Taylor and other leaders paid their commanders.[28]

Indeed, Taylor and the NPFL were not the only ones who realized that taxing was a profitable enterprise. ULIMO-K (United Liberation Movement for Democracy-Kromah faction) also managed immigration and customs, taxing traders and monitoring those who crossed into their territory.[29] During the war:

> Fighters took food from villagers as a form of direct tribute, but they also supervised or took levies from gold and diamond-mining, rubber-tapping and palm oil manufacture ... by civilians who then had to pay at least a part of the proceeds to the fighters who ruled them. Where foreign firms were operating with heavy equipment, factions would simply tax them for the right to export rubber or logs.[30]

In some cases, these were official fees, paid into Ivorian and Swiss bank accounts; in other cases, logging companies were directed to pay the salaries of the port managers and the expenses for Taylor's National Security Agency, and also to generate electricity in the east of the country.[31] In setting up checkpoints to provide borders with parts of Liberia held by other factions, Taylor and the NPFL had begun to engage in basic forms of statebuilding by securing their territory, and providing public goods.

In creating Greater Liberia, Taylor was able to assert some control over this area, and also to protect local infrastructure to a degree. This early behavior is also consistent with statistical analyses showing that the longer an autocrat is in power, the more robust the property and contract rights regime.[32] Critically, Taylor thought of himself *as a president-in-waiting, not as a bandit.* Early on in the war, he saw his future as being tied to the territory and he was anxious that the economy continue to be as productive as possible.[33] Taylor behaved as we might expect an aspiring statebuilder to behave.

---

[27] William Twaddell (1996).　　[28] Stephen Ellis (1999), p. 141.
[29] Ibid., p. 135.　　[30] Ibid., p. 143.
[31] William Reno (1998), p. 96.　　[32] Stephen Ellis (1999), p. 143.
[33] Christopher Clague, Philip Keefer, Stephen Knack and Mancur Olson (1996).

Even while Taylor's NPRAG government controlled swaths of countryside, fighting between the various factions continued on and off. There were three transitional governments before the Abuja II Accord agreement was signed in 1996, bringing with it the first real hope of lasting peace.[34] Finally, in 1997, Liberia held an election which was handily won by Charles Taylor. Taylor captured 75 percent of the votes with 85–90 percent voter turnout.[35] Many international observers were stunned by this result, but Liberians themselves were neither surprised nor alarmed.

There are several theories explaining why Liberians gave Taylor such an overwhelming victory. The most plausible of these is that Liberians were hoping to placate Taylor by giving him the prize that he so desperately wanted; the darker side of this theory was the implicit threat that the NPFL would take the country back to war if Taylor was not elected. There was even some anticipation that having finally secured the presidency, Taylor might focus on governing rather than fighting. Those hopes were quickly dashed.

Taylor was now a different man: the Charles Taylor who had once sought to impose accountability and proper financial management in running the government's General Services Agency (GSA) was gone. In his place was a warlord hardened by years of brutal fighting and keeping his enemies at bay. Similarly, the once-stable and functioning Liberia was now militarized and deeply divided. The Liberia that Taylor took over in 1997 was not the same Liberia that he had once dreamed of leading.

Laying the Foundation for Extralegal Groups

The exploitation of natural resources by nonstate actors marked a critical juncture: it was the point when the state lost control over the management of its natural resources—*and* the accompanying profits and taxes. The economic activities of the various fighting factions transformed the nature of the local economy in five different ways—with visible effects across the rubber, timber, and diamond industries.

First, natural resource extraction by the factions created new local trading networks for rubber, timber, and diamonds. Over time, fighters developed a knowledge base and familiarity with these commodities and their markets. This facilitated the emergence of extralegal groups. Indeed, some of these trading networks specialized in smuggling resources across the country or across international borders. The conditions of war had taught participants in these markets how to take their business underground when necessary—particularly when UN sanctions were imposed on diamonds (2001) and

---

[34] Terrence Lyons (1999), Chapter 3.
[35] Friends of Liberia (1997), Terrence Lyons (1999), p. 55.

timber (2003). The pressure from these commodity bans forced these trading networks to adapt in order to survive. Some of these markets and networks went dormant before shutting down entirely, while others grew more nimble and resilient as a result of sanctions.[36]

For better or worse, Taylor democratized the exploitation of resources by opening up the markets to a diverse range of participants and demonstrating the viability of artisanal exploitation. In creating these new networks and markets, the wartime trade in timber, diamonds, gold, and rubber proved that natural resources could be profitably exploited by individuals with little experience in these sectors. As these sectors opened up, with opportunities for everyone to participate, they were no longer the exclusive domain of Congo elites and large corporations. The ways in which some industries were organized made it especially easy for individuals to enter and to prosper. For example, by the time war had ended, many ex-combatants were familiar with how the informal rubber and diamond industries worked and had the skills and experience to profitably participate in them. Some had firsthand experience in these industries and others knew friends or fellow fighters who had worked within these sectors. This knowledge and these networks constituted part of the war economy legacy.

Second, Taylor's commercial exploitation of the countryside through the NPRAG, the NPFL's rebel government, revealed the extent to which the Liberian state had lost control of its territory. The widespread participation of so many different fighting factions in the exploitation of natural resources revealed the state's vulnerability. Although the Liberian state had once been perceived as having a firm grip on the monopoly of force, the outbreak of war shattered that belief. The state had lost its aura of invincibility. Despite a hard shell of military might, the state was shown to possess a soft underbelly.

Third, Taylor and the NPFL rebels normalized the illegal extraction of natural resources. During the war, many people participated in natural resource extraction. Sometimes this occurred on public land and other times, it happened on private land. While there might have been the odd bit of private mining or logging before the war, the scale of private resource exploitation vastly increased during the war. Tapping, mining, and logging became commonplace. There was little, if any, social approbation associated with it, partly because people did not view the state as the rightful owner of the resources on the land. Even people at the highest levels of government were engaged in these activities.

For the emergence of extralegal groups, what is worth highlighting is that these activities had been normalized by the end of the war: the illegal extraction of natural resources did not transgress social norms. During the war,

---

[36] Lee Jones (2015) offers a penetrating critique at the failure of economic sanctions regimes.

nonstate actors felt empowered to take control of the country's resource areas and the profits that came with them. To a large extent, these norms carried over into the post-conflict period, making it socially acceptable to take on employment that was formally considered illegal. This leaves a post-conflict government with a substantial challenge: how to regain control over these natural resource rents and change perceptions about the social acceptability of these types of activities.

Fourth, Taylor made ad hoc taxation common practice. Not only were people expected to provide food to fighters and pay checkpoint taxes during the war, but for those who traded in natural resources, there were all manner of unofficial taxes including a port tax, a land tax, a volume tax, and an export tax. In the logging industry, official fees and taxes could be waived in exchange for a bribe to the appropriate official. The ways in which the resource industries were set up in wartime meant that people were accustomed to paying these unofficial tributes. When it came time for extralegal groups to start taxing, it was already an established practice.

Finally, Taylor and other faction leaders showed that they could operate successfully without the backing of a recognized state, proving that government backing was not necessary for commercial success. Even as a rebel leader, there were foreign companies that were willing to do business with him. The success of these operations revealed that the framework of trust provided by the state was not needed for the commercial sector to thrive. Indeed, the existence of these arrangements posed a problem for the Interim Government of National Unity (IGNU) which was already struggling to assert its authority. These arrangements threatened the legitimacy of the Liberian state, and undermined its role as intermediary and commercial guarantor. The next sections will examine how these types of practices affected the dynamics of the individual sectors.

Rubber

The NPFL's control of Greater Liberia gave Taylor access to opportunities in the rubber industry. After taking over the Firestone plantation in 1990, Taylor negotiated an agreement with the company's executives whereby the NPFL would provide "protection" for the rubber plantation in exchange for "tax payments" that included "income taxes, social security payments, and rent, equipment and rice, valued at U.S. $2.3 million,"[37] as well as military and logistical support.[38]

---

[37] Maeve O'Boyle (2014).
[38] Associated Press (1992); M. De Montclos (1996), Truth and Reconciliation Commission of Liberia (2009); Maeve O'Boyle (2014).

Both parties appeared to benefit from this arrangement: Firestone could be assured that its valuable capital assets would be protected from damage and Taylor would not only receive his protection payment, but the NPFL also gained a degree of control over the plantation's workers and could sell rubber abroad through Firestone's business connections.[39] Rubber also had to be processed for export and Taylor was able to collect a 25 percent tax on this part of the production process as well.[40] According to Taylor, control of Firestone netted the NPFL U.S. $1 million to $2 million every six months.[41] As journalist Elizabeth Blunt notes,

> They had everything a rebel army would want. They had fuel supplies. They had generators. They had communications. They had food, and they had nice facilities. They had clinics and they had really nice houses. So it was a very, very good base to operate from.[42]

All told, the deal that Taylor struck with Firestone was remarkably successful, netting Taylor millions of dollars personally, and providing the Freedom Fighters (as the NPFL styled themselves in the early days) a secure operating base for launching attacks into Monrovia. Taylor himself admits how critical Firestone was for him at that juncture in the war because the company provided both the financial resources and the foreign currency that were needed to keep fighting.[43]

Despite the security agreement, Firestone was exporting at a fraction of its prewar levels. Instead, private tappers worked the Firestone plantation and privately sold on their production for export. As Philippa Atkinson noted, "Fighters organise much of the illegal tapping of abandoned plantations, with forced labour sometimes used."[44]

Firestone was unhappy that others were tapping its rubber without compensation and then selling it back to them for processing. Consequently, they pushed the Liberian government to institute a ban on rubber exports—which it did. These sanctions succeeded in eliminating the independent tappers, but they were soon replaced by members of the various armed factions who realized that there was money to be made.[45] For example, the Liberian Peace Council (LPC) took over the LAC plantation in 1993 and allowed its fighters to profit from the rubber industry in order to maintain their loyalty.[46] Despite the rubber sanctions that had been put in place, Malaysian, Korean, and Lebanese buyers operated freely, easily circumventing the controls in place.

Liberians even invented their own unique form of rubber exploitation during this period by collecting buried rubber waste from the Firestone

---

[39] William Reno (1998), p. 100.
[41] Charles Taylor (2009b).
[43] Charles Taylor (2009b).
[45] See Stephen Ellis (1999), p. 128.
[40] Philippa Atkinson (1997), p. 10.
[42] Maeve O'Boyle (2014).
[44] Philippa Atkinson (1997), p. 10.
[46] William Reno (1998).

plantation. It was sold for reprocessing at U.S. $50 per tonne. Rubber "miners" called this substance "bouncing diamond."

Interestingly, it was not only the Liberian factions who were involved in the rubber industry. From March 1993 onwards, ECOMOG peacekeepers were also making a tidy profit by taxing all cargo that came through the ports. For example, it was alleged that in 1993–4, ECOMOG taxed up to 1700 tonnes of rubber per month for export.[47] Later, in 1996, Atkinson showed that one shipment of rubber was taxed by ECOMOG at U.S. $4000 (roughly half the value of one container).[48] On top of this basic fee, 25 percent of the shipment value was paid in US dollars and then refunded to the company in Liberian dollars at the official prewar 1 to 1 exchange rate—this amounted to an unofficial 25 percent tax. The evidence suggests that there were ECOMOG peacekeepers who were also willing to turn a blind eye to the government-imposed rubber sanctions for the right price.[49]

The role of ECOMOG is important here because it illustrates how a criminalized war economy briefly became a criminalized peace economy during the lull in fighting between 1997 and 1999. Arguably, these same dynamics contributed to Liberia's return to war in 1999.

When ECOMOG peacekeepers arrived in Liberia, they fought aggressively against Taylor's NPFL rebels in a bid to impose peace on the country. At the same time, their enthusiastic participation in the local war economy contributed to the buildup of conflict capital in the country. Indeed, some ECOMOG peacekeepers had clearly developed a stake in the local war economy; instead of helping to destroy the country's conflict capital, many were activating it instead. It was notable that Liberians openly mocked ECOMOG's intentions by referring to it as Every Car or Moving Object Gone. At the time, the ECOMOG peacekeepers were the only actors with the military capacity to dismantle Liberia's wartime networks. Yet not only did peacekeepers fail in their mission, but they also became enmeshed in the local war economy, profiting handsomely in the process.

As illegal rubber tapping expanded, it became clear that the transitional governments at the time were powerless to stop it, or deliberately chose not to. Industry knowledge and networks were being developed, showing how fighters could profitably (if illegally) tap rubber or profit from its taxation. The many modes of taxation laid out a financial model for survival, and knowing that even major companies like Firestone and LAC could be incentivized to cooperate with rebel factions and buy their rubber only enhanced the viability of creating a resource enclave. Importantly, ECOMOG and other rebel groups showed that the rubber industry had low barriers to entry. In this way, the economic potential of the rubber sector became apparent to all. This was a proof-of-concept test for future extralegal groups.

---

[47] Stephen Ellis (1999).   [48] Philippa Atkinson (1997), p. 10.
[49] Stephen Ellis (1999), p. 168.

Timber

While the rubber industry provided Charles Taylor and the NPFL with a comfortable stream of income, it was the logging industry that turned out to be the most profitable and the most integral to maintaining military control over the country. As a rebel leader, Taylor quickly learned to exploit the timber industry during the early years of the civil war.[50] Not only did revenues from logging concessions contribute to Taylor's war chest, but later on, he was able to use his connections to these same timber companies to provide employment for members of his militias.

The practices of the timber militias—especially with coercive labour, violent taxation, and controlling territory—created local conditions that were friendly to the emergence of extralegal groups. As with the rubber sector, the timber concessions that Taylor negotiated with foreign firms during the war would have proven to ex-combatants that logging was a viable business. Again, Taylor's control over vast swaths of Liberian forestland would also have demonstrated how easily a group of fighters might seize territorial control of a logging area. And just as it was true that rubber companies were willing to work with rebel groups, foreign firms were also willing to buy timber from Liberian timber companies, despite a history of abusive practices.

Timber Concessions

In the early days of the war, Taylor's plan was simple: sell concession rights to foreign logging firms in Greater Liberia and collect taxes on timber exports. As part of the concession package, Taylor provided military protection to his logging clients.[51] During this period from November 1990 to October 1992, logging companies operated in much the same way as they did before the war, paying a variety of taxes to Taylor's NPRAG government including land tax, volume tax, export tax, and port tax.[52] Timber exports had fallen substantially from the prewar days, but companies still managed to log up to 200,000 cubic meters of timber worth approximately $20 million in 1992 alone.[53] While Taylor's timber empire in the countryside was substantially weakened after ECOMOG's 1993 bombing of Greenville and Buchanan, about a dozen or so logging firms remained, relying on close relationships with local faction leaders to do business.[54]

---

[50] For more on Taylor's pre-1997 exploits in the timber industry, see pp. 95–7, Silas Siakor (2002).

[51] Peter Cooper (1992).   [52] Philippa Atkinson (1997), p. 11.

[53] William Reno (1998), p. 95.

[54] Liberian environmental NGO Green Advocates has referred to these companies as "The Dirty Dozen." See Alfred Brownell (2007a) and Philippa Atkinson (1997), p. 11.

After he assumed the presidency in 1997, Taylor formalized his control over the country's forests with the passing of the National Forestry Law in January 2000. With few exceptions, this law gave ownership of all of the country's forests to the government.[55] Executive Order No. 4 further consolidated Taylor's control over timber concessions. This decree put the Ministry of Finance in charge of collecting 50 percent of Land Rental fees and 98 percent of stumpage fees.[56] In theory, the remainder was supposed to be collected by the Forest Development Authority (FDA), but in practice, the Taylor government had issued all manner of exemptions, and allowed suspicious tax losses and side payments.[57] The result was that logging concession fees, timber taxes, and all manner of related revenues were siphoned away from official government channels.[58]

For example, in his examination of official FDA statistics, Silas Siakor found that revenues from the FDA's 5 percent Export Duty could not be accounted for (see Table 4.1). He estimated that if these revenues had been collected, the FDA would have received an additional $10 million.[59] Related data revealed other discrepancies: a substantial proportion of felled logs and sawn timber from 1997–2001 remained unaccounted for—these logs were felled, but were never declared for export. The estimated market value of these missing logs ranged from U.S. $62 million to $183 million (Table 4.2).[60]

Table 4.1. Official timber production and revenues, Liberia 1997–2001[61]

Year	Round Log Production Vol. (m³)	Freight on Board (FOB) Value of Exports (US$)	Reported Assessed Revenue (Government Taxes and Fees) (US$)	Unpaid 5% Export Duty (US$)
1997	74,976	7,525,594	1,032,481.50	376,280
1998	157,098	12,288,133	2,975,353.37	614,407
1999	353,543	23,418,567	5,677,572.94	1,170,928
2000	934,160	67,505,473	20,730,046.05	3,375,274
2001	982,292	79,883,927	19,036,132.99	3,994,196
	2,502,069	190,621,694	49,451,586.85	9,531,085

[55] UN Panel of Experts on Liberia (2001), para 329. Exceptions included community and private forests that had been replanted.

[56] Stumpage fees are paid to the land owner on a per-tree basis for the right to harvest timber.

[57] UN Panel of Experts on Liberia (2001), p. 72.   [58] Ibid., p. 71.

[59] Silas Siakor (2002), p. 11.

[60] Estimates varied depending on the species of wood. For detailed calculations and assumptions, see p. 12, ibid.

[61] Figures obtained from FDA as reported by p. 10 and p. 12, U.N. Panel of Experts on Liberia (2001). The Reported Assessed Revenue figure includes government fees and taxes charged for reforestation, conservation, forest research, severance, land rental, as well as the Industrialization Incentive Fee and the Forest Product. Figures supported by Silas Siakor (2002).

Table 4.2. Missing logs[62]

Year	Production Volume (m³)	Export Volume, Round logs & Sawn timber (m³)	Round Logs Unaccounted for by Volume (m³)	Estimated value of logs, for Ekki species, US $85/m³	Estimated value of logs, for Iroko species, US $250/m³
1997	74,976	49,463	25,513	2,168,600	6,378,300
1998	157,098	80,646	76,452	6,498,400	19,113,000
1999	353,543	207,472	145,771	12,390,500	36,442,800
2000	934,160	637,401	290,750	24,713,800	72,687,500
2001	982,292	773,613	194,107	16,499,100	48,526,800
Total	2,502,069	1,748,595	732,593	62,270,400	183,148,000

While logging played a role in financing the NPFL rebels during the first part of the civil war, it was really during the post-1999 period that the trade in timber became critical to Taylor's operations. During his presidential years, Charles Taylor's control of the country's forests was uncontested. Logging concessions were frequently negotiated by Taylor on a personal, quid pro quo basis. Many of the logging firms that Taylor had made arrangements with were later accused of committing human rights abuses. The most notorious among these was the Oriental Timber Company (OTC).

The Oriental Timber Company

OTC was the largest and most important of Liberia's timber companies. After setting up in 1999, the company provided financial, military, and logistical support for Taylor's activities, shoring up his domestic support base with cash payments and, when necessary, providing violent enforcement. The company also played a critical role in the arms-for-timber trade.

There were two official shareholders in OTC: Guus van Kouwenhoven and Global Star Trading. Van Kouwenhoven, a Dutch businessman, was the president of the company and its public face. He controlled 35 percent of OTC.[63] The other documented OTC shareholder was Global Star (Asia) Trading Limited, a company based in Hong Kong but with Indonesian roots through its parent company Djan Djajanti.[64] Djan Djajanti serviced the Asian market. Through the 1990s, Asia had developed an enormous appetite for all raw materials, including timber. China, in particular, was importing large

[62] Silas Siakor (2002). For estimates of missing revenue based on tree species, see p. 11, Silas Siakor (2002).
[63] Public Prosecutor (2006), 7(2).
[64] It is unclear whether Global Star existed as anything other than a shell company. The link to the Djan Djajanti Group in Indonesia was made through documents presented at the Ruprah trial. See pp. 25–7, Global Witness (2002).

quantities of timber indirectly through OTC.[65] In Liberia, Global Star was represented by Joseph Wong Kiia Tai, who was also the son of Djan Djajanti's chairman.

There was also an unofficial third shareholder: Charles Taylor. Here, the relationship between van Kouwenhoven and Taylor becomes important— their shared history stretched back to the early days of the civil war when van Kouwenhoven ran the TIMCO logging company behind the lines of Taylor's NPFL rebels. Theirs was a cooperative relationship, though it was clear that van Kouwenhoven deferred to Charles Taylor.

At his trial, van Kouwenhoven revealed that 50 percent of his own OTC royalties were paid to Taylor. According to "Mr. Gus," as he was known in Liberia:

> Taylor did not have a financial interest in OTC, but in myself... He called for me and told me that it was understood that the Liberian government and OTC had an official tax relationship. The regular government budget was not sufficient and they would ask business men for financial aid.[66]

Taylor confirmed his interest in OTC when he openly declared that "no one will be permitted to disturb its operations. This is my pepperbush."[67] He went on to warn "officials not to harass investors."[68] In declaring OTC his personal golden goose, he forbade local authorities and FDA staff from demanding bribes and other favors from OTC management, as was customary. A proverbial joke in Liberia was that OTC really stood for "Only Taylor Chops."

OTC's operations in Liberia were substantial.[69] Van Kouwenhoven's personal correspondence indicates that in August 2002, roughly $10 million had been invested into operations.[70] Taylor awarded OTC (through its subsidiary Liberian Forest Development Company) the largest timber concession in Liberian history. Initially, the company was granted a 1.24 million hectare concession in the southeast. A second concession was later granted, bringing the total concession area to 1.6 million hectares. The FDA reported that this constituted 42 percent of the country's productive forests.[71] Combined with his other timber concessions from the Royal Timber Company, van Kouwenhoven controlled a concession area of 3 million hectares. This constituted 79 percent of Liberia's productive forest areas. Further, OTC was given the right to manage the port of Buchanan, which effectively meant that the company also controlled the country's timber exports because round logs could only be exported via Buchanan. To obtain these concessions, van Kouwenhoven

---

[65] Ibid., p. 13.   [66] Public Prosecutor (2006), Section 7.2.
[67] Silas Siakor (2002), p. 16.   [68] Global Witness (2002), p. 25.
[69] See Amnesty International (2006), p. 23 and Public Prosecutor (2006), Section 7.2.
[70] The official investment was declared at $110 million.
[71] UN Panel of Experts on Liberia (2001), p. 72.

reportedly paid Taylor a commission of between U.S. $3 million and $5 million.[72] According to Sanjivan Ruprah, a West African diamond dealer and personal friend of Guus van Kouwenhoven's, export revenues exceeded the initial investment within fourteen months.[73]

Taylor's Timber Militias

After claiming the presidency, Taylor began restructuring the army in earnest. He forced 2500 soldiers into retirement and replaced them with NPFL fighters whose loyalty to him had already been battle-tested.[74] He stuffed the Liberia National Police (LNP) with his supporters. The idea of integrating fighters from rival armed factions into the new structure was out of the question.[75]

Taylor also established Anti-Terrorist Units (ATUs) that reported directly to him rather than through the official Armed Forces of Liberia (AFL) chain of command. These groups effectively served as private militias accountable only to Taylor. By maintaining these different blocs of fighters scattered throughout the country, under the command of different leaders, he was able to ensure that no individual commander would wield enough power to threaten his position. The role of the ATUs was unambiguous: they fought *for Taylor*, not necessarily for the government. When Taylor did not need these militias, they were employed as private security guards for concession holders such as the Oriental Timber Company (OTC) and other timber companies.[76]

Thus, the timber militias arrangement served three purposes: they fought on Taylor's behalf, they provided security for the timber companies, and they provided gainful employment for a core group of fighters who had loyally fought for Taylor for many years. These three functions were inseparably intertwined. By physically protecting the timber concessions of the favored few and suppressing any local dissent, the timber militias also protected the revenues that paid for the Taylor administration. Conversely, by continuing to fight for Taylor and defending his regime, the militias were also protecting the

---

[72] The exact arrangements for this payment are unclear. Global Witness reported that between August and October 1999, the Ministry of Finance was ordered by Taylor to provide a receipt for $3 million to OTC even though the Ministry itself did not receive any of this money, implying that at least $3 million was paid upfront. However, van Kouwenhoven also admitted that he was asked by Taylor to make an advance payment of $5 million toward "future taxes." Global Witness 2002. Thereafter, Taylor was paid royalties on a regular basis. Taylor made many requests: "He asked us to send a number of tractors to his farm, or he said that he wanted a road, that he needed electricity and he would ask me if I could advance the money. He also simply asked for payments." See p. 17, UN Panel of Experts on Liberia (2001); p. 72, Public Prosecutor (2006); and 7(2), Truth and Reconciliation Commission of Liberia (2008b).
[73] Amnesty International (2006), p. 25.
[74] John-Peter Pham (2004), p. 177.
[75] Festus Aboagye and Alhaji M.S. Bah (2005).
[76] Forest Concession Review Committee Phase III (2005).

timber companies' interests and their right to log. This kept the ex-NPFL fighters paid and busy, preventing them from plotting against Taylor.

It was a symbiotic relationship: Taylor found work for his unemployed fighters, and OTC could be confident of meeting its security needs in an otherwise insecure environment. Approximately 63 percent of the 2398 Liberians employed by OTC were ex-combatants.[77]

Most of the time, the militia members worked for the timber companies as part of the security personnel or as general duty staff, but at any given moment, Taylor could also call upon them to fight. Although each company had its own separate security force, the commanders of the militias were expected to coordinate their actions for cross-border operations and attacks against the Liberians United for Reconciliation and Democracy (LURD) and the Movement for Democracy in Liberia (MODEL) rebel groups.

Several companies employed the private militias including: Oriental Timber Company (OTC), Royal Timber Company (RTC), Maryland Wood Processing Industry (MWPI), United Logging Company (ULC), Bureaux Ivorian Ngorian (BIN), Mohammed Group of Companies (MGC), Salami Molawi Incorporated (SMI), and Jasus Liberia Logging. While the human rights abuses of the various militias were legion in the areas where they operated, the Oriental Timber Company and its militia, the Navy Division, were the most infamous among them.

The Navy Division

Of all the timber militias, the Navy Division was reputedly the most brutal and best organized. Officially, it operated as part of the Liberian military, but in practice, it was autonomous. With 1500 members, the militia was commonly known as the Navy Rangers. They were led by Lt. General Roland Duo. Duo, in turn, took his orders from Charles Taylor vis-à-vis military matters, while also managing the militia for van Kouwenhoven as OTC's Chief of Security.

Under Taylor, Duo was the Chief of Staff of the Navy Division, as well as Director of the NPA (National Port Authority) and the Liberian Seaport Police. In these official capacities, he was in charge of the country's ports, including Buchanan, which was where OTC shipped its logs overseas. The Navy Rangers also operated their own private prison known as "Break Water" where people were routinely tortured, killed, and raped.

When Guus van Kouwenhoven stood trial in Dutch courts for war crimes, he explained how OTC and the Navy Division came to operate together:

> At that time I asked my Indonesian business partners how we should set up the security of OTC in Liberia... I then discussed this matter with Charles Taylor. I told him that we had to arrange for a number of armed security men. Taylor

---

[77] Global Witness (2002).

indicated that he did not want OTC to employ its own security guards and he said that he himself would arrange for armed security officers for OTC. Subsequently [Roland Duo], being the former chief of staff of the army, of the Navy Division, came to OTC for security, because the war had ended.

...The agreement was that Charles Taylor would send people that would receive payment from OTC. So the intention was that former fighters would be deployed and paid by OTC, because the government did not have money for that. [Duo] also received payment from OTC. [Duo] was both chief of staff of the NPA and director of security of OTC.[78]

Joseph Kpagbor, a former commander of the Navy Division, provided a practical example of how the OTC–Navy Division link operated in practice: "OTC and the militias supplied us with arms and uniforms...we had a rule that if you went to be paid you have to go to the battle front and fight and when you come you will get $150.00 and two bags of rice."[79]

The Navy Rangers were legendary in their cruelty when serving as a government militia. Although they were more restrained while providing security for OTC, they still resorted to gunfights in disputes over concession area boundaries. The fighting was especially intense if the concession area was being seized from a company that was actively engaged in logging, or if the boundary in dispute was shared with one of Taylor's favored timber companies. In a January 2000 letter from a regional FDA worker to the Managing Director of the Forest Development Authority, it was noted that the Navy Rangers were taking over concessions by force, after which Taylor would then award OTC the concession rights to these areas.[80] Sometimes, this would require using force to displace villagers from their homes to make room for new logging operations.

Armed guards were posted at logging sites to prevent the FDA, government officials, and local residents from entering logging areas; checkpoints were set up to extort money from area residents. At the Buchanan port, armed OTC militia members patrolled the area. Their presence alone was often enough to suppress any local dissent or criticism of logging operations.

OTC also coerced local people into working for them: in areas under company control, citizens were not permitted to farm their own land unless they also worked for OTC. Milton Teahjay dared to challenge this policy and subsequently found his village burnt to the ground.[81] Further, the logging companies were known to assault those who protested, conducting public floggings as well as other forms of torture.[82] For example, Mike Massa was beaten to death at Break Water "for gathering unwanted log stumps at the port to make charcoal."[83]

---

[78] Public Prosecutor (2006), Section 7.1.
[80] Alfred Brownell (2007a).
[82] Folo-Glogba Korkollie (2002).

[79] Joseph Kpagbor (2008).
[81] Global Witness (2002), p. 12.
[83] Alfred Brownell (2007a).

When serving in its role as a militia force, the Navy Division was even more violent. The head of the Navy Division, Roland Duo, was accused of spearheading the 2002 Mahare Bridge Massacre in Bomi County. In this incident, 355 civilians were killed because they lived in the Bomi Hills, the home base for the LURD rebel group. After Duo's militia group captured the area in 2002 on behalf of Taylor, all local civilians were viewed as LURD supporters. First, the men were harshly beaten, and then anyone who was left—old men, women, and children—was rounded up and methodically killed.[84] Survivor James Kabah testified that they were lined up and shot, ten at a time.[85]

Arms for Timber

As the UN arms embargo against Liberia took effect, the timber industry took on new significance. Not only was it valued for the income that it generated for the Taylor regime, but it also provided a means of circumventing the arms embargo. OTC arranged for weapons, ammunition, and armaments to be delivered to Taylor's fighters.[86] In exchange, OTC was allocated lucrative timber concessions and military protection by Taylor's forces.[87]

For his business dealings with Taylor and his role in OTC, van Kouwenhoven was arrested by the Dutch authorities in March 2005 and charged with committing war crimes and importing arms into Liberia. On June 7, 2006, van Kouwenhoven was acquitted of the war crimes charges for lack of evidence, but was convicted and sentenced to eight years imprisonment for contravening the UN arms embargo on Liberia. On March 10, 2008, this judgment was overturned by the Dutch Court of Appeal, citing that the prosecution's witnesses were unreliable. In 2010, this judgment was subsequently overruled by the Supreme Court and the case was sent back to the Court of Appeal for a new trial.[88] Finally, on April 21, 2017, van Kouwenhoven was once again found guilty—and this time, he was also convicted as an accessory to war crimes. He was sentenced to nineteen years in prison.[89] Yet even while this verdict represents an international victory for prosecuting corporate complicity in international crimes, within Liberia, the question remains whether this decision will renew a call for further transitional justice measures to be taken.[90]

---

[84] See UN Panel of Experts on Liberia (2001), p. 75; Public Prosecutor (2006); Truth and Reconciliation Commission of Liberia (2008a).

[85] Truth and Reconciliation Commission of Liberia (2008a, 2008b).

[86] See July 28, 2006, Trial transcript: 7(28)–7(62), 8, 9.

[87] For his role in sanctions busting, van Kouwenhoven was listed as an arms dealer in violation of UNSC Resolution 1343. He was also put on the UN Travel Ban list and placed on the U.S. Denied Person List. See OCR Compliance (2004) and UN Security Council (2004).

[88] The Hague Justice Portal (2010).   [89] Fred P.M. van der Kraaij (2017).

[90] Ruben Carranza (2017).

Diamonds

The diamond sector also rose to prominence during the civil war with a thriving cross-border trade as well as local mining interests. Although Liberia itself was only a small producer of diamonds, it borders on Sierra Leone, a country known for its gem-quality diamonds. A combination of export taxes and sanctions on rough diamonds in Sierra Leone turned Monrovia into a major transit hub for trafficking diamonds out of Sierra Leone and into Belgium's international diamond markets.

Taylor and the NPFL played an especially important role in encouraging the cross-border diamond trade: Taylor was fully complicit in the RUF's violent exploitation of the Kono diamond mines in neighboring Sierra Leone. As documented by numerous human rights organizations, Taylor was closely allied with Foday Sankoh and the RUF. Taylor provided Sankoh with arms and a supply route from Liberia in exchange for Sierra Leone's prized diamonds.[91] After being mined in Sierra Leone and transported to Liberia, the rough diamonds were then sold (in mayonnaise jars) to dealers in Monrovia who imported them legally into Belgium. From there, they were cut and polished before entering the retail market.[92] Sanctions, in this case, did succeed in making it more difficult for the RUF to directly obtain weapons and ammunition, but they also meant that Sankoh now had to rely on Taylor for armaments.

Within Liberia, other factions such as the NPFL, ULIMO-J, and even the ECOMOG peacekeepers were highly involved in alluvial diamond mining. For example, in the mid-1990s, ULIMO-J controlled Bomi County and the diamond mines in the area. Reno notes:

> ...local commanders distributed opportunities to mine alluvial diamonds and gold to maintain control over fighters... ULIMO-J fighters and commanders also profited from a transit trade in diamonds from illicit operations in Sierra Leone... [Roosevelt] Johnson acted as a local purchasing agent, providing fighters with ammunition and immediate payment for stones. Ammunition and guns, which ULIMO-J sold to fighters, established the young fighters' right to engage in this commerce, set up roadblocks to collect tolls, or loot local farms... Both Johnson and ECOMOG's Nigerian commanders were in a position to offer protection to miners. Both vied for the opportunity to do so, in return for which they received a portion of mining profits.[93]

With or without a functioning state, it was clear that the diamond sector had become a thriving commercial success. The globalization of supply chains meant, in practice, that there were no serious impediments in getting "Liberian" diamonds to market.

[91] For details on Taylor's relationship with the RUF, see the judgment on the Charles Taylor case Special Court of Sierra Leone (2009).
[92] Ian Smilie, Lansana Gberie and Ralph Hazelton (2000).
[93] William Reno (1998), p. 104.

CONFLICT CAPITAL IN THE FIGHTING FACTIONS

As the fighting continued during the civil war, conflict capital accumulated. In the postwar period, ex-combatants continued to activate this capital as they formed extralegal groups. As the case study chapters will go on to show, Liberia's extralegal groups were rooted in the ex-combatant community. Leaders and core members were ex-combatants or were closely allied to ex-combatants. For this reason, it is important to understand who fought in the war and how the various factions related to one another.

Fighters

Liberia's armed factions largely consisted of part-time, ad hoc fighters rather than dedicated, full-time, professional fighters.[94] The irregular nature of warfare in Liberia has been underscored by the involvement of civilians, some of whom played a larger role in the conflict than their unarmed status might indicate. During the earliest stages of the war, civilians volunteered to shelter and feed fighters, and helped them navigate their way through the bush. Later on, civilians were forcibly recruited to fight,[95] other times serving as porters, "bush wives," or sex slaves.

In this war, there existed a spectrum of participation, sometimes coerced and sometimes not. A perpetrator in one instance might easily be a victim in another instance. Ellis notes: "many fighters were simply ordinary people... all factions retained close links with Liberian society and many people participated in an armed force at some stage of the war, acting out of fear or self-interest, without ever becoming hard-core fighters."[96]

While there were certainly full-time combatants fighting on all sides of the war, Taylor estimated that approximately 85,000 picked up arms under the banner of the NPFL at one point or another.[97] While Taylor may have been exaggerating, this figure is viable depending on how membership is defined. Taylor himself has highlighted the "drop-in" nature of his fighters:

> There are thousands of people that come fight and because we are not running a regular paid army...they may fight for a month or two and the guy is gone maybe back to his village to go and take care of his farm.... I'm saying there's just thousands of people that if we were to do an emergency call in because of a major problem and say all of those that fought before please come back, they will come

[94] In her influential book *New and Old Wars*, Mary Kaldor (1999) argued that conventional warfare with its clearly defined battlefields and trained fighters was on the wane. Importantly, she pointed to the increased use of irregular forces.

[95] Kristen Cibelli, Amelia Hoover and Jule Kruger (2009).

[96] Stephen Ellis (1999), p. 134.   [97] Charles Taylor (2009a), p. 24873.

back. But this is not any conventional army where you've got people ready and willing. It was always a situation where people could come and go[98]

One important consequence of having so many ad hoc fighters is that many people fought in the war at one point or another—even those who did not consider themselves to be fighters. Many who did not fight became victims of violence. And many others still, young and old, witnessed horrific acts. Through continuous exposure, entire communities became desensitized to the use of violence during the course of the war.[99] Participants, victims, witnesses—were incrementally building up their conflict capital as violence was socialized into their everyday activities. Acts of brutality that would have once been considered appalling became commonplace.

One image from my collection of Liberian civil war photographs embodies how attitudes toward violence changed as the war progressed. The photo features a long line of several dozen refugees, most of them carrying their possessions on their heads. Toward the bottom right corner of the photo is a man's body lying by the side of the road, legs splayed out and head bloodied. His shirt is open, his chest is bare, and his shoes are immaculately white. Of the two dozen or so refugees who are standing in line, there are only two children staring at the body. Everyone else is staring straight ahead, seemingly indifferent. The violence that was wrought upon this man was scarcely worth a second glance.

This indifference toward violence did not manifest itself overnight, but through repeated episodes. Even when war ends, these attitudes do not simply revert back to their prewar state. Instead, the buildup of conflict capital through the course of civil war perpetuates what Christina Steenkamp terms a "culture of violence."[100] The longer the war, the more socially ingrained the norms of violence become, and thus, the slower the rate of decline for the stock of conflict capital.

Core Alliances

Liberia's extralegal groups were created from the remnants of the fighting factions. Membership has largely derived from the core alliances in Liberia's civil war. These are illustrated in Figure 4.1. The flow chart shows how the core constituent groups formed the same alliances over the course of the war. For example, the Krahn-Mandingo alliance was maintained throughout the war in several guises. The Krahns dominated the AFL and then went on to form the LUDF, which then joined with an armed group of Mandingos to become

---

[98] Ibid., p. 24874.
[99] There is a growing literature on atrocities in civil war that integrates a psychological and neurological understanding of how humans respond to violence. See Kieran Mitton (2012, 2015).
[100] Chrissie Steenkamp (2005).

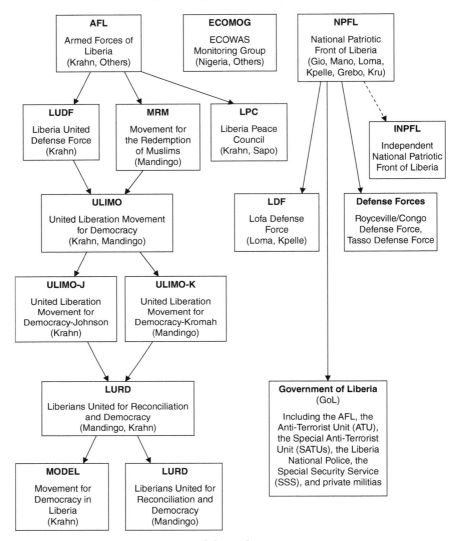

Fig. 4.1. Major fighting factions, 1989–2003

ULIMO, and then splintered off to form ULIMO-J, the remains of which reunited with its Mandingo counterparts to form LURD, with the Krahn faction splitting off yet again to form MODEL.

While these alliances sometimes broke down, Figure 4.1 sketches out their rough trajectories.[101] Factions that fought one another on one occasion would

---

[101] N.H. Lidow (2016) offers a deep and detailed history of Liberia's seventy-three rebel movements and militias (1980–2003).

later band together to defeat a common enemy on another occasion. Ethnicity also played an important, but not always definitive, role in the formation of some groups and alliances. Ellis notes that:

> in most circumstances this mobilisation of ethnic identity was more rhetoric than reality, as every faction included substantial numbers of fighters of diverse ethnic origin and ethnic allegiance became really important only when a local grievance, rooted in local history and land disputes, became caught up with national factional activity.[102]

At times, there was as much fighting within factions as between them. Consequently, cohesion within each of the groups varied across space and time. Even at the faction level, trust was not guaranteed. Desperation, camaraderie, loyalty, and coercion each played an important role in maintaining group cohesion. Even after the war ended in 2003, levels of conflict capital remained high and the threat of violence lingered. Peace was not assured and there was a general sense that the country could tip over into war again, at a moment's notice. The local balance of power still favored the fighters. But commerce required stability. The irony was that only those with coercive power would be able to provide that stability.

Fighting Factions and Ethnicity in Extralegal Groups

In this study, civil war allegiances formed the basis for the extralegal groups that followed. Although the structures of the fighting factions do not map directly, some commanders did form extralegal groups as the country transitioned out of conflict. As with any new enterprise, commanders recruited loyal and capable colleagues to join them. It was not uncommon for extralegal groups to include ex-combatants from outside of the dominant faction. This echoed the fluidity of the alliances that formed and dissolved during the civil war. For example, in the Guthrie Group, most of the ex-combatants had fought for LURD, but some had fought for MODEL and others for the Taylor government. In this case, what mattered most was a shared background as an ex-combatant. Civilians who were not associated with wartime factions would have found the environment particularly difficult because these groups had a reputation for casual violence.[103]

Membership in an extralegal group was not defined strictly by ethnicity either. In some cases, such as the Sinoe Group, core members were mostly from the local area and thus the composition of the core group was predominantly Wedjah.[104] However, very close by, the neighboring BOPC Group had

---

[102] Stephen Ellis (1999), p. 105.   [103] Alfred Brownell (2007b).
[104] UNMIL Civil Affairs Officer for Sinoe County (2005); UNMIL Security Officer for Sinoe County (2005).

a diverse ethnic mix. The leadership was Tassu, but ex-combatants and miners came from all over Liberia and other parts of West Africa. Local interviews revealed that some miners had traveled from as far away as Guinea, Mali and Sierra Leone.

THE END OF WAR

In between the firefights, the quest for peace in Liberia continued, usually in fits and starts. Successive peace agreements were negotiated, signed, and then ripped up. All in all, sixteen ceasefire and peace agreements[105] were signed and broken between 1990 and 2003 before the Comprehensive Peace Agreement (CPA) was eventually agreed upon in Accra on August 18, 2003. The nation wearily celebrated but remained skeptical that the peace would hold.[106] Taylor's Vice President, Moses Blah, temporarily took over as head of state, until businessman Gyude Bryant was officially installed as Chairman of the National Transitional Government of Liberia (NTGL) on October 14, 2003.[107] Taylor himself left for exile in Nigeria, then plotted his escape when his arrest looked imminent. He was eventually apprehended and turned over to the Special Court for Sierra Leone and charged with war crimes. The judges subsequently found him guilty of aiding and abetting war crimes and he was sentenced to fifty years in jail. In 2013, he appealed his case and lost. The British government agreed to take him and he is currently serving out his sentence in Frankland prison, in the English city of Durham.

The 2003 peace agreement mandated that political power was to be shared between four groups: the three fighting factions (LURD, MODEL, GoL) and civil society representatives. Cabinet positions in the NTGL and seats in the National Transitional Legislative Assembly (NTLA) were divvied up accordingly, as were management positions for the Public Corporations and the Autonomous Agencies and Commissions.[108] While the CPA brought peace,

[105] For a detailed list of peace agreements, see Footnotes 70 and 71 in the Introduction.

[106] This skepticism was well grounded: Former UNMIL Special Representative of the Secretary General, Jacques Paul Klein reported that MODEL and LURD were disappointed with the accord because they felt that the UN had "stolen their victory." See Jacques Paul Klein (2006).

[107] Klein also indicated that Ellen Johnson Sirleaf had the votes needed to lead Liberia during the transitional period, but the factions were afraid of her because they believed she would prosecute them. Consequently, they settled on Gyude Bryant as a compromise candidate. See ibid; also see Morten Bøås (2005).

[108] Each of the three fighting factions was allocated five ministries while civil society was allocated six ministries (arguably less important ones). For the allocation of cabinet posts, see p. 40 of National Elections Commission (2005). For the allocation of seats in the National Transitional Legislative Assembly, see p. 20 of the CPA. Government of Liberia, Liberians United for Reconciliation and Democracy, and Movement for Democracy in Liberia (2003).

Table 4.3. UNMIL annual budget 2003–11[109]

	UNMIL Budget (USD)
August 2003–June 2004	$564,614,300
July 2004–June 2005	$822,106,000
July 2005–June 2006	$722,542,100
July 2006–June 2007	$704,321,400
July 2007–June 2008	$688,383,400
July 2008–June 2009	$603,760,800
July 2009–June 2010	$561,031,500
July 2010–June 2011	$524,052,800
July 2011–Jun 2012	$525,612,730
July 2012–Jun 2013	$496,457,800
July 2013–Jun 2014	$476,329,800
July 2014–Jun 2015	$427,319,800
July 2015–Jun 2016	$344,712,200
July 2016–Jun 2017	$187,192,400

the transitional government itself had a legitimacy problem. In the words of Jacques Paul Klein, the former head of UNMIL: "The main problem with Accra was that it turned over the government to three sets of thugs."[110]

As the country moved tentatively from a peace agreement in 2003 to democratic elections in 2005, the international community spent billions of dollars in humanitarian aid and invested billions more in reconstruction assistance. A conservative estimate of donor spending would average at least U.S. $1 billion annually in the decade (2003–13) after the war ended.[111] The cost of Liberia's UN peacekeeping mission alone amounted to well over half a billion dollars annually for the first nine years of the mission (Table 4.3). This figure does not include spending from other important UN agencies such as UNDP, the World Food Programme, or UNHCR; nor does it include aid from bilateral donor agencies, international financial institutions, international nongovernmental organizations (NGOs), Economic Community of West African States (ECOWAS) operations, or the many millions generated by the Consolidated Appeals Process (CAP). Many more billions in debt forgiveness was also granted by the World Bank and the IMF.

In 2014 and 2015, humanitarian assistance surged again as the Ebola virus struck Liberia, Sierra Leone, and Guinea. Governments, international health

---

[109] These figures were obtained through the UN's peacekeeping operations budgets for the United Nations Mission in Liberia (UNMIL). See A/C.5/58/35 (2003–04), A/C.5/59/18/REV.1 (2004–05), A/C.5/60/27, (2005–06), A/C.5/61/22 (2006–07), A/C.5/62/23 (2007–08), A/C.5/63/23 (2008–09), A/C.5/64/15 (2009–10), A/C.5/65/15 (2010–11), A/C.5/65/19 (2011–12), A/C.5/66/18 (2012–13), A/C.5/66/18 (2013–14), A/C.5/68/26 (2014–15), A/C.5/69/24 (2015–16), A/C.5/70/24 (2016–17) in UN Dag Hammarskjöld Library (2017).

[110] Jacques Paul Klein (2006).

[111] This estimate does not imply that this money was spent in the host country.

officials, aid agencies, and NGOs all responded slowly to the emergency, and the virus wreaked havoc through the Mano River region killing 4809 people in Liberia, 3956 in Sierra Leone, 2543 in Guinea, and infecting another 28,646 people in the region.[112] Donors provided humanitarian aid and crisis health-care, but funds were not always effectively targeted.[113]

Democracy at Last

When the war ended, an uneasy calm settled over the country as daily life regained a semblance of normality. In the first few years, the goal was to re-establish basic security and political stability in order to hold elections by October 2005, as dictated by the 2003 peace agreement. But in the months and weeks leading up to the election, there was an unmistakable tension in the air. After fourteen years of civil war, no one could be sure that the fragile peace that had settled over Liberia would prevail.

At the time, I was in the country doing fieldwork and I distinctly remember feeling optimistic but still very worried. In the weeks leading up to the election, both the optimism and the worry intensified each time I traveled back to Monrovia from other parts the country. By day, the city gave off a comforting sense of normality: a bustling street life, lively markets, and even occasional traffic jams. By night, the main streets resembled a ghost town. There were no people and no cars on the roads. The downtown area was blanketed in darkness save for the headlights of an occasional UN vehicle. It felt like a city under lockdown. Daytime Monrovia gave me hope, but nighttime Monrovia suggested that the city still lived in fear, even two years after the war had officially ended.

On Saturday, October 8, a few days before the 2005 election, the leading presidential candidates held marches. The largest of these was for George Weah, the former footballer. From the roof of my guesthouse, I was able to watch hundreds of thousands of people marching in support of his candidacy. Tubman Boulevard overflowed with marchers from 7 a.m. through to mid-afternoon. Although the atmosphere was festive, there was an edge to the crowd. By this point, I had been in the country long enough to sense that emotions were running high and that the mood could turn ugly in a matter of seconds. This moment and others like it served as a reminder that elections, no matter how free or fair, could not guarantee peace.

---

[112] World Health Organization (2016).

[113] For example, the U.S. government spent $1.4 billion on Ebola treatment units, mostly in Liberia. However, the clinics were barely used because the number of infected patients dropped dramatically before construction could be completed. See Norimitsu Onishi (2015).

The country's big test came on October 11, 2005. Election day had arrived. Monrovia was on edge and Liberians and foreigners alike were skittish. The possibility of violence erupting was on everyone's mind. Some international organizations had even taken the precaution of sending expatriate staff to neighboring Freetown or Accra in case violence erupted. There was an implicit understanding that the fighting factions were still active and that faction leaders might be asked to remobilize on election day.

Fortunately, the voting itself was quiet, orderly, and uneventful. Liberians voted with joy. Election day was declared an official holiday and the streets outside polling stations were lined with people waiting to cast a ballot. Some queued up at dawn; others walked for five or six hours in the scorching sun to vote.

The ballots were tallied and former football star George Weah won the first round, with 28 percent of the vote. World Bank bureaucrat Ellen Johnson Sirleaf came in second with 20 percent of the vote. None of the candidates won an outright majority in the first round so a presidential runoff election had to be held.

In spite of Weah's lead during the first round of voting, it was Ellen Johnson Sirleaf who ultimately won the November 8 presidential runoff.[114] It was a clear victory for Sirleaf with 59 percent of the votes vs. Weah's 41 percent. In response to his defeat at the polls, Weah lodged formal complaints of electoral fraud and led a series of demonstrations and protests in the capital for two months.[115] Some of these protests turned violent, though they faded in intensity as time wore on.[116]

During these periods of anger and unrest, the country seemed particularly vulnerable. George Weah had a core of support in the country's youth and ex-combatant community. His glamour as a former football star made him a favorite of the former fighters. With the contested electoral results came fears that a new cycle of violence might begin. Yet in the end, after intense international pressure was brought to bear on Weah, he finally withdrew his charge of electoral fraud. This paved the way for Ellen (as she is popularly known in Liberia) to assume office on January 26, 2006.

Ellen's election to the Liberian presidency was notable on many fronts: she was the first female elected head of state in Africa; she was a highly educated technocrat; and she was the favored candidate of the international community. Initially, her prominence on the world stage heightened the expectations of Liberians, some of whom hoped that the election of the U.S.' favored candidate would lead to the immediate transformation of the country. As is common in electoral settings, both the president's promises and her voters' expectations

---

[114] Results from the second round of voting on November 8, 2005: Ellen Johnson Sirleaf: 59 percent; George Weah: 41 percent. Although Weah lost the 2005 election, he ran (unsuccessfully) for Vice President in 2011, before finally winning the election for President in 2017, against Joseph Bokai.

[115] Lane Hartill (2005).   [116] Josephus Moses Gray (2005).

were unrealistic. Reconciling voters' hopes with reality has underscored the two-steps-forward-one-step-back nature of rebuilding a war-torn state. Despite the many problems of the Sirleaf administration, Ellen has been successful in consolidating the country's hard-earned peace.

Indeed, one of her highest priorities when she took office was to disband the Guthrie Group and to reclaim the plantation. Without her early direct intervention and politically skilled handling of this matter, it is not clear that this region would have been pacified. Not only would the Guthrie Group still exist, but it is likely that even more extralegal groups would have developed on still more rubber plantations and in other sectors of the economy.

CONCLUSION

This brief history of Liberia's civil war puts the country's extralegal groups into context. It has highlighted the various ways in which civil war taught ex-combatants lessons of coercion, governance, commerce, negotiation, and violence. In summary, this chapter identified five ways in which the civil war and the war economy created conditions and practices that were conducive to extralegal groups.

First, the exploitation of natural resources created local markets and trading networks specific to these commodities, making it easy for extralegal groups to revive these networks rather than having to construct them from scratch. Second, the commercial adventures of Taylor's NPFL and other fighting factions undermined the perceived invincibility of the state. Third, the illegal exploitation of natural resources became so widespread during the war that it became acceptable and even commonplace to participate in their extraction. Fourth, wartime taxation practices reduced resistance to illegal taxation and created a norm of "taxation": extralegal groups expected individuals to pay the taxes they imposed—however arbitrary—and individuals themselves expected to pay them. Finally, the workings of the war economy revealed that it was possible to circumvent the state altogether and that there were plenty of foreign companies who were willing to work directly with nonstate actors.

Chapters 5–7 will focus on extralegal groups in the rubber, diamond, and timber industries, and the ways in which the political economy of war interacts with post-conflict dynamics.

Part III

Economic Sectors

5

Rubber

"We know they have power and control over their people, including influence on the county superintendent."

UNMIL Civil Affairs Officer, referring to the Guthrie Group on the Guthrie Plantation[1]

"The guys have actually launched a rubber war. They are prepared to fight to the end to take over these farms as their own."

Firestone plant protection agent[2]

Since Liberia's first plantation was established in 1906, rubber has been one of the most important sectors of the economy, but also one of its most controversial. With the signing of the Firestone concession agreements in 1926, the rubber industry and the country's political development became intimately intertwined. From Firestone's takeover of the country to the use of forced labor to the long-standing turmoil over labor conditions,[3] Liberia's rubber industry encapsulates many of the tensions that have existed in the government's historic relationship with the United States, with multinational companies, and with its own citizens. Many of these tensions laid the foundation for extralegal groups.

Even after Charles Taylor was forced into exile in Nigeria and the Comprehensive Peace Agreement brought an official end to the civil war in August 2003, the political atmosphere in Liberia remained thick with tension. As UN peacekeepers took control of security and fanned out across the country, the political situation gradually stabilized. However, there were important exceptions to the general improvement in the security climate. One of the most notable exceptions was the rubber sector—some of the country's major rubber plantations remained unstable for years after the war ended. Even as the UN was disarming and demobilizing the fighting factions, two of the country's major rubber plantations were controlled by ex-combatant groups. These

---

[1] Ministry Liaison UNMIL Civil Affairs Officer (2005).   [2] *The Analyst* (2006a).
[3] International Labor Rights Fund (2005).

areas operated beyond the control of the National Transitional Government of Liberia (NTGL) and UNMIL peacekeepers.

Given that Liberia's natural resources had been used to finance the civil war, the UN Security Council was specifically concerned that resource revenues might be used to reignite the conflict. To address this potential problem, the Security Council decided that part of UNMIL's mandate would be "to assist the transitional government in restoring proper administration of natural resources."[4] Originally, the primary targets of this particular directive were Liberia's timber- and diamond-producing areas, but during the post-conflict period, it was the rubber plantations that posed the most significant challenge to the government's authority. It did not seem to matter what incentives were offered or what threats were made, ex-combatants and their associates refused to give up their control over the Guthrie and Sinoe rubber plantations. The Firestone security guard quoted at the start of this chapter was not the only person who felt that a rubber war was imminent. It was a worry shared by many. Four of Liberia's seven major rubber plantations were illegally occupied at some point in the aftermath of the civil war. Even in 2009, six years after the civil war had officially ended, the government still had not managed to regain control over the Sinoe Rubber Plantation (SRP).

Among the four illegally occupied plantations, the most significant threat to peace was posed by the situation on the Guthrie Rubber Plantation. This plantation was taken over by ex-combatants from March 2003 to September 2006. After the war ended, former fighters from LURD, as well as MODEL and the Government of Liberia (GoL) jointly controlled rubber tapping as well as the sale of rubber on the plantation for a period of three and a half years. During this time, ex-combatant leaders fought UNMIL peacekeepers when they attempted to reclaim control of the area, and they regularly threatened the government and the peacekeepers with violence. When the government finally regained control of the area in September 2006, a report by Landmine Action UK indicated that the situation on the ground remained unstable:

> [the] potential threat of hostilities with the Plantation...were paramount if the Joint Securities [UNMIL and the Liberia National Police] were not very careful. Former Generals Prince B. Seo, Joseph Nyumah along with other lined commanders and loyalists made frightening and threatening remarks which talked about disarming the Namibian UNMIL Soldiers that fired at them...But, if all other intervention fails, they will have no alternative, but to disarm the UNMIL and cause serious havoc in this part of the country, thus making it ungovernable [*sic*].[5]

Out in the southeast of the country, the situation on the SRP also proved to be an enormous challenge for both the Bryant transitional government and the Sirleaf administration. Six years after the signing of the Comprehensive Peace

---

[4] UN Security Council (2003a).   [5] Landmine Action UK (2006).

Agreement, the Liberian government was still unable to assert its authority over this area. Instead, a group of ex-combatants, with the cooperation of key community leaders, continued to control the plantation's rubber production, as well as the surrounding area. The leader of this ex-combatant group, Paulson Garteh, aggressively asserted his right to rule over the Sinoe plantation.[6] He claimed to be both judge and police on the plantation, and he declared himself to be "God" during a radio interview in June 2005.[7]

Both the Guthrie and Sinoe situations serve as vivid examples of how extralegal groups emerge, develop, and become entrenched. In this chapter, the theoretical framework will guide the analysis of the Guthrie and Sinoe groups, as well as the failure of two other nascent extralegal groups in the rubber sector. At the sector level, the framework predicts that extralegal groups are most likely to develop in the rubber sector because of the relatively low barriers to entry requiring little capital and minimal skills. At the level of the individual extralegal groups, the framework predicts that they will emerge in locations where there is both a demand for contract enforcement and a supply of ex-combatants available to meet this demand. The framework also predicts that the tax collection process will strengthen them organizationally and that these groups will develop their own local power bases, facilitated by bribing and coercing local authorities. This chapter will compare the predictions of the framework with how these groups actually evolved.

This chapter has five sections. The first section briefly describes Liberia's rubber industry, providing context for how the various groups operate. The second and third sections will discuss the Guthrie and Sinoe Rubber Plantations respectively. The fourth section will examine the Cavalla and Cocopa plantations where attempts at establishing extralegal groups were less successful. Finally, this chapter will conclude with a brief comparison of the challenges faced by each of the plantations.

LIBERIA'S RUBBER INDUSTRY

Rubber is a critical commodity for the Liberian economy. In addition to Firestone, there are other large industrial rubber plantations, along with a number of smaller, private rubber farms. Yet even as other sectors of the economy developed, rubber remained a very important cash crop. Liberia only has a tiny share of the global rubber market, but this still amounted to approximately U.S. $70 million in 2005 or 13 percent of the country's official GDP of $550 million.[8] Rubber became particularly important after timber

---

[6] UNMIL Human Rights (2006).   [7] Ibid., p. 28.
[8] U.S. Department of State (2006).

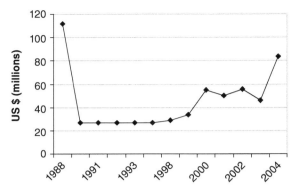

Fig. 5.1. Liberia rubber exports during the war (1988–2004)

sanctions went into effect in July 2003. By the time the war ended in August 2003, rubber had become Liberia's most important legal export (Figure 5.1).

The Rubber Tapping Process

In Liberia, rubber trees are grown in the millions in order to harvest the milky latex that seeps out of after it has been cut. To access the latex, all that is required is a knife, some plastic cups for collection, and acid. Tappers either purchase these supplies on credit or they are provided as part of a sharecropping arrangement.

Tappers are typically assigned to tap a set number of trees each day. To do this properly, they need to place a thin spiral cut of just the right thickness and depth in order to achieve optimal latex flow without wounding the tree. Over the next few hours, liquid latex seeps out of the cut and is collected in a plastic cup. Although it can take months or even years to master the technique, it is certainly possible to tap rubber with very little experience—the trade-off is that the tapper will need to proceed carefully or risk damaging the tree. It is also possible to make multiple cuts to a tree in a practice that is commonly known as "slaughter tapping"—this leads to greater yields in the short run but leads to the early death of the tree in three to five years. (Rubber trees typically survive for thirty years.)

Slaughter tapping is important to this discussion of extralegal groups because those that are insecure about their ability to maintain control over an area will have greater incentive to slaughter tap. Consequently, the prevalence of slaughter tapping provides a good indication of how confident an extralegal group is that it will continue to retain control over an area. For example, if an extralegal group feels certain that it will retain long-term control of a plantation, then it is more likely to encourage careful tapping practices. However, if it is unsure about future tenure, then more slaughter tapping is expected; without an assurance of lasting control over the area, the incentive is to "loot" the trees by extracting as much as possible as quickly as possible.

After tapping, the latex is collected. It is strained and concentrated by adding acid, and then put through a centrifuge which removes water and increases the rubber concentration. Most of this liquid latex eventually makes its way to the Firestone plant for processing and the concentrated latex is then shipped to the US.[9] While the tappers wait for the liquid latex to accumulate, they return to the trees that were tapped the day before to collect the solid latex that has coagulated at the bottom of the cup—these are "cup lumps." The cup lumps are collected and granulated into little crumbs and later processed into different grades of solid rubber.

A typical tapper, often working with the help of children and other family members, will usually tap and collect latex from 1100 or more trees each day, earning an average daily wage of U.S. $3.19.[10] The work is grueling and best-suited to those in good physical condition. Nonetheless, the rubber industry is one of the few industries that has been able to provide steady formal employment. Approximately 7.5 percent of the population relied on the rubber sector for their livelihood.[11]

International Prices

Another critical factor that impacted the Liberian rubber industry was the rise of global commodity prices. From 2001, many commodities, including rubber, experienced dramatic increases. To illustrate, prices from Figure 5.2 show that when the war ended in the fall of 2003, the futures price for one kilogram of TSR20 (Technically Specified Rubber, a standard rubber product) was roughly U.S. $1. As the country emerged out of civil war, the rubber market began to boom. Three years later in 2006, the price of rubber had almost doubled to $1.95. We saw another peak in 2008, as global rubber prices hit $2.53. The following year, prices dropped back to $1.80. But shortly thereafter, prices surged again to new highs, topping out at $4.52 in 2011 before gradually declining to $1.38 in 2016.

---

[9] There are also two other companies with latex processing plants—the Liberian Agricultural Company (LAC) and Weala Rubber Company—but Firestone's is the largest.

[10] Using the Alien Tort Claims Act, a lawsuit was filed by the International Labor Rights Fund in the U.S. against Bridgestone-Firestone for their operations on the Firestone plantation in Liberia. The company was accused of "forced labor, the modern equivalent of slavery." Although the case was not permitted to proceed as a class action lawsuit, it did set a precedent in allowing a child labor claim to be brought forward under the Act. For further details on the case, see Chapter 5 in Daniel E. Lee and Elizabeth J. Lee (2010).

[11] In 2000, approximately 25,000 people were employed in the rubber industry. Each of these workers was estimated to support nine dependents, for a total of 225,000 reliant on the rubber industry (out of a population of 3 million). See UN Security Council (2001a), para 42.

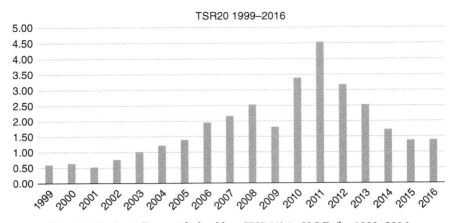

Fig. 5.2. Technically specified rubber (TSR20) in U.S.D./kg 1999–2016

However, for salaried rubber tappers in Liberia, these price increases did not improve their daily wages—salaries were not impacted by the ups and downs in the international price of rubber. On the plantations controlled by extralegal groups, the situation was different because there was greater wage flexibility. It is likely that the increase in the price of rubber on international markets contributed to the influx of ex-combatants and others onto the rubber plantations.[12] Notably, it was the leaders of the extralegal groups, rather than the tappers, that stood to gain the most from these price increases. They assumed the risks but also benefited from the rewards which came with global price fluctuations. As prices increased, extralegal groups found that they had an even greater incentive to maintain control over their territory for as long as possible. Figure 5.2 is a graph of historical prices for Technically Specified Rubber (TSR20). It serves as a rough guide to global price fluctuations during the post-conflict period.

THE GUTHRIE GROUP

Taking Over the Plantation

In March 2003, near the end of the civil war, LURD Generals Joseph Nyumah and Mohammed Tarrawally and those under their command took over the

---

[12] An alternative explanation for the presence of extralegal groups in the rubber sector can be attributed to the dramatic rise in international rubber prices. However, this explanation does not account for the presence of these groups in other sectors of the economy where international prices did not experience such increases.

territory in and around the Guthrie Rubber Plantation. According to Fayiah Williams, the Camp Master of Kissi Camp, Nyumah and Tarrawally originally asked to buy the cup lumps from their camp. At that point in early 2003, the official concession holders had abandoned the Guthrie plantation because of the war and residents were tapping profitably for themselves.

Soon after, Nyumah realized that the trade in rubber was lucrative and convinced a group of LURD fighters to help him take over the plantation. He sent Sumo Dennis, a LURD major at the time, to look after his business interests at Guthrie. Dennis assumed full territorial control over the plantation. At roughly the same time as the factions were negotiating the peace agreement, he began to integrate thousands of ex-combatants from different fighting factions as well as key political supporters of LURD and MODEL into the Guthrie network. Estimates of ex-combatants on the plantation varied. Some estimated that there were 15,000 on the plantation while UN officials suggested that the figure was lower than 5000.[13] These numbers peaked between the war's end in August 2003 and June 2005.

This large group of ex-combatants was led by the Central Committee of the Ex-Combatant Welfare Committee. The ECWC later became known as the Top Brass Ruling Council before changing name again to the High Power Ruling Council (HPRC). The HPRC was led by Sumo Dennis and included the most senior commanders on the Guthrie plantation, almost all of whom were former LURD commanders. Later, the HPRC tried to formalize its role on the plantation by forming the National Veteran Rehabilitation Project (NVRP), with the goal of claiming NGO status. There was substantial overlap in membership between the ECWC, HPRC, and NVRP. Given this overlap, I refer to this group collectively as the Guthrie Group. However, extralegal group membership also extended broadly and loosely, to include, for example, those who demonstrated public support by participating in one of the group's protests or riots.

On the plantation, the population had swollen to 32,000–38,000 inhabitants by 2005 in the years after the war.[14] Many of these were local residents who gradually returned after the war ended. Many of these local residents were seasoned rubber tappers. Some of them tapped side-by-side with the ex-combatants— but not without fear. When Sumo Dennis took over the Guthrie plantation, he used his group of ex-combatants to extend his reach throughout the plantation, and eventually persuaded and coerced all the local tappers to submit to his authority.

As time passed, Sumo Dennis grew increasingly confident of his abilities to take on UNMIL. Eventually, he demanded control of Guthrie for three years as

[13] For example, an estimate of 3700 was drawn from a June 2005 UN report on the Guthrie plantation. See UNMIL (2005a).
[14] Ibid.

a precondition to giving up the plantation to the government without a fight. Dennis was confident of his authority over the area, "forcing observers to believe that the demand may have grown out of the conviction that they have a fighting edge over the government or UNMIL or both."[15] One ex-combatant on the plantation issued a foreboding warning: "The big people just causing noise for nothing. Some of them know what they can get from us there. If they not be careful, we will fight them. Some of us will die before we leave from here."[16] This resistance to leaving the Guthrie plantation was also echoed by other influential ex-combatants.[17]

For the first time in fifteen years, political stability was in sight. The Liberian government and the international community had much to lose if Dennis and the Guthrie Group followed through on its threat. So much had already been invested in the country's stability that the threat to reignite local violence was taken very seriously. But the Guthrie Group did not need to take the country back to war; its members simply needed to stir up enough violence to make the country look unstable and ungovernable. This would give them the leverage that they needed over the transitional government.

Ultimately, the Guthrie Group succeeded in retaining control of the plantation for three and a half years—from the period preceding the signing of the CPA in August 2003 through the entire tenure of the transitional government, and right into the first year of Ellen Johnson Sirleaf's administration.[18] Only in September 2006 did the government finally reclaim physical control over the Guthrie plantation.

Emergence

When General Nyumah and LURD first took over Guthrie in spring 2003, LURD and MODEL were marching toward the capital from the northwest and southeast respectively. The fighting was intensifying and Taylor's forces had lost a lot of ground. There was little government authority outside of Monrovia and the country was in the middle of a civil war. A victory by LURD and MODEL looked likely and imminent. Based on this assessment, Nyumah, Dennis, and the rest of their fighters gambled that taking over the Guthrie plantation early on would give them a good chance of keeping control of it after the war ended.

Given these conditions, the emergence of the Guthrie Group can be explained as a deliberate strategy of stationary banditry, facilitated by a buildup of conflict capital. This supports a supply-led emergence explanation: a small group of soon-to-be-unemployed fighters went searching for an economic

---

[15] *The Analyst* (2006b).   [16] Gibson W. Jerue (2006).
[17] *The Analyst* (2006c).   [18] UNMIL (2005a).

opportunity and took advantage of one in the rubber sector. If these were civilians (rather than ex-combatants) in peacetime rather than wartime, we would recognize them as entrepreneurs of sorts. The key difference, of course, is that the members of the extralegal group had recourse to violence.

Let us consider a counterfactual: Would the Guthrie Group have been established if the war had continued to rage on, beyond the spring of 2003? Perhaps, but the size of the group would certainly have been considerably smaller. Without the influx of unemployed fighters that followed when the war ended, the demand for extralegal governance in this area would not have been as strong. Consequently, alternative governance structures (chiefs, local administration, police, elders, politicians) could have been more viable. For this reason, it is unlikely that this extralegal group would have developed to the extent that it did.

In taking over the Guthrie Rubber Plantation, Nyumah made a rational calculation. With the end of the war in sight, taking control of one of Liberia's largest rubber plantations would be more profitable than continuing to loot his way into Monrovia.[19] While UN sanctions on diamonds and timber had been in place since 2001, there were no sanctions on rubber, making the plantation an even more attractive target. It helped that the international price of rubber rose substantially in 2003 and that the major rubber companies (Firestone, Weala, and Salala) were not scrutinizing the ways in which their rubber was being sourced.

Second, the emergence of the group was helped by an existing LURD command structure and the social bonds that had already been established between former fighters. The operations of the Guthrie plantation were initially structured according to that hierarchy. This buildup of conflict capital is important because it shaped the interactions among group members, and also between the group and the local community. Conflict capital helps explain why the Guthrie Group became an extralegal group (with violent capabilities) instead of an informal business enterprise (without violent capabilities).

As the operations on the plantation grew, so did the need for credible, third-party regulation. Up to 38,000 people flooded Guthrie as it became one of the few places in Liberia where it was possible to earn a living during the post-conflict period. For masses of ex-combatants, Guthrie presented a clear employment opportunity for those without any skills or education. When LURD first took over the Guthrie plantation during the war, the fighters numbered in the hundreds; by 2005, these numbers had swelled to as many as 15,000. However, the rapid growth of such a large (potentially violent) group in the post-conflict period created an environment with few enforceable rules.

As the tapping community grew, the camp leadership took on an increasingly important conflict resolution function. Even though the Guthrie Group

---

[19] Rubber Sector Expert (2007).

was not created to meet the need for contract enforcement and conflict resolution (as hypothesized in the framework), it ended up providing an important local governance function. They prescribed how conflicts were to be dealt with, depending on who the disputing parties were. Conflicts between ex-combatants were dealt with by the camp's ex-combatant leader or the chief of security. Appeals, along with unresolved and continuing disputes were then escalated to Sumo Dennis. For civilian disputes, these were handled primarily by the camp master, and then escalated to Sumo Dennis if necessary, though this rarely happened in practice. For disputes between civilians and ex-combatants, it was the camp master who was responsible for providing a resolution. In practice though, if the camp master was not an ex-combatant, the conflict would be dealt with by the camp's ex-combatant leader, and then escalated to Sumo Dennis where necessary.

Before the war, the chief and village elders were responsible for local governance and general conflict resolution in the Guthrie region. The social dynamic shifted considerably after the war though and a substantial proportion of ex-combatants did not respect the power of these local authorities. For example, in conflicts between ex-combatants and civilians, the town chief of nearby Gbah, Saa J. Sillu, would invite former commanders to assist in settling disputes so that commanders could enforce the decisions that were reached. The local magistrate judge for Gbah suggested that the problem was even more severe: whenever he would issue summons to an ex-combatant to appear in court, he usually received a personal threat. In this respect, Sumo Dennis and the leaders of the Guthrie Group demonstrated that they were able to fulfil the need for credible, internal regulation inside the camp. In fact, they were the *only* ones capable of serving this function at that point in time.

Despite these nascent attempts at providing governance, it is important that the Guthrie Group and its role on the plantation is not romanticized by those who champion for local governance approaches. The leaders of the group often served as police, judge, and jury, ruling on conflicts and authorizing beatings of those accused of selling rubber outside of the normal camp channels. The Guthrie Group succeeded in ruling with authority, but its legitimacy was derived from its brutal effectiveness.

What is remarkable about the Guthrie Group is that Sumo Dennis had begun operations with a small group of LURD commanders, but then expanded membership to include generals, commanders, and ex-combatants from all three warring factions, foreign militias like the Kamajors, and even local civilian tappers.[20] The inclusion of non-LURD members is particularly important because it shows that the group became flexible enough to absorb newcomers—even those who had fought against LURD not so long ago. For

---

[20] UNMIL (2005a).

their part, civilians were expected to conform with the practices of the extralegal group: namely, they were expected to participate in protests, even violent ones, to help the group retain control of the plantation.

Development

On the Guthrie plantation, the most common business arrangement was a 50–50 split between those who "owned" the tasks and those who did the rubber tapping. Tappers received 50 percent (though in practice, this often amounted to 35–40 percent) of the price set by Sumo Dennis while the commanders who controlled the task received the remaining 50 percent.[21] Further down the supply chain, the leadership and the task holders would resell this rubber to agents from Firestone, Weala, LAC, and later, to the Interim Management Team, charging a separate "tax" on the agents for this transaction. In financial terms, this meant that each tapper could produce 10–15 bags of rubber each month, with each bag worth $15. Of the $150–$225 that tappers collected, they kept 35–50 percent of their rubber revenues.

Depending on the camp, the profits would then be distributed according to production or rank. Tappers expected to receive their share of profits after deductions for rice and other "expenses." However, there was a lot of variation in how tappers from each of the twenty-one camps were treated. One civil society leader reported that in some camps, civilian tappers received a bag of rice and a promise of payment which was never fulfilled; in other camps, the 50–50 arrangement was honored and tappers might make as much as a few hundred dollars each month (but usually much less).[22]

Problems

The fact that tappers, both civilian and ex-combatant, were not reliably being paid, was a particular focal point for local disputes. When the Guthrie Group (consisting of generals and commanders) was unable to pay its tappers, the usual compensating arrangement was for them to tap for a week or two without being taxed—the problem was that the commanders always had the option of seizing this rubber as well. When those who are purportedly in charge of contract enforcement violate contracts themselves, there is little recourse that can be taken. This type of behavior further exacerbated tensions between tappers (many of whom were local civilians) and the Guthrie Group—and it also

[21] Peace Building Resource Center (2005); Landmine Action UK (2006).
[22] Rubber Sector Expert (2007).

undermined the ability of the Guthrie Group to resolve disputes. All too often, the senior leadership were perceived as exploiting their role as regulators. For their part, tappers would occasionally secretively tap for themselves in a process that was referred to as "fast dubbing." This was usually done by civilians or low-ranking ex-combatants who would tap the rubber, cook it, and sell it in a 24–48-hour period in a bid to bypass the regular forms of taxation.

While relations were often tense between the ex-combatants and the original Guthrie residents, in principle, the taxation method that the Guthrie Group employed should have strengthened these relationships. By offering a 50 percent equity stake in their production, the Guthrie Group could have theoretically created a local base of support for their continued occupation of the plantation—this was significantly more money than they were making before. This 50–50 profit-sharing model had the potential to create a loyal local support base among the residents if it had been consistently adhered to and enforced by the leadership—but it was not.

Structure

The Guthrie plantation consists of three estates; each estate contains several camps (approximately sixteen in total) and the camps are subdivided into areas called tasks. Senior commanders from each of the three warring factions were responsible for allocating tasks (each consisting of approximately 520–600 rubber trees) to their generals and commanders. The generals and commanders would then recruit low-ranking fighters, former Guthrie employees, and various locals to do the actual rubber tapping.

Each of the twenty-one camps had a leadership committee with a camp master, a deputy, an ex-combatant leader, a youth leader, a chief of security, and a women's leader.[23] In the leadership committee, the camp master, and the ex-combatant leader tended to be the most powerful. The ex-combatant leaders were chosen by the top leaders of the Guthrie Group. The camp masters were sometimes chosen by the Guthrie Group and other times they were selected by local residents; some were civilians and some were ex-combatants. Indeed, most of the camp leadership positions were filled by ex-combatants. Outside the camp leadership structure, there were also powerful rubber coordinators who reported directly to Dennis and the Guthrie Group leadership about each camp, providing information on the tappers and their "sponsors," as well as on the general rubber trade.

---

[23] Ironically, this governance structure is almost identical to the composition of community councils that were subsequently established by NGOs and international organizations as part of local peace and reconciliation processes.

Although some form of camp-level structures would have been re-established even if ex-combatants had not taken over the plantation, these organizational structures are noteworthy given that all of the fighting factions had significant discipline problems during the war. In spite of these problems, Dennis and the Guthrie Group successfully expanded their authority across the plantation's twenty-one camps and built a relatively coherent and powerful organization with direct control over this community, while instilling greater unity between the generals and low-ranking ex-combatants in the process. This expansion of control through tax collection suggests that the corresponding growth in the tax base increased the group's organizational abilities, as suggested by the extralegal groups framework.

In addition to the 50–50 tax, there were other levels of taxation as well. Locally, many tappers paid a de facto rice tax since some task holders sold their rice at a significant mark up; there was also a de facto monopoly "tax" since all tappers were forced to sell their rubber to the task holders for a fraction of the market price. For example, in 2004, tappers would sell a ton of rubber for U.S. $65 to the Guthrie Group member who owned the task; this person would then turn around and sell it to Firestone or another company for $250. Prices began to soar and by late 2006, Firestone was paying as much as U.S. $800–$900/ton for that same ton of rubber while task holders were offering tappers as little as $85–$125/ton.

Yet another tax that was imposed was the $200/ton charged by the Guthrie Group along with a $1000 registration fee paid by every rubber broker/agent who conducted business on the plantation. Finally, there was a truck tax collected at the Klay check point: pickup trucks were charged $25–$50 for each load; light trucks paid $75; and heavy trucks paid $150–$200. Abraham Keita, a local truck driver, expressed the local mood this way: "Ex-combatants here have become law unto themselves collecting fees from the drivers for operating transport around the plantation."[24] Data from a Landmine Action UK study[25] suggests that the proceeds from these taxes were roughly distributed to the Guthrie Group leaders as follows: Chairman: 45 percent; Co-Chairman: 20 percent; Secretary: 15 percent; Chief of Security: 10 percent; Assistant Chief Security: 5 percent; Attaché: 10 percent; Ordinary Ex-Combatants: 1–2 percent.

In absolute terms, the amounts of money being generated by the extralegal group were small. Sumo Dennis was estimated to have earned between U.S. $10,000-$15,000 per month in 2004 and early 2005.[26] This amount likely increased with a seasonal rise in production levels and an increase in the price of rubber. These are not large amounts, but in Liberia, where most people were surviving on less than $1/day, $10,000 was a fortune. To compare, even the

---

[24] IRIN (2006a), p. 28.   [25] Landmine Action UK (2006).
[26] UN Joint Mission Analysis Cell (2005i).

country's civil servants were being paid only U.S. $20 per month when they were paid at all. (Later, wages rose to $30/month). Ex-combatants who had opted to participate in the DDR programs would have received $30 per month for the period they attended training (six to nine months). By comparison, rubber tapping was considerably more lucrative. As a result, many ex-combatants registered and received their disarmament payment, but dropped out during the demobilization or reintegration stage and headed to Guthrie to tap rubber. By local standards, the profits generated by rubber tapping on the Guthrie plantation were substantial enough to sustain a small fighting force.[27]

Even though the tax collection system was not created with the intention of building an administrative system, the assortment of taxing mechanisms ended up creating a structure with a clear hierarchy, a stable source of income, and multiple sources of information to maintain accountability. Taxes provided substantial financial benefits for the leadership of the Guthrie Group which increased the loyalty of its profit-sharing members and made them more willing to fight. The taxation/profit-sharing structure bound the group together in common cause and the tax collection structure built up organizational capacity that otherwise would not have existed.

Entrenchment

As an extralegal group develops, its primary goal is to retain territorial control for as long as possible without a confrontation from the government. The theoretical framework suggests that an extralegal group is most likely to adopt a medium-term time horizon of three to five years. During this period, the network will seek to maximize its returns. In the case of the Guthrie Group, the available evidence supports the prediction that it adopted a medium-term time horizon. The Guthrie Group and its supporters did not behave like looters with short time horizons, but they also did not make long-term investments in public goods or public institutions. Their outlook represented something in between: they did not loot local residents; but they chose to slaughter tap, which would have maximized their gains in the three- to seven-year timeframe.

Incredibly, by November 2004, they had enough clout and power to negotiate a deal with the General Resources Corporation—which legally owned the concession rights—whereby 450 ex-combatants would have been retained as tappers or as security guards.[28] In exchange, GRC would be permitted to set up

---

[27] By way of example, in 2005, Liberian child soldiers were being recruited by their former commanders to fight in neighboring Côte d'Ivoire for a onetime payment of $300–$400. See Human Rights Watch (2005).

[28] UN Joint Mission Analysis Cell (2005i).

offices and checkpoints inside Guthrie and buy rubber. Looking back, this was an immense achievement for an extralegal group. If the leaders had agreed to this deal and stuck with it, they would have consolidated their gains and achieved a degree of economic security. But they rejected the deal, presumably because they felt that they could do better.

There is an interesting counterfactual here. During the period when the group controlled the Guthrie plantation, George Weah was the leading candidate for the Liberian presidency. His core constituency was Liberia's youth—particularly the ex-combatant community.[29] This was his most significant support base. If Weah had won the presidential election, it would have been difficult for him to act against ex-combatant interests and forsake their support. The framework predicts that even if Weah's administration was unwilling to cooperate, the Guthrie Group would have safeguarded its interests through bribery and coercion—as was the case with the National Transitional Government of Liberia. Hence, if Weah had won the election, the Guthrie Group would have had a good chance of retaining control of the plantation. If the Guthrie Group had held on to power under these circumstances, the extralegal groups framework predicts that the Guthrie Group would have adopted a long-term timeframe and changed their operations to tap more sustainably.

The framework also predicts that extralegal groups with medium-term time horizons will attempt to prolong their tenure by co-opting state institutions. There is evidence of this behavior with Guthrie Group leaders. Indeed, the Guthrie Group employed several creative tactics in an attempt to convert their medium-term control into long-term control. First, they tried to justify their occupation with a very literal interpretation of Article VI, §6 of the Comprehensive Peace Agreement which states: "All combatants shall remain in the declared and recorded locations until they proceed to reintegration activities or training for entry into the restructured Liberian armed forces or into civilian life."[30] The Guthrie Group interpreted this clause to mean that ex-combatants had the right to occupy the plantation while they were "waiting" to participate in the UNMIL disarmament and demobilization stages. Even though the Guthrie ex-combatants had been extended the same opportunity to participate in the national DDR process as other former fighters, they put forward this argument as justification for their presence on the plantation.

Another tactic that the Guthrie Group used to prolong their tenure was to set up an NGO, the National Veteran Rehabilitation Project (NVRP),

---

[29] See Johanna Söderström (2013) for a perceptive discussion of how ex-combatants felt betrayed by the electoral experience of 2005, and how their attitudes towards democracy evolved over time.
[30] Government of Liberia, Liberians United for Reconciliation and Democracy and Movement for Democracy in Liberia (2003).

to replace the Guthrie Group and legitimize the collection of taxes on the plantation. As an internal security report from the UN observed:

> All indications lead us to suspect that each of the above issues is a mechanism of delay employed by the ex-combatants at Guthrie Rubber Plantation. This would be in keeping with their previous pattern of behaviour. The ex-combatants' goal is likely to stalemate the [election] registration process and postpone their potential relocation until after the election in October. By waiting until after the election, they may be betting on their ability to capitalize on their political power increasing their odds of remaining permanently at GRP [Guthrie Rubber Plantation].[31]

Even when a government takeover was imminent and it was clear that the Rubber Planters' Association of Liberia (RPAL) would assume management of the plantation, the Guthrie Group continued with its tactics of coercion and delay. "Let me make it very clear that the plantation could remain ungovernable if the government forced us out without giving us sufficient time to pack and evacuate," said Prince Welleh, a leader in the Guthrie Group. This veiled threat was made during a press conference shortly before the government was expected to reclaim the plantation in 2006. Welleh then went on to suggest that if the ex-combatants were not granted ninety days to leave the plantation then they would resort to armed robbery and threaten the local population. Some ex-combatants also insinuated that any local residents who dared to tap rubber under the new RPAL management would be subjected to violence[32] while others threatened to use acid against the peacekeepers.[33] These sorts of violent threats had succeeded in the past and the Guthrie Group expected them to be effective again. Past interactions with the transitional government and the international community had proven that the most effective way of drawing attention to their cause was through violent protest, and if necessary, by using violence in the community. The quotation at the start of this chapter also shows that UNMIL understood the level of control exerted by the Guthrie Group.

Still, the Guthrie Group's most useful tactic for changing their time horizons from medium-term to long-term was to bribe and coerce national and local politicians into prolonging the illegal occupation of the plantation. During the two years the transitional government was in power, this effort was quite successful: a number of Cabinet ministers and senior government staff were allegedly bribed into delaying the repossession of Guthrie. For example, bribes ranged from a few drums of gasoline all the way up to a vehicle. The group was also actively involved in politics. In addition to publicly backing George Weah, the Guthrie Group supported senatorial candidate,

---

[31] UN Joint Mission Analysis Cell (2005j).   [32] Jimmey C. Fahngon (2006).
[33] McCarey Marshall (2006).

Richard Devine (Liberia Action Party) because he favored allowing the ex-combatants to remain on the plantation.[34] Devine won his election.

Another indication that the Guthrie Group had adopted a medium-term strategy was evidenced in its pattern of taxation. During the course of 2006, when it became clear that the new Sirleaf administration was intent on reclaiming the plantation, the group's leaders instituted additional layers of taxation. The extralegal groups framework predicted that the Guthrie Group would become more rapacious as its future status on the plantation became more uncertain—and this was in fact the case. With less incentive to keep their tappers satisfied (for future tapping), the group's leaders kept an increasingly larger share of profits, against the protests of their tappers. At this time, the Guthrie Group was paying its tappers $85–$125/ton where it once paid $65/ton, but it was selling the same ton of rubber for as much as $800–$900—a dramatic increase from the $250/ton it used to receive. Most of the markup ended up as "taxes" to the Guthrie Group.

Admittedly, it is difficult to differentiate between rapacious behavior that is induced by the possibility of a government takeover and rapacious behavior that is simply opportunistic. However, it was clear that civilian and ex-combatant tappers were well aware of market prices and knew that they were receiving a declining proportion of revenues. It was also clear that the Guthrie Group became less disciplined and the number of violent incidents increased as the government threatened to take over with greater and greater credibility. These behaviors are consistent with the framework's predictions.

There was also a noticeable change in how local civilians felt about relations with the Guthrie Group and the ex-combatants. In 2005, they reported that relations were "generally fine," but a year later in March 2006, they reported that "the situation has seriously degraded in time and they fear for their own safety as well as for the state of the plantation."[35] Extortion of businesses and robberies were on the increase—again, this is consistent with the theoretical framework. When the Guthrie Group was confident of its tenure, it behaved more peaceably. The extralegal groups framework suggests that this is because the group has a stake in the plantation's future. However, as it watched its chances of holding on to the plantation slip away, some members of the group, especially ex-combatants at the tapper level, felt that they would benefit more from a direct looting strategy. The leaders themselves were no longer incentivized to stop the looting either—and neither the police nor UNMIL were prepared to step in.

At this point, both the transitional government and UNMIL considered the Guthrie Group a significant security threat—one that was capable of disrupting the peace. One important consideration was that the army had been

---

[34] UN Joint Mission Analysis Cell (2005j).   [35] IRIN (2006a).

completely dissolved and was being rebuilt from scratch (in consultation with the American military contractor DynCorp).[36] In August 2006, the month the Guthrie takeover was scheduled to begin, there was no Liberian army to speak of. The first class of recruits had only just begun training.[37] Despite the departure of many ex-combatants, there were still at least 500 to 1000 fighters who still occupied the Guthrie plantation in the spring of 2006.[38]

UNMIL's Weak Response

Not only was Guthrie deemed a security threat for Liberian nationals, but even UNMIL peacekeepers treated the plantation as a no-go zone. While Guthrie was being illegally occupied, the area had been off limits for most Liberians and internationals. Even though the Guthrie Plantation was considered one of the country's most serious security threats, UNMIL did not intervene. As early as October 26, 2004, Jacques Klein, the Special Representative of the Secretary-General and head of UNMIL, formally urged Chairman Bryant to restore law and order on the Guthrie Plantation and offered UNMIL's support, but the NTGL still did not take action against the group.

Privately, UNMIL officials have cited three reasons for not taking a more active role in ending the occupation in the early years of the peacekeeping mission. First and foremost, Liberia's transitional government was not politically committed to evacuating the ex-combatants from Guthrie. Second, UNMIL did not want to risk a violent confrontation when the political situation was still very fragile; they stressed that it was paramount that the security situation appear stable during this period because further violence would have upset not only the Liberians but also could have potentially destabilized Liberia's neighbors in the Mano River region, causing great alarm to all of the major donor countries. Third, some officials argued that UNMIL did not have the mandate to root out the Guthrie Group (or other groups like it).

In an interview about his tenure as the head of UNMIL, Jacques-Paul Klein said that the Guthrie Group should have been directly confronted early on in the mission. The problem, he said, was that "I had no executive power. I could make demands, but I had no authority to enforce them."[39] Klein saw this as a central problem of his tenure: he thought that Liberia should have been administered as a protectorate of the UN for two years, with Liberian deputies, in a structure similar to that of the UN Transitional Administration in Eastern Slavonia.

---

[36] For an insider's account of DynCorp's role in Liberia, see Sean McFate (2013).
[37] Fully staffed, the army would still only consist of 2000 soldiers.   [38] IRIN (2006a).
[39] Jacques Paul Klein (2006).

A year later, the transitional government signed a deal with Agro Resources Corporation which explicitly included the ex-combatants in the new management agreement[40]—this was a clear effort by the state to co-opt the interests of the group and to convert their lucrative medium-term interests into less profitable, but steadier long-term interests. Even though the leaders of the Guthrie Group ultimately put an end to the deal, this formal recognition in the agreement acknowledged the de facto power enjoyed by the Guthrie Group within the boundaries of the plantation. If the group was unimportant or did not pose a substantial threat to the country's political stability or indeed the government itself, then *no such concession would have been made.*

Another key reason that the NTGL officials allowed the group to continue occupying the plantation was that they were concerned with what the ex-combatants would do if they had to earn their livelihood some other way. The possibilities were worrisome: the Guthrie Group could have reconstituted itself as a local militia; it could have resorted to banditry; or its members could have sold their services as mercenaries, heading east to fight in Côte d'Ivoire. From a security standpoint, the Guthrie Group had the potential to cause a security crisis and jeopardize a still fragile peace process. Remarkably though, the Liberian government managed to reclaim the plantation.

Statebuilding by the State

Shortly after Ellen Johnson Sirleaf took over the presidency, she made the Guthrie occupation one of her top priorities. The head of UNMIL, Alan Doss, was also extremely concerned about the security situation on the plantation and UNMIL had already established an internal working group to address the Guthrie situation. It consisted of UN representatives from Civil Affairs, Civilian Police, Human Rights and Protection, Humanitarian Coordination, Joint Mission Analysis Cell (JMAC), Political Planning and Policy, and Reintegration, Rehabilitation, and Recovery. Given their common concern, Sirleaf and Doss created the Rubber Plantations Task Force in February 2006, barely a month after she was inaugurated. This sent an early signal to the Guthrie Group leaders and to other extralegal groups that the new president would not be sympathetic to their demands.

The Task Force was led by the Ministry of Agriculture but had broad representation from across a number of government ministries and UNMIL units. From the government, this included the Ministries of Agriculture; Finance; Gender and Development; Internal Affairs; Health and Social Welfare; Justice; Labour; Planning and Economic Affairs; the Liberia Rubber Development Authority; the Environmental Protection Agency; the National

---

[40] UNMIL Human Rights (2006).

Security Agency; the Liberia National Police; and the National Commission for Disarmament, Demobilization, Rehabilitation and Reintegration. From UNMIL, this included Human Rights and Protection; Civil Affairs; Public Information; Legal and Judicial Support; Political Planning and Policy; Corrections; Gender; Environment; Reintegration, Rehabilitation, and Recovery; Military; Administration; UNPOL; and UNDP. The Rubber Planters Association of Liberia was also a member.

The Task Force consulted widely, speaking to communities, local officials, politicians, NGOs, and the rubber companies themselves. This process of cautious data-gathering, consultation and consensus-building by the Task Force helped to build up a constituency for change—not only on the Guthrie plantation, but across Liberia's seven major plantations (including the SRP which is discussed below). In short, the Task Force helped build the political will within the government and within UNMIL to take action against both the Guthrie and Sinoe Networks. The recommendations that emerged from their May 2006 report were clear: the plantations had to be secured, illegal rubber tapping halted, and the ex-combatants peacefully removed with some form of compensation. The suggested timeframe for these actions was one month.[41] An interim management body would then take over while the status of the concession contracts was clarified. The Task Force suggested a six- to twelve-month timeframe for putting in place long-term arrangements for the plantation.

The Sirleaf government systematically followed through on the recommendations, broadcasting its intentions to reclaim the plantation through the media and also through site visits (backed up by UNMIL peacekeepers). The Guthrie Group had already been in negotiations with UNMIL, discussing the conditions under which its members would leave Guthrie and participate in DDR programs. But as expected, Guthrie Group leaders continued to stall for time, threatening retaliation against the government and against all those who dared to cooperate with the government and UNMIL. For the government, the belligerence of the group was alarming, even though there was little doubt that UNMIL peacekeepers could have successfully quelled an armed insurrection on the plantation at this point. Still, the government of Liberia itself did not have the military or police capability for handling this situation. This possibility of violence remained a cause of great national concern. Without UNMIL, the government would not have been able to reclaim Guthrie.

Repossessing Guthrie

Given the conclusions of the Rubber Task Force, and the risk that Guthrie was perceived to pose, there were two options available to the Sirleaf government:

---

[41] Rubber Plantations Task Force (2006).

confront or co-opt. Both of these are described earlier in the book in the theoretical framework chapter. In this case, the repossession of Guthrie took place in stages, beginning with co-option before preparing for confrontation. First, create divisions between ex-combatant tappers and the Guthrie Group leadership through a gradual process of attrition. This was done through a combination of enticements (DDR package) and threats (forcible eviction). Second, having weakened the group militarily and having introduced internal conflict, it is then possible to threaten the leadership with confrontation.

The repossession began with an official ceremony on August 16, 2006 which was attended by local officials and UNMIL Head Alan Doss. At the ceremony, the Liberia National Police, unarmed and nervous, officially reclaimed the plantation on the government's behalf, while UNMIL peace-keepers stood nearby at the ready. In the end, there was little resistance—the government and UNMIL had announced several times that this was going to happen, and had prepared the ground by offering DDR packages to those who were eligible. Following the ceremony, UNMIL immediately began to build an on-site camp, with housing and office space. UNMIL began regular patrols of the plantation.

Interestingly, *even before repossession had taken place*, the local and international press immediately declared the operation a success. Local headlines that morning read: "Government reclaims rubber plantation from former fighters," "UNMIL, Gov't Takes Guthrie Today," "UNMIL Takes Over Guthrie, But."[42] It is important to note here that Liberia's newspapers are underfunded and many were known to accept bribes in exchange for favorable coverage or placement. Given the timing, it is likely that some of the early favorable media coverage was orchestrated in this way.

At this stage, an interim management team was also put in place, led by RPAL. Unfortunately, the installation of the new managers only angered the Guthrie Group further because some of the RPAL leaders were former Taylor advisors. For some ex-LURD members, it felt as if history was repeating itself with Taylor's networks reasserting themselves once more.[43]

After the initial reclaiming by the government and UNMIL, ex-combatants were given two more weeks to leave. By September 1st, some had left, but others remained. Another deadline was set for September 15th. This time, the ex-combatants were told that after September 15th, they would not be permitted to tap or sell rubber on the plantation and that UNMIL and the local police would enforce this deadline. By the end of September, the Sirleaf government had regained control of the plantation with UNMIL backing. By mid-October, RPAL had begun rubber production.

---

[42] Jennie K. Fallah (2006); IRIN (2006b); *The Analyst* (2006c).
[43] Landmine Action UK (2006).

In a twist of irony, after reclaiming the plantation, the government ended up using the Guthrie Group's camp-level organizational structures. After the leaders had physically left the plantation, some ex-combatant tappers remained and sold their rubber to RPAL. RPAL bought rubber directly from the tappers themselves, and in the early days of the takeover, they offered to pay the tappers *more* for the rubber than the Guthrie Group leaders had been paying. This tactic facilitated the government's takeover and firmly placed civilian loyalties on the government side. Still, in the lead-up to the planned takeover, there was great concern that Guthrie Group leaders would mobilize ex-combatants to fight the reclamation.

One Guthrie Group leader threatened: "I control all the work in this Estate, all of these children report to me, they are tapping my rubber. If I say disarm, they disarm, if I say we go to the Ivory Coast, they will go to the Ivory Coast."[44] These were worrying claims. UNMIL Head of Mission Alan Doss expressed the difficulties of the situation: "Reform carries risk. There are winners, but there are also losers—those who perhaps have lost what they saw was their right."[45] While some had previously registered in the DDR process and were given the chance to re-enter the program, other ex-combatants had no alternatives and everything to lose when the government repossessed the plantation.[46]

Although the plantation was successfully reclaimed by the Liberian government in the end, this result was by no means a foregone conclusion. If George Weah had been elected president; if President Sirleaf had not made the rubber sector a top priority; if the Guthrie Group had enforced its own 50–50 rule; or if any one of a number of things had happened differently, then the group might have been able to retain control of the plantation. In spite of this success, it was never clear that the Liberian government had the capacity to successfully coordinate and implement a project on this scale. Certainly, internal UN documents revealed a deep skepticism in the ability of the Liberian government to follow through.

In the years following the 2006 government takeover, there were high expectations of the interim management team. Unfortunately, the operations were beset with problems. Repeated demonstrations occurred, many of them violent, as tappers complained of unpaid wages. The presence of ex-combatants also remained, though they were now controlled by former NPFL leaders rather than LURD. In the end, at least one leader of the Guthrie Group, a former LURD commander, regained significant power on the plantation.[47]

---

[44] Ibid.   [45] Heidi Vogt (2007).
[46] Responding to this danger, Landmine Action UK developed an extensive rehabilitation and reintegration program, targeted specifically at those who remained unregistered. Hundreds of ex-combatants received training under this program, which was modestly successful at reintegrating hardened ex-combatants into civilian life, though the program was also very expensive. For a full assessment, see Christopher Blattman and Jeannie Annan (2011).
[47] Jaremey R. McMullin (2013), p. 212.

While no ex-combatant group reclaimed outright control of Guthrie, workers grew increasingly unhappy and the condition of the plantation deteriorated. In August 2009, the Malaysian agricultural conglomerate Sime Darby signed an $800 million agreement with the Liberian government which included the rehabilitation of the Guthrie plantation. The company assumed control of Guthrie on January 1, 2010, but within six months, it had already found itself at the center of several labor controversies.[48]

THE SINOE GROUP

The SRP is located in the far-flung southeast of the country, a six- to ten-hour road journey from Monrovia during the dry season. During Liberia's six-month rainy season, the area is virtually inaccessible except by helicopter. Far from the capital as well as the country's eastern border and lacking reliable road access, Sinoe County is one of Liberia's most isolated regions. Even though Sinoe County is sparsely populated, there were an estimated 3000–5000 residents on the SRP in mid-2005 and as many as 10,000 people were spread out among the plantation's seven camps by February 2006.[49]

When the war ended in August 2003, the Sinoe plantation was occupied by MODEL fighters, but by March 2004, General Wallace had evacuated the rebels from SRP and handed it back to the original concession holder: the Mesurado Corporation. In turn, Mesurado hired RUBREMICII to manage the plantation. RUBREMICII officially took control of the plantation shortly thereafter.

However, by June 2004, Paulson Garteh, an ex-MODEL and ex-LPC general, had violently kicked out the management company and taken over SRP with the support of ex-combatants and the local community. The former "General Satan" remained in charge of the plantation until he was arrested for robbery and local assault in May 2006.[50] He was later released on bail in Monrovia and reportedly fled to Côte d'Ivoire with about twenty ex-combatants from the Sinoe plantation (UN Panel of Experts on Liberia 2006).[51] Garteh was then replaced by Leon Worjlah, another ex-combatant known locally as "White Flower."

For several years, the government and UNMIL made a series of attempts to regain control of the plantation, but without success. Part of this effort included putting in place a local ban on rubber produced from the Sinoe

---

[48] Matthias Daffah (2010); Horatio Bobby Willie (2010).

[49] As estimated by Jackson Paul, the Comptroller for the Sinoe Rubber plantation. See Green Advocates (2006).

[50] Garteh is recommended for prosecution in the TRC Final Report for "massacre, torture & extortion." See Truth and Reconciliation Commission of Liberia (2009), p. 346.

[51] UN Panel of Experts on Liberia (2006).

plantation. The ban was enforced by a Joint Security Team which included UNMIL peacekeepers. At a checkpoint in nearby Nyenfueh Town, UNMIL troops were instructed to intercept all rubber shipments. The leaders of Sinoe's extralegal group worked around the ban by avoiding the roads and transporting the rubber down the Sinoe river by canoe into Greenville. Once there, they would sell their rubber and purchase their supplies (knives, chemicals, buckets and cups) from LAC and Firestone agents.

The plantation stayed in the hands of ex-combatants until November 29, 2009 when local LNP officers (backed up by the LNP's specially trained Emergency Response Unit) officially reclaimed it on behalf of the government.[52] On December 18, 2009, the government signed an interim management agreement with Lee Network Enterprises.[53]

Emergence

After MODEL evacuated the plantation in March 2004, many ex-combatants remained in the Greenville area waiting for the Disarmament and Demobilization process to begin. Official DDR statistics show that there were some 1300 ex-combatants in Sinoe County at this time.[54] Some of them were tapping rubber while they occupied the plantation and the number of ex-combatants and local residents tapping on the plantation gradually increased as the security situation improved during the spring of 2004. With more and more tappers on the plantation, and many of them ex-combatants, the framework predicts that competition leads to an extralegal group emerging to meet a need for credible regulation and dispute resolution. The available evidence from Sinoe supports the framework's logic.

At the end of the war, even though there was an existing local authority structure in place—the Sinoe Legislative Caucus—caucus members did not command the same authority as the ex-combatant leaders. This was a particular concern since it was not until many months after the CPA was signed that UN peacekeepers were finally deployed to Sinoe County. Further, the disarmament and demobilization of fighters in the area did not begin until October 24, 2004— over a year after the war had officially ended.[55] Local civilian leaders received little respect from the ex-combatants themselves, giving rise to a governance vacuum.

Stepping into the vacuum on behalf of the Sinoe Group was Paulson Garteh. He was the most powerful and charismatic of the ex-combatants; this ex-MODEL

---

[52] The Emergency Response Unit is an armed division of the Liberia National Police specially trained to handle situations requiring the use of weapons and for dealing with riots and natural disasters.

[53] Bill E. Diggs (2009).   [54] UN Humanitarian Information Centre for Liberia (2005).

[55] UN DDR Resource Centre (2008).

general eventually became the manager of SRP. He commanded a loyal group of about forty ex-combatants with a fearsome reputation[56]—the group was large enough to be intimidating. What distinguished Garteh from other ex-combatants were his political charisma and his local roots. He was originally from the area and was sympathetic to the concerns of the Wedjah community. By the time the plantation was handed over to the RUBREMICII company in March 2004, Garteh had already established himself as a local leader. He spoke out publicly several times against the company's management, asserting that Mesurado's repossession of SRP in 1987 was illegitimate. He argued that after the government confiscated SRP in 1980 following the Doe coup, it had no right to simply give the plantation back to Mesurado. Instead, the plantation should be entrusted to the community until there was a democratically elected government in place. Further, he claimed that Mesurado had received the concession under dubious circumstances in the first place in 1970, stirring up community support for a takeover.[57]

In June 2004, even though RUBREMICII had the legal authority to manage the Sinoe plantation, it had little enforceable authority on the plantation grounds. By this point, it had become clear that the community was not going to allow RUBREMICII to operate. Part of the problem was due to the company's ownership—Roland Massaquoi, a close associate of Charles Taylor and a former Cabinet minister, owned RUBREMICII and was seen by the Wedjah as part of the ruling Congo class.

Instead of allowing RUBREMICII to return, Garteh convinced his Wedjah kinfolk and the Sinoe Legislative Caucus to take over the plantation and distribute the proceeds from rubber sales back to the community. The Caucus appointed him General Manager. With the support of community leaders and his group of ex-combatants, Garteh formalized this arrangement by creating the Wedjah Rubber Corporation (WRC) which later morphed into the Citizens' Welfare Committee (CWC), and was also known as the Wedjah Citizens Interim Management Team. For simplicity, I refer to this group in its various guises as the Sinoe Group.

Development

There is limited information on the taxation structure of the Sinoe Group. In February 2006, the environmental NGO, Green Advocates, conducted a

---

[56] IRIN (2006c).

[57] After agreeing to establish a banana plantation on the Sinoe land, the Afrikanische Frucht Companie (AFC) planted rubber trees instead and the government decided that it would have to pay $1.5–$1.8 million in taxes. The AFC left Liberia and Stephen Tolbert, the Finance Minister at the time and the brother of President Tolbert, supposedly bought out the AFC concession and paid the AFC taxes that were owed to the government.

workshop in Greenville where the Comptroller for the plantation, Jackson Paul, stated that they collected "only a monthly due of one-bag of rubber" worth L.D. $450.00 or U.S. $8.00 directly from each tapper.[58] Paul estimated that there were approximately 10,000 registered tappers on the plantation which would have resulted in U.S. $80,000 per month in taxes. In comparison, the Sinoe Group's taxes on rubber agents who were buying the rubber from the tappers were more substantial. Local journalist Patrick Kamor stated that the standard tax for brokers who wanted to purchase SRP rubber was U.S. $100; on top of that, the Sinoe Groupwas also collecting 25 percent of what the rubber brokers bought and were keeping it as a tax.[59] The Citizens of Wedjah, a civil society group, suggest that a conservative estimate of the tax burden on rubber brokers would be $150–$250/ton[60] which would have netted the Sinoe Group an additional U.S. $20,000–$40,000 per month.

This tax structure contrasted sharply with that of the Guthrie Group's 50–50 arrangement with its tappers. On the Sinoe plantation, the strategy was to focus taxation at the broker level. The $8/month flat tax was reasonable and consistently applied compared to Guthrie's tappers who were taxed much more heavily, and more *directly*. Rather than taxing the tappers, who the Sinoe Group needed onside, they instead focused on taxing the brokers, which was logistically easier, and also saved them from imposing a heavier burden on their tappers.

Based on internal UNMIL documents, the group had a clear organizational hierarchy that included a Chairman/General Manager, Co-Chairman, General Secretary, Treasurer, Committee Agents, and Camp Supervisors. Initially, the group's stated plan in 2005 was to maintain seven camp divisions, provide schools and health clinics and staff them with teachers and health workers.[61] It was expected that the rubber taxes that were collected would pay for these services. While these taxes were collected on behalf of the community, in the end, none of the money was ever spent on public goods. Most of these funds have reportedly been privately redistributed into the hands of the Sinoe Group, which included Garteh, his deputy and successor Leon "White Flower" Worjlah. A proportion of this money was also used to buy the continued cooperation of national politicians, various members of the Sinoe Legislative Caucus, and other local authorities.

Nonetheless, what was interesting about the tax structure on SRP was that its leaders offered people a financial stake in their own production—just like the Guthrie Group. But in contrast to Guthrie, the WRC leadership did not exploit the situation to the same extent as the Guthrie leaders. On the Sinoe plantation, taxes were more affordable and were applied more uniformly and predictably across the board for both tappers and brokers. As a result, even though the community knew that taxes were being paid to "the Big Men," they

---

[58] Green Advocates (2006).   [59] Rebecca Murray (2009).
[60] Public Agenda (2008).   [61] UNMIL Civil Affairs (2005b).

were still able to earn a livelihood and thus had a substantial stake in sustaining the occupation. In short, *the leaders of the extralegal group had succeeded in aligning their interests to those of the tappers.* In this respect, the group had expanded to encompass not only the leadership, but also rank and file tappers. The size of the network grew, as was demonstrated by the violent demonstrations supporting the Sinoe Group's right to occupy the Sinoe plantation. This willingness to fight made it a much more powerful organization to deal with in political and security terms. As the January 2007 revolt against the Interim Management Team demonstrated, Garteh and the Sinoe Group had succeeded in building a local power base that would not simply bow to interests in Monrovia.

Another interesting observation about the flat tax policy ($8/tapper per month) was that it changed the balance of power within the organization in an unexpected way. In the early days of the takeover early in 2004, it was Garteh, his ex-combatants, and the members of the Caucus who were clearly in control. Over time though, the balance of power changed as security improved and political tensions across the country eased. As more time passed, coercive force became less important. The changing balance of power became apparent when civilian tappers and local residents became emboldened.

Entrenchment and Statebuilding

As with the extralegal group on Guthrie, the available evidence suggests that Garteh's Sinoe Group was reasonably confident of its ability to maintain a medium-term presence. Although the group did not engage in widespread looting as a group of roving bandits might, neither was it fully invested in the long-term future of the plantation. Slaughter tapping was common in spite of the concerns expressed by long-term residents who understood how destructive the practice was.[62]

Sinoe Group leaders also built a governance structure for collecting taxes and resolving disputes, though it was not as hierarchically organized as that of the Guthrie Group. Interestingly, data from UNMIL security reports from 2004 to 2007 suggest that there was better personal security on the Sinoe plantation and that the Sinoe Group provided a more stable environment for business. But this came at a cost: when Garteh was asked what was done with criminals on the plantation, he went so far as to say that he personally served as both police and judge.[63] Further, an UNMIL report observed that as of July 2005,

---

[62] UNMIL Civil Affairs (2005d).   [63] UNMIL Human Rights (2006).

there are no community benefits like clinics, schools, hand-pumps, wells and toilets, and the community infrastructures are depleted and in a deplorable state, including those in the camps in the plantation. Access to the plantation is becoming increasing impassable as the roads and bridges have not been repaired since the civil war erupted in December 1989.[64]

In short, no physical investments had been made in local public goods, and no efforts had been made to establish local institutions to provide these goods.

The Sinoe Group also successfully employed two tactics to delay a government takeover. The most important of these was to cast doubt on the validity of the concession agreement that was officially held by the Mesurado Corporation. It did this by reminding the Wedjah population that Mesurado had never fulfilled the provisions for community benefits as agreed to under the original Afrikanische Frucht Companie (AFC) agreement to establish a banana plantation.[65] Garteh and the Sinoe Group fully exploited these tensions—to the extent that even after RUBREMICII and community representatives managed to negotiate an agreement which would have allowed for the return of the company, this extralegal group still managed to hold onto control of the plantation by convincing the community that their views and rights had not been properly represented in the agreement, and by alleging that the 1990 death of certain Wedjah citizens was the fault of RUBREMICII.[66]

Despite vociferous condemnation of the Sinoe Group by the transitional government and by UNMIL, the Sinoe Group still managed to obtain the cooperation of at least one key politician, NTLA member Victor Queah. At a critical juncture in 2005, Queah was able to direct the local police to shut down the plantation and install Paulson Garteh as the head of the plantation.[67] The extent to which Queah was involved in or beholden to the Sinoe Group is unclear. He may have been involved since its inception or he may have been bribed as part of the group's organizational strengthening process. What is apparent is that Queah's intervention further delayed Mesurado's (and by extension RUBREMICII's) ability to control the SRP for at least two months. It is also likely that Queah helped steer control of the plantation toward Garteh's group. Further, confidential UNMIL documents revealed allegations that local police officers were complicit in the rubber trade and that they were deliberately undermining the ban on rubber coming from SRP.[68] For their part, the police have countered that they were not aware of the local ban, and that rubber brokers forced their way through the checkpoint. These forms of co-optation are consistent with the entrenchment of extralegal groups. Local politicians and government officials were being coopted into the Sinoe Group's sphere of influence.

---

[64] UNMIL Civil Affairs (2005d).   [65] Ibid.
[66] UNMIL Civil Affairs (2005b).   [67] UN Joint Mission Analysis Cell (2005k).
[68] UNMIL (2005b).

Even when the Minister of Agriculture and the Minister of Justice arrived on the plantation in January 2005 to suspend all operations and reassert RUBREMICII's legal right to operate, Garteh simply led the ex-combatants in a revolt against them. A few days later, the Sinoe Legislative Caucus wrote a letter to the Minister of Agriculture overturning his decision to give Mesurado and RUBREMICII—the legal contract holders—their concession back. Garteh delivered the letter personally.[69] The letter and its delivery were both notable acts of defiance—they showed that Garteh was operating from a position of strength. The Sinoe Group dictated the terms for management of the Sinoe plantation and there was nothing the national Minister for Agriculture could do to change the situation on the ground.

From the Wedjah perspective, the legitimacy of the Minister's claims were questionable anyway. Monrovia's Congo rulers had taken their lands away decades ago, and now, the community felt that it was simply reclaiming what was rightfully theirs. Garteh was not just providing "dispute resolution", he was also tapping into a bitter mistrust of the state and deep-seated resentment of the ruling class.

Even when there were outstanding warrants for Garteh's arrest, he continued to manage the plantation. As an UNMIL Human Rights report observed:

> Local authorities lack sufficient logistic support or facilities to detain high-risk prisoners such as Mr. Garteh. The limited operation of the Courts in Sinoe County to date also raises the likelihood that if he were arrested, the case would not proceed in accordance with the law and human rights standards, leading to impunity for these serious offences.[70]

Certainly, by February 2005, Garteh was confident in his ability to assert full authority over the plantation and that local officials, including the police, would defer to him. By this point, local officials may have ceded authority out of fear or out of genuine support, or they may have been bribed into submission as part of the extralegal groups' organizational strengthening process. Unfortunately, there is no evidence available that differentiates between these possibilities. It is also unclear whether the Sinoe Group increased tax rates after the Memorandum of Understanding was signed on April 14, 2005 allowing for the return of RUBREMICII. On the other hand, the local population certainly believed that the takeover was imminent and increased their rate of "Gorbachev"—that is to say, they were tapping as much as possible as quickly as possible before the arrival of the new management team.[71] These actions were consistent with a medium-term time horizon: as the window of opportunity began to close shut, the extralegal group was expected to take as much as possible in the remaining time. Interestingly though, no evidence has

[69] UNMIL Human Rights (2006).   [70] Ibid., p. 24.
[71] UNMIL Civil Affairs (2005a).

emerged that the Sinoe Group increased their tax rate or introduced new taxes at this point—running counter to the predictions of the framework.

While the security threat posed by the Sinoe Group was initially not as serious as that on the Guthrie plantation, over time this became a bigger challenge for the government in its attempt to assert authority over the territory. Certainly, in terms of using military force, UNMIL peacekeepers could have easily crushed the Sinoe Group if threatened,[72] but it was not belligerent toward UNMIL or the government. Nor were there the same types of security problems as existed on the Guthrie plantation.

In May 2006, the Joint Government of Liberia-United Nations Rubber Plantations Task Force formally recommended that the Sinoe plantation be secured immediately. But the government did not have the capacity to reclaim the plantation. It was several years later before the Sinoe plantation was finally repossessed at the end of 2009.

Shortly after the success of the Guthrie takeover in September 2006, the Sirleaf administration attempted to install an Interim Management Team on the Sinoe plantation. In January 2007, the Sinoe Group reached a deal with the district commissioner of Sinoe County to set up an interim management committee. They agreed that the commissioner would gradually take over the plantation, and that members of the Sinoe Group would be able to continue tapping rubber, but that they would be levied a tax of U.S. $65/ton. In exchange, these tax revenues would be used to enhance public welfare on the plantation.[73] In late January of 2007, there was a violent revolt against the new management team involving 250 people. There was an unconfirmed report that one person was killed, though White Flower denied this. Although there were reportedly no firearms in use, people brandished machetes, sticks, and acid.

In the end, the arrangement lasted six weeks and $130,000 in tax revenue was collected. When no improvements to the plantation were made, the Sinoe Group ended the deal and kicked them out. UNMIL officials believed that Sinoe's district commissioner had never had the authority to make this deal in the first place, and that he had kept the funds for himself.[74]

Security problems on the plantation continued through early 2007 and it soon became clear that the government would not be able to repossess SRP. In fact, the government's lack of success on this front indicates that the Sinoe Group had successfully developed a local power base that was able to resist government authority. Yet local support for the Sinoe Group waned over time. The group had made promises about spending money on local development, but group members allegedly pocketed the money instead. The opportunity for providing public goods and bottom-up statebuilding had been wasted. People's cynical notions about government corruption and greedy politicians were confirmed once more.

---

[72] UNMIL Civil Affairs (2005c).   [73] Shawn Blore (2007).
[74] Ibid.

The Community Fights Back

In an unexpected move in June 2008, local residents organized themselves and demanded a full accounting of the tax money that had been paid to the WRC. Several clashes occurred between community members and the Sinoe Group. When those who had allegedly stolen the money (mostly local officials) provided only excuses about where the funds had gone, the Citizens of Wedjah complained directly to the Minister of Agriculture.[75] "White Flower" Worjlah and the Sinoe Group were subsequently forced out by the community, the Superintendent, and the Sinoe Legislative Caucus.

In the extralegal groups framework, entrenchment follows the development stage. However, in this case, there was a bottom-up demand for actual "tax" accountability coming from local residents, and it came at the expense of their own personal safety. According to the framework, speaking out against an extralegal group is unlikely because it is dangerous, and risks angering the Sinoe Group's leaders—with potentially violent consequences. In this moment of speaking out, it could be argued that an attempt at a bottom-up process of statebuilding and empowerment had begun—even if it did not ultimately yield the desired results.

As the government and UNMIL peacekeepers attempted to regain control over the plantation, UNMIL officer Eric Perry said that members of the Sinoe Group "were a little hostile, and they wanted to form part of any eventual management team or concession [t]hat was coming."[76] As the government and UNMIL failed in its successive attempts to regain control over the rubber plantation, the extralegal group grew increasingly confident of its ability to maintain control of the area. By 2008, the Sinoe Group was fully entrenched in the local political economy. Given the isolated location of the Sinoe plantation, it seemed unlikely that the government would be able to successfully project its power into an area as remote as this.

In November 2008, the County Superintendent for Sinoe, Sylvester Grigsby, moved to have Worjlah (Garteh's deputy) and eight other members of the Sinoe Group arrested after a confrontation with local police in which someone was shot, and a house and a car were set on fire. Worjlah "White Flower" and the other members of the group were charged with arson and intent to commit murder. At this point, the plantation's operations were completely shut down. It was not clear whether the situation would improve because the group had been weakened or whether its members would choose to retaliate with violence. The violent confrontations also made it difficult for UNMIL to act because its neutrality would have been compromised if it had supported Grigsby's actions by acting against the Sinoe Group and its supporters. But by February 2009, the Sinoe Group leaders were released without charge.

[75] Zeze Evans Ballah (2008); Public Agenda (2008).
[76] Rebecca Murray (2009).

In 2009, UNMIL officer Eric Perry reported that, "The local community residents were begging for intervention because since 1990 there has not been any social service provisions—there were no schools, no clinics, absolutely nothing."[77]

The theoretical framework suggests that once an extralegal group becomes entrenched, it becomes difficult to destroy it or co-opt it—yet contrary to expectations, several of its leaders were arrested. What happened? The answer can largely be found in the steep drop in international rubber prices from 2008 to 2009 (see Figure 5.2). The decline in prices made it more difficult to continue paying government officials who needed to be paid. Meanwhile, the decline in revenues was compounded by the fact that local tappers had exhausted the rubber trees through continuous slaughter tapping.[78]

What is most interesting about the Sinoe Group was that there was a brief period during which it had succeeded in transforming itself into an organization that resembled a modern cooperative. There were opportunities for members to jointly manage operations, and there was some degree of community legitimacy (though this support was fleeting).

The group also had another key attribute of a cooperative—which was that it allowed its members to directly partake in profits. Yet it was operating outside the law laid down by the government in Monrovia. At that point in 2006 and 2007, the group could have chosen to commit itself to bottom-up statebuilding. And indeed, that is exactly what it had originally promised to do—but it broke its own promise and group members pocketed the profits instead. For six years, the Sinoe Group managed to maintain control of the plantation, in spite of repeated government efforts to reclaim it.

When Superintendent Grigsby finally moved to have Worjlah and the Sinoe Group leaders arrested, a space was finally created for bottom-up statebuilding. But that is not what happened. Instead, locals allege that Grigsby himself picked up right where Garteh had left off: the original Citizens Welfare Committee was renamed the Sinoe Trust Fund.[79] The Fund began charging a tax of $100/ton of rubber. The previous pattern of taxation that had been set out by the extralegal group had morphed into a standard model of corruption with the Superintendent allegedly pocketing a substantial portion of the tax money for himself in exchange for authorizing the SRP's activities. For local tappers, one pattern of entrenched corruption had simply been replaced by another.

In response, the Ministry of Agriculture then blocked the Sinoe Trust and appointed its own interim management team. In early 2009, the two groups

---

[77] Ibid.

[78] The international price of rubber (TSR20) dropped from U.S. $2.50/kg in 2008 to $1.80/kg in 2009, but the local price drop was more dramatic.

[79] *The Analyst* (2008); Rebecca Murray (2009).

struggled for control of the Sinoe plantation.[80] It was not until late 2009 that the dynamic shifted in favor of the government.

On November 30, 2009 local police officers, with the assistance of the Emergency Response Unit of the Liberia National Police, assumed control of the plantation. Two weeks later on December 15, Minister of Labour Tiawan Gongloe and Minister of Agriculture Florence A. Chenoweth gave the official order to end illegal tapping on the Sinoe plantation. A few days later, an interim management agreement was signed with the Lee Network. After years of ex-combatant control and veiled threats of violent uprisings if the Sinoe Group was ever to be displaced from the plantation, the transition turned out to be uneventful. Having learned from the Guthrie operation, the government co-opted most of the local tapping population into the new arrangement. Six years after the war had officially ended, the Liberian government finally had full control over its territory again.

But why had Sinoe taken so long when the Guthrie plantation had been reclaimed so much earlier? Clearly, the contestations over ownership and management—both legal and physical—created uncertainty. And even when the Ministry of Agriculture confirmed that Mesurado was the rightful owner in 2005, it was unclear whether this decision had the support of the rest of Cabinet. Only in 2007 did the Ministry of Justice back up this decision, confirming that the plantation was owned by Mesurado. At that point, the Sirleaf government asked UNMIL to reclaim the plantation in order to install an interim management team (as on Guthrie). However, the UN was unwilling to do so unless the Liberian government was going to ensure that any interim team would be held to account for financial management and community development. For its part, the Sirleaf administration did not want to be seen "reclaiming the plantation from the combatants to hand over to the Tolberts, a prominent Americo-Liberian family."[81] The result was a stalemate: UNMIL refused to reclaim Sinoe for the government, just as the government did not want to be perceived as pushing UNMIL to do. During this time, the Sinoe Group grew stronger, and tensions continued to build.

OTHER PLANTATIONS

In addition to Guthrie and Sinoe, there are five other major rubber plantations spread out across Liberia: Firestone, LAC, Cavalla, Cocopa, and Salala. Yet extralegal groups did not develop on all of the major plantations, but only on Guthrie, Sinoe, and to a lesser extent, on Cocopa and Cavalla. Delving deeper into the rubber sector, another question arises: Why did extralegal groups develop on some plantations, but not others?

---

[80] U.S. Department of State (2009).   [81] Ibid., para 24.

The theoretical framework predicts that extralegal groups are most likely to develop in the economic sectors with the lowest barriers to entry. The logic of this argument is predicated on the motivations of individuals with a capacity for violence but limited skills and capital, thus leading them to self-select into sectors that are easy to enter such as rubber tapping. However, given the large number of rubber farms both large and small, these individuals also need to make an additional choice of plantation. Which plantation should they choose?

In choosing a plantation, it is reasonable to assume that these individuals apply the same criteria again: which plantation has the lowest barriers to entry? For ex-combatants who were already occupying a rubber plantation, staying in place would have made the most sense. However, some plantations were clearly seen as more vulnerable than others. At least part of this perception of vulnerability depended on the status of the plantation's ownership and management contracts. Where ownership and management contracts were in dispute, concession holders were not providing the same level of security—companies contesting ownership did not have the same incentives to guard an investment that might end up in someone else's hands. Consequently, plantations without secure contracts and ownership structures attracted more individual ex-combatants. In turn, the larger the number of ex-combatants that are headed to a specific place, the stronger the signal to other ex-combatants that a particular plantation is vulnerable to takeover. In some cases, official operations ceased completely as the occupation by extralegal groups was sorted out; the subsequent turmoil over management and control also made it easier for extralegal groups to reorder the local economic landscape.

Of the cases where there have been either attempted or successful extralegal rubber groups, a key condition links them together. What Cavalla, Cocopa, Guthrie, and Sinoe all had in common was that their concession and management arrangements were in dispute at the end of the war and the legitimacy of these agreements was constantly being challenged by the local population, competing companies, and various levels of government.

In contrast, on plantations where management contracts were secure, companies spent substantially more on security arrangements and maintained tighter control over their operations. For example, taking over the Firestone rubber plantation was not perceived as a realistic possibility—the company had an airtight contract with the government of Liberia which it was willing to legally and physically enforce. There was no ambiguity about the status of the contract. This provided the proper incentives to invest in and protect the plantation; in turn, this made it unlikely that there would be an unwanted influx of rubber tappers and thus, no demand for extralegal groups.

Table 5.1 shows that at the end of the civil war in August 2003, most of the major rubber plantations were in the midst of either an ownership or

Table 5.1. Status of concession and management contracts at the end of war[82]

	Cavalla	Cocopa	Sinoe (SRP)	Guthrie	LAC	Firestone	Salala
Concession Holder on Aug 18, 2003	Disputed. SIPEF vs. Government	Disputed. Liberia Company (LIBCO) vs. Government	Disputed. Mesurado	Government	LAC (owned by Inter- cultures)	Firestone (Bridgestone)	Salala (ACOMO)
Management Agreement as of Aug 18, 2003	Disputed. SIPEF vs. MODEL	Disputed. RUBREMICII vs. Government	Disputed. RUBREMICII vs. Mesurado	Disputed. General Resources Corp. vs. Agro Resources	LAC	Firestone	Salala
Aug 18, 2003 Occupied by Extralegal groups	MODEL Yes	GoL militia Attempted	MODEL Yes	LURD Yes	MODEL No	Firestone No	Salala No

82 See Rubber Plantations Task Force (2006), p. 4.

management dispute or both. The exceptions were LAC, Firestone, and Salala—the same plantations where extralegal groups did not develop. On the other four plantations, there were attempts to establish extralegal groups—with mixed success.

The concession dispute over the Guthrie plantation illustrates how the uncertainty of the ownership situation created a disincentive to protect the plantation itself. Court documents laying out the case between the General Resources Corporation (GRC) and the Government of Liberia show that UNMIL was unwilling to remove Guthrie's extralegal group and provide security in the area.[83] Consequently, GRC was not going to make its promised U.S. $1 million investment in the plantation. In turn, this led to the government cancellation of GRC's contract, creating further uncertainty in the ownership status of the plantation. The result of all this was that no stakeholder was incentivized to consider the Guthrie Plantation's long-term interests.

So far in this chapter, the focus has been on the extralegal groups that successfully formed on the Guthrie and Sinoe plantations. This following section will briefly discuss two less successful attempts to establish extralegal groups on the Cavalla and Cocopa plantations. While the focus of this book is on extralegal groups that have succeeded, it is also important to note that extralegal groups can also fail. Indeed, it is likely that many more extralegal groups have failed in Liberia and that we know little about them precisely because of their limited lifespan.

Cavalla Rubber Plantation

The Cavalla plantation is situated next to the border with Côte d'Ivoire, close to the port city of Harper. At the end of the war, much of the southeast was controlled by MODEL forces, including the Cavalla plantation. After being managed by a succession of companies throughout the civil war, MODEL commanders eventually gained control of the area and put Camille Chrafeddine in charge of the plantation from the end of the war through to September 2004.[84] Like the Guthrie and Sinoe plantations, Cavalla was occupied at the end of the war by ex-combatants. MODEL's goal was to retain control of the plantation, just as their counterparts had done on the Guthrie and Sinoe plantations.

MODEL and Chrafeddine were lucky: the ownership and management of the Cavalla plantation was under dispute. Officially, the Belgian company SIPEF owned at least 50 percent of the Cavalla concession in partnership with the Liberian government; however, it was unclear as to whether SIPEF

---

[83] General Resources Corporation (2006).   [84] *Maryland County News* (2007).

also owned the other 50 percent of the concession. SIPEF contends that it had paid $2 million toward a loan that the Liberian government owed a Belgian company in exchange for the other 50 percent of the company. The transaction supposedly went through the Liberian company LPCC, but when the company went bankrupt, the $2 million could not be found. During this time, while the ownership and management were under dispute, MODEL took full advantage of the uncertainty, installed Chrafeddine, and established its own structure of control.[85]

Unfortunately for Chrafeddine, different factions of ex-MODEL fighters competed for control of the plantation in the aftermath of the war.[86] These factions were unable to unite and no single faction was able to dominate; this lack of unity prevented any single group from conclusively taking over. Without a dominant group to quell the violence and establish stability, UNMIL had no choice except to respond with force. There were months of firefights before UNMIL prevailed.

In September 2004, UNMIL finally reached the Harper area and peace-keepers forcefully disarmed the MODEL fighters.[87] At the time, even though the war had already ended, UNMIL was still in the process of pacifying the country and consolidating control. Peacekeepers had a Chapter VII mandate, and though some parts of the country were peaceful, this was by no means true throughout the country. Overall, the security situation was still quite tenuous, and the instability on the Cavalla plantation added to Liberia's political uncertainty.

Given the weakness of the transitional government, UNMIL had to decide whether it would confront, co-opt, or ignore the different extralegal groups which were trying to take over the rubber plantation. Far from Monrovia, and with the worry of ex-MODEL rebels defecting to fight in Côte d'Ivoire, UNMIL had greater freedom to act on its Chapter VII mandate and used its military power to definitively root them out of Cavalla. Without this commitment from UNMIL peacekeepers, ex-combatants would not have ceded the Cavalla plantation back to the government. It was only after UNMIL's intervention that the Maryland Legislative Caucus and the NTGL was able to force Chrafeddine off the plantation.

The theoretical framework also suggests that once a group has built up a local power base and become entrenched, it is unlikely to give up local control without some resistance. Accordingly, while the reclamation of Cavalla was ultimately successful, different nascent extralegal groups on this plantation continued to pose a threat to the local security situation for several years after the initial government takeover in 2004. There is evidence that some

[85] On December 1, 2007, the Cavalla plantation was taken over by Salala Rubber Industries. See ibid.
[86] Global Witness (2004a).   [87] UN DDR Resource Centre (2008).

ex-combatants tried unsuccessfully to re-take the plantation in March 2006.[88] According to an UNMIL officer who was familiar with the situation, this was not the first time that the ex-combatants had attempted to regain control of the plantation after they had been forced to hand it back to the local authorities.[89]

After UNMIL finally secured the Cavalla plantation in the fall of 2004 and handed it back to Gyude Bryant, head of the transitional government. The NTGL initiated a new bidding process for the management of the plantation. Soon after, Agro Management Associates was awarded a contract to manage the plantation for four years.[90] However, the situation on the plantation itself was still not stable. The management agreement came to be disputed as a result of a flawed bidding process, which in turn jeopardized the management agreement for a further six months. In addition, there was also a major labor dispute over unpaid wages that eventually led to a workers' strike in early 2005.

In the end, what was critical to the successful takeover of the Cavalla plantation was that the confrontation occurred early in the development of the extralegal group, when it had not yet developed substantial organizational capacity through taxation, and before it had become deeply entrenched in the local fabric. It was also significant that violent conflict between competing extralegal groups created more violence than was tolerable to UNMIL—rather than having one extralegal group resolve disputes and enforce contracts, the conflicts between multiple extralegal groups only further jeopardized the peace.

The success of the Cavalla reclamation can also be evaluated in light of UNMIL's willingness to confront the extralegal group (See Chapter 2, Table 2.2). At this stage of the post-conflict transition, UNMIL was the de facto government, and it was in a strong position to make decisions on the dismantling of armed groups because it had the UN mandate to do so. This particular case demonstrated the effectiveness of treating the problem early in the life cycle of the extralegal group—even at the risk of losing peacekeepers' lives.

Cocopa Rubber Plantation

The Cocopa plantation is located in the northeast corner of the country, in Nimba County, close to the border with both Côte d'Ivoire and Guinea. Like Sinoe and Cavalla, Cocopa is also far from the capital; during the rainy season, it is virtually unreachable by road. The region is remote enough that national authorities in Monrovia do not have any real control over it, and in addition, the ownership and the management of the plantation were both in dispute.

---

[88] World Food Programme (2006).   [89] UNMIL Civil Affairs Officer (2007).
[90] Maggie Daems (2004); UNMIL Human Rights (2006).

In 1949, the Liberia Company (LIBCO) signed a concession agreement with the government for forty years. In 1967, this contract was extended for another forty years with the proviso that a set percentage of the plantation would be cultivated by 1987. In the middle of the civil war in 1996, LIBCO sublet the plantation to the company RUBREMICII,[91] which was owned by Roland Massaquoi, the Minister of Agriculture at the time. When the war ended, the nature of these agreements came under dispute.

Through the second part of the civil war, there was a clear command structure in the GoL forces that controlled the area, but this structure gradually disintegrated after the war ended. At the end of the war, Government of Liberia forces occupied the Cocopa plantation. In this area, the DDR process began in August 2004, but by April 2005, groups of GoL ex-combatants were roaming around like bandits, looting everything in sight.[92] No single group was able to dominate the area and short-term interests reigned supreme.

By the summer of 2006, there appeared to be as many as ten different groups that were either competing for control of the plantation or regularly stealing tapped rubber and other valuables.[93] At one point in May 2006, the plantation was so overrun with looters that it had to be shut down for almost a week. This assortment of groups was tapping illegally, stealing from local residents, and terrorizing plantation workers. They were reportedly armed with "machetes/cutlasses, knives, single barrel guns, and AK-47 rifles."[94] In August 2006, former GoL commanders including Washington Clay and Buku Vaye made the most serious attempt to take over the plantation, injuring several people and causing an evacuation of the area around the plantation.[95]

As the government's reclamation of the Guthrie plantation looked more and more imminent through the summer of 2006, the various Cocopa groups knew their time was limited given the government's aggressive stand. They responded by intensifying their looting and attacks. As the frequency and severity of attacks increased through the end of the year, there was less and less to loot. Soon, workers were abandoning the area because the security conditions had deteriorated dramatically.[96] There was nothing left to take. These events bear out the predictions of Olson's roving bandit model.

Returning to the theoretical framework, part of the process in the successful formation of an extralegal group requires the consolidation of control over an area. This was never achieved on the Cocopa plantation. Those, like Washington Clay, who wanted to take over the plantation and run Cocopa the same way that the Guthrie Group were doing, were simply unable to unite

[91] RUBREMICII also has formal management rights over the Sinoe Rubber Plantation.
[92] Mensiegar Jr Karnga (2005).
[93] Michael Kpayili (2006); Marcus Malayea (2006); Ishmael F. Menkor (2006).
[94] *The Analyst* (2006a).
[95] Solomon Gaye (2006); Michael Kpayili (2006); Marcus Malayea (2006).
[96] Public Agenda (2006).

or subdue the other groups sufficiently to create order and monopolize violence in the area. Too many groups wanted to provide extralegal governance and none of them prevailed.

CONCLUSION

This chapter provides the first practical test of the extralegal group framework. The evidence from the rubber sector demonstrates that the theory was relatively successful at explaining the development and entrenchment of extralegal groups but that the evidence for the emergence stage was mixed (as with the emergence of the extralegal group on Guthrie).

The tentative findings from this chapter support the hypothesis that areas with high concentrations of ex-combatants (as predicted by low barriers to entry for a particular economic activity) encourage the emergence of extralegal groups. The Guthrie and Sinoe Groups exemplified the most successful of these entities, developing and strengthening their organizational capacity through the tax collection process. The end result was that these extralegal groups briefly created independent power bases that undermined national and international peacebuilding, local security, territorial consolidation, and central statebuilding efforts.

In spite of the cycle of entrenchment predicted by the theoretical framework, the Guthrie Group and the Sinoe Group demonstrated how an extralegal group that appears to be entrenched *can be dismantled or co-opted and shifted toward a path of state-led statebuilding.*[97] While the strategy for dealing with the Guthrie situation was complex, the Sirleaf government's handling showed that success is possible. First, the careful process of building a political consensus at the national level, as well as a community consensus, established a legitimate case for more active intervention measures by the government. Next, the divide-and-conquer strategy that whittled away at the loyalties of ex-combatant fighters (through DDR incentives) shrank the group's active support base. The final takeover by the police was backed by a robust security presence from UNMIL. Among the low-level group members who remained, local tappers were co-opted by offers to purchase rubber at slightly higher prices than those being offered by the Guthrie Group.

Having learned from Guthrie, the government employed a similar multi-stage strategy with Sinoe—though this effort was not as neatly executed and suffered numerous setbacks. On the Sinoe plantation, the legitimacy of the extralegal group had already been chipped away for several years by the time

---

[97] Note that statebuilding, simply by virtue of being state-led, does not necessarily lead to an improvement in outcomes. Other actors may actually be better placed to serve the public interest.

the government reclamation process began in earnest in 2009. The national consensus for action against the group had long been established by the findings of the 2006 Rubber Task Force. When the County Superintendent unexpectedly jumpstarted the process with the arrests of Worjlah "White Flower" and associates, the balance of coercive power shifted away from the Sinoe Group, and the organization was unable to recover from its loss of leadership. The subsequent government takeover—conducted by the national police *without* UNMIL support—proceeded uneventfully. The lessons of Sinoe and Guthrie suggest that a coordinated, multi-staged approach to dismantling entrenched extralegal groups can work well, provided that there is political support at the local and national level, and robust security provisions in place.

From the Cavalla situation came a different lesson: a direct, physical confrontation of an extralegal group is more likely to succeed in the earliest stages of emergence, when there is a single actor (in this case, UNMIL) that has a mandate to use force. While other difficulties ensued after UNMIL became less directly involved with Cavalla, the initial reclamation of the plantation was a success.

A comparison of the qualitatively different outcomes on Sinoe vs. Guthrie suggests that the outlook on extralegal groups need not be dire. Local ownership—through the leadership structure and through profit-sharing—merits further consideration for those interested in strengthening the state, and also for those who want to preserve the public interest. In the first instance, it is important to note that there were fewer complaints about Garteh and the Sinoe Group leadership as compared to Sumo Dennis and the Guthrie Group. The fact that Garteh was from the area and was a member of the local ethnic group likely caused him to moderate his interactions with the local population. The other way in which local ownership may have mattered is in the taxation arrangements: taxation was more predictable and Sinoe tappers kept more of their profits, creating an important alignment of interests with the leaders of the Sinoe Group. This reinforced the strength of the group and provided a financial incentive for the broader membership to stand behind the Sinoe Group leadership.

Another issue that was briefly discussed in this chapter is why extralegal groups developed successfully on some rubber plantations but not others. The evidence points to two related factors: how secure the concession ownership and management rights were perceived to be and whether the concession holder maintained a robust security presence on the plantation. Both of these factors affected where individual ex-combatants' decided to begin tapping.

Finally, this chapter also spoke briefly to nascent extralegal groups that never fully developed. Why did the attempts on Cavalla and Cocopa fail? Aside from the obvious efforts of UNMIL in restoring government authority and the internal conflicts on each plantation between an assortment of groups, it should also be noted that local populations did not share in profits. When

UNMIL assumed control, there was little local resistance. On Cocopa, in particular, none of the groups had local support, nor did they try to cultivate any. More than anything else, they were locally branded as "rogues"—a catch-all term used to describe thieves and people who have committed a crime. Ultimately, their poor standing made it difficult to mount a successful resistance when the government decided to reclaim the plantation.

While there has been some success in confronting and co-opting extralegal group in Liberia's rubber sector, success has been more elusive in the country's diamond sector. Chapter 6 will focus on extralegal group formation in the diamond industry and illustrate the difficulties that public-minded officials and civil society organizations face in breaking out of the entrenchment stage.

6

Diamonds

The diamond industry has long posed a challenge to government authorities in West Africa. From mining to taxing to exporting, West African governments have struggled to control the supply of diamonds within their territories.[1] In the late 1990s and early 2000s, the problems surrounding the informal diamond economy achieved global ignominy as the diamond trade was implicated in the civil wars of Angola, Sierra Leone, and Liberia. Since this time, researchers have been untangling the relationship between diamonds and civil war using a variety of methodologies including statistics and GIS mapping;[2] qualitative country case studies;[3] as well as interdisciplinary syntheses.[4] The primary focus of this literature has been the civil war context.[5] Early studies focused on the correlation between diamonds and civil war onset and civil war duration using cross-national datasets. The evidence from these studies has been mixed. Building on the early theoretical claims made by Philippe Le Billon,[6] Lujala, Gleditsch, and Gilmore conducted a finer-grained analysis to show that the *type* of diamond deposit matters: kimberlite (primary) diamond deposits reduce ethnic civil war while alluvial (secondary) diamonds increase the risk of civil war.[7] Other analyses have examined how diamonds are used to finance conflict.[8]

---

[1] William Reno (1995).

[2] On diamonds and civil war onset, see Michael L. Ross (2004a); Michael L. Ross (2004b); Macartan Humphreys (2005); Päivi Lujala, Nils P. Gleditsch and Elisabeth Gilmore (2005); Halvard Buhaug and Jan K. Rod (2006). On diamonds and the duration of war, see Paul Collier, Anke Hoeffler and Mats Soderbom (2004); James D. Fearon (2004); Michael L. Ross (2004a); Michael L. Ross (2004b). On diamonds and the severity of war, see Päivi Lujala (2009).

[3] On Angola, see Tony Hodges (2001); Philippe Le Billon (2001a); Rafael Marques and Rui Falcão de Campos (2005). On Sierra Leone, see Paul Richards (1996); David Keen (2005); R. Maconachie and T. Binns (2007).

[4] See Philippe Le Billon (2001b), Philippe Le Billon (2008).

[5] Exceptions include R. Snyder and R. Bhavnani (2005) and F. K. Nyame, J. A. Grant and N. Yakovleva (2009).

[6] Philippe Le Billon (2001b).

[7] Päivi Lujala, Nils P. Gleditsch and Elisabeth Gilmore (2005). See also R. F. Tusalem and M. K. C. Morrison (2014).

[8] Douglas Farah (2004); Philippe Le Billon (2008).

But diamonds are not destiny. Neighboring Guinea shows how diamonds can sit alongside abject poverty without triggering civil war,[9] while Botswana demonstrates how a country's institutions of private property can immunize against war, and create the conditions for high levels of economic growth.[10] More generally, Boschini, Pettersson and Roine[11] find that the diamond curse only applies to countries with low-quality institutions, and that countries actually benefit from diamonds if their institutions are sufficiently robust.

Yet even as the resource curse literature has delved deeply into the macroeconomic pitfalls of an overreliance on natural resources,[12] this literature's implicit assumptions concerning statehood, government, legal frameworks, and the macro-economy typically do not apply to postwar countries. Resource curse theories cannot easily be adjusted and applied to weak states like Liberia, and the resource curse literature has begun to recognize these deficiencies and limitations. Gradually, it is shifting away from cross-national regressions and toward micro-level studies that are better able to identify causal mechanisms and the conditions in which they apply.[13] How, then, can we build on the diamonds and conflict literature to understand the role of diamonds in a *post-conflict* setting? What happens to diamond mining areas after war?[14] Are these areas of rising tension and instability, as some have suggested?[15]

This chapter tackles these questions through the lens of extralegal groups, testing the framework using the BOPC Group in Liberia's diamond mining industry. It builds on the violent conflict and natural resources literature, incorporating insights that take into account a country's overall resource profile, its mode of extraction, its geographical location, and a resource's physical properties to understand how they affect the emergence, development, and persistence of extralegal groups. I examine three ideas that arise from the literature.

First, some scholars have argued that individual resources should not be considered in isolation but, rather, in relation to the rest of the economy. A country's mix of resources matters: the sectors in which extralegal groups are most likely to emerge are those with the lowest barriers to entry relative to other sectors.[16] Second, the mode of extraction is important because the easier it is to extract a resource, the greater the pool of unskilled labor who will be attracted to the sector, creating a greater need for local contract enforcement and dispute resolution. In the diamond sector, this means that alluvial (rather

---

[9] M. D. Bah (2014).

[10] James A. Robinson, Daron Acemoglu and Simon Johnson (2003).

[11] A. D. Boschini, J. Pettersson and J. Roine (2007).

[12] R. M. Auty (1993); R. M. Auty (2001); Jeffrey D. Sachs and Andrew Warner (2001).

[13] E. Nillesen and E. Bulte (2014).

[14] Practitioners have invested more effort in this question. For example, civil society groups created the Diamond Development Initiative: http://www.ddiglobal.org

[15] S. A. Wilson (2013); M. D. Beevers (2015).

[16] D. Michael Shafer (1994); Terry Lynn Karl (1997); R. Snyder and R. Bhavnani (2005).

than kimberlite) diamond mines will facilitate the emergence of extralegal groups. In both relative and absolute terms, the barriers to entry for alluvial diamond mining are low as compared to kimberlite mining.

Third, Philippe Le Billon argues that the distance from the resource area to the capital is critical for reasons of control. Even for a relatively small country like Liberia, Le Billon's argument matters because short distances can take a deceptively long time to travel. This physical and social distance from the capital effectively means that diamond mining areas in the periphery essentially govern themselves. This physical buffer gives extralegal groups room to grow, develop organizational structures, and build up local networks of influence.[17] Finally, a resource's physical properties are important to the development and persistence of extralegal groups. The fact that diamonds have a high value-to-volume ratio makes them easy to smuggle and difficult to tax—giving extralegal groups an advantage in evading government bodies seeking to reclaim control of the trade.

In testing the framework in Liberia's diamond sector, the dynamics of the BOPC case show how diamond mines can continue to pose security problems long *after* the war has ended. Specifically, this chapter will demonstrate that diamond mining areas are still vulnerable to takeover even after war has ended, and that these enclaves become potential hotspots for conflict recurrence. In one sense, it is not altogether surprising that an important source of conflict financing becomes a site of continued conflict in the aftermath of war. But it is important not to forget that we can trace the source of this conflict, in part, back to how we categorize claims of legitimacy: who is mining legally or illegally, formally or informally, legitimately or illegitimately? *These are not simply claims of law, but claims of power.* In Sierra Leone, for example, a coalition of mining companies, the state, and traditional chiefs pushed for more industrial mining at the expense of local, artisanal miners, intensifying community conflict.[18] The characterization of artisanal diamond mining as an "illicit" activity also feeds into the international community's desire to sanitize the industry—even at the expense of miners' livelihoods[19] and schooling opportunities.[20] This is a reminder that wartime economies interact with weak state capacity and informal institutions in complex ways—with long-term implications for statebuilding.

The chapter is divided into two sections. The first section describes Liberia's diamond industry in both historical and operational terms, and will ground the analysis that follows. The second section tests the extralegal groups framework against the BOPC Group, the only extralegal group to emerge in the diamond sector. The chapter concludes with a brief assessment of how well the theoretical framework predicts the general behavior of the BOPC Group.

---

[17] Philippe Le Billon (2001b), p. 570. [18] S. A. Wilson (2013).
[19] Philippe Le Billon (2006); S. J. Spiegel (2015).
[20] R. F. Tusalem and M. K. C. Morrison (2014).

LIBERIA'S DIAMOND INDUSTRY

In Liberia, diamonds have a long and storied history. They were first discovered in the country in 1934, but prospectors soon determined that there were no commercially viable mines. Prospecting efforts continued, but it was not until the 1950s that diamonds played a substantial role in the local economy. This change arose primarily because large deposits were discovered next door in Guinea and Sierra Leone, leading to massive quantities of stones being smuggled into Liberia whereupon they were officially exported to Belgium.[21] When tighter export controls were imposed by the government of Sierra Leone in the 1960s and 1970s, diamond exports dropped. In the domestic mining sector, prospecting activity had dried up entirely by the 1980s.[22]

Despite the fact that commercial diamond mining never took off in Liberia, there are several known diamondiferous zones in Liberia.[23] The largest of the three areas is in the western part of the country along the Lofa river basin. It stretches across the counties of Lofa, Gbarpolu, and Grand Cape Mount. The second diamond mining area is located in Nimba County starting just north of Saclepie and ending around Saniquelle—it is about a quarter the size of the Lofa diamondiferous area. The third and newest diamond mining zone is located in the southeast, in Sinoe County, on the premises of the BOPC plantation. While diamond mining later became an important part of the Liberian economy, it is critical to remember that the size and quality of Liberia's diamonds in these areas has never reached the standard of those in Sierra Leone and Guinea.

It was not until the late 1990s, during the civil war, that Liberia became a diamond smuggling hub once again. In neighboring Sierra Leone, the Revolutionary United Front (RUF) in Sierra Leone was mining diamonds to finance a brutal civil war.[24] Next door in Liberia was Charles Taylor, a close ally and political supporter of the RUF. When the Security Council imposed sanctions on Sierra Leonean diamonds in 2000, Taylor assisted the RUF in creating a workaround by selling them arms in exchange for diamonds.[25] These diamonds were then sold to local dealers and exported out of Monrovia. In response, the Security Council extended sanctions on rough diamonds to include those originating from Liberia as well.[26] While the sanctions were

---

[21] Diamonds were smuggled to Liberia because it was the easiest place in the region to obtain U.S. dollars and dealers wanted to be paid in a hard currency.

[22] Lansana Gberie (2004).   [23] Ministry of Lands Mines and Energy (2000).

[24] Ian Smilie, Lansana Gberie and Ralph Hazelton (2000); John L. Hirsch (2001); David Keen (2005).

[25] Panel of Experts on Sierra Leone (2000). In fact, during Charles Taylor's trial at the Special Court for Sierra Leone, the prosecution argued that Taylor had command and control power over the RUF, thus indirectly controlling the Kono diamond mines (Initiative Open Society Justice (2013)). Ultimately, the court did not accept this argument.

[26] UN Security Council (2001b), B6.

inconvenient for the Taylor regime, they did not put an end to diamond exports. Instead, diamonds that were once openly carried into Belgium were simply being smuggled past Belgian customs officials.

Even though UN sanctions on the importation of rough diamonds originating from Liberia were put in place in March 2001, this embargo—intended to prevent Sierra Leone's diamonds from reaching international markets—was often and easily evaded.[27] Separately, the pace of diamond mining within Liberia actually picked up after the war ended in 2003—even though diamond sanctions remained in place. While a small number of mining companies received official licenses from the Ministry of Lands, Mines and Energy (MLME) to conduct exploratory mining, most of the diamond mining initiatives were illicit operations run by small-scale artisanal enterprises.[28]

Sanctions and Extralegal Groups

The UN embargo on rough diamonds affected extralegal groups in several ways, in spite of the fact that the country's domestic diamond mining industry was not the original target of the sanctions.[29] Sanctions created three indirect problems. First, by driving the diamond trade underground, sanctions forced the government out of a regulatory space that it otherwise would have occupied after the war ended. This had consequences for the diamond trade in the postwar period: UN sanctions were only partially successful at halting the flow of diamonds out of Liberia because the government had no mechanisms in place for regulation. Consequently, when the war ended, the UN diamond embargo was kept in place while Liberia faced the challenges of a growing domestic diamond mining sector. However, the government was caught in a bind: it could not regulate the industry because formally, the diamond industry was not supposed to exist. How could the government be expected to regulate an industry that it was responsible for prohibiting? In this way, sanctions created a regulatory power vacuum. This was an opportunity ripe for exploitation.

The second problem created by diamond sanctions was that they exposed UNMIL's unwillingness to act against the BOPC Group. The diamond embargo inadvertently revealed how poorly sanctions were actually enforced, and they revealed UNMIL's ambivalence in "assist[ing] the transitional

---

[27] Ibid.

[28] In Liberia, mining rights are owned by the state and a license from the Ministry of Lands, Mines and Energy is required to operate a mine. With the exception of exploratory licenses, the Ministry did not authorize any diamond mining licenses during this time.

[29] Liberian-mined diamonds were only included within the sanctions regime to close a potential loophole ensuring that Sierra Leonean diamonds could not be passed off as Liberian diamonds.

government in restoring proper administration of natural resources."[30] In its multiple failed attempts to shut down the BOPC mines, UNMIL lost reputational credibility at the local level. These failures dealt a blow to how the UN was perceived in Sinoe County, where BOPC was located. Not only did UNMIL's failure to act encourage the BOPC Group, but it also demonstrated to Liberians that sanctions would not be enforced because the UN lacked the political will or the professional capacity—or both—to enforce sanctions. These problems only served to strengthen extralegal groups more generally, and the BOPC Group specifically.

The third problem with UN sanctions was that they incentivized the creation of smuggling networks. The more stringently the diamond embargo was enforced, the more creative these networks became and the more difficult they were to detect. As diamond smugglers gained greater experience at operating illicitly because of the sanctions regime, they were also developing personal relationships and building social capital that would facilitate illicit transactions in the future. By the time the BOPC Group emerged in the post-conflict period, the smuggling networks and organizational infrastructure for the clandestine diamond industry were already in place. In short, sanctions spurred the creation of these networks and unintentionally strengthened them, benefiting the BOPC Group.

The Global Market and the Domestic Market

From 2005 through 2016, global diamond production has fluctuated from a high of 177 million carats (2005) to a low of 120 million carats (2009).[31] Since 2010, global diamond production has stabilized at roughly 130 million carats (Table 6.1).[32] Relative to other diamond producers, Liberia's industry is quite small. While production has been gradually increasing since the end of the war, even with its highest production levels in 2015, Liberia is still only producing 69,000 carats worth U.S. $31 million. Globally, Liberia produces only a tiny fraction of the world's diamonds.

Domestically however, the diamond industry has been an important part of Liberia's postwar economy. In spite of UN sanctions imposed on Liberian diamonds in 2001, mining continued throughout and after the war, contributing substantially to the informal economy. To put the relative importance of the diamond industry into perspective, Liberia's formal GDP in 2004 was

[30]   UN Security Council (2003b).
[31]   Yury Spectorov, Olya Linde, Pierre-Laurent Wetli, et al. (2012); Olya Linde, Aleksey Martynov, Ari Epstein and Stéphane Fischler (2016).
[32]   Olya Linde, Aleksey Martynov, Ari Epstein and Stéphane Fischler (2016).

Table 6.1. Official Liberia rough diamond production 2007–15[33]

	Volume (carats)	Production Value (USD)
2007	21,700	$2,657,542
2008	47,007	$9,891,785
2009	28,368	$11,260,573
2010	26,591	$15,954,534
2011	41,932	$16,183,202
2012	41,985	$16,164,275
2013	53,699	$19,680,742
2014	65,822	$28,175,134
2015	68,576	$31,459,636

estimated at $492 million[34] while the value of Liberia's domestic diamond production was estimated at $13 million to $50 million annually.[35]

Another consideration is that the mining industry has been a major employer in a subsistence economy. During the war, it was estimated that 20,000 to 30,000 Liberians were dependent on the alluvial diamond trade.[36] In the postwar period, 10,000 to 50,000 people worked in the diamond sector. Critically, the alluvial diamond mining keeps busy those who would be the most capable of challenging a weak government, and it supports the livelihoods of up to 450,000 dependent family members.[37]

The Diamond Value Chain

After the stones are mined, most rough, uncut diamonds usually make their way to Antwerp, Belgium or a smaller regional trading centre. They are then sorted and sold in batches to a small and select group of firms called "sightholders," who then sell them to diamond traders, who further sort them by size and quality. Higher quality stones are provided with a Kimberley Process certificate to prove their origin before being sent out to be cut and polished, primarily in India.[38] They are then sold at one of twenty-eight registered diamond bourses around the world.[39] Here, wholesalers and

[33] Kimberley Process (2015).
[34] This figure underestimates economic activity in Liberia because it fails to measure the informal and illegal economies, which are both sizable. For example, the GDP figure would have failed to include the diamond industry while UN sanctions were in place.
[35] As estimated by the Kimberley Mission of Experts, February 14–18, 2005. See p. 40, UNDP Liberia (2005). A more conservative estimate of $10–17 million has been offered by a member of the Panel of Experts. See Caspar Fithen (2005), Woodrow Wilson Center (2006).
[36] Panel of Experts on Liberia (2002).   [37] UNDP Liberia (2005), p. 40.
[38] For more information on the Kimberley Process, see http://www.kimberleyprocess.com
[39] World Federation of Diamond Bourses (2017).

Table 6.2. The global diamond value chain for 2010[40]

	Value added at each stage (USD billions)	Value at each stage, as % of production value	% of Value Chain
Production value	12.0	100%	19.9%
Production sales	0.3	103%	0.5%
Sales by sightholders/dealers	0.2	104%	0.3%
Cutting & Polishing	5.0	146%	8.3%
Polished diamond sales by dealers	0.7	152%	1.2%
Jewelry manufacturer sales	16.8	292%	27.9%
Retail sales	25.2	502%	41.9%
TOTAL	60.2		

retailers can buy them either as loose stones or pre-set in jewelry. In the final step of the supply chain, consumers purchase these diamonds from retailers.

Yet not all parts of the supply chain are created equal. Table 6.2 shows the "value added" at each step. The largest increase in value occurs at the retail level where diamonds are significantly marked up. To put this table into perspective, it is helpful to evaluate the numbers in light of the size of the global diamond industry. From 2007 to 2016, the worldwide sale of rough diamonds varied from a low of U.S. $8 billion in 2009 to a high of $16 billion in 2014.[41] In contrast, between 2005 and 2013, the annual retail value of the diamond jewelry industry ranged from a low of $59 billion (2009) to a high of $81 billion (2015).[42]

In this study, the term "production" is central. In many countries, the producer is simply a mining company and production value represents the diamond sales of the company. But there are other cases, especially in Africa and in artisanal mining communities, where the term "producer" masks another supply chain. In these cases, a rough diamond may change hands several times before it reaches a person who would be formally considered a "producer." The producer hierarchy, as it operates in Liberia and other parts of West Africa, is discussed in greater detail below.

The Political Economy of Mining

In order to think about the producer supply chain, it is necessary to first understand the physical process of mining. There are two types of diamond

---

[40] See p. 22, Gerhard Prinsloo, Yury Spectorov and Olya Linde (2011).
[41] Olya Linde, Aleksey Martynov, Ari Epstein and Stéphane Fischler (2016), Figure 4.
[42] Statista (2017b, 2017a).

deposits: kimberlite (primary) and alluvial (secondary). With kimberlite deposits, diamonds are typically buried in deep rock. If these diamond pipes reach the surface, wind and water erosion scatter the diamonds to create alluvial deposits along shorelines and river banks.

With kimberlite deposits, a significant capital outlay (usually in the range of millions of dollars) is required to import the equipment needed to excavate, blast, drill, and crush the ore. For this reason, kimberlite diamonds are usually mined by companies because the barriers to entry are too high to be mined by individuals. In contrast, alluvial diamonds can be mined with or without expensive equipment. For artisanal mining, this process typically entails digging deep pits into an area where a river or stream might have passed.

In its most basic form, alluvial mining is back-breaking work. Diggers typically work in teams as small as four and as large as twenty. Usually, tasks are rotated within the group; they begin by digging massive pits that are several meters deep, removing the layers of rock and soil that lie over the diamondiferous layer. This process lasts from a few days to three weeks. The piles of gravel that have been dug up are then washed by hand using sieves. Any diamonds that are left in the sieve are picked out. In some groups, the concentrate may be sifted twice by a second group member with more sorting experience to ensure that a diamond is not mistaken for a pebble and accidentally discarded.

In Liberia's forests, the mining pits are three to four meters deep. In other parts of West Africa, the mines may run as deep as twenty or thirty meters. Many miners work waist-deep in water and mud as they dig and sift for diamonds. Some groups have access to a pump which is used to lower the water level while other groups make do without.

The Supporter System

In Liberia and other West African countries (Guinea, Sierra Leone, Côte d'Ivoire), the supporter system is used in artisanal diamond mining.[43] In simple terms, supporters provide the financing while the diggers provide the labor. Framed optimistically, the supporter system is a venture capital arrangement whereby diggers offer their labor in exchange for daily rice rations (about 0.5 kg) and the opportunity to sell any diamonds they find to their "supporter." Those working under more generous arrangements may also receive a daily allowance of U.S. $0.10 to $0.50.[44] Much depends on luck: a

---

[43] For a comprehensive overview of the system, see Alfred Zack-Williams (1995) and Gavin M. Hilson (2006).

[44] Robert Powell and Mohamed Yahya (2006).

digger might go for months without finding anything only to suddenly stumble upon a bonanza of gemstones.

Viewed critically, however, the supporter system exploits the poor by selling desperate people the dream of striking it rich. Diggers receive subsistence wages in exchange for hard manual labor. Yet even if a valuable stone is found, diggers are forced to sell it to their supporter.[45] The supporter sets the price for the diamond, takes a share of the profit, pays the on-site supervisor or pump owner, and distributes the remainder to the diggers. All mining operations have an on-site supervisor who enforces these rules. The supervisor could be the mine owner (the person who owns the concession and all of the diamonds that are mined), or the supporter's agent, or the dealer's agent.[46]

A typical diamond transaction might see revenues shared as follows: On-site supervisor 10 percent, Supporter/Broker 45 percent, Diggers 45 percent.[47] Yet this breakdown is deceiving because diggers are forced to accept the selling price set by the Supporter/Broker. In the supporter system, diggers have no leverage because they are completely reliant on the Supporter/Broker to finance the operation.[48]

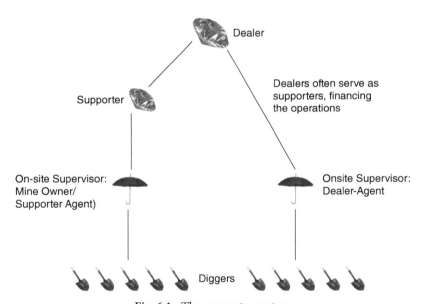

Fig. 6.1. The supporter system

---

[45] Ibid.   [46] Mohamed Yahya (2007).
[47] Based on interviews with diamond diggers, see BOPC Diggers' Focus Group (2005). Also see expert interviews with Mohamed Yahya (2007) and UNMIL Human Rights Officer (2005).
[48] UNDP (2005).

Diggers are usually very poor—too poor to finance their own mining activities. In Liberia's diamond mines, some diggers are ex-combatants, but many are not. Most are either local farmers who are mining in the off-season while others are nomadic miners from other parts of Liberia or West Africa.[49] Diamond mining is a regional industry in West Africa; any hint of a new diamond mine can lead to instant migration across the region's porous borders.[50]

In absolute terms, the barriers to entering the Liberian diamond mining industry as a digger are very low.[51] Ultimately, all that is required are shovels, spades, sieves, tents, and rice. Sometimes equipment is provided by the supporter. Sponsoring a small group of diggers for a few months of work could cost as little as a few hundred dollars.[52] For a larger group of diggers with more equipment, it may cost a supporter several thousands of dollars in operating expenses before the venture becomes profitable. Given the lack of available capital in the postwar period, the pool of potential supporters (local businessmen or diamond dealers) is limited in a small country like Liberia.

On-site supervisors act as intermediaries, keeping a close eye on the operation on a day-to-day basis, ensuring that any diamonds that are found make their way back to the supporters. On-site supervisors represent the supporter's financial interests in the project and usually work on a commission basis. It is also possible for diggers to finance their own operations, though this is less common and occurs perhaps 20–30 percent of the time.

Further up the chain, in the relationship between supporters and dealers, it is the dealers who set the price of stones. In West Africa, dealers are predominantly Lebanese. In Monrovia, most of them can be found on Randall Street in the downtown area. These dealers maintain a de facto oligopoly in the region, effectively depressing the price offered for rough stones. The dealers export the uncut stones to Antwerp or another diamond trading hub. The price at which these diamonds sell once they are exported to Antwerp represents the "production value" referred to in Table 6.2.

Within such a system, supporters often provide some form of "unemployment insurance" to their diggers.[53] For example, diggers who contract malaria are still fed and given medicine. In theory, diggers can also abandon their "masters" at any point in time to work at another mine or for a different employer. In practice, this is often not possible though. Conversely, if a mine is not profitable, a supporter can close up shop and abandon the diggers without financial compensation.

---

[49] Robert Powell and Mohamed Yahya (2006).
[50] Alfred Brownell (2005); Alfred Brownell (2007b).
[51] However, certain skills are helpful. For example, the ability to quickly distinguish a rough diamond from a pebble: these look similar to an untrained eye. The historical involvement in the regional diamond industry of some groups (such as Mandingos) confers a production advantage. Yet even though spotting more diamonds makes a group more profitable, it is still physical labor that drives artisanal mining.
[52] Mohamed Yahya (2007).   [53] Diamond Company Manager (2009).

THE BUTAW OIL PALM COMPANY (BOPC) GROUP

There are three regions in Liberia that have been actively mined for alluvial diamonds: Lofa Bridge, Nimba, and BOPC.[54, 55] Following the theoretical prediction that extralegal groups are likely to emerge in alluvial diamond mines (but not kimberlite mines), this section focuses on the Butaw Oil Palm Company (BOPC) plantation and the extralegal group in this area. The goal of this section is to test how well the theoretical framework predicted the development of this particular extralegal group.

While there is some evidence that other extralegal groups also emerged in the Lofa Bridge and Nimba regions, this chapter focuses on BOPC. Under ideal conditions, all three alluvial mining areas would have been analyzed and compared to provide the most comprehensive picture of the alluvial diamond sector. Unfortunately, this was not possible for logistical reasons in the immediate aftermath of the war. The paucity of information about these other areas made it particularly difficult to triangulate information from multiple, reliable sources. The biggest difference between BOPC and the other two mining areas was that it received a much larger influx of miners in the postwar period. The framework suggests that conditions on BOPC were more likely to facilitate extralegal groups compared to other alluvial diamond mining areas of Liberia, since demand for contract enforcement capabilities would have been more sought after.

Background

BOPC is located in Sinoe County, in the southeast of Liberia, far from Monrovia and big city life. The plantation itself covers a vast territory of 850,000 acres (or 3440 km^2) and the diamond mining site is near the Upper Taso/Baffu Bay area of the plantation.[56] To reach the mining area, it is a three-hour (50 km) drive from the county capital of Greenville through miles of bush to reach the point in the road closest to the mining town of Shampe. From there, it is a full day's hike to reach the gateway town that services the various mining camps located deep in the bush. Considering its location in the middle of rural Liberia, the town offered an impressive range of goods and

---

[54] UNMIL's Greenville office was extremely helpful in conducting research on this area, as was Alfred Brownell of Green Advocates.

[55] A number of kimberlite mining areas have also been recently discovered, and, as hypothesized, they have not hosted any extralegal groups.

[56] Before the civil war erupted, BOPC was once an important oil palm plantation and processing facility, but the focus of the plantation shifted to alluvial diamond mining in the spring of 2005.

services by Liberian standards: cold beer, basic supplies, a movie club, and even a brothel. When I visited in 2005, business was booming.

The rise of BOPC as a mining concern began when the firm Royal Company was given a gold mining license by the Ministry for Lands, Mines, and Energy on May 31, 2005. The company had already conducted exploratory work in the area and rumors had emerged that the company was in fact searching for diamonds and not gold on the BOPC lands. Once Royal began their operations, it became obvious that this was indeed the case: the diamond mining machinery imported into the area did not escape local notice. Facing an uproar from local residents, the Ministry moved to quickly cancel Royal's mining license, but by this time, word had spread throughout West Africa that the BOPC area was rich with diamonds.[57] The influx of miners began almost immediately—despite UN sanctions in place against the export of rough diamonds from Liberia.

Migration to the region soon became overwhelming. By mid-June of 2005, there were approximately 5000 people in and around the plantation.[58] Thereafter, hundreds of people poured into the mining site each day. Hopeful miners arrived in Greenville carrying supplies that would last them for several months in the bush. In spite of an official ban on mining activities in the BOPC area by the Ministry, the number of miners continued to increase steadily. UNMIL and local authorities variously cajoled and warned the miners to stop mining and leave the area. They were ignored. By that time, many people had confirmed that diamonds were indeed plentiful. The crowds kept pouring in.

In mid-July, 2005, estimates of the mining community on BOPC had risen again. By August, the UN and others estimated that between 17,000 and 24,000 residents were occupying an area that had previously housed fewer than 500 people. The UN also estimated that 90 percent of BOPC's new migrants were ex-combatants.[59] This analysis would have varied depending on how "ex-combatant" was defined and how the status of any new arrival would have been determined. Consider, for example, that many of those who fought in the war were "irregular fighters"—those who were only occasionally mobilized for major battles.[60] While 90 percent seems an improbably high estimate, the proportion of newly arrived miners with combat experience was nonetheless substantial.

In early August 2005, there was a brief respite from the population influx as a spontaneous mass evacuation occurred in the wake of a deadly cholera outbreak. It is estimated that hundreds of people died during this period.[61]

---

[57] The license was cancelled on June 8, 2005.
[58] UN Joint Mission Analysis Cell (2005f).
[59] UN Joint Mission Analysis Cell (2005d).
[60] See the section on Fighters in Chapter 4 for a more detailed discussion.
[61] In the midst of the crisis (August 15, 2005), the death toll ranged from 29–135. See p. 6, UNMIL and World Health Organization (2005).

Within the mining community, the fatalities were attributed to "demons." Shortly thereafter, ritual sacrifices were performed and the area was considered "cleansed." Miners swiftly repopulated the area. By early September 2005, the population had swelled back to 10,000–15,000 and mining activities resumed apace.[62] When the rainy season ended in November 2005, population estimates for the area had reached as high as 50,000. Even in June 2008, the population estimates for Paris camp, the largest of ten or so mining sites on the plantation, had an estimated population of 10,000.[63]

Emergence and Early Entrenchment

In 2005, the BOPC population swelled, deflated, and swelled again, bringing out tensions between the original non-mining community and the newly arrived miners, as well as between the miners themselves. Inevitably, the sudden rise in population, commercial activity, and wealth created numerous personal and business disputes.

The BOPC area housed a high concentration of ex-combatants engaged in an activity that the government could not regulate. Nonetheless, the diamond trade persisted in this environment, even though there was no secure way to enforce business agreements given the myriad problems with the police, the judiciary, and the rule of law. For example, as miners flooded BOPC in the summer months of 2005, violent disputes over diamonds broke out in the area with at least one documented stabbing death.[64] In addition, the government also reported a series of "armed clashes" which resulted in fatalities.[65] In spite of these violent episodes, diamond mining continued.

In the absence of other governance mechanisms, the extralegal groups framework posits that an entity will emerge to provide dispute resolution and contract enforcement, and that this entity is backed up with coercive force. Evidence from the BOPC situation supports this stage of the framework.

The group's behavior suggests that the BOPC Group did not emerge consciously as an organized entity. Instead, disputes arising from the influx of residents required intervention from those who had the authority to enforce a resolution—namely, powerful ex-combatants. Some of these ex-combatants had been appointed chiefs during the course of the civil war. Locally, these new chiefs were loyal to two local powerbrokers: Nelson Paye and MacDonald Tarpeh. These men were critical to the leadership of the BOPC Group.

---

[62] See UN Joint Mission Analysis Cell (2005e); UN Joint Mission Analysis Cell (2005g); UN Joint Mission Analysis Cell (2005c).
[63] Panel of Experts on Liberia (2008a), para 115.
[64] UN Joint Mission Analysis Cell (2005d).
[65] UN Joint Mission Analysis Cell (2005h).

Both Paye and Tarpeh had served as NPFL commanders during the early part of the civil war and they later became generals in MODEL. Tarpeh had once been appointed by MODEL to serve as the Acting District Superintendent for Sanquin Statutory District; Paye became an employee of the Ministry of National Defense when the war ended.[66] Both men were prominent commanders in Sinoe County during the civil war and were regarded as powerful figures in the community; both commanders had strong ex-combatant followings.[67] Tarpeh was named by the Truth and Reconciliation Commission as a war criminal.[68] Each one was in a strong position to draw on the conflict capital that they had each built up over the course of fourteen years of civil war.

Paye set up a mining camp for himself (named Paye Camp).[69] It was monitored by trusted ex-combatants who had previously fought under his command, and the BOPC Group as a whole was managed by Tarpeh. Tarpeh himself was a member of the Tassu, the ethnic group based in the BOPC area; this was critical for obtaining the support and cooperation of local community leaders. In fact, the group's leadership structure included key community leaders such as the town chief and the town mayoress.[70]

When disputes among the new arrivals arose on BOPC, it was the town chief who formally resolved them. However, it was Tarpeh's coercive authority that reinforced these decisions. For example, disputes over women were not uncommon. Newly arrived diggers would rent "wives" from the local brothel. These women would live with the miner for a fee and the brothel owner would also receive a fee. When miners disputed over a "wife," the brothel owner would attempt to settle the dispute first. If this effort was unsuccessful then those diggers who shared the same supporter would ask their supporter to resolve it. If they had different supporters, they would turn to the town chief, seeking backing from Tarpeh or Paye. Effectively, Tarpeh and Paye resolved these disputes by expressing their preference for one side or the other. This network of implicit coercive support gave the BOPC Group its coercive authority.

Other Sources of Local Authority

How else might we explain this local regime? Rather than crediting the BOPC Group's coercive authority, it is possible that the diggers and the community admired the group rather than feared it. An alternative or complementary explanation is that the BOPC Group may have been perceived as a traditional authority, rather than simply just a coercive one. Yet this seems unlikely given that the

---

[66] UNMIL (2005e).   [67] Ibid.
[68] Truth and Reconciliation Commission of Liberia (2009).
[69] UN Joint Mission Analysis Cell (2005d).
[70] Ibid.; UNMIL (2005d); Panel of Experts on Liberia (2006).

presence of Tarpeh or Paye was critical to settling disputes. This also seems unlikely given the lack of influence of other chiefs from neighboring districts.

In principle, there were several other actors that could have provided local governance: representatives of the central government, the UN, and former (civilian) chiefs and elders. Yet in the years after the war ended, these actors were either unable or unwilling to provide basic governance functions. Government officials in Monrovia did not have the capacity nor the political will to shut down the BOPC mines, but neither could they regulate an activity that they had legally banned. As in other parts of the world, the UN was unwilling to become involved in conflicts that were viewed as "local."[71] And even traditional chiefs and elders who had once served as local mediators no longer wielded much authority in their areas. The Clan Chief of Sinoe County, Emannuel S. Wesseh, expressed how powerless he felt throughout the war years and how this feeling persisted even when the war ended:

> I personally suffered as a chief from all the factions. The NPFL enter my town... As soon as they entered there was no chiefs' business... Everybody became commander...
> So they asked for food, you give them food. If nobody around to carry their loads to the next town, you will carry their load, because you are in their hands and so there were not respect for the chiefs. They say sit down old man, you on the ground now they called you papay. And you are on the ground doing your papay work. And then there were no respect at that time. Because the war way is still in our children... And now there is no chiefs elected, all the chief that were from the war time are still chiefs. No one has come to be elected as chief. So the respect for chiefs are not there.[72]

Another explanation for the emergence of the BOPC Group is that it formed to provide security for the community in an environment of insecurity. This is a common response in areas of insecurity. In Peru, the rondas campesinas (self-defense patrols) filled such a void; in South Africa, the vigilante justice group Pagad meted out vigilante justice; in Guatemala, it was the Civilian Self-Defense Patrols (PAC); in Iraq, Sons of Iraq groups formed in Baghdad neighborhoods in order to protect themselves against local Shi'a militias and the police; in Sierra Leone, the civil defense forces were formed to protect local civilians from the RUF and the AFRC. Even in other parts of Liberia, community patrols of ex-combatants formed in places like Voinjama. However, it was clear that these groups were not formed in self-defense. Self-proclaimed civil defense groups are typically open about their vigilante and patrolling activities—but this was not how the BOPC Group behaved. It never justified its existence with community patrols or local surveillance, not even rhetorically.

---

[71] For another discussion on the UN's reluctance to get involved in local conflicts, see Séverine Autesserre (2010, 2014).

[72] Emannuel S. Wesseh (2008).

Development

Critically, the BOPC leadership (which incorporated ex-combatant leaders as well as local authorities) set up a successful taxation system and applied it to everyone who entered the plantation grounds. In contrast to rubber, timber, and iron ore, it was much more difficult to tax the profits from diamond mining because diamonds can easily be smuggled off-site. To counter the smuggling problem, the BOPC Group decided to tax the *opportunity to mine*. Miners were charged U.S. $50 for access to plots measuring roughly 3 meters x 3 meters in size.[73] Each plot was typically shared by three to six miners. BOPC Group representatives patrolled the camps on a daily basis to ensure that there was no encroachment of boundaries. When the miners returned after the cholera outbreak in August 2005, they found that the plot price had increased to U.S. $100.[74] The increased fee did not seem to be induced by the prospect of an imminent government takeover; rather, it was a supply and demand issue. Fifty dollars was not affecting the demand, so it became clear that there was scope to increase prices. Even those who had previously established plots had to pay an additional fee.

Further, the BOPC Group also charged an entry fee of L.D. $100 (roughly U.S. $2) to access the BOPC site. Not only were miners required to pay this entry fee each time they entered the site, but so were all those who provided supplies and entertainment.

In contrast to the disorganization that I observed in other parts of Liberia, the BOPC tax collection system was set up in an organized manner. Ledgers were used to keep track of miners and maintain a written record of those who had paid their entry and mining fees. Through the process of collecting these taxes, the BOPC Group institutionalized itself. It strengthened its internal organizational capacity as well as its financial capacity. At the same time, taxation created a sense of order and also helped to consolidate the group's dominance over the area. Those who refused to comply had their campsite shelter destroyed and were evicted by local "bush devils"—community members dressed in traditional costumes, donning devil masks. In Liberia, bush devils are powerful symbols and invoke deep-seated fear as well as respect. Being chased out of the area by a bush devil is considered to be harsh punishment; it is equivalent to being cast out of society.

While these institutions may sound foreign, most societies have institutions that serve similar purposes: tax collection, enforcement, and punishment. In place of America's IRS (Internal Revenue Service) and the UK's HMRC (Her Majesty's Revenue & Customs), tax collection is performed by a BOPC Group leader; rather than being enforced by the courts, it is enforced by

---

[73] UN Joint Mission Analysis Cell (2005b).   [74] UN Joint Mission Analysis Cell (2005d).

ex-combatant leaders who form part of the BOPC leadership. Instead of paying a severe fine like in developed countries, the offender's belongings are destroyed; instead of arresting the tax evader, this person is physically and socially evicted from the area by the bush devil.

Yet it was not only the enforcement policies that made tax collection so uniform, but also the physical remoteness of BOPC, even within a relatively isolated county. The hike into the village of Shampe takes several hours from the nearest road: new arrivals are easy to spot. This is an important point because the literature on diamonds suggests that the diffuse nature of alluvial diamonds makes it difficult for the state to maintain control over the resource. In fact, this spatial argument about the control of resources would benefit from more nuance. While the diffuse nature of the diamond deposits is important, what is critical for state control is access to the mining area via roads and other exits. If access to the area is physically restricted, it then becomes easy to set up a checkpoint. In the case of BOPC, there was only one route through the bush into the mining zone. Circumventing this route and clearing a new one would have been physically difficult—and all newcomers would eventually be spotted anyway. There was only one way into BOPC and that was through Shampe town—a single entry and exit point allowed the BOPC Group's tax policy to be more easily enforced.

Further Entrenchment

"Entire communities are benefiting from this industry. They are eating too."

Former County Superintendent, commenting on BOPC[75]

"Townspeople don't know about mining business. We are entertaining people; they come here to buy salt and pepper."

Clan Chief, BOPC[76]

As taxation on BOPC grew increasingly lucrative through the summer of 2005, the BOPC Group acquired more and more resources with which to bribe any official who dared to question its activities or its authority. After a few months of regular "tax" collection, UNMIL reports suggested that the BOPC Group had grown substantially in both power and influence. Liberian government officials at the tribal, county, and possibly national levels were personally profiting from the "taxes" being collected.[77] Correspondingly, the group also became increasingly intransigent about revealing where its tax revenues had gone.[78] As mining continued, the BOPC Group's influence continued to increase.

---

[75] Former County Superintendent (2005).   [76] Clan Chief (2005).
[77] UN Joint Mission Analysis Cell (2005a); UNMIL (2005c).
[78] UNMIL (2005f).

The Ministry of Mines, Lands, and Energy set one deadline after another banning diamond mining, only to find its pronouncements continually ignored. For example, on June 27, 2005, the County Superintendent confirmed the Ministry's initial ban on all gold and diamond mining at a town hall meeting in Shampe. At this time, the Superintendent provided a ten-day grace period but also stated that anyone who remained on site after July 7, 2005 would be arrested. On July 8, the day after the deadline, another town hall meeting was held to ensure that the ban had been enforced. At that meeting, almost every single local official in attendance agreed that the ban had been upheld and that the miners were leaving the plantation. This included Macdonald Tarpeh (in his role as the District II Commissioner), the Shampe Town Chief, the Upper Clan Chief for District II, the Tassu Tribal Spokesman, the Tassu Mayoress, and the Tassu Paramount Chief. The Tassu Mayoress stated that she had recorded the names of 4282 people who had voluntarily left the camp, and the Tassu Tribal Spokesman said that he had worked with the youth leadership to evacuate another 1500 people from BOPC.

The contrasting quotes at the start of this section illustrate the tensions and what was at stake. On the one hand, the community was thriving economically because of all the illegal diamond mining. On the other hand, consistent denial and the pretense of cooperation was key to maintaining the status quo.

Yet there was clear evidence that officials were not telling the whole truth. Local residents had reported that few people had left the site and that more people were actually entering BOPC than leaving. Government and international representatives were even able to observe for themselves the arrival of new miners entering the site with sufficient supplies for a long-term stay.[79] Not only were new miners entering the BOPC site, but local authorities were publicly telling bold-faced lies to national officials, and also to UNMIL—with no visible consequences.

In an internal memo, UNMIL itself remarked that: "It is unclear whether any deadlines or directives from the government will be heeded since illegal miners, dealers, and buyers, have professed a strong belief that UNMIL and the government do not have the capacity to enforce these."[80] It became apparent that the National Transitional Government of Liberia (NTGL) had neither the political resolve nor the capacity to follow through on its proclamations to shut down BOPC. So the government's hands-off approach continued. The group wanted permanent control over BOPC and they had the support of local authorities.

Interestingly, this evidence provides support for the framework but also diverges from it. The need for local contract enforcement and some form of regulatory authority in this environment set the stage for the emergence of the

---

[79] UNMIL (2005e).   [80] Ibid.

extralegal group—which is consistent with the framework. However, in the case of the BOPC Group, the local authorities were involved from the outset rather than being compromised when the BOPC Group gained organizational and financial strength.

While the theoretical framework shows the three stages of extralegal groups as being sequential, this was not the case with the BOPC Group where Emergence and Entrenchment occurred in parallel. This effectively meant that local authorities were financially benefiting from the mining activities right from the beginning instead of waiting until after taxation had strengthened the group's organizational clout. The effects of early entrenchment were most apparent when UNMIL and other international actors demanded that diamond mining on BOPC be stopped immediately, and local leaders simply ignored them.

In the theoretical framework, the issue of compromised local authorities comes to a head when the state needs its agents (local authorities) to reassert control over the area. On BOPC though, emergence and entrenchment happened together. Given its nascency, the extralegal group did not initially pose a threat to government or to the state, so it was left alone. Instead, it was only later on, as the BOPC Group became wealthier and better organized, that entrenchment really began to undercut the government's plans.

Local Security Threat

There were also signs that the BOPC Group presented a significant local security threat. Given the unstable political situation in 2005 leading up to the October election, the worry was that the BOPC threat would have a domino effect on other, similarly volatile areas such as the Guthrie and Sinoe rubber plantations.

An internal UNMIL report noted that one of the two local police officers that had been assigned to cover Shampe was "stripped of his uniform and almost beaten by a group of people . . . for trying to enter the gold and diamond mining area."[81] This incident underscored the volatility of the situation. While there is not sufficient information to determine if the BOPC Group had orchestrated it, the important thing is that the miners and local residents *believed* that the incident was set up as a show of force by the group's leaders. Although this explanation was contested, it was viable, in part because the individual did not die in the incident. This indicates that something held the mob back from doing what many angry Liberian mobs often do—which is to beat the targeted individual until they are dead or nearly so.

---

[81] Ibid.

In another incident, the Joint Security Team in Sinoe made confidential plans to establish a new checkpoint at the Sinoe Highway entrance of BOPC—only to find this information quickly leaked. By the time the Security Team realized that their plans had been made public, the BOPC leaders had already charted and cleared an alternative route to the mining site.[82] The Joint Security Team consisted of representatives from the County, UNMIL, the police, the Ministry of National Security, the National Security Agency, and the Bureau of Immigration and Naturalization, so the information could have been leaked by anyone, but UNMIL suspected that the information was most likely to have been shared by local officials.[83]

Certainly, it was clear to the local community and the miners that anyone who dared to work against the interests of Tarpeh and the BOPC Group would pay a price for their disloyalty. This message was further reinforced when the Superintendent of Sanquin Statutory District was threatened with physical harm and death by Alfred Payne[84] (a former NTGL commander and a former leader in the Tassu defense force) and Arthur Dworh. The superintendent had dared to defy the BOPC Group by speaking out about how diamond mining was continuing in spite of the ban. Later, he attempted to find out about the tax money that had been collected on BOPC—neither of these actions made him popular with the BOPC Group.[85] Notably, this was the only local official who was willing to publicly speak out against the BOPC Group.

The State's First Response: Ignore

After an extralegal group has developed some organizational and financial capacity, the theoretical framework suggests that it will adopt a medium-term time horizon for territorial control. In the case of the BOPC Group, the actions of the leaders suggest that they were reasonably confident of their tenure over BOPC in the medium term. They did not try to tax the miners at unreasonable rates as would be expected if they only had short-term expectations. Yet the leadership also did not behave as if it expected to hold on to BOPC in the long run. Outside of basic security, the only other public good that the Group assisted with was securing space for a much-needed public marketplace.

For its part, the NTGL never displayed a genuine interest in stopping the mining. The government paid lip service to international concerns by enacting a local ban on diamond mining after the initial influx of miners began, but it made little effort to enforce the ban. Indeed, at the time that the BOPC Group was emerging, the NTGL may have had *de jure* authority over the area, but it was so weak militarily that it could not have enforced the ban anyway.

---

[82] Ibid.
[83] UNMIL Civil Affairs Officer for Sinoe County (2005); UNMIL Human Rights Officer (2005).
[84] Also referred to as Alfred Pyne. [85] UNMIL (2005f).

UNMIL could have provided military support to help the NTGL enforce the diamond mining ban and in fact, the Special Representative of the Secretary-General (SRSG) Jacques Klein was asked by Lands and Mines Deputy Minister Fayia for assistance in monitoring the BOPC situation. However, Klein declined on the grounds that it was not in UNMIL's mandate and claimed that the mission lacked the resources to undertake this problem.[86] Thus, without the clear support of local authorities and UNMIL, a direct confrontation with the BOPC Group was simply not a realistic option for the NTGL.

When President Sirleaf first took office in January 2006, the BOPC situation was one of several ongoing crises confronting the government. The BOPC diamond mining operations still showed no signs of letting up and the newly elected government had to decide how to respond. Yet faced with many urgent problems and the need to quickly fulfill campaign promises, the situation at BOPC was initially not seen as a priority. During most of 2006, the BOPC Group simply continued as before, with key members acting as arbiters of disputes and indirectly providing contract enforcement as well as some degree of public order. Tax collection also continued during this period.[87] When diggers had finished mining one plot, they would pay the requisite tax for a new plot and continue mining.

When the Sirleaf administration confronted the problem, it found itself with three choices: it could ignore the group, co-opt it, or confront it. Each of these choices carried its own risks. The biggest concern was that a confrontation would result in violence and consequently destabilize the country or damage Liberia's reputation for recovery with the international community. This risk was real and significant. Indeed, it was argued in Chapter 2 that the dynamic that emerges between extralegal groups and their national governments is that of a race to build organizational and financial capacity—if not managed carefully, this race could lead directly to a return to war.

An Attempt to Co-Opt

By early 2007, there were signals that UN sanctions on the export of rough diamonds would soon be lifted. At this point, co-opting the BOPC Group became a viable option for the government. In anticipation of the moment that sanctions were to be lifted, a survey team from the MLME visited Paris camp on the BOPC plantation in March 2007. This visit posed several problems that illustrate the difficulties of co-optation. In the first instance, the BOPC Group and its Tassu leadership became angry that the Ministry was granting mining licenses without consulting them or asking their permission when the area in

---

[86] Global Witness (2006).   [87] Mohamed Yahya (2007).

question was considered traditional to the Tassu. Further, the team from MLME also did not communicate to the miners why the site visit was taking place. The miners only knew two things: that they were each to be charged U.S. $260 in order to have their claim legally surveyed and registered with the government, and that the official who sent the team was James Konowa. At the time, Konowa was Assistant Minister for Mines, Mineral Resources Development and Conservation. He was also infamous among the miners for accepting bribes in exchange for doling out prime mining concessions. Members of the mining union had complained in the past about Konowa, but to no avail. When they found out that he was the one who had sent the team, the miners became noticeably hostile.[88]

An Unsuccessful Confrontation

Having upset the leaders of the BOPC Group *and* the miners, the Ministry's survey team faced an angry crowd of thousands. Police backup was called in from Greenville, but the surveyors from MLME remained vastly outnumbered. After a few days on BOPC, the government surveyors and the police were forced to retreat—at machete point. Soon afterwards, Konowa was fired—ironically not because of his incompetent handling of the BOPC visit, but because he was charged with corruption.

Through poor planning and unintended consequences, the Sirleaf government had accidentally triggered a confrontation with the BOPC Group. Through this confrontation, the government had also unwittingly revealed how weak its hand was. As articulated by researcher Shawn Blore, "The survey incident should serve as a strong signal to the Ministry of Lands and Mines. Post civil-war, neither the ministry nor other Liberian authorities are strong enough to enforce their dictates in the field by decree."[89]

In summary, the trajectory of the BOPC Group's development followed a path that was similar to that laid out in the theoretical framework. While it did not match up at every stage, the logic and behavior of this extralegal group are broadly consistent with the theoretical framework.

CONCLUSION

To put the BOPC Group into local context, this chapter began with a description of Liberia's diamond industry and its links to smuggling networks. It argued that the institution of UN sanctions laid the foundation for the emergence of extralegal groups. The chapter then described the local mining industry and the

---

[88] Shawn Blore (2007).   [89] Ibid.

inner workings of the supporter system before testing the extralegal groups framework against the case of the BOPC diamond mining group.

The evidence from the BOPC Group reveals strengths and weaknesses in the extralegal groups framework. As predicted, the need for an entity to resolve disputes and mediate local business transactions was met by a group that was backed informally with coercive power. As the group began to tax, its organizational capacity strengthened, thereby increasing its local influence. These tax revenues were allegedly used to sway the interests of local author-ities. In these ways, the evidence from BOPC is consistent with the theoretical framework.

On the other hand, this case also shows that the three stages of emergence, development, and entrenchment are not as neat in practice as they are in theory. These stages can actually blend into one another or occur in a different order. In this case, local community leaders and other authorities formed part of the BOPC Group from the very beginning. At this point, emergence and entrenchment occurred jointly. This was followed by the development stage, and then deeper entrenchment—by which time the BOPC Group was able to lay claim to a substantial local power base, creating a significant security threat with potential spillover effects into other areas.

Overall though, this exploration of the BOPC Group and Liberia's diamond industry illustrates how this extralegal group posed a significant security threat at different times, certainly at the local level, and arguably also at the state level too. At the same time, this case study also demonstrates that local governance structures, even if they are "extralegal," can still be useful for improving local security, and perhaps even form a nascent version of local statebuilding.

7

Timber

"Even though the checkpoint is gone, they still stop and pay their taxes out of fear, in case the rebels come back."

UNMIL Regional Officer, Zwedru[1]

From the air, Liberia is a country of bright green abundance. Approximately 45 percent (4.3 million hectares) of the county is covered in forest.[2] In fact, the largest remaining contiguous portion of the Upper Guinea forest can be found in Liberia. In the north and northeast, the Upper Guinea forests cover Lofa and Bomi counties, and in the south and southeast, the remaining tract of these forests stretches across Rivercess, Grand Bassa, Sinoe, Grand Gedeh, Maryland, Nimba, and Grand Kru counties. As a result, Liberia's timber industry has long been one of the most important sectors in the national economy. While forestry has always played an important economic role in Liberia, it was only during the civil war that the industry rose to economic prominence. Through the 1990s, the world's appetite for timber and other natural resources increased rapidly. In spite of the civil war that was raging across large swaths of the country, Liberia was well positioned to take advantage of the commodities boom because of its openness to foreign investors and its historical links to global commodities markets.

By the late 1990s, logging revenues contributed 20 percent of the country's GDP; by 2000, timber made up a staggering 50 percent of Liberia's export revenues.[3] In 2001, as the war flared up again after a period of dormancy, the export of round logs alone was worth U.S. $120–$240 million.[4] Between 1997 and 2001, the production of round logs increased by a factor of thirteen (Figure 7.1). China and Europe were particularly enthusiastic consumers of Liberian timber.

---

[1] UNMIL Regional Officer (2005).   [2] James W. Doe (2005), p. 3.
[3] Shawn Blore (2007), p. 9.
[4] Official exports of round logs were valued at U.S. $80 million, but the UN Panel of Experts estimated that the official exports figure "underestimate[d] real exports by 50–200%". See Panel of Experts on Liberia (2001), para 321.

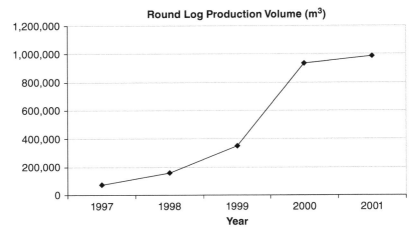

Fig. 7.1. Round log production, 1997–2001

All of this changed abruptly after the UN placed sanctions on Liberia's round logs and timber products in July 2003. As discussed in Chapter 4, the timber sector played a strategic role in financing the Taylor regime during the civil war. After sanctions were imposed, commercial logging virtually ground to a halt as all of the large multinationals left Liberia and took their equipment with them. A few firms were able to evade sanctions and continued shipping by land rather than by sea, choosing to export via neighboring countries,[5] but most companies closed down their operations.

Because timber revenues were perceived to be financing the country's civil war, the shutdown of Liberia's logging industry was widely viewed as an example of how targeted sanctions could succeed.[6] According to official statistics from Liberia's Forestry Development Authority (FDA), the value of the timber trade dropped from over $100 million during the war to $4 million by the time the government had regained full control of its territory in 2006.[7] Although these figures underestimate the size of the industry, they still illustrate the serious drop-off in production after sanctions were imposed.

John Woods, the Managing Director of the FDA during this period, suggested that once timber sanctions were lifted, annual forestry revenues would eventually reach U.S. $15 million to $20 million a year and that 7000 new jobs would be created.[8] The UN Panel of Experts reached a similar conclusion,

---

[5] Global Witness (2005c).
[6] For an exploration of the unexpected and unintended consequences of economic sanctions, and how they fail to achieve their intended political objectives, see L. Jones (2015).
[7] Panel of Experts on Liberia (2006), p. 14.   [8] IRIN (2006d).

suggesting that up to 10,000 people would eventually find work in the forestry sector[9] (though these were optimistic estimates).[10] By 2010, Kamara et al. estimated that 3850 worked in pit sawing and 1500 people worked in retail pit sawn timber, with some additional jobs as timber traders.[11]

While Liberians waited for timber sanctions to be lifted, there was still a burgeoning domestic market to be served when the war ended—especially as post-conflict reconstruction was taking place. Without a commercial logging sector, this demand was met by artisanal loggers, more commonly referred to as pit sawyers. (Pit sawing is also referred to as chainsaw milling.) In the post-conflict period, it was pit sawing that began to pose problems for the state. The state's inability to contain the operations of these groups—in open contravention of Liberian laws—highlighted the fact that the government was incapable of controlling its domestic affairs. Having a nonstate armed group provide regulation for the local logging industry only underscored the significance of the problem. Later, as the logging industry matured and government capacity increased, extralegal groups also adapted. In some cases, they partnered with timber companies—some of whom had been active during the war but had assumed new corporate identities—taking advantage of legal loopholes like Private Use Permits (PUPs). Once it became obvious that this class of permit was being exploited, companies simply switched to another type of logging permit, Community Forest Management Agreements (CFMAs) in order to maintain a veneer of legality.

The problems in the timber sector were manifold and intertwined. As discussed in Chapter 2, in the section on Entrenchment, the state had a weakest link problem. In a remote part of the country like River Cess, the government's determination to tackle extralegal groups was only as strong as its weakest link. The UN Panel of Experts outlined the problem for the timber sector:

> Rule of law is particularly difficult to implement in the leeward counties (outside Monrovia), where slow decentralization undermines the establishment of effective governance. Regional offices, for LNP [Liberia National Police] and the Forestry Development Authority (FDA), for example, have been difficult to maintain because of poor infrastructure and the fact that employees must travel back to the capital to receive salaries. A lack of rural policing undermines the Government's ability to enforce regulations on, for example, natural resources. This facilitates criminal economic networks that exploit unemployed youth, many of whom are ex-combatants.[12]

These were ideal conditions for an extralegal group.

---

[9] Panel of Experts on Liberia (2006), p. 16.   [10] P.L. Shearman (2009).
[11] Jangar S. Kamara, Edward S. Kamara, Letla Mosenene and Francis K. Odoom (2010), p. 177.
[12] Panel of Experts on Liberia (2007), p. 9.

This chapter examines the pit sawing sector and the extralegal group that emerges from the logging industry. The focus is on the Nezoun Group, based in River Cess County, another remote region of Liberia. This chapter tests the theoretical framework against this group. It is divided into four major sections. The first section surveys Liberia's local pit sawing operations in the River Cess area and describes how these operations are structured. The second section examines how UN timber sanctions and the FDA's domestic ban on logging affected the logging industry. The third section compares the development of the Nezoun Group against the extralegal group framework, taking into account the role of conflict capital. The fourth section examines how the confusion in the ownership of timber concessions paved the way for the Nezoun Group.

PIT SAWING IN LIBERIA

In spite of the dominance of commercial logging firms in exporting timber, small-scale logging has long been common practice in Liberia. Locals refer to the practice as pit sawing. In simple terms, pit sawing refers to cutting down trees by hand using chainsaws. No other mechanized equipment is used. Instead of expensive machinery such as skidders (for transporting cut trees to the loading site) and feller bunchers (for cutting and gathering trees), manual labor is used to fell and de-limb trees, transport them to the roadside, and lift them onto truck beds. Since pit sawyers do not have access to road-building equipment or skidders, they are forced to log in forests that are close to major roads, usually within a ten- to fifteen-minute walk to the roadside.[13] An additional difference is that pit sawyers do not always process their logs in sawmills because of local transportation difficulties or expensive sawmill fees. In these cases, pit sawyers opt to mill their wood using a chainsaw at the stump site. Consequently, they end up producing planks that are of lower quality than those processed in sawmills.

Originally, this type of small-scale artisanal logging was carried out by locals who were supplying the domestic timber market for construction and furniture. In the past, the market for pit sawn timber had been limited, but in the post-conflict period, it assumed new importance as other sectors of the economy shrank.

Whereas the big industrial logging firms once supplied local markets, the imposition of sanctions meant that Liberians had to buy their timber from domestic pit sawyers in the years after the war ended. There were no other

---

[13] Francis Colee (2009).

sources. Even though the practice of pit sawing did not directly violate the UN timber embargo, it did undermine the Security Council's end goals as stated in Resolution 1521:[14]

> Urg[ing] the National Transitional Government of Liberia to establish its full authority and control over the timber producing areas, and to take all necessary steps to ensure that government revenues from the Liberian timber industry are not used to fuel conflict

Yet despite the Security Council's expressed desire for the NTGL to establish government control over Liberia's forests, UNMIL peacekeepers did not actively patrol the logging areas. In 2005, as the government began to ask the UN for the easing of sanctions, an official of the Liberian Forest Initiative (an initiative led by the US Forest Service) reported that the country's forests remained unsafe because of ex-combatant logging activities.[15]

To add to the contradictions in policy, UNMIL peacekeepers in charge of monitoring the timber sector were allegedly profiting from trucks full of timber that had to pass through the UNMIL checkpoint at the city of Buchanan, on their way to Monrovia. These practices were confirmed by local sources including the county's UNMIL Civil Affairs officer and circumstantial evidence from a Global Witness briefing.[16] Informal conversations with local residents and local NGOs who operated in the areas suggested that these practices were common knowledge. Complicating matters further is the fact that the UN and other international actors who had pushed for stringent enforcement of timber sanctions had likely purchased banned pit sawn wood for their own projects and construction purposes—contravening the government's ban on domestic logging.

The Crew

A basic pit sawing crew consists of eight to twelve people (see Figure 7.2). As the timber makes its way from the forest to the retail timber depots on the outskirts of Monrovia, other actors are brought in. The capital equipment costs for getting started in pit sawing are relatively high compared to rubber tapping and diamond and gold mining (see Table 7.1). Accordingly, only those with access to substantial capital can afford to begin logging. Often, the owners of the chainsaws are not the actual operators.

For example, in one pit sawing village near White Flower, a few hours drive from Tubmanberg, one pit sawing camp had roughly a dozen people onsite. Unusually, the operator owned his own saw. Logging expert Francis Colee

---

[14] UN Security Council (2003b), p. 4.   [15] Global Witness (2005b), p. 28.
[16] Ibid.; UNMIL Civil Affairs Officer for Grand Bassa County (2005).

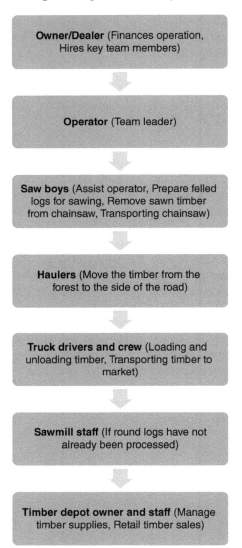

Fig. 7.2. Pit-sawn timber labor supply chain

from the Liberian NGO Green Advocates found that only a small fraction of operators in the River Cess area owned their own chainsaws.[17] In most cases, the operators worked for dealers who financed multiple pit sawing teams. For example, Global Witness documented a visit to an operation with two camp-sites, six chainsaws, sixty-one male workers, and three women. The person

---

[17] Francis Colee (2008).

Table 7.1. Pit sawing expenses, River Cess County[18]

Operation	No. of people	Labor Costs (USD per week)	Other Expenses (USD)	Monthly Cost (USD)
Operator	1	$150		$600
Haulers	4	$100		$1600
Saw boys	3–5	$37.50		$450–$750
Cook	1	$25		$100
Truck drivers, truck rental, and crew		$1500		$6000
Chainsaw/Pit saw		–	$1500 to $1800	–
Fuel, lubricant, maintenance			$500/week	$2,000
Waybill			$360 each	$1440
Truck toll			$160/truckload	$640
Checkpoint clearance			$8/truckload	$32
Total expenses	$12,862 (up to $13,162) + one-time chainsaw cost of $1500–$1800			

financing the operation was based in Monrovia.[19] This was common: Monrovia businessmen would band together and register with the Liberian Pit Sawyers Association of Monrovia. This allowed them to obtain a permit from the FDA to begin logging. The operator who was responsible day-to-day would typically be a mid-level commander (typically, a rank of "general") while the saw boys and haulers were usually made up of rank and file fighters. After the timber was processed at the logging site, it was then sold at timber markets in Monrovia (Red Light, Sinkor, Bushrod Island).

A standard truckload of pit sawn timber (typically 600 pieces) was worth U.S. $2500 to $5000, depending on the size of the boards.[20] Each team could produce roughly one truckload a week for a monthly income of $10,000 to $20,000. Some networks were found to be using trailers and other large vehicles that were able to transport much larger quantities of timber (up to 1000 pieces).

Estimates of what it costs to operate a pit sawing team varied. Moses Gbarpodolu,[21] Manager of Chain of Custody at the FDA, suggested a minimum of $5000/month, while Colee[22] estimates $12,750/month. These figures suggest that each team could make a monthly profit of up to $15,000. This was a sizeable sum in a rural area where most people lived on less than $1/day. While it is difficult to determine the exact number of pit sawing teams that operated during the early post-conflict years, the FDA and UNMIL estimated

---

[18] Adapted from ibid.   [19] Global Witness (2005c), p. 21.
[20] $2500 according to the Panel of Experts; $3354–$4620 according to Colee; $5000 according to Global Witness. See Panel of Experts on Liberia (2005b); Francis Colee (2008); Global Witness (2005c).
[21] Moses Gbarpodolu (2007).   [22] Francis Colee (2008).

that in 2006, there were about 1000 pit sawyers (most of them ex-combatants) operating in about two hundred areas across Liberia.[23] Estimates put the number of pit sawyers operating across Liberia at approximately 6000 people, with 3500 of them located in River Cess County.[24]

UN SANCTIONS, THE FDA BAN, AND POST-CONFLICT TIMBER

While timber revenues helped fuel the Liberian civil war, timber sanctions imposed by the UN Security Council helped end the war. With the passing of UN Security Council Resolution 1521 in 2003, sanctions on round logs, timber, and other forest products were finally put in place, cutting off one of Charles Taylor's most valuable sources of revenue. The UN and NGOs like Global Witness were able to demonstrate that the Liberian timber industry was propping up a violent regime and fomenting war in neighboring countries. Nonetheless, during this period, commercial logging continued at a furious clip—right up to the point that the UN Security Council placed sanctions on the export of round logs and timber products from Liberia. It was only after sanctions officially took effect in July 2003 that industrial logging finally stopped. After the war ended, the Liberian government lobbied intensely to have sanctions lifted. Following extensive discussions and negotiations with the UN and the international community, timber sanctions were provisionally lifted on June 20, 2006. They were fully lifted on September 19, 2006.

While UN sanctions are issued internationally, there are no international authorities to enforce them. Instead, sanctions constitute an export ban for the country in question and an import ban for other countries; it is up to individual countries to enforce UN sanctions. In practice, this is often difficult to do for legal, logistical, and capacity reasons. Consequently, the UN has no leverage over business activities within the borders of a country under UN sanctions.

In Liberia, while UN sanctions officially banned the export of round logs and timber products, sanctions only applied to exports and technically should not have affected domestic logging. Instead, it was up to the FDA to regulate the local forestry sector. To comply with UN sanctions, the FDA instituted a pit sawing ban in 2000 (FDA Regulation #26- The Ban on Pit Sawing/Power Chain Sawing) which remained in place until 2012, when the government finally decided to regulate the industry through Chain Saw Milling Regulation #115-11. During

---

[23] Panel of Experts on Liberia (2005b), p. 12.
[24] Panel of Experts on Liberia (2008b), p. 27 and Francis Colee (2009).

the twelve years that the ban was in place, pit sawing occupied a gray zone. Technically, it was considered an illegal activity—and it remained illegal even after UN sanctions were lifted. Yet for all intents and purposes, government officials turned a blind eye to the trade and the ban was ignored.

Even within the FDA, there was substantial confusion about the official stance on pit sawing. In 2004, some FDA representatives were taxing timber that was transported by truck, but not on foot, while other officials in Monrovia were denying that taxes were being charged at all.[25] The policy banning pit sawing was restated in November 2004—with little effect. Even the FDA itself did not take its own ban seriously: it set up a system to charge for permits and taxed timber shipments into Monrovia even while the ban was still in place. *In spite of its own ban on pit sawing,* tax revenues derived from this practice made up about half of the FDA's budget in 2004 and 2005.[26] John Wood, the head of the FDA at the time, matter-of-factly acknowledged that even though pit sawing was illegal, it was still critical to the economy given the absence of other employment opportunities.[27]

In 2005, annual pit sawing permits were reportedly being issued for $200 apiece. By 2007, this price had risen to $500 plus an additional $700 tax on the team.[28] An additional tax of $0.60/piece of cut timber was also being charged, amounting to roughly $360 per truckload. In an interview at the FDA, Moses Gbarpodolu, the Chain of Custody Manager, indicated that he was aware that the government was taxing an activity that it had declared illegal, but he also felt that a pragmatic approach was warranted. If people were going to cut the timber anyway, reasoned Gbarpodolu, then the government should charge them for this privilege.[29] This approach was supported by the Liberia Forest Initiative (LFI), which helped devise the monitoring system, with UNMIL checkpoints and forest patrols.

Yet the problems arising out of these contradictory policies also *undermined the authority of the FDA and created a space for corruption.* A Panel of Experts report in 2006 suggests that under the National Transitional Government of Liberia, forestry officials pocketed bribes from pit sawyers in exchange for not charging official FDA taxes and fees. Global Witness reported similar allegations made against the FDA officer in the eastern city of Harper: new administrative fees were being arbitrarily imposed on pit sawyers at the local level and it was not clear that these fees were making their way back into the government treasury. A common complaint of the pit sawyers themselves was that FDA staff operated in the regions "only to extract bribes and transport bush meat".[30] The extent to which FDA officers had taken advantage of pit sawing fees was evidenced by the difference in revenues *after* the FDA was

---

[25] Global Witness (2004b), p. 7.   [26] Francis Colee (2009).
[27] AllAfrica.com (2009).   [28] Forest Development Authority (2007).
[29] Moses Gbarpodolu (2007).   [30] Panel of Experts on Liberia (2005b), p. 22.

forced to tighten up its fee collection processes. During 2004 and 2005, when FDA policy was unclear, Liberian pit sawyers paid less than $80,000 in government fees, whereas in the first nine months of 2006 alone, over $485,000 was collected.[31]

At one point, ex-combatants in the pit sawing industry were so angry with the bribes being exacted by FDA officials that when several of the FDA's regional offices reopened in February 2004, they rioted in Buchanan and directly threatened violence against the FDA team in Zwedru.[32] Given that there was still fighting going on in some parts of the country in early 2004, and the factions had not yet been fully disarmed, these threats to the still-fragile peace process were taken very seriously.

Demand for Basic Governance

The acrimonious relationship between the FDA and local pit sawyers is important because it demonstrates why General Kofi and the Nezoun Group became so influential during this postwar period. The conflicts between pit sawyers, local communities, logging companies, and the FDA made it difficult to operate a logging business: some form of on-the-ground regulatory authority was needed.

These events also illustrate in concrete terms why the notion of extralegality is useful. There is no commonly enforced legal standard. What is legal is flexible and adaptable depending on the circumstances and the connections of the parties involved. In these various disputes, it is not clear who is corrupting who—at times, *ex-combatants appear to be organizing against corrupt government officials.* This underscores the point made at the start of the book: there is nothing about the state that is inherently good, and making assumptions about who is a "good" actor or a "bad" actor based on the state/nonstate dichotomy creates problems. What *was* clear was that the government and its representatives were themselves party to the problem, rather than serving as impartial referees.

Moreover, UN timber sanctions and the FDA ban remained in place even after the war ended. After foreign logging firms left Liberia, local networks stepped in to supply the local timber market. Between July 2003 and June 2006, domestic timber was supplied almost entirely by local pit sawyers. Business was brisk: much of the country's infrastructure and housing stock had been destroyed. As the prospects for stability improved, construction began anew and people desperately needed materials to rebuild.

---

[31] Panel of Experts on Liberia (2006), p. 15.
[32] Panel of Experts on Liberia (2004), p. 30.

During this period, local pit sawing networks were dominated by ex-combatants for three reasons. First, as suggested by the extralegal groups framework, the barriers to entering the industry were relatively high (compared to rubber and alluvial mining), but not prohibitively so, particularly for commanders who had accumulated enough wealth to invest in a chainsaw. Second, there was the matter of industry experience: ex-combatants, especially those who had been employed in Taylor's timber militias, were more likely to be familiar with the logging industry and to have the necessary pit sawing skills. Third, there was the matter of conflict capital. Even after the war ended, the sector was still viewed as the purview of Taylor and his associates. The timber industry had a wartime reputation as being violent and dangerous. In the immediate aftermath of the war, with the atrocities of war still fresh in their minds, civilians were reluctant to participate in pit sawing given its association with the most brutal elements of the Taylor regime. UNMIL civil affairs and military observers in the region confirmed that, at least initially, only other ex-combatants would have been willing to work in these conditions.[33]

For these reasons, there was likely a higher concentration of ex-combatants operating in the industry as compared to the rubber tapping and alluvial diamond mining industries (though all three industries were closely associated with the fighting factions). These conditions benefited an influential ex-NPFL commander, allowing him to take control of the Nezoun area (also known as Nizwein or Km85) and to systematically tax the local timber trade.

CONFLICT CAPITAL AND THE NEZOUN GROUP

With its endless acres of forests, one of Liberia's prime pit sawing regions has been River Cess County. This part of the country is considered isolated, even by Liberian standards. Its distant location has traditionally made it difficult for the FDA (and other government agencies) to regulate logging in this area. Even before the FDA's regional offices were looted during the civil war, the closest FDA authority was located in Greenville, at best a two- to three-hour drive away (four to six hours in the rainy season). Historically, this part of the interior has been too far away from the capital to warrant political attention. During the civil war, the area was known because it was a key outpost for the Oriental Timber Company's (OTC's) operations. Within River Cess, there are several pit sawing areas: the most prominent among these include Yarnee district and the road from Nezoun (close to the former OTC camp) near Sayah town.

---

[33] UNMIL Regional Officer (2005).

Table 7.2. The Nezoun Group

	The Nezoun Group
Period of emergence	Wartime
Armed	Yes
Ready to engage in violence	Numerous threats of violence, but limited use of actual violence
Initial organizational strength	Loosely organized, but still a cohesive unit based on combatant relationships; originated as a network of fighters loyal to General Kofi
Organizational structure	Hierarchical, but with freedom to leave and re-enter the group
Activities	Taxation of local timber industry, also direct logging
Entrenchment	Explicit and implicit threats to local population; bribing of local authorities, FDA, peacekeepers

In 2005, UNMIL estimated that there were at least one hundred pit sawing teams in the county, and most of these pit sawyers had once belonged to timber militias.[34] In 2005, the two districts of Central River Cess and Timbo had more than twenty separate pit sawing camps set up, each one with approximately five chainsaws in operation. During this time, it is estimated that five to twenty truckloads of timber were sent from River Cess to Monrovia each day.[35] While it is difficult to estimate the value of this trade, by these estimates, daily timber revenues from these two areas alone was worth anywhere from U.S. $12,500 to $100,000. However, getting the timber out of these areas and into Monrovia came with an obstacle: timber trucks had to travel through territory that was informally controlled by Bob Kofi Zah, a former wartime commander locally known as General Kofi.

This discussion will focus specifically on the timber trade in River Cess County near Nezoun,[36] which was home to the extralegal group controlled by General Kofi. Members of the extralegal group included twenty to fifty ex-combatants from the River Cess area. However, it taxed from a much bigger base of local pit sawyers. In this discussion, I use the extralegal groups framework to consider the activities and behaviors of this group. The legacy of conflict capital will also be discussed vis-à-vis the operations of the Nezoun Group.

Emergence

During the war, General Kofi and the fighters that were loyal to him fought with a number of different factions during the course of the war. These rebel

---

[34] Panel of Experts on Liberia (2005a), para 126.   [35] Ibid.
[36] It is not actually based in Nezoun, but Nezoun is the nearest prominent town that appears on maps of Liberia.

factions included the LPC (Liberia Peace Council), Charles Taylor's NPFL, and MODEL. General Kofi himself was recognized as a critical military leader in the region. Kofi is Bassa, the dominant ethnic group in the area; he is a local; and he has deep connections throughout River Cess County. These factors would have helped him while serving as a quasi-governor for the county during the civil war years, especially in providing dispute resolution and informally setting the rules for the treatment of local civilians.

As the war was ending, Kofi and a small group of youths and ex-fighters began to collect logs left by the OTC. Shortly afterwards, Kofi began his own logging operations and used some of these former fighters to supervise his local pit sawing operations. Over time, Kofi's group came to dominate the local timber trade.[37] Alfred Brownell, head of the environmental NGO Green Advocates in Monrovia, came to refer to the Nezoun Group as the "local timber mafia."[38]

The Nezoun Group appears to have emerged out of the need for local dispute resolution between the Forest Development Authority's tax collectors and ex-combatant pit sawyers. Consistent with the theoretical framework, the revival of local logging created conflict between community residents, Kofi's pit sawyers, outside pit sawyers, and the FDA. There was a clear demand for contract enforcement and dispute resolution within the local logging sector— creating a space that Kofi's Nezoun Group could fill. Conflict capital played a critical role here: the personal networks and military command structures that had developed locally through the war remained intact after the war. Employment prospects in River Cess County were meagre and local ex-combatants trusted General Kofi. His name still commanded fear, respect, and loyalty in the community.

After the war ended, General Kofi continued to serve as a local authority figure and to resolve the disputes arising between local communities, logging companies, pit sawyers and the FDA. As a traditional leader from the community, he had the legitimacy to resolve local conflicts. As the local Big Man, he was also in a position to redistribute the benefits of logging back to the local community—if and when he chose to do so. Kofi, as head of the Nezoun Group, served as the local mediator and power broker. He was in a position to declare how benefits should be shared, who was or was not entitled to bush meat, what to do if food or planks of timber were stolen, how to handle delayed payment, and how to respond when fights broke out over wives and girlfriends.

His role was not without controversy though, especially since his questioning of pit sawyers about the legality of their operations sometimes resulted in the confiscation of their timber as punishment. Under the leadership of

[37] Panel of Experts on Liberia (2005a), para 127; Panel of Experts on Liberia (2006), p. 41.
[38] Alfred Brownell (2010).

General Kofi, "ex-combatants [we]re involved in the trade in almost all the activities like cutting, sawing, loading, and transporting the logs and mediating between community people and traders."[39]

Under ideal circumstances, the FDA or another government entity would have been able to provide business regulation, dispute resolution, and basic forms of governance to the timber sector. But given the reality of postwar financial and capacity constraints, it was clear that the government had neither the desired capacity nor the legitimacy to do any of these things properly. Indeed, the relationship between the Nezoun Group and the FDA was already tense because they were effectively competing against each other for the right to tax.

On the one hand, the FDA staff themselves were perceived as corrupt by locals; on the other hand, FDA staff could not afford to be confrontational with these groups because they were worried that some of the pit sawing teams were armed.[40] The only thing they could do was to remind these armed pit sawing crews that Section 18.16a of the National Forestry Reform Law prohibits armed security guards from working under a Forest Resources License.[41]

Another potential source of regulatory authority should have been the Liberia National Police (LNP), but they were weak, and did not command local respect. UNMIL noted in their county profile of River Cess: "Many a time, people refuse[d]...court arrest in [the] event of LNP acting alone. In such instances, LNP needs the support of UNMIL military to carry out their duties."[42] The profile continued, describing how ex-combatants posed a particular problem because they "denied state authority from time to time." Given these difficulties, dispute resolution had to be enforced by someone who commanded local respect, such as General Kofi and the Nezoun Group. The problem was that this dispute resolution function also allowed Kofi to activate his conflict capital, making it more difficult for peace to fully consolidate in River Cess.

But dispute resolution and contract enforcement were not the only considerations. There was a parallel dynamic that explained the Nezoun Group: it was itself a business entity formed to extract local resources. Like the Guthrie Group, operations had begun during wartime, and then continued on as an informal business when the war ended. General Kofi had been directing his own logging operations in River Cess and had recruited his former fighters to join him in the Nezoun Group. The Nezoun Group was not only a regulator, it also ran its own logging enterprise.

---

[39] UNMIL Civil Affairs (2005e).
[40] Interestingly, the FDA had no problem charging these same teams $400 for pit sawing permits.
[41] Forests Monitor (2008).   [42] UNMIL Civil Affairs (2005e).

These two dynamics jointly drove its emergence: Nezoun Group as local dispute resolution specialists and Nezoun Group as business enterprise. It is difficult to say which dynamic was more important. Reflecting on the counterfactual, if there had not been a need for contract enforcement and dispute resolution, it is unlikely that the Nezoun Group would have established such a dominant presence. Yet even if the group had not been involved in the logging business, something like the Nezoun Group would probably still have arisen to meet the need for local business dispute resolution. Here, the emergence of the group does not follow the theoretical framework exactly, but provides part of the explanation.

There is also the possibility that the Nezoun Group emerged to provide security for local citizens. This seems unlikely though, given that the group made no claims about providing local security at any point. So while security might well have been a secondary reason, it was unlikely to be the primary reason for the existence of the Nezoun Group. It was also telling that no security tax was collected—only a timber tax—from the local population, even though collecting such a tax is typical for local security provision.

The theoretical framework also predicts that some unemployed youth and ex-combatants will gravitate to pit sawing—but not in the same numbers as rubber tapping and diamond mining. Pit sawing is a capital-intensive endeavor compared to rubber tapping and diamond mining. Consequently, there are limited opportunities for participation because the barriers to entry are higher, which means fewer entrants into the sector. With fewer pit sawyers, there should be less conflict, and thus, less of a need for extralegal groups.

Further, pit sawing should be evenly dispersed across the country's vast forest lands, minimizing conflict between different crews. However, a key factor in choosing a logging site is proximity to existing logging roads. Because logs need to be carried by hand, pit sawyers are usually located within a ten- to fifteen-minute walk from a logging road. Consequently, pit sawing teams ended up clustering near existing logging roads since these were most advantageous for transporting lumber, especially given the lack of heavy machinery available for moving and lifting logs. As a result of this clustering, there has been conflict and competition in the areas in and around Nezoun. These conflicts were likely aggravated by Taylor's militarization of the timber industry and the armed status of some local ex-combatant pit sawyers. For example, an interview with a senior FDA official revealed that dispute resolution services were needed in negotiating the boundary between one pit sawing team and another.[43] There were also conflicts with the local population that had to be dealt with, including compensation claims from area residents for logging activities.[44]

---

[43] Senior FDA Director (2005).   [44] UNMIL Civil Affairs (2005e).

Development

While General Kofi and members of the Nezoun Group participated directly in pit sawing themselves, they also began to charge taxes at Yapa Town toward the end of 2003, as timber trucks left River Cess County, just after the war ended. Although Kofi's Nezoun Group began collecting timber taxes at Yapa Town, this arrangement was later replaced by an "official" taxing system set up by county officials, which included the superintendent and members of the Liberian legislature, and had the consent of the FDA. Officially, these tax revenues were supposed to be collected by the Wood Toll Committee on behalf of the FDA and county officials in order to fund local development projects. In practice, however, it was the Nezoun Group that collected these funds on behalf of the Wood Toll Committee. General Kofi was the chair of the committee.

Not only were pit sawyers being taxed by the Nezoun Group, but a subtle, yet important shift occurred through the introduction of the Wood Toll Committee. By linking General Kofi's Nezoun Group to the government's official Wood Toll Committee, "taxation" became official, and the government was now responsible for this money. Extralegal governance had metamorphosed into official government corruption.

Each time a truckload of timber left Yapa Town, a tax of U.S. $160 was paid to the Wood Toll Committee. This money was supposed to be deposited into an official account, but interviews conducted in the area suggest that the revenues from River Cess were never deposited and further, that the existence of the account was questioned by local residents.[45] Indeed, the whole taxation scheme was reformed in 2006 because there were allegations of corruption and mismanagement.

Two years after the signing of the CPA, an interview with an UNMIL official in the region revealed that even though the checkpoints in the area had formally been dismantled, timber trucks were still stopping voluntarily and paying the tax.[46] As suggested by the quote at the start of this chapter, this UNMIL official believed that the practice had continued out of respect and fear of General Kofi and the Nezoun Group. Pit sawyers viewed this tax as serving a dual function: first, as a protection payment because they feared General Kofi's men and the consequences of *not* paying the tax; and second, as an insurance policy, in case the country returned to war, they would have already banked these payments toward future protection.

Later, the timber tax regime was again reconfigured and the FDA instituted a new scheme under which it charged U.S. $800 for each sawing license, again collected by the Nezoun Group on behalf of the Wood Toll Committee.

---

[45] Rivercess County Residents (2010).   [46] UNMIL Regional Officer (2005).

At some checkpoints, the group also collected wood planks as another form of taxation. In some cases, this timber was made available to NGOs for public works, but most of it was resold or used personally by those collecting it.[47] Essentially, General Kofi and his associates were taxing the timber trade— allegedly on behalf of the government—and doing so in an increasingly organized and systematic manner.

The "tax" money collected by the Wood Toll Committee on behalf of the FDA—perhaps all of it—remains unaccounted for and most likely ended up in private hands. In theory, the FDA taxes had been designated for development, but this money was actually being funneled back into the hands of the Nezoun Group and its expanding network of local authorities. While Kofi collected the taxes, local officials would approach Kofi directly for their cut. Unfortunately, it is not clear how this money was distributed among local officials and members of the group. Nevertheless, these informal actors wielded substantial influence in the community.[48] In light of the group's power over other local actors, it is unlikely that any of these tax revenues were ever remitted to the government.

Although there were clear indications that members of the Nezoun Group profited from the taxes being collected, it is difficult to assess whether the group grew stronger organizationally as a result of the tax collection process. One piece of evidence supporting organizational strengthening is that when the Nezoun Group first began to tax, only the extralegal group members were benefiting. However, as local authorities became involved in tax collection, the group expanded. The tax regime became quasi-official; it was sanctioned by the FDA even though it was common knowledge that most of the money was going to Kofi, a group of local officials, and senior members of the Nezoun Group.

While the group did grow stronger as a result of taxation, the dynamics of the Nezoun Group suggest two related mechanisms for organizational strengthening. One of these is articulated in the framework: the *process of collecting* taxes created organizational strength and capacity. Another possible mechanism is that collecting taxes actually *drew local authorities closer* to the Nezoun Group to access a share of the revenues—it is possible that it was this bond to local authorities that improved the group's capacity and finances. In all likelihood, both mechanisms were probably at work: early entrenchment occurred together with strengthening tax collection. Of course it is difficult to evaluate whether the Nezoun Group was controlling the local officials or whether local officials came to control Kofi's Nezoun Group, and to what extent this relationship may have changed over time.

Certainly, in the period immediately following the end of the war, the group was able to take advantage of its high levels of conflict capital. In September

[47] Global Witness (2005a); UNMIL Civil Affairs (2005e), p. 30.
[48] Christine Cheng (2012).

2004, the situation was tense—a full year had passed since the CPA had been signed—a report from Global Witness noted that "much of the interior remain [ed] under the control of armed ex-combatants, preventing the deployment of government representatives and preventing critical oversight of natural resources and security."[49] During this time, the financial and organizational capacity of the Nezoun Group also grew[50] as taxation expanded to include not only the group's pit sawing crews but anyone who drove through the region's major road arteries.

Entrenchment

Once an extralegal group is established, the framework suggests that its leaders will go to great lengths to hold onto the area under its control, including corrupting local authorities and threatening violence in a bid to guarantee access. There is evidence that this occurred with the Nezoun Group. For example, the local population knew that taxes were being collected from the many trucks full of timber leaving the area each day. When locals complained about this in January 2005, General Kofi "threatened to burn down Yapa town if they questioned his authority."[51] Kofi was arrested locally (though it is not clear what he was charged with) but was released shortly afterwards. His threat was taken seriously—General Kofi had a brutal wartime record. Yet even if the political will within the government had existed to address this threat, the local authorities did not have the capacity to follow through: Nezoun only had six poorly equipped police officers, and in practice, only one or two would actually be working. In July 2007, there were only two dilapidated police stations for all of River Cess County.[52]

Aside from persistent taxes and the direct threats of violence against locals, there was another telling indication of the Nezoun Group's local entrenchment. This extralegal group had persisted despite multiple governmental efforts to prohibit pit sawing and reassert territorial control over Liberian forestland, and also despite the fact that regaining control over natural resource areas has been a critical part of UNMIL's mandate. While the broader ex-combatant pit sawing lobby was undoubtedly influential in the government's decision to accept pit sawing despite its own official ban, General Kofi and the Nezoun Group likely helped shape this decision. At the time, both the

---

[49] Global Witness (2004b), p. 10.

[50] It is possible that the group grew stronger because influential local officials were attracted into its ranks when they recognized the taxation potential. Under this scenario, organizational capacity was not developed "in-house" but instead through attracting outside "talent." Yet there is little evidence that this occurred at a meaningful scale.

[51] Panel of Experts on Liberia (2005a).

[52] County Development Committee (2007), p. 10.

Ministry of Agriculture and the FDA had both been allocated to MODEL as part of the terms of the Comprehensive Peace Agreement. Given that General Kofi had recently fought for MODEL, it seems reasonable to expect that he would have lobbied MODEL Cabinet members to allow pit sawing to continue uninterrupted through the tenure of the NTGL. Later, General Kofi began organizing community demonstrations against companies who had been given logging concessions in the area. These demonstrations were aimed at protecting the group's core economic interests and also to enhance his reputation as a community "protector."

The Nezoun Group's relations with the local population have also been tense. Certainly, in the immediate aftermath of the war, locals were still frightened of General Kofi and his "boys"—the memory of bloodshed was still fresh enough that people did not dare to openly defy the group. General Kofi was an important local elder and still retained legitimacy because of his "local protector" status.[53] And yet, over time, local residents were also becoming vocal about the fact that the group was collecting "taxes" without any benefits being returned to the community. When those tensions escalated in January 2005, the repercussions of letting the Nezoun Group evolve without any state intervention or regulation became apparent: the state realized that it could not control the group, even when it threatened violence. This makeshift strategy of accommodation gave rise to a semi-autonomous network that was willing to use violence, and capable of holding the government hostage to its demands. Although the Nezoun Group did not pose a threat to the survival of the Liberian state or the Liberian government, it was still powerful enough to cause a violent episode that would have destroyed Liberia's façade of peace. This would have been disastrous for the country.

There is little doubt that the Nezoun Group had the cooperation of some well-placed local officials. However, the group also needed the help of Sector One peacekeepers in order to be able to send their timber shipments through. Interestingly, when UNMIL peacekeepers in Buchanan were asked directly about timber being transported from Nezoun to Buchanan, they denied that there was any significant timber movement even though it would have been impossible to ignore the multitude of timber trucks passing through that checkpoint on a daily basis.[54] To be fair, there was no political will to stop the domestic timber trade since it did not seem to be fueling any organized rebel movement. Consequently, some local UNMIL peacekeepers opted to turn a blind eye to the timber shipments and others chose to impose their own version of a checkpoint tax instead.

---

[53] For example, in this retelling of his role in the war, Kofi casts himself as community protector. See Tod Whitwer (2009).

[54] Global Witness (2005a).

Opportunities for Statebuilding

Like Liberia's other extralegal groups, the Nezoun Group established a local power base and successfully controlled the local timber trade. But beyond creating a stable environment for local trade, it did not go any further in providing public goods. With the decline of the Nezoun Group's conflict capital, there was an opportunity for the government to transform the pit sawing industry into a sustainable community forestry sector, providing local employment, and importantly, a share of timber taxes for public goods. At that moment though, there was so little trust in government. And the government had neither the desire, capacity, nor credibility to carry out this type of reform.

To restore local confidence, someone had to do some statebuilding—even if the state itself was not interested in leading it up. At the local level, the Nezoun Group had the most significant governance capabilities in terms of its capacity for violence and tax collection. It also had a stronger local presence and substantial local influence. The group was actually well placed to expand its authority not just to rule, but to govern. This transition though, of *rebalancing and aligning individual material interests of a powerful elite and mapping them on to a collective, public interest*—is one of the defining challenges of building a state.

In contrast, the state also had an opportunity to strengthen governance through the FDA, the police, and local officials. Yet even though Monrovia officials agreed with the international community that statebuilding was the most desirable outcome, the reality was that people found it extremely difficult to trust the state. Given the abuses that the Taylor government had wrought upon the area, the predatory nature of the Doe regime, and the years of pervasive insecurity in between these periods, any government would have had an impossible time convincing local residents that things were going to be different in the future.

Further, FDA officials and local authorities further undermined central statebuilding by collecting tax money and keeping it for themselves.[55] This type of behavior further reinforced why Liberians, especially those in rural areas, found it difficult to trust Monrovia officials. The local view was that their tax money had still not delivered any *local* public goods. The international emphasis on *statebuilding at the national level had come at the expense of delivering public goods at the local level.*

Gradually, the power of the Nezoun Group and of General Kofi faded. They became less belligerent. As a new post-conflict order emerged, the conflict capital of the Nezoun Group also declined. The various factions—including ex-MODEL fighters who belonged to the Nezoun Group—went through the

---

[55] Panel of Experts on Liberia (2006).

DDR process. Their capacity for violence declined and the peace began to feel more settled. This created space for local activists to build up their own social capital. Steve Joe, a local human rights campaigner of the Concerned Citizens Caucus of River Cess County, began challenging Kofi. Over several years, he mounted a campaign of social awareness and began a dialogue with Kofi. He lobbied local authorities, elders, village chiefs, and paramount chiefs. As time passed, the community's fear of General Kofi gradually declined. Steve Joe and his coalition of civil society activists negotiated with Kofi and the Nezoun Group for many years to give up their activities. Today, Kofi is a farmer in River Cess County. This was a rare case where a respected local activist was able to directly challenge private interests—and win. But it was done locally, and gradually, over many years. It was not externally imposed.

Wartime Statebuilding

Interestingly, timber companies such as OTC that operated during the civil war period *did* provide public goods; a senior official of the Forest Development Authority confirmed that they also acted as local authorities, providing limited humanitarian services and building local infrastructure.[56] For example, they dug wells and installed hand pumps; in other instances, they installed electricity, built schools, hospitals, markets, and roads, and maintained bridges. They also provided local security, though these timber militias were primarily focused on guarding the forestland and not the local population. Clearly the provision of public goods by the timber companies cannot compensate for the abuses suffered by residents. However, it does illustrate that the central government does not have a monopoly on statebuilding or public goods provision. The relationship between van Kouwenhoven's OTC, the state, and local communities was more complicated than we might have been led to believe.

Indeed, these contrasting behaviors between the Nezoun Group, the FDA, and private timber companies illustrate how statebuilding activities can be effectively carried out by nonstate actors. Donor governments assume that the state is best equipped to provide public goods, but this is not always true in conflict or post-conflict situations. Foreign advisors, particularly those with Western assumptions about what the state is and what it should be, would do well to remember that the civil servants can be just as corrupt as ex-militia members, particularly if there are no clear ways to hold rulers to account.

---

[56] Senior FDA Director (2005).

CONCESSIONS UNCERTAINTY
AND EXTRALEGAL GROUPS

When the civil war finally ended in 2003, Liberia's forests and forestry institutions were in shambles. To give the sector a fresh start, the transitional government established the Forest Concession Review Committee in July 2004. The members of the Committee came from the Liberian government, Liberian civil society, and from the international community. This was the third attempt in recent memory to overhaul the forest sector—the two previous attempts led by the FDA had ended in failure.[57]

The Committee's task was to verify each of the forest concessions on Liberia's books and determine whether each one should be upheld or cancelled.[58] The findings were illuminating. The chaos of the sector is best illustrated by the fact that timber companies had been allocated logging concessions that comprised *two and a half times the total amount of forest area in the entire country*. Put another way, the same logging areas had been awarded to multiple firms at different points in time. As a result, President Sirleaf signed Executive Order No. 1 and cancelled all of the country's forest concessions just a few days after taking office in 2006.

A "debarment list" also emerged out of the second stage of this process, identifying seventeen companies that had provided support to timber militias, participated in or assisted with the arms-for-timber trade, or caused instability in the country. These companies and their principals were officially banned from the timber sector. Not surprisingly, OTC and Guus van Kouwenhoven were both on this list. The final stage of the concession review also revealed a disturbing finding: only 14 percent of taxes owed by the country's timber companies had actually been collected—a further $64 million was still owed in back taxes.

This confusion around the ownership of the concessions is important because it affected the Nezoun Group's incentives, as well as the government's incentives to engage in statebuilding. For two and a half years after the war

---

[57] Forest Concession Review Committee Phase III (2005), p. 2.

[58] The three-stage process began by assessing the legal status of the concessionaire. This required proof of incorporation and a business certificate, as well as a legal concession contract and that there be no conflicting claims on the concession area. The second stage was to check for "threshold behaviour" such as involvement in the arms-for-timber trade. The third and final stage consisted of evaluating compliance with financial obligations to the state, rule-of-law obligations, community obligations, and labor law obligations. Forty-seven of the country's seventy timber companies participated in the review.

The vetting process was rigorous by developing country standards—perhaps unfairly so given that no other companies in Liberia were being held to such a high standard and no company operating in Liberia at the time would have been able to meet all of these criteria. In the end, not one single company was able to pass the first stage of the concession review process. See ibid., pp. 12–25.

ended, it remained unclear which companies had rights over which parcels of land. Even after all concessions were formally cancelled in early 2006 and the government regained *de jure* control over all of the timber areas again, it was still not yet possible to assert any kind of meaningful territorial control over these areas.

The lack of clarity in ownership rights had several consequences that made it easier for extralegal groups to establish themselves. First, there were no companies to deter pit sawing crews from logging on their land; with local permission from local chiefs and/or the Nezoun Group, it was theoretically possible to log almost anywhere in River Cess County. Second, the fact that no pit sawing groups had any legal or verifiable claim over any particular area meant that there was also a greater need for regulation and dispute resolution between them. Third, confusion over concessions also made it easier for extralegal groups to emerge because it was never clear what entity owned the logging concession when multiple firms had each been granted the right to log in the same area during the Taylor years. Without the certainty of undisputed ownership, no firm will move to protect its asset for fear that it will lose the ownership battle and another company may reap the benefits instead. The Nezoun Group itself faces a similar problem: the lack of clear ownership in the post-conflict years has meant that the state and the Nezoun Group were more reluctant to engage in statebuilding because it was not clear who would reap the long-term benefits of these efforts. The government had little incentive to invest seriously in public goods since any future logging concession contracts would have included some form of investment in local development; similarly, the Nezoun Group's uncertainty about its ability to retain long-term authority over the taxation regime would also have minimized its incentives to provide other kinds of public goods with longer term benefits.

CONCLUSION

This discussion of the Nezoun Group supports two of the three stages of the extralegal groups framework. Regarding the group's emergence, the evidence suggests that it grew out of an existing resource extraction business as well as a need for internal regulation after the war ended and it was no longer clear who was in control of the countryside. Here, conflict capital helps explain the success of the Nezoun Group in providing contract enforcement and dispute resolution services in dealing with local pit sawing groups, local communities, and the FDA. In considering the development and entrenchment stages, the behavior of the Nezoun Group is consistent with the theoretical framework. The operations of the Wood Toll Committee (effectively run by the Nezoun Group) demonstrated the hold that this group had over the local timber trade.

The Nezoun Group also became locally entrenched, as predicted by the framework. Because of the fact that the group was closely tied to local authorities, dislodging it was difficult. As the situation stabilized over time though, the Nezoun Group's conflict capital gradually diminished and the social capital of the community gradually strengthened. Over the course of the next decade, community activists succeeded in slowly eroding the group's conflict capital, and with the help of local activist Steve Joe, the Nezoun Group was dismantled.

A key conclusion from this chapter is that the state is not always the most appropriate entity to engage in statebuilding. In this instance, not only did the FDA prove itself incapable of providing basic governance functions, but its corrupt practices reinforced local cynicism toward central government. Even the Nezoun Group, as problematic as it may have been, was viewed more favorably by many locals than the FDA in the years following the war.

For those concerned with the practicalities of statebuilding, this is an important point: in donor countries, the traditional assumption has been that public goods and services can only be delivered by the government. What this chapter reveals is that under certain circumstances, particularly when the state is weak, a peacetime government may be so deeply mistrusted that other entities turn out to be better positioned to engage in statebuilding and to do the work of governing—even where these entities are nonstate armed groups.

Change is apace in Liberia's timber industry. Certainly, the flagrant abuses of the past created a strong impetus to reform the operations of the entire industry. Even though extensive measures have been undertaken to reimagine and reconfigure the timber industry, new ways of circumventing the rules were devised, as with the exploitation of the Private Use Permits. The jury is still out on whether industry reforms have been successful. Even if government-led reforms are unsuccessful in the short run, evidence from the Nezoun Group shows that it remains possible for the government and civil society to gradually co-opt these extralegal governance structures and re-anchor local statebuilding efforts.

Part IV

Trade Makes the State

8

Conclusion

Extralegal Groups are Statebuilders

This book began in the forests, mines, and rubber plantations of a country that had been torn apart by years of civil war. It started with observations from the field: groups of ex-combatants were providing basic governance functions in order to facilitate trade in natural resource areas. In examining the dynamics of these groups through the course of this book, this study of extralegal groups has shone a spotlight on the political economy of post-conflict transitions—as a mutually constitutive local and international process. To unpack these dynamics, I presented a theoretical framework for analyzing the logic of extralegal groups—their emergence, development, and local entrenchment. In the theoretical framework, I argued that an extralegal group provides contract enforcement and dispute resolution in order to create a stable commercial environment. The group builds up capacity through taxation, and uses its clout to locally embed itself. Having explored the sectoral dynamics of extralegal groups in Liberia in Chapters 5–7, I now turn to theories of state formation to place extralegal groups in a broader historical context.

The underlying dynamic that drives the emergence of extralegal groups is the need to trade—but trading is difficult when the environment is unstable. To overcome this problem, an extralegal group offers contract enforcement and dispute resolution. In essence, it asserts order and a raw form of justice, by taking control over the judgment and punishment of disputes, and regulatory functions. Unintentionally, an extralegal group has constituted the *kernel of the state* and has become a de facto statebuilder. If a crude summary of Tilly's argument is that "War made the state, and the state made war,"[1] then in today's globalized world, it is *trade that makes the state*.

However, it is not only the visible governance functions of extralegal groups that are worth noting, but also their hidden functions. Extralegal groups *consolidate coercive authority, socialize and subjugate populations into*

---

[1] Charles Tilly (1975), p. 42.

accepting an outside ruler, and remove the right of the individual to judge disputes and enforce punishment. Again, the underlying desire to trade is important. Without the motivation to trade, these functions—both visible and hidden—would not have taken hold so quickly or been as readily accepted. In these ways, *extralegal groups establish norms of compliance and cooperation with the local population.*

In this concluding chapter, I begin by reviewing the theoretical insights that emerge from the case studies of Liberia's extralegal groups in the rubber, diamonds, and timber sectors. These insights set the scene for a discussion of statebuilding as an evolutionary process, rather than a defining historical moment. In the second section, I explore the ideas of Hobbes and Locke to reflect on Western understandings and assumptions about statehood, state formation, and statebuilding processes. Then, I take a step back to provide historical context for the role that extralegal groups play in the longue durée. The third section argues that extralegal groups do not only provide visible governance functions, but that they also provide hidden statebuilding functions that underpin order and justice in the state. In the fourth and fifth sections, I tackle the thornier problem of how the international community conceives of statebuilding, and I offer a set of principles for responding to extralegal groups. The sixth section discusses other country contexts where the concept of extralegal groups should prove illuminating. I discuss the theoretical framework's applicability to other country case studies and its applicability to "peaceful" states like Colombia, Kosovo, and Mexico, before offering some final reflections.

THEORETICAL INSIGHTS

The evidence from Liberia supports the logic of each individual stage as outlined in the theoretical framework. However, while the framework was useful for thinking through how individual incentives (the micro-level) interact with national and regional political economies (the macro-level), the case studies on the rubber, timber, and diamond sectors also revealed that each of the framework's stages were not sharply defined in practice, and that the stages could occur in a sequence other than (i) emergence (ii) development (iii) entrenchment. For example, with the BOPC Group, the emergence and entrenchment stages occurred together as local community leaders and ex-combatant leaders joined together to form the extralegal group. The development stage came later, followed by further entrenchment. The empirical evidence also highlights the importance of social and political context. Extralegal groups do not arise in a vacuum; their emergence is inevitably rooted in key historical moments.

Extralegal Groups Are Not Necessarily "Bad"

In addition to testing the utility of the theoretical framework, the resource case studies (rubber, timber, diamonds) also yield some interesting insights. First, extralegal groups are not necessarily "bad" actors. Indeed, the overall effect of these groups may actually improve local statebuilding outcomes. However, the human desire to categorize people as good or bad masks the complexities of the situation. Rather than simply dismissing these groups as "peace spoilers,"[2] it is more useful to ask: What functions do extralegal groups serve?[3] Characterizing them as "bad" obscures the necessary functions they provide. The implicit process of judging these groups implies that there is a fixed standard to which they are being compared. Rendering a judgment of "bad" infers that extralegal groups are bad in comparison to something else. This begs the question: What are they being compared to? Here, again, an implicit standard of Western stateness is being unrealistically imposed.

An extreme characterization of this perspective suggests that if extralegal groups were removed, a high-functioning, democratically elected, redistributive, and development-minded local administrative order would organically emerge after war. This is clearly a caricature, but *in judging an extralegal group, the default comparison is to the states who set these standards*, the ones that most readers are familiar with: capable, responsive, and resilient constitutional liberal democracies.[4] In other words, "good" states; states that purport to operate in the interests of its citizens.[5]

Most readers of this book live in these trusted, strong, and stable states, and their ideas—*our* ideas—about stateness are likely to be anchored in contemporary notions of high-capacity statehood. In these states, public interest is elevated above personal interest. Legal and constitutional protections are deliberately put in place to separate personal gain from public interest. The prevailing norm is that state actors prioritize doing right by their citizens. In this framing, the state becomes an expression of collective good. However, such a framing can also imply that extralegal groups are the obstacle that prevent a stable, public-interest-oriented state from arising.

The reality is very different. A more realistic alternative to an extralegal group is a state-backed coercive force. For a minute, just imagine all of the previous predatory and exploitative behaviors of the police, the military, the legislature that the Liberian people have been subjected to. Consider the many attempts of local populations to resist these behaviors over time. Now ask

---

[2] Stephen J. Stedman (1997).   [3] David Keen (1998).
[4] The resilience of these democratic regimes is being tested by Brexit and Trump. See Jeff Colgan and Robert Keohane (2017).
[5] But see Paul Krugman (2017) on Donald Trump's $1.5 trillion tax bill.

yourself: Do extralegal groups pose a greater threat than a state that has a history of predation and exploitation?

Extralegal groups tread the fine line between business entity and private militia, emphasizing business in some cases and coercion in others. There is no template for the relationship between extralegal groups and the communities they live in. As the Guthrie Group, the Sinoe Group, the BOPC Group, and the Nezoun Group made clear, these are specific to the local community and will evolve over time. It would be an oversimplification to stress that these groups are "bad" for post-conflict statebuilding when in fact their relationships with local communities are more complex and multilayered.

If we focus on the functions of extralegal groups, the empirical case studies in the rubber, diamond, and timber sectors show that, in the short run, these groups can play an important stabilization role immediately after war. They offer local dispute resolution, contract enforcement, and regulation in pursuit of a stable trading environment. They also offer employment and status, occupying the time of those who are most likely to rearm. This is not to say that they are virtuous actors or that their behaviors are acceptable, but rather that they need to be analyzed with greater objectivity rather than rejected wholesale because of their nonstate status.

Group Ties Matter

Evidence from extralegal groups in Liberia suggest that strong ties between the extralegal group leaders and the local community can mitigate the potential for exploitation. For example, where the Guthrie Group's taxation policies were quite rapacious, those of the Sinoe Group were considerably less so. Further, there were also fewer violent clashes (assaults, violent disputes, etc.) on the Sinoe plantation as compared to the Guthrie plantation.

One potential explanation for this difference in outcomes is that the leaders of the Guthrie Group had no ties to the area whereas leaders of the Sinoe Group did. On the Guthrie Rubber Plantation, the extralegal group leaders separated themselves from local residents. The influx of new arrivals also meant that the population was more heterogeneous, whereas on the Sinoe Rubber Plantation, the leaders were of the same ethnicity as locals. This difference between their behaviors suggests that leaders with stronger local ties felt more constrained in their taxation practices. For example, it is easier to impose and enforce social sanctions on those within your own ethnic group as compared to those outside the group.

While this example presents only one case, and only one of many possible explanations for differences in the group's behaviors, strategies, and local responses, it is nevertheless consistent with experimental results from social psychology that emphasize the important role that group identity can play. For example, experiments demonstrate that empathy for others is highly correlated with how strongly an individual identifies with her in-group. In an experiment that randomly assigned individuals to opposing teams for an online game, and then followed up by reading anecdotes about the other team, an interesting result emerged: the stronger the feelings of group identity, the less empathy the individual would have for the opposition. This held true even for people who rated as having highly empathetic personalities.[6] Emile Bruneau, one of the study's authors, noted: "The more an individual's team affiliation resonated for them, the less empathy they were likely to express for members of the rival team . . . Even in this contrived setting, something as inconsequential as a computer game was enough to generate a measurable gap."[7]

However, evidence from the Nezoun Group suggests that the importance of community ties requires further probing. What is the nature of the relationship? How strong is the tie? How are relationships affected by violence and armed conflict at the individual and group levels? General Kofi, the de facto leader of the Nezoun Group, maintained deep local ties to his area, was of the same ethnicity (Bassa) as local residents, and was enmeshed in informal local authority structures. Yet initially, there were few constraints on his power.[8] General Kofi threatened local residents when they resisted him in the years immediately following the end of the war. But over time, as peace took hold, Kofi responded to community activism, and a decline in his own legitimacy. It took time, but the in-group restraint mechanism later came into full effect.

Here, civil society leadership in an environment of declining conflict capital provides a more convincing explanation. As the General's conflict capital peaked at war's end, and gradually diminished, his grip on the community loosened over time, and his role and influence were more easily contained. At the same time, local civil society was developing greater influence in an environment where conflict capital was gradually depleting. In this changing milieu, environmental activist Francis Colee has argued that civil society leaders like Steve Joe played a critical role in "converting" General Kofi.[9] But of course, it is unclear the extent to which Kofi's changing attitudes should be attributed to external pressures vs his own internal changes. While group ties appear to have had a mitigating effect on exploitative taxing regimes in Sinoe and BOPC, the situation in Nezoun suggests that this influence remains contingent on other factors.

---

[6] M. Cikara, E. Bruneau, J. J. Van Bavel and R. Saxe (2014).
[7] Jeneen Interlandi (2015).   [8] Rivercess County Residents (2010).
[9] Francis Colee (2015).

Entrenchment is a Corruption Equilibrium

Evidence from the sectoral case studies suggests that even where extralegal groups initially emerged to serve a basic governance function (e.g., internal dispute resolution), the result was that local institutions (state, police, judiciary, local authorities) ended up beholden to the extralegal group. Because they were weak and lacking in capacity after the war, and local institutions had a long history of personalization in West Africa, it was not surprising that state institutions could be undermined with relative ease.

A different way to characterize the entrenchment dynamic is as a multi-player Nash equilibrium whereby no player can improve her position by changing only her own strategy. In short, players cannot improve their lot by abandoning their corrupt practices. Of course, this characterization of entrenchment is a bit simplistic. Plainly, some of the case study dynamics reveal that government officials and extralegal groups can also have mutually beneficial partnerships. In other cases, it is difficult to untangle who is co-opting who—is the extralegal group co-opting government officials or vice versa? It is difficult to discern which party has the upper hand in these transactions.

What we do know though is that (1) power usually does not rest solely in the hands of official representatives of the state; and (2) the balance of power can shift between and across different sets of actors over time. *Assuming that a given power configuration remains static neglects the fluidity of the post-conflict window and the potential for change.* In a place like Liberia and in other states where Big Man patronage politics still dominate, change cannot reasonably be expected overnight. This is true even where extralegal groups established somewhat symbiotic (though still problematic) relationships with local populations, as with the Sinoe Group and the BOPC Group. Having focused on extralegal groups as a local, post-conflict phenomenon, the following section will take a step back to consider their role in the broader state formation process.

ESCAPING THE STATE OF NATURE

When the word "ungoverned" is uttered, it conjures up associations with anarchy, barbarity, and vengeance. It suggests disputes that end in bloodshed, vigilante killings, and violent chaos. There is a sense of the primitive and the backward that accompanies those who are ungoverned. If we trace these associations back in time, we end up at Thomas Hobbes' idea of the state of nature, a condition where states did not exist. For Hobbes, the state of nature was synonymous with a state of war, which meant a disposition to fighting.[10] According to Hobbes, the ultimate realist, a "state of warre" exists between hostile countries unless there is "assurance to the contrary."[11]

In Hobbes' own words, "during the time men live without a common Power to keep them all in awe, they are in that condition which is called Warre; and such a warre, as is of every man, against every man."[12] Before society, there was "continual fear and danger of violent death, and the life of man [is] solitary, poor, nasty, brutish, and short." In Hobbes' version of the state of nature, life is so cruel that the only escape is to concede all your rights to the sovereign in exchange for having your life protected.

In contrast, John Locke's state of nature bore little in common with Hobbes. For Locke, the state of nature was more benign and allowed for coexistence. At its core stands the human capacity to reason. People have positive interactions with each other; rules exist and are enforced because human beings can reason with one another. Hence, there is no need for the kind of maximal, all-powerful state that Hobbes envisaged. Nevertheless, Locke's version of the state of nature had a fatal flaw: it lacked access to impartial justice. In Lockean terms, the state of nature implied a state that could never achieve full justice.

I discuss the state of nature here in order to establish a conceptual baseline for what happens in the absence of strong central state authority. After all, a civil war is one manifestation of the state of nature. A post-civil war transition can be read as an attempt to escape the state of nature, again. Hobbes and Locke bring us back to first principles—what do we need from a state? Clearly, they each offered strikingly different renderings of the state of nature. One resembles continuous civil war while the other is more akin to the relatively peaceful relations of the American Frontier. But despite their very different views of human nature, both philosophers still viewed *the state as the solution* to the problems imposed by the state of nature. Hobbes saw a need for order and Locke saw a need for consistent and impartial justice. Differences in how the state is perceived today—for example, in U.S. debates on small government—can partly be traced back to these contrasting visions between Hobbes and Locke. Escaping the state of nature becomes important because these early philosophical foundations provided the justification for the

---

[10] Thomas Hobbes (1651), The First Part, Chapter XIII, "For WARRE, consisteth not in Battell onely, or the act of fighting; but in a tract of time, wherein the Will to contend by Battell is sufficiently known...So the nature of War, consisteth not in actuall fighting; but in the known disposition thereto, during all the time there is no assurance to the contrary. All other time is PEACE."

[11] This is also the underlying assumption for Kenneth Waltz's neorealist model of international relations. See Kenneth N. Waltz (1979).

[12] See Thomas Hobbes (1651), The First Part, Chapter 1.13. To be clear, Hobbes' interpretation of Warre was not limited to fighting but would be more accurately labeled insecurity.

existence of the state and also the kind of state that is needed—its core responsibilities, its powers, and its limits.

The Myth of the "Good" State and State as Savior

For those who view governments largely as a force for good, it is difficult to imagine the state as posing the biggest threat to its own citizens. If the state of nature is as Hobbes described it to be, then in a Hobbesian world, the most vital function of the state is to save us from ourselves. Only an almighty sovereign can deliver people from inevitable war. But in order to do the job properly, the sovereign must be given total power. Thus, for Hobbes, the state is cast as savior. It is endowed with an inherent goodness because the alternative is so deplorable.

Compared to Hobbes, Locke's conception of statehood is more limited, and does not have the absolute authority of Hobbes' Leviathan. Nevertheless, the state is infused with a sense of moral good because it provides impartial justice. For Locke, the state only exists to provide three things: common laws, impartial judges, and the ability to enforce rulings. When the sovereign power violates the covenant of impartial justice and takes on the role of both participant and judge, then the people have an obligation to remove this authority from power. In this conception of the state, *whenever the sovereign power becomes corrupted and loses its legitimacy, it is overthrown by the people.* In this way, the legitimacy of the state is built into Locke's system.

These philosophical foundations for justifying the nation-state are integral to Western notions of statebuilding. Both Hobbes and Locke offer a paradigm of benevolent statehood. For Hobbes, an all-powerful state is the only way to prevent anarchy and destruction; for Locke, the state is good because its provision of impartial justice gives it legitimacy and there is a self-regulation mechanism for flushing out corrupt officials.

Centuries later, for politics scholars and policymakers from rich, developed countries, this quality of "goodness" and the desirability of the state have become so deeply ingrained that they are rarely even questioned. The political legacy of these ideas underpins the international policy community's approach to statebuilding such that the prevailing assumption of policymakers, from *both* developed and developing countries, is that states are inherently "good" and that the need for a strong state is a given. These convictions are then confirmed when we turn to countries mired in civil war (e.g., Somalia), and find that they often lack a strong central state authority.[13]

---

[13] Séverine Autesserre (2009).

The justification for the state project appears self-evident: civil wars are more prevalent in states that are deemed fragile or weak or failing.[14] For example, a cursory examination of ongoing civil wars reveals significant overlap with the list of countries that do poorly on measures of state legitimacy, public services, human rights and rule of law, and the security apparatus.[15] Seen in this light, the task of building the state is translated into a technical project focused on institutions and capacity. The relationship with the citizenry is cut out. In this way, the process is depoliticized and made ahistorical. Statebuilding is sanitized.

Rethinking the desirability of a strong state and being able to question the state paradigm itself requires empathy for a life lived differently—from the perspective of those in another country or culture, or those who have different coloured skin and a different set of social, political, and economic values.[16]

Those who live as part of the majority in strong, functional states appreciate that competent governments can provide significant social, political, and economic benefits to its people. For those who have never been oppressed or persecuted by the state, even obvious problems such as institutionalized racism or sexism can be framed as anomalous state behavior.[17] And interestingly, even for those who have been systematically discriminated against by the state, it is still possible to disaggregate monolithic "state" behavior into more nuanced views, as with African Americans' faith in the U.S. federal government alongside their hostility toward local and state governments.[18] In these ways, exceptional behavior can be framed as isolated problems to be corrected over time, preserving the core reputation of the nation-state.

For these reasons, imagining a state that preys on its citizens and applies justice unequally is particularly challenging when decision makers in the international community have largely been exposed to its protective benefits. For these reasons, the imagined ideal state is strong because the global policy discourse is being shaped by individuals who have had overwhelmingly positive experiences with well-functioning states.

This collectively lived experience sways us to create strong states so that others will also benefit from similar conditions. In the twenty-first century, it is easy to forget that we are the beneficiaries of long and convoluted statebuilding processes, and that it took most countries many centuries to get to this point.

---

[14] Fund for Peace and Foreign Policy Magazine (2016).

[15] It is not clear which way the causal relationship works, if a causal relationship can be established at all.

[16] There are important exceptions to this. African Americans are more likely to mistrust state authority because they have been systematically mistreated by them. See Alice Goffman (2015) and Shayla Nunnally (2012).

[17] For example, consider the institutional injustices raised by social movements such as #BlackLivesMatter in the U.S.'s post-Ferguson context, and #AmINext on behalf of murdered aboriginal women in Canada.

[18] Shayla Nunnally (2012).

Micro-Processes of Statebuilding

In the international statebuilding literature, there have been robust debates about how to "do" statebuilding after war since the 1990s. While the early agenda for addressing the challenges of postwar environments was set by Boutros Boutros-Ghali's *An Agenda for Peace*,[19] it soon became apparent that state weakness would complicate efforts at peacebuilding and conflict prevention. A number of research agendas developed in response to the "state problem," including literatures on weak and failed states,[20] liberal peacebuilding,[21] international transitional administrations,[22] shared sovereignty and trusteeships,[23] hybrid orders,[24] the political economy of statebuilding,[25] nation-building,[26] and historical approaches to statebuilding.[27] This dialogue is rooted in the politics and international relations literature.

In contrast, the state formation literature takes a different approach to states, viewing their emergence as path dependent, and largely driven by internal, country-specific dynamics. This approach has been more influential in sociology, economic history, and geography.

Sociological approaches to state formation have underscored that it takes centuries, rather than years or decades, to "make" a functional state. This framing treats state formation as a process whereby a state "learns" through its own institutional memory, and gradually builds enough resilience and adaptive capacity to survive internal and external change. It may be brutal, but it is through the rebellions, riots, revolutions, uprisings, civil wars, palace coups, genocides, and the process of violently killing masses of its own people that enables the state to learn, and to develop the capabilities to respond to various challenging conditions. These are the episodes that test and define a society, a sensibility, a culture. In historical terms, it is useful to frame these periods of (dis)organization and mobilization as the *micro-processes of statebuilding*. The activities

---

[19] Boutros Boutros-Ghali (1992).

[20] I. William Zartman (1995); Jack A. Goldstone, Ted Robert Gurr, Barbara Harff, Marc A. Levy, et al. (2000); Jennifer Milliken and Keith Krause (2002); C. T. Call (2008); Ashraf Ghani and Clare Lockhart (2008); C. T. Call (2011); Fund for Peace and Foreign Policy Magazine (2016), Susan Woodward (2017).

[21] Roland Paris (2004); Roland Paris 2010; Susanna Campbell, David Chandler and Meera Sabaratnam (2011); D. Zaum (2012).

[22] Simon Chesterman (2004); Richard D. Caplan (2005).

[23] James D. Fearon and David D. Laitin (2004); Stephen D. Krasner (2004); James Mayall and Ricardo Soares de Oliveira (2011).

[24] Volker Boege, Anne Brown, Kevin Clements and Anna Nolan (2009); David Chandler (2009); Lee Jones (2010); Roger MacGinty (2010); Oliver P. Richmond and Audra Mitchell (2012); Roger MacGinty and Oliver Richmond (2016).

[25] Roland Paris and Timothy D. Sisk (2009); Mats Berdal and Domink Zaum (2012); Louise Anten, Ivan Briscoe and Marco Mezzera (2015).

[26] Keith Darden and Harris Mylonas (2012).

[27] Toby Dodge (2006); Cameron G. Thies (2007); Meera Sabaratnam (2013).

of extralegal groups are best understood in this way—as one of many micro-processes of statebuilding that cumulatively add up to the nation-state.

Sometimes, these micro-processes of statebuilding (riots, rebellions, wars, social movements, extralegal group activities), and their corresponding responses from civil society can restore state–society relations to a tolerable equilibrium. But other attempts to restore the balance may fail, and fail spectacularly. It is common for different constellations of elite actors to make the same mistakes over and over again for decades or centuries—and over time, that state, and its corresponding society, will stagnate or decline.

But statebuilding is not always recognizable as such when it occurs. It can be difficult to identify in the moment, and sometimes, the formative nature of these processes can only be appreciated in hindsight. Yet short-term activities that are illiberal in nature do not necessarily prevent a liberal end state from arising in the long run. Rather than prescribing one set path for building a robust and resilient state, it is important to recognize that for any given state, there are many different potential statebuilding paths—not all of which will result in a secular, constitutionally liberal state and some of which will most certainly result in despotic and illiberal regimes. This may be difficult for Western actors, in particular, to accept.

For European state formation, Tilly argued that it was war that drove state-making.[28] As nation-states began to expand and take over the war-making process from the fifteenth to seventeenth centuries, key war-fighting tasks were outsourced to mercenaries and financiers. From the eighteenth century to the mid-nineteenth century, rulers then sought to control both troops and finances through a process of nationalization. This period built the social cohesion—the "imagined community"—needed to establish stable nation-states.[29] During this time, rulers also needed to bureaucratize their control over coercion (armies, navies, materiel) and institutionalize capital-raising processes (taxation) practices. Tilly's assertion was that the organizational form that was best able to take advantage of these processes and geopolitical norms of the time turned out to be nation-states.

Today, the nature of armed conflict is different and globalization has changed relations between and within nations. The conditions and logic of Tilly's state-making processes do not apply,[30] though many, like the anthro-pologist Ronald Cohen, have cogently argued that warfare is a necessary, but not sufficient condition for state formation.[31] At best, the relationship between warfare and state-making is contingent and ambiguous in the contemporary

[28] But see Steven Pincus and James Robinson (2016) for an account of Britain's state formation processes that de-emphasizes the role of war.
[29] Benedict R. Anderson (1983).
[30] Tilly (1990) himself does not claim that his processes apply to contemporary states (Ch. 7). See also Anna Leander (2004).
[31] Ronald Cohen (1984), p. 332.

context.[32] At worst, others have convincingly demonstrated that warfare hinders the state-making process.[33]

Such a longue-durée[34] approach to state formation contrasts starkly with contemporary statebuilding practices which are evaluated annually or, more generously, every five to ten years. This difference in approach suggests that there needs to be a fundamental reassessment of what is realistically achievable during a cycle of post-conflict statebuilding.

State Failure and "Ungoverned" Spaces

Today, the study of contemporary politics and international relations assumes statehood as a basic element of the discourse. The nation-state system means that virtually all populations on the planet have moved beyond the state of nature[35] and there is a baseline expectation that everyone on the planet belongs to a state.[36] With the establishment of social contracts between sovereign authorities and citizens, as well as a common institutional framework (the nation-state), discussions of the state of nature can seem anachronistic in contemporary politics.

Since the terrorist attacks of September 11th on New York City and Washington D.C., the state of nature debate has been revived in a different guise. Subsequent attacks targeting Westerners and Western capitals have complicated and also intensified these debates. State failure and "ungoverned spaces" raise the specter of terrorist hideouts and training grounds.[37] Here, the term "ungoverned" and "failure" both have Hobbesian implications: destructive anarchy, uncivilized savagery, barbarity. The tone of this discourse has become so intransigent that Susan Woodward has even argued that the concept should now be read as *ideology*. Colloquial usage of the term "ungoverned spaces" in particular is stereotypically bound up with radical Islamist terrorism. Yet the reality of day-to-day life in an ungoverned area encompasses

---

[32] See also the mixed results of Brian D. Taylor and Roxana Botea (2015).

[33] For example, see Thierry Gongora (1997); Paul Collier (2007).

[34] Fernand Braudel (1958).

[35] Nevertheless, at least 10 million people in the world are stateless. See UNHCR (2015).

[36] A notable exception includes the 100 million strong population of an area in Southeast Asia referred to as Zomia, which includes populations who have purposefully chosen not to participate in the modern nation-state. See James C. Scott (2009).

[37] For example, the U.S. Department of Defense established an Ungoverned Areas Project. A number of other prominent think tanks such as the Rand Corporation, the Centre for Strategic and International Studies, and RUSI have also explored this subject, especially with respect to its effects on terrorist networks. Also see Anne L. Clunan and Harold A. Trinkunas (2010) and Stewart Patrick (2010).

a wide range of experiences.[38] Some of these spaces have no links to formal governance structures (i.e., not governed by a central state, like Zomia);[39] other spaces might have competing systems of governance, but not one that dominates, resulting in violent contestation and high levels of violence and insecurity (e.g., parts of Afghanistan, Libya, Syria, Iraq); others still are properly governed, but remain autonomous from an internationally recognized central state authority (e.g. Somaliland).[40]

In the discussion that follows, I will show that Hobbes' and Locke's ideas about the state are deeply embedded in how we think about global order. The arguments they put forth about what happens in the absence of the state, and hence, what the functions of the state should be, provide the foundation for the ideal type states that serve as standard reference points, and the implicit metrics by which states are judged today, and the importance of being "civilized."

Order and Justice: The Kernel of the Modern State

Combining Hobbes' and Locke's core ideas on how to escape the state of nature, and drawing on Weber's notion of statehood, we can conceptualize the modern state as a political community with two organizing principles: order and justice. Together, these form the *kernel of the modern state*.

(1) Order: A monopoly on the legitimate use of force; and
(2) Justice: Reliable access to impartial justice.

But how do we achieve these aims? How do we produce societies that are both orderly and just? These two building blocks of the state will not simply emerge, fully formed. *Citizens have had to fight for these core functions of the state*, and they have had to put continuous pressure on government officials to make these governance functions work for the benefit of the people. *Order and justice did not develop all at once, but were fought for* in stages *over time*. Here, we return to extralegal groups because they reveal the contradictions of how order and justice mechanisms can easily take an illiberal turn, and they show us what state formation processes look like *in practice*.

This book has focused on the governance functions provided by Liberia's extralegal groups. On the Guthrie plantation, the Sinoe plantation, on BOPC,

---

[38] See Anne L. Clunan and Harold A. Trinkunas (2010). See Jeff Garmany (2009) and Graham Denyer Willis (2015) for a different perspective on how governance is provided in a Brazilian favela (shantytown), a space that is commonly viewed as having minimal or no state presence.
[39] James C. Scott (2009).
[40] For an insightful discussion relating nonstate governance to processes of statebuilding, see Volker Boege, Anne Brown, Kevin Clements and Anna Nolan (2009).

and in Nezoun, the emphasis has been on dispute resolution, the enforcement of those decisions, and the internal regulation of local commodities markets. The need for these functions underscored how trade catalyzed the earliest stages of both order and justice provision. But these only constitute the *visible* functions of statebuilding. In this section, I focus on the hidden contributions to statebuilding made by extralegal groups.

The Hidden Contributions of Extralegal Groups

This book began by presenting extralegal groups as security threats—entities that have the power to threaten a war-to-peace transition. I started the book in this way because this was how I had been introduced to these groups, and this was also the way in which they presented themselves to the world. If the transition from war to peace had to be retold as a fairy tale, extralegal groups would have undoubtedly been cast as the evil villains. Yet once we stop labelling extralegal groups as mere thugs or "rogues," a narrative of survival, livelihoods, and governance provision emerges. With the passage of time, leaders of extralegal groups no longer seem as villainous as they were once made out to be, and indeed, the actions of their members and supporters appear rational, even sensible. The fairy tale gets flipped on its head, in part because of contrasting views of the state—what it is, what it was, what it should be. Locally, extralegal group leaders can be cast as Robin Hood figures, redistributing wealth from the rich to the poor.

Returning to the fairy-tale analogy, we can think of the conventional extralegal groups story as being told by a powerful but unreliable narrator with a particular worldview. Unwrapping this story layer by layer, and tackling many of its built-in assumptions—from the perspectives of the groups themselves, the Liberian government, and international policymakers—has been the focus of this book. In the end, we find that international policymakers, especially those in the West, have different baseline standards for state behavior, and many have not considered that processes of state formation and statebuilding typically take several centuries or more.

Up to this point, I have shown that extralegal groups do more good than harm for the statebuilding process because they keep the most hardened of ex-combatants occupied and employed; they provide dispute resolution and contract enforcement in governance-poor environments; they regularize the practice of tax collection (even if "tax revenues" are not spent on public goods); and they facilitate the creation of markets.

Here, I will extend the argument to the *hidden* elements of statebuilding: in resolving disputes, extralegal group leaders essentially act as "judge and enforcer." If we break down this function into its constituent parts, extralegal groups are performing three *hidden functions* which solidify the kernel of the state:

(i) Order: Consolidating coercive authority in a given territory;
(ii) Order: Socializing the population into accepting a ruler; and
(iii) Justice: Removing the right of the individual to judge and enforce punishment in disputes to which they are party to.

These are crucial but unseen functions of contemporary statebuilding. Where Hobbes emphasized order as an organizing principle, and the importance of an all-powerful state in the name of ending war, extralegal groups consolidated authority in a defined territory, and then socialized the population into accepting a governing authority.[41] Where Locke stood for impartial justice, extralegal groups shifted the norms of dispute resolution by moving populations away from individual vigilante justice and toward third-party judgment and enforcement. These attitudinal shifts—toward creating order and resolving disputes—are critical for building states. In these ways, extralegal groups should be viewed as contributing to the state formation process. Let us consider each of these hidden functions in turn.

Consolidating Coercive Authority and the Civilizing Process

The task of consolidating coercive authority in a given territory is a long, drawn-out process that typically takes place over the course of centuries rather than decades. In areas where coercive authority is fragmented, extralegal groups move to aggregate and consolidate its use for commercial purposes. In this way, extralegal groups create space for the existence of a state-like entity after a period of intense violence where local authority may have been heavily contested, deeply fragmented, and variable in its penetration. For better or for worse, local populations are forced to accommodate this aggregation and consolidation of coercive authority.

Both the international statebuilding and state formation literatures largely agree that establishing a state monopoly over acts of violence by armed groups is a necessary first step to building an effective state. In *The Civilizing Process*, Norbert Elias describes the two foundational stages of state formation.[42] Dietrich Jung summarizes this two-stage process as follows:[43]

1) In the first phase, a factual monopoly of physical force is established. An increasing number of people lose direct access to the means of force, which progressively become centralized in the hands of a few and thus placed outside open competition.

---

[41] See also Reyko Huang (2016) on the institutional and social legacies of war.
[42] Norbert Elias (1982).   [43] Dietrich Jung (2008), p. 35.

2) In the second phase, this relatively private control over the monopoly of physical force tends to become public, i.e. it moves from the hands of state-makers into a political setting of legal institutions and appointed rulers under the control of the public.

Elias refers to the first stage as the "monopoly mechanism" and the second stage as the "royal mechanism." The first stage is about establishing the monopoly on force, while the second stage focuses on creating institutions for the legitimate use of that force. This broadly approximates the approach of international statebuilders: halting violence must come first, and the building of institutions should follow.

Yet, the more power that is aggregated and concentrated into a single entity, the more important it becomes for this power to be subjected to close scrutiny. Extralegal groups can continue to use coercion and repression to rule, but those who want to retain their power *with* the people's acceptance must build trust in order to establish a consistent set of rules and consistent enforcement. Elias' civilizing process begins with the threat of coercion, but eventually evolves into bargaining and trust-building between parties. We can treat this back-and-forth dialogue as a *process of legitimation*.

Socializing Populations to Accept a Ruler

While the international statebuilding literatures focuses on the state and its institutions, it neglects the other side of this process: that people need to be socialized into accepting a ruler. Or, put differently, there is no human today who is brought up with unrestricted freedom. From birth, every human is subjugated to a ruling authority—in most cases, the state; in other cases, community leaders. For most people, belonging—in all senses of the word—to the state is a given. It is difficult to imagine living in a world where the default is to *not* be ruled. Indeed, most of humanity has been socialized or subjugated (to varying extents) to accept the idea of being ruled.

Yet if we return to the conditions of human life before the existence of organized society, there were no rulers. For both Hobbes and Locke, a ruler is a social construct. In Hobbes' world, rulers must be imposed on the people for their own good, to save them from themselves and the human tendency toward violence. For Locke, one's starting assumption is that individuals can peacefully coexist in a self-directed and leaderless system. In both systems, populations must be socialized into accepting a ruler.[44]

---

[44] Self-organizing systems abound in nature. See Stuart A. Kauffman (1993). In economic systems, see for example, Robert Sugden (1989) on spontaneous order.

Looked at differently, it is also possible to frame this process as one of social Darwinism: as a story of human domestication. In evolutionary biology terms, we are all the descendants of those who were successfully socialized into being ruled. In Darwinian terms, we may all share a genetic or epigenetic trait that offered a survival advantage to being ruled—a marker in our DNA that has facilitated or induced the agglomeration of larger and larger human communities, in areas that have become increasingly densely populated.[45] In order for these human communities to grow, those of our ancestors who could not be socialized into being ruled simply did not survive the domestication process and did not pass on their genes.[46] If we think about extralegal groups as one in a series of micro-processes of statebuilding, then it is possible to recognize their role in this socialization/subjugation process.

Shifting Away from Self-Enforcement of Norms

Although Hobbes and Locke fundamentally disagreed on the premises underpinning the state of nature, one thing they did agree on was that individuals in the state of nature were able to mete out justice on their own behalf in the event of a dispute.[47] Civil war environments often produce areas of contested authority that resemble state of nature conditions.[48]

When these contested spaces persist over a long time, individuals learn to "resolve" disputes and impose justice as they see fit. This can include acts of vigilantism and revenge, meted out by neighbors acting on past grievances.[49] This anarchical environment persists until an active authority is established. In these conditions, extralegal groups serve the purpose of *shifting the norm so that individuals are no longer meting out their own punishment*. This allows individuals to turn to extralegal groups as a third party when disputes get serious. In this way, extralegal groups shift expectations and norms of dispute resolution and contract enforcement.

For statebuilding, what is essential here is that *third-party enforcement requires putting one's fate into the hands of another*. As problematic as the conduct of such a third party may be, the extralegal group moves dispute resolution away from the individual and into the hands of a jointly

---

[45] For an evolutionary biology perspective on violence, see Mike Martin (2018).

[46] Consider for example, Dimitri Belyaev's Farm-Fox Experiment. See Lyudmila Trut (1999).

[47] See Chapter II, Of the State of Nature, Sections 7 and 8, John Locke (1690).

[48] Many areas that experience civil war do not experience contested authority. Rebels or the state may have a very strong grip on different parts of the country. For example, see Zachariah C. Mampilly (2011); Kimberly Zisk Marten (2012).

[49] Civil wars provide an opportunity for neighbors to act on past grievances and settle long-standing feuds. See Stathis N. Kalyvas (2006).

acknowledged authority. Critically, in acknowledging this authority, the individual is giving up her right to decide her own fate. Edmund Burke expresses this argument poignantly:

> One of the first motives to civil society . . . is, *that no man should be judge in his own cause.* By this each person has at once divested himself of the first fundamental right of uncovenanted man, that is, to judge for himself, and to assert his own cause. He abdicates all right to be his own governor. He inclusively, in a great measure, abandons the right of self-defense, the first law of Nature. Men cannot enjoy the rights of an uncivil and of a civil state together. That he may obtain justice, he gives up his right of determining what it is in points the most essential to him. That he may secure some liberty, he makes a surrender in trust of the whole of it.[50]

This shift away from individuals rendering judgment in their own disputes and enforcing punishment is the precursor to what Locke called impartial justice and what we now think of as being the rule of law. In a post-conflict environment, this ideal seems naïve given the illiberal nature of extralegal groups.[51] However, I argue that what extralegal groups are unconsciously doing is *incrementally socializing a population* toward an ideal of impartial justice.

In creating rule of law, the first step is to take away the right to judge and punish oneself and to give it to another party. Ideally, this right is given to an impartial entity rather than an extralegal group whose interests are clearly biased. Indeed, for Locke, the third party *must* be impartial in order for the authority to be useful. Yet Locke's formulation is idealized. What is more realistic is for broad acceptance of rule of law principles to occur in stages. We can expect that the establishment of a "judge-like entity" will be separate from attempts to inject impartiality, and separate again from efforts to impose consistency and predictability on how those rules are applied.

Even where impartiality is not achievable in the short run, taking away the authority to judge oneself and personally impose punishment remains an important first step. Extralegal groups push populations in this direction, despite the fact that their behaviors and decisions exhibit bias. In the long run, extralegal groups will evolve and be replaced. The role of "judge" will grow and evolve; norms of impartiality will solidify into laws. This behavioral shift, away from the state of nature and self-enforcement of rules and toward third-party judgments, is a vital step in statebuilding.[52]

---

[50] See p. 88, Edmund Burke (1790).

[51] For Hobbes, the illiberal nature of extralegal groups is less problematic as long as the primary goal—escaping the state of nature—can still be achieved.

[52] With the invention of the blockchain, the nature of contracts may change so substantially that the role of "judge" will be forced to adapt.

RETHINKING THE INTERNATIONAL COMMUNITY'S APPROACH TO STATEBUILDING

Most of this book has focused on the actions of extralegal groups, and the individuals that lead them. I have argued that extralegal groups can contribute positively to the statebuilding process—but not always visibly or in ways that are desired by external actors. The ways in which these kinds of groups are often characterized—as peace spoilers and violent economic predators—and the ways I have written about them in this book—as complex actors with evolving roles—can partly be attributed to different assumptions about states and statebuilding.

To begin, the term "statebuilding" is commonly used as shorthand for a process of externally led statebuilding, usually in post-conflict countries. Substantively, this form of external intervention has critics and enthusiasts. Some see statebuilding as a neutral, technical exercise of capacity building while others intuit neo-colonialist overtones of Western domination,[53] and not without reason.[54] For patriots, statebuilding is but a poor substitute for the more aspirational "nation-building."

Significantly though, there is a common denominator to these discussions: that external actors should lead the statebuilding process.[55] Lead statebuilders include external actors like the UN or the World Bank, regional actors like the African Union, and influential states or former colonial powers such as the U.S., the U.K., and France. Despite the rhetoric of local ownership[56] and the reform of aid processes to fragile states through the New Deal,[57] the term statebuilding still implies external leadership. In contrast, the notion of "state formation" also speaks to a statebuilding process but emphasizes an *internal evolution of state-society relations.*[58] Conceptually, state formation is less politicized and its analysis tends to be applied to wealthy, developed states in the international system, such as Europe's nation-states.[59] With some important exceptions,[60] the

---

[53] On statebuilding as empire-building, see David Chandler (2006).

[54] Sebastian Mallaby (2002), James Fearon and David Laitin (2004).

[55] Researchers have been most preoccupied with their own country's influence in this process and have tended to focus on this (predominantly Western) perspective. Further, the external agents involved in statebuilding are influential recurring actors in the international system and consequently, they receive more attention in the literature.

[56] Sarah von Billerbeck (2017).

[57] International Dialogue on Peacebuilding and Statebuilding (2011).

[58] This is not to say that the international statebuilding literature does not recognize the importance of domestic actors.

[59] Charles Tilly (1992).

[60] For example, see the OECD DAC Do No Harm report, James Putzel (2010). See also Diane E. Davis and Anthony W. Pereira (2003); Volker Boege, Anne Brown, Kevin Clements and Anna Nolan (2009); Berit Bliesemann de Guevara (2012).

literatures on externally led statebuilding and internally driven state formation overlap surprisingly little despite the potential for fruitful engagement.

Infusing the statebuilding discourse with insights from the state formation literature will help align statebuilding theory with statebuilding practice. For this shift to occur, it is important to change how donors, policymakers, and researchers think and write about statebuilding.[61] This is challenging though because it requires international statebuilders to tolerate belief systems that conflict directly with Western sensibilities and may be blatantly illiberal.

Building up such a common, pluralistic discourse requires acceptance of the following:

- Statebuilding is a long-term process and states take different amounts of time to build the kernel of the modern state;
- Given the social nature of states, a state's given rate of learning at each particular stage increases exponentially as late entrants learn from the experiences and mistakes of early entrants;
- The path to modern statehood need *not* be planned and deliberate;
- For statebuilding to be sustainable, it must be internally driven rather than externally mandated;
- Not all states aspire to be liberal;
- Each step of a statebuilding path does not need to be liberal in order to achieve a liberal end state.

Even while the broad strokes of statebuilding are similar, contemporary approaches to statebuilding still fail to recognize that today's "successful" states did not evolve out of deliberate state formation strategies, but rather that the nature of these processes were highly contingent and organic. *Nor were Western states themselves consistently liberal at every stage in their history.*

Strengthening the State Is a Double-Edged Sword

International program and policy actors have largely internalized the primacy of the state system—governmental actors are privileged with unquestioned authority, no matter what atrocities they have committed. This can be summarized as: "the state knows best." For example, we can see this assumption expressed when only national governments can serve as interlocutors to the international community. This shows how the international community subtly confers legitimacy to the side of the government. In this way, the system is rigged to protect states' interests and ensure their survivability.

---

[61] See Christine Cheng, Jonathan Goodhand and Patrick Meehan (2018).

Western efforts to strengthen and stabilize states also need to be historically contextualized. Since World War I, the public rhetoric of international relations has gradually shifted away from a purely geo-strategic view of national interest toward a justice- and human rights-based conception. Some states have fully and successfully embraced this shift and have changed their institutions to reflect this new value system, while other states remain more traditionally rooted in a hard power outlook. As communism fell by the wayside and nationalism became bloody, richer states have adopted this new human rights and justice framework, in part to keep alive a dream of political utopia.[62]

One implication of this broad shift in how states justify their own behaviors is that statehood has now become imbued with *the potential for "doing good" and "civic-mindedness"* in a way that did not exist a century ago. These rhetorical aspirations are now assumed to be universal—irrespective of whatever kind of state previously existed.

The problem with this view of the state is that it evaluates the state *as it should be*, not *as it is*. The government of the day is not always benevolent, and rather than viewing state strengthening as the silver bullet to ensuring stability and security, it is more accurately described as a double-edged sword. The tools of the state can be used to secure and support the population, but they can also be used to coerce and extort.[63] Part of transitioning out of war includes securing borders and control over territory, but strengthening state capacity in these particular dimensions also facilitates repression and exploitation. Rather than focusing solely on building up the coercive power of the state (for example, through security sector reform initiatives),[64] international actors need to invest equal resources in improving inter-group relations and state–society accountability mechanisms.

Problems with the Liberal Template

In attempts to rebuild the state, there are two concerns with the involvement of external actors. First, in the literature, there has been a conflation of terms: statebuilding has come to be automatically associated with a certain *type* of statebuilding—the Western, liberal kind. There has been scarcely any room for negotiation on this front. The way in which international actors are tasked with implementing the liberal vision today leaves no scope for deviation or accommodation with non-liberal practices—even where it is clear that social and political practices of governance will not change overnight. There is no

---

[62] Samuel Moyn (2010).
[63] Robert Bates (2008), Daron Acemoglu and James Robinson (2012).
[64] For a thorough discussion of SSR in Liberia, see Sukanya Podder (2013) and Sean McFate (2013). For a more general discussion of the transformative effects of SSR, see Monica Duffy Toft (2010b).

latitude for other statebuilding paths that have not strictly hewed to liberal capitalist norms, as with the developmental trajectories of China, Malaysia, Brazil, Turkey, or South Korea for example.

The problem is further compounded because a rigidly liberal version of statebuilding demands a standard of internal consistency that is impossible to attain. Compromising the liberal standard results in losing the moral clarity and righteousness of the liberal vision, so "difficult" actors who do not conform have no place in this version of statebuilding, and are instead treated as pariahs, or "rogue states."

Statebuilding has become shorthand for a "liberal" vision of the state that implies:

(a) Conformity with Western values and the liberal template (elections + free markets);
(b) Statebuilding leadership from international (read Western) actors;
(c) The moral righteousness of the liberal vision of the state; and
(d) The inherent benevolence of the state.

A second implication of linking statebuilding with the liberal template is that governments and the international community are expected to respond to extralegal groups in a specific way. A monopoly on violence must first be established by eliminating these groups because of the threat that they pose to national security. The liberal template demands this because these coercive, nonstate groups are viewed as security threats, first and foremost.

The international response to extralegal groups has highlighted that there is little space for them to be incorporated into the official statebuilding narrative. This is partly because they are tainted by war, partly because they sit outside state structures, and partly because they threaten national security, even where they offer local security. There is an overall attitude of "West knows best" when it comes to post-conflict statebuilding that can be perceived as righteous and arrogant. A dogmatically liberal vision prevents a more honest and realistic conversation about how Weberian bureaucratic values might clash with how a post-conflict state is *actually* run.

The term "statebuilding" is being used in ways that assume a single clear path to full "stateness," when in fact, there may be multiple paths, each of which is strewn with different kinds of hazards. A more flexible approach would acknowledge the following points:

(i) Statebuilding's ultimate aim is to provide public governance goods; the nature of these goods need not conform to Western values, and the delivery mechanisms need not be liberal;
(ii) Statebuilding can be driven by citizens and civil society as well as by government officials and external actors; and
(iii) The presumed benevolence of the state is derived from Westerners' own perceptions of and their own relationships with Western states.

A Universal Metric for Statebuilding

I began this book by defining statebuilding as a process of building local institutions to provide public goods. I focused on statebuilding in its earliest stages. In assessing statebuilding success, *it is important to stress improvements in the daily lives of citizens rather than the institutional shells which mimic signals of stateness but lack substance.* In this regard, the problem is that sometimes state capacity is built up, but does not serve the citizens in whose name the state is being constructed. Contemporary approaches to understandings of and practices of statebuilding emphasize institution-building rather than the public goods and social services that these institutions are expected to deliver. Policy thinking on statebuilding "success" stresses the existence of institutional capacity rather than citizen satisfaction with these institutions. *We measure capacity rather than the improvement in the lives of citizens.*

In theory, it is possible to reclaim the term "statebuilding" and use it in a way that frees it of its Western imperial baggage and its assumed superiority and righteousness. One potential metric for measuring statebuilding success *is the ability to provide to all citizens equal access to essential governance goods (e.g., security, rule of law) and to distribute these goods fairly through impersonal institutions.* This aligns with the two core elements that make up the kernel of the state: a monopoly on legitimate force and access to impartial justice. Using this measure as an acid test, all states—rich and poor, democratic or not—show room for improvement, and can be compared along the same statebuilding spectrum.[65]

In this spirit, extralegal groups can be evaluated against more realistic expectations for the Liberian state rather than Western standards of stateness. By eliminating the Successful/Failed *binary* that is inherent in the contemporary statebuilding discourse, it becomes possible to frame statebuilding in a way that does not simply place rich, developed states on a pedestal, as the sole model that all other countries should aspire to.

POLICY PRINCIPLES FOR DEALING WITH EXTRALEGAL GROUPS

How should government officials and international policymakers respond to extralegal groups? Should these groups be dismantled as soon as they begin to emerge? Given that they threaten the use of violence in communities and that

---

[65] For example, see 16.3 of the Sustainable Development Goals: "Promote the rule of law at the national and international levels and ensure equal access to justice for all."

they hinder the consolidation of state authority, it follows logically that they should be destroyed. If the goal is to build a Western rational-bureaucratic state, then the first task is to strengthen the state by helping it to re-assume a monopoly over the legitimate use of force.

However, one of the underlying arguments in this book is that state strengthening should not be the default response. States are not inherently "good" and deserving of international support, and neither are all nonstate actors inherently "bad" and deserving of condemnation. Between these extremes, there are many ways for governments and international actors to respond. The problem is that the "good" intentions of external actors do not necessarily lead to improved outcomes for citizens. Critically, the international community should not be viewed as the "savior" in the narrative of post-conflict transitions, nor should they view themselves as saviors.

Providing a single policy prescription would be antithetical to the spirit of this study. However, extralegal groups can pose a real challenge to postwar societies, and local and international actors will feel the need to respond. This section discusses five policy principles, each aimed at improving the everyday lives of regular citizens in the affected communities. Notably, not all of these principles are compatible with the aims and interests of external policymakers and government elites.

Principle 1. Support Domestic Political Legitimacy, with an Eye on Second Order Effects

Responding to an extralegal group requires an understanding of how politically legitimate the group is perceived to be by its host community, and the extent to which the former has fused with the latter.[66] Higher levels of local political legitimacy will make it harder to displace the group.

Extralegal groups are not all alike. The nature of the relationships between extralegal groups and their host communities will vary. Some extralegal groups maintain exploitative relationships and others are more transactional in their approach, while others still, rely on social ties to their communities. Some communities will share deep ties and an ability to mobilize, while others will be easily divided. Uniformity should not be assumed in how extralegal groups treat local populations—assuming that all extralegal groups are exploitative based on the experiences of one extralegal group would be a mistake. Indeed, even to assume that the *same* extralegal group will behave consistently over time would be unwise.

---

[66] The problem of legitimacy raises questions about what is considered legitimate, and who gets to decide. While these are clearly critical issues that are wrapped around the exertion of power, I set aside these questions because they take us beyond extralegal groups.

From the perspective of local communities, these gradations in political legitimacy—across groups, between leaders, over time—are implicit. Even for national leaders, there is an understanding that different extralegal groups can have different kinds of relationships with their local communities—even while they may be publicly denouncing *all* extralegal groups as national security threats. Any efforts to improve the accountability of these groups to their communities, to the government, or to other legitimized institutions, should be broadly encouraged. Here, changes in the Nezoun Group brought about by Steve Joe and local activists serve as a reminder of how public interest can be injected into the power structure.

For outsiders, it may be particularly difficult to assess levels of local political legitimacy. But properly surveying this political landscape is crucial. For international actors in particular, extra care must be taken in assessing an extralegal group's political legitimacy. Otherwise, international actors will be prone to eliciting the kinds of responses others think they want to hear. For example, if the international community's narratives about these groups is that they are threatening, then they will likely be fed anecdotes that affirm these views. Instead, international actors need to create the space for honest answers, and be ready to embrace the contradictions that this may entail.

Accurately assessing levels of domestic political legitimacy is critical to formulating a strategic response in post-conflict transitions, but it can mean different things in different locales. A Western diplomat's conception of domestic political legitimacy will be different from that of a Liberian grass-roots activist or the head of a local mining firm. Importantly, *democracy does not necessarily imply legitimacy*, and *non-democratic arrangements do not automatically equate to illegitimacy* (see Table 8.1).

Accordingly, even though an extralegal group lacks legitimacy in the eyes of international actors, it may still be viewed as locally legitimate because it provides a semblance of local order through regulation, dispute resolution, and contract enforcement.

Table 8.1. Desirability of regime characteristics by Western standards

	DEMOCRATIC	NON-DEMOCRATIC
LEGITIMATE	**Most desirable** E.g., Free, fair, open, and transparent political campaign and elections	**Less desirable** E.g., Traditional or religious rule through chiefs, elders, Poro and Sande societies
ILLEGITIMATE	**Less desirable** E.g., Violent campaign period followed by rigged elections	**Least desirable** E.g., Militia rule using terrorist tactics and repression, as with the RUF in Sierra Leone, the Shining Path in Peru, or the LRA in Uganda

Principle 2. Prioritize Livelihoods

In many respects, this is a book about livelihoods and survival after war. As noted in the opening chapters, the problem of employment is particularly acute for hardened ex-combatants, who are often poorly educated and also stigmatized because of their status as former fighters.[67] Nevertheless, desperate people find their own employment by voting with their feet—even if this means acting outside of the law. Right after the war ended in 2004, Liberia's formal unemployment rate was 85 percent.[68] Liberians—ex-combatants and civilians alike—were willing to take jobs anywhere doing just about anything. Extralegal groups were simply a by-product of the situation, born out of the individual livelihood incentive structures that were in place at the time. *In the aggregate, these individual decisions shape the trajectory of local governance and statebuilding.*

For the most part, the modern peacebuilding template consists of reforming state institutions, with electoral democracy, economic liberalization, and security sector reform at its core. Institutional reform is tackled from the top down. Similarly, the economic dimensions of statebuilding after war that are put forward by the IMF and the World Bank through their Poverty Reduction Strategy Plans (PRSPs) focus on technical reforms of the country's financial and economic systems. In contrast, the livelihoods of the country's citizens receive little attention—the rationale being that employment will resolve itself once the right macro-economic structures are put in place. With the fundamentals in place, the reasoning is that it will then be possible to grow the economy, which in turn will improve livelihoods.[69]

To fully appreciate why livelihoods are low priority, another factor to take into account is that developing countries have large informal economies, yet the IMF and the World Bank use the same set of macroeconomic and socioeconomic indicators to examine countries *at all stages of development.* This has significant policy implications. For example, if economists use the formal unemployment rate as their key indicator for employment, they will miss the fact that a large proportion of the population works in the informal sector. Even where the unemployment rate has been adjusted to incorporate informal sector work, a focus on the rate itself means that it is easy to overlook the

---

[67] Unfortunately, DDR programs also have a poor track record when it comes to the economic reintegration of ex-combatants. Liberia's program was no exception. DDR training programs taught the same skill set (auto mechanic, soap-making, tailoring, carpentry, etc.) to thousands of people. But when these individuals attempted to join the workforce, they found that their newly acquired skills were ill-suited to the demands of the local labor market.

[68] While this figure overstates the unemployment problem (it ignores the informal sector which absorbs roughly one-third of the workforce), it still provides an important indication of the severity of the situation. See Government of Liberia (2004).

[69] In fact, we have seen in recent years that economic growth and employment rates have been decoupled from one another, and that globalization has amplified the unequal distribution of wealth within countries.

precariousness and insecurity of work. Rather than focusing solely on formal macroeconomic indicators, an emphasis on *livelihoods*—in the formal and informal sectors—can provide some redress.

A further problem is the overemphasis on foreign direct investment (FDI) which tends to bring large and reliable payments into government coffers. Large investments in developing natural resources, for example, are seen as critical to restoring the country's economic viability and are prioritized and supported by international actors. In theory, this makes sense. Governments need stable tax revenues in order to deliver public services. However, the process of attracting large FDI projects is often riddled with corruption—with little or no benefit being delivered to the average citizen.

This push for FDI has come at the expense of sectors that provide more local jobs such as the agricultural sector, small and medium enterprises (SMEs), the informal economy, and the illicit economy. Sectors that do not bring FDI are treated as second- or third-order concerns, without considering their impact on local livelihoods. This often makes the transitional no-war-no-peace phase more tenuous than it needs to be.

A livelihoods approach to the economy—including more accurate measures of informal economic activity and more of a focus on lowering short-term unemployment rates—would better address lingering sources of tension. For example, reopening local markets or creating temporary public works projects can build on skills learned from DDR programs and reshape the local political economy. These kinds of initiatives put livelihoods at the center of a peaceful transition.

Principle 3. Build Trust in the State. Focus on Local Public Goods Provision

A different way for policymakers to approach extralegal groups is to recognize their contribution to providing order, rather than focusing exclusively on its members' violent pasts. By changing the nature of their local role, it may even be possible to fundamentally alter the group's essential character.

If the core aim is to improve the daily lives of citizens, then focusing on the actual ability of the actor in question to provide governance is critical. In post-conflict contexts, the state is not always the most capable actor. Highlighting this capacity gap will heighten tensions with post-conflict governments because the practical implications of such a shift would imply greater scope for these functions to be provided by nonstate actors. Moving away from a strictly state-centric view of governance provision will provoke a set of questions about who *can* and *should* provide public goods. In some cases, this might mean that these governance functions end up being supplied by international or local NGOs, or by private companies. In other cases, this might mean that governance functions are provided by extralegal groups, which are perceived as illegitimate.

Setting aside these concerns momentarily, if policymakers focused on the ability of providers—state or nonstate—to perform critical governance functions, then it is also possible that the nature of the groups themselves can be forced to evolve over time. The question that then arises is: Can outsiders play a supportive role in creating accountability between citizens and actors who are otherwise viewed as illegitimate?

Theoretically, we can expect that if an extralegal group is perceived by locals to be fair in its provision of governance goods, then the *form* of that group will eventually adapt to reflect a fair process. In short, if the group can be induced into performing its governance functions fairly, then that group will set up a structure that is also fair. Instead of trying to eliminate the group, the focus is to induce, constrain, hold to account, and incentivize it to perform its governance tasks fairly, by using whatever tactical levers are available. The target is the group's governance provision rather than its outlaw status. If policymakers set aside their pre-conceptions of the "extralegal" label and instead prioritize the quality of governance provision, then form may follow function. Over time, building up social and community constraints should affect how the group behaves.

Principle 4. Do Not Judge Based on Western Standards

For external actors, most of whom are from outside the region in which they are working, responding to extralegal groups means evaluating and passing judgment on behaviors that are rooted in cultures, traditions, religions, or value systems that are very different from those where they come from. What is considered to be a corrupt practice in one country may be viewed as an everyday activity in another country. For example, in responding to extralegal group activities in Liberia, local actors see a big difference between "taxing" with community redistribution and "taxing" without community redistribution. The former is perfectly acceptable whereas the latter can get you killed by a lynch mob. The emphasis lies in whether the money is redistributed—or not. However, for those who are accustomed to impersonal state institutions, these "taxation" practices would be viewed as illegitimate in and of themselves because only the state is seen as having the right to tax.

The problem of imposing what might be considered "basic" institutional standards in one country becomes further complicated when the rule of law is not firmly in place and laws are not uniformly applied within a country.[70] In these situations, what is considered legal or illegal can be subject to interpretation because the application of law is itself malleable.

---

[70] For example, see the Rule of Law Index, World Justice Project (2015).

Similarly, there is overlap in formal, informal, and even criminal activities. The same activities can be interpreted very differently depending upon the context. Consider the timber sector: trade in commercial lumber is a formal, thriving industry in Liberia. Nonetheless, some of the logs that end up in the lumber yards were harvested informally, without proper permits or tax payments to the Forestry Development Authority, and without local permissions from local tribes. Depending on one's perspective, these logging activities can be viewed as part of the formal economy (through the retail trade), the informal economy (gray market), or as part of the criminal economy (black market). Needless to say, treating an activity as "informal" has different implications than treating it as "illegal" or "criminal." Yet making a judgment on whether these extralegal group activities qualify as informal or criminal relies on a contextualized understanding of both the social and legal framework of a society.[71] If the interest is peace and stability, the issue is not only whether the activities were deemed illegal by black letter law standards in high-capacity Weberian states, but also whether standards of legality are perceived to be applied fairly.

Principle 5. Extralegal Groups Can Evolve

This study demonstrates that there is substantial variation in extralegal group behavior and capacity, over time and across space. The ways in which government officials and international policymakers respond to extralegal groups should depend on the behaviors of the group. Some will respect local communities and use minimal violence while others will not. Some leaders and groups will be able to provide governance functions effectively while others cannot. Some will tax fairly and consistently and others will not. The difficulty lies in assessing which extralegal groups can be successfully converted into statebuilders and which ones cannot, bearing in mind that within the category of "extralegal," all groups should not be tarred with the same brush.

BEYOND LIBERIA: EXTRALEGAL GROUPS IN OTHER SETTINGS

This book introduced a framework for analyzing extralegal groups. While the framework proved useful for understanding the political economy of Liberia's war-to-peace transition, its applicability to other countries requires further exploration. With that caveat in mind, there is evidence that the framework is

---

[71] For a seminal discussion on social norms and practices around the world, see William G. Sumner (1906).

useful in its constituent stages because extralegal groups exist in varying stages of maturity in other countries. This poses interesting possibilities for future research.

The framework could be tested on post-conflict cases such as Kosovo, Colombia, and Afghanistan. In Kosovo, the goal would be to search for evidence of territorial control over certain types of trade (e.g., cigarette and gasoline smuggling) based on splinter groups of the Kosovo Liberation Army (KLA) and their associates. There are indications that entities resembling extralegal groups operated in the region in its postwar recovery period.[72] In Colombia, the demobilization of the paramilitary group Autodefensas Unidas de Colombia (AUC) gave birth to the Urabeños in the mid-2000s. As the AUC was dismantled, local fighters re-organized into criminal gangs and fought each other for control of the cocaine trade. Gradually, they built up a membership of thousands and successfully shut down the northwest of the country in a one-day armed strike in 2016.[73] In Afghanistan, former militia commanders, criminals, and tribal leaders have banded together to create intricate networks supporting the heroin trade, with some Afghan leaders becoming warlord-governors in the process.[74]

Taking the concept of extralegal groups beyond Liberia broadens the applicability of the theory to other types of fragile state situations such as Somalia, Brazil, Mexico, Haiti, East Timor, and the Democratic Republic of Congo.[75] In all of these countries, there have existed forms of extralegal groups powerful enough to threaten the state. For example, in Somalia, there are indications that the pirate syndicates have evolved in a way that is consistent with the extralegal groups framework being proposed.[76] In Brazil, the favelas of Rio and São Paolo operated as micro-states controlled by drug trafficking gangs with their own territorial boundaries, service delivery, and contract enforcement systems until recent "Pacification" programs were implemented beginning in 2008.[77] In Haiti as well, criminal gangs in Port-au-Prince were once so powerful that they were entrenched in the country's political structures.[78]

Similarly, in the case of powerful and violent drug cartels operating along the U.S.–Mexican border, the stages of extralegal group development and

---

[72] R. T. Naylor (2001); M. Pugh (2004); Michael Pugh and Neil Cooper (2004); Aida A. Hozic (2006).

[73] Christine Cheng and Jorge Delgado (2017).

[74] Jonathan Goodhand (2011); Dipali Mukhopadhyay (2014).

[75] A related analysis examines gangs as nonstate armed groups, drawing on the conflict literature. See Jennifer Hazen (2010).

[76] Mohamed Ahmed (2009); David Anderson (2009); Jeffrey Gettleman (2009).

[77] On security in the favelas, see Enrique Desmond Arias and Corinne Davis Rodrigues (2006); Ben Penglase (2009). For a critique of the recent Pacification processes, see Robert Muggah and Albert Souza Mulli (2012).

[78] Michael Dziedzic and Robert M. Perito (2008).

entrenchment resonate with how these cartels operate. Their methods have been so successful that Mexico was briefly discussed as a possible failed state.[79] With respect to extralegal group development, the taxation structures put in place by drug cartels substantially strengthened their organizational abilities— especially in terms of demarcating territory and establishing local loyalties.[80] These structures are active not only on the streets of Mexico's cities, but also throughout Mexico's prisons.

In choosing a strategy of coexistence, this sequence of events is consistent with a central government's choice to ignore extralegal groups, allowing them to grow unhindered for several decades, only to find itself facing an untenable situation where they are so deeply embedded in the local political economy that they become impossible to root out or reign in. This meant that when President Felipe Calderón decided to launch his aggressive strategy against the cartels and reclaim control over those regions in 2006, he faced an efficient and violent organization that was capable of penetrating local police forces and the powerful Mexican military.

FINAL REFLECTIONS

In this book, I have shown how extralegal groups establish primitive forms of order and justice in order to create the conditions for trade. Without intending to, they create the kernel of the modern state by directly providing basic governance functions of contract enforcement and dispute resolution. Extralegal groups also offer vital but hidden statebuilding functions of consolidating coercive force, by socializing the population into accepting a ruler, and moving the citizens away from vigilante justice. At the same time, they also pose a clear threat to national security: they are decisive actors that determine whether a country recovers from war or relapses back into armed conflict. These tensions coexist.

This study has unpacked the structures and incentives of these groups, deriving a contextually based account of their behavior that explains their emergence, development, and entrenchment in rational actor terms. The trajectories of these groups reveal the complexity of post-conflict transitions and the challenges that extralegal groups pose to war-torn societies. Using extralegal groups as a window into the post-conflict environment, the framework developed here has highlighted where post-conflict governments and the international community have leverage to empower citizens and civil society to demand accountability—and where they do not. It has also revealed how

---

[79] For example, see George Friedman (2010); George W. Grayson (2010).
[80] Robert Bunker (2010).

international institutions are each constrained by forces within their own organizations, as well as by the politics of the country in question.

In this book, I have introduced the concept of conflict capital to demonstrate that an act of violence—committing it, being victim to it, even passively observing it—has sociological and physiological effects that must be reckoned with, at the individual and group level. I have shown how the framing of actors and events can deeply affect the trajectory of peace for a community—the difference between being labelled a blood diamond mining town vs an artisanal mining center matters deeply for local livelihoods. I have explored the myth of the "good" state and deconstructed why statehood resonates so deeply within the international community. I have made the case for a more pluralistic approach to governance that acknowledges the wide variety of actors that provide de facto governance, including those that are illiberal. I have referred to historical precedent to show how patterns of exploitation echo down the generations, turning victims into perpetrators. I have demonstrated that an end to war does not necessarily mean an end to violence, and that peace should not be treated as a binary concept, but as a continuum. And I have shown that resources are not destiny, and that community activists can join together to demand local accountability from their leaders.

Creating a peaceful state is complex and highly contingent. In the words of former UN Secretary-General Dag Hammarskjöld: "The pursuit of peace and progress cannot end in a few years in either victory or defeat. The pursuit of peace and progress, with its trials and errors, its successes and setbacks, can never be relaxed and never abandoned." In Liberia, as in other post-conflict societies, the hope is that a vibrant and sustainable peace will prevail and endure.

9

Coda. Research Design Scaffolding

"You never see the mistakes, or the struggle."
Carol Dweck[1]

This is not a traditional chapter on research design and methodology. Rather than leaving you, the reader, with the impression that this project was neatly and logically conceived in its entirety—as it has been presented up to this point, hopefully—this chapter is premised instead on the idea that designing a research project is an inherently messy process. The opening quote from social psychologist Carol Dweck captures how scholars tend to present their work— as a finished whole, without discussing any of the mistakes or the struggle that went into its creation. Scholarly norms of presenting published work often mask valuable lessons on how research is actually conducted. Here, I take a more analytically transparent and reflective approach.

The concept of "research design scaffolding" that is referred to in the title of this chapter suggests that a certain amount of construction goes into academic research.[2] Rather than discarding this foundational work as tangential, irrelevant, or as undermining the final result, I propose that unveiling this scaffolding— in a way that explains how and why the project evolved—can provide an additional standalone contribution to understanding the subject matter. By discussing the rationale and the thinking that goes into refining a research question, the hope is that other scholars will be encouraged to lay bare more of their thought processes where it is practical and ethical to do so.[3] This is not a call for greater data access or production transparency.[4] Instead, this

---

[1] Megan McArdle (2014).

[2] Research design comprises the research question and the research methodology that is used to answer it.

[3] See the revised rules in the 2012 American Political Science Association Ethics Guide and the Journal Editors' Transparency Statement, Political Science Journal Editors (2014). See also, the Symposium on Transparency in Qualitative and Multi-Method Research, Tim Büthe and Alan M. Jacobs (2015).

[4] I hold significant reservations about data access and production transparency for qualitative research, especially for ethnographic and conflict research. For further discussion, see Katherine

discussion focuses on constructing the research question, rather than generating or interpreting the data that lead to the findings. The ways in which we choose and refine a research question itself deserve to be demystified.

Does this chapter reflect a gendered approach to research design? Perhaps. I am proposing a retrospective reflection on the overall project that emphasizes a collaborative, rather than confrontational, approach to learning from the research process. Rather than maintaining the fiction that the final, published version of the research design has remained the same since the project was first conceived, I will argue that social scientists need to be less adversarial and more iterative in creating a common body of knowledge.

CHANGING THE CONVERSATION: THE FICTION OF TIDY RESEARCH

In most scholarly books on politics, the discussion of research methodology tends toward a straightforward description of the methods used, with limited discussion about the challenges encountered and the many iterations that a research design typically passes through. Interestingly, it is often in the preface or the acknowledgments of a book, where unexpected research obstacles are most likely to be frankly discussed. Only in the preamble, in this unofficial commentary, is there a hint of how much a project has changed over time, or how logistical challenges led to major changes in the research question.[5] In this same spirit, this chapter builds on this tradition by proposing that scholars be given the intellectual space to formally share and discuss the design and methodological evolution of a major research project—especially the critical junctures in a project when important research design choices were made.

Research is an iterative process and early iterations can provide valuable insights into the black box of research design. Nevertheless, it is unsurprising that scholars do not reveal more about their research design process, the ways in which they choose their research questions, or their motivations for choosing a particular line of inquiry.[6] Pointing out the weaknesses in how a study is designed can undermine the credibility of the results and provide fodder for critical attacks. Because of the fact that it is the perceptions of other scholars that ultimately drive prestige[7] and success in the academic world, the incentives are such that being open about research design scaffolding could do more

---

Cramer (2015); Nancy Hirschmann, Mala Htun, Jane Mansbridge, Kathleen Thelen, et al. (2015); Sarah Elizabeth Parkinson and Elisabeth Jean Wood (2015); Victor Shih (2015).

[5] For example, see Smith's Preface in D. J. Smith (2007).

[6] On understanding the motivations of politics scholars and the role that political activism played in the research of leading scholars, see G. L. Munck and R. Snyder (2007).

[7] On the academic prestige economy, see K. Coate and C. Kandiko (2013).

harm than good to an academic career.[8] For those who are seeking to convert a Ph.D. thesis into a book, the common advice from book publishers is to minimize or even eliminate the methodology section altogether.[9]

In the study of politics, the typical approach to research design and methods focuses on explaining *how* the chosen method was used to answer the question posed. Indeed, scholars typically approach the discussion of methods with care.[10] However, much is left unsaid, as MacGinty points out:

> Our research is taking place in the real world. Not in some laboratory, or using a dataset that someone else has collected. These problems are the ones faced by many NGOs, INGOs, international organisations and academics in their research and yet...and yet...we rarely hear about these problems. Why not? Is it because they only conduct research in perfect environments? Or is it because they tend to mask many of the practical difficulties that they face in order to give the impression that their research is robust and trustworthy?[11]

THE RESEARCH QUESTION

The classic format for presenting politics studies underemphasizes the iterative nature of research itself, saying little about the choice of research question.[12] The starting point for the investigation is the research question[13] and the end point is articulated in the findings. The research methods describe how the author gets from A to B.

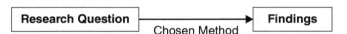

Often, the classic approach is sufficient and deriving the chosen research question adds little value. Indeed, presenting tangential information can obscure the research question and its central findings, confusing the reader in the process.

---

[8] On Twitter, the conversation based on the hashtag #overlyhonestmethods has revealed the extent to which scholars have purposely misinterpreted, strategically purged, blatantly ignored, and advantageously skewed their data to suit their desired findings.

[9] K. Kelsky (2011); P. Dunleavy (2014).

[10] There are many excellent examples of thorough discussions of research methodology in conflict settings, and reflections on how this can be conducted ethically. For example, see E. J. Wood (2014). For an example of how research methodology is thoughtfully discussed, see J. R. McMullin (2013), p. 7. See also Appendix A: The Ethnography of Rebel Organizations in J. M. Weinstein (2007).

[11] Roger MacGinty (2014), also see comments at the end of this post.

[12] Sometimes, especially with technical or quantitative research, the author might also explain why one method was chosen over another.

[13] Hui's discussion of the research question that was *not* chosen is consistent with the spirit of this chapter. Victoria Tin-bor Hui (2005), p. 7.

Nevertheless, the choice of starting point is still important because embedded within a research question are a set of assumptions about the world, how it works, how the author believes it *should* work, and where the author sits in relation to the subject matter. The topic, the research question, and the research design are not neutral; they reflect an author's values, and these values can also shift during the course of a project.[14] The matter of how scholars arrive at that supposed starting point is usually something of a mystery—a conjuring trick of sorts. *The research question is framed for the reader so that it seems preordained, when in fact, there were many research questions that could have been posed, and many different ways of answering the same research question.*

To explore this notion, this chapter now takes you back to the Introduction again to interrogate the evolution of the research question of this book. Where the classic approach presents the research question as a given, this chapter treats the research question and the corresponding search for an appropriate method to answer that question as a combined iterative process.

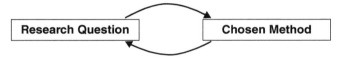

At the start of a research project, most scholars start out with a variety of questions that they want to answer and then they go through an iterative process of discovery, pondering, testing, elimination, and refining before they settle on The Research Question that is formally presented as the starting point of the study. A lot of learning goes on in this process that is hidden from the reader. This chapter unpacks how the research question itself is derived and examines the iterative process that underlies it.[15]

To provide an analogy, think about how algebra is taught. In solving an algebra problem, it is always important to show your work. For example, on an exam question worth ten marks, it is possible to get the final answer wrong, but to still get nine marks out of ten by showing all the steps leading up to it. The key principle here is that demonstrating how the answer is derived is just as important as the answer itself.

Despite these reminders, this advice to *show your work* is not always heeded in algebra. Students have different styles of doing math. Some prefer to leave scraps of their thinking along the way, writing out only the elements that cannot be solved in their heads. Other students work through the algebra problem and then erase everything except for the final answer. Then there are

---

[14] Timothy Pachirat (2015).
[15] Nordstrom's reflective ethnographic approach in questioning how we study war and what is deemed worth studying also resonates with the approach of this chapter. See C. Nordstrom and A. C. G. M. Robben (1995); C. Nordstrom (2004).

the high achievers, who logically link the original question to the final answer with all of the key steps in between (and no tangents). Others still might start off trying to answer the question, veer off in the wrong direction, then cross out those parts that were incorrect before trying another line of reasoning, and then crossing that out too if it did not work out. These students are inevitably the messiest, leaving a wake of algebraic destruction behind them as they meander toward the final answer.

In constructing their research questions, politics scholars resemble the students who erase all of their work after arriving at the correct answer—the research question is simply taken as given. A scholarly study begins by justifying the research question, by placing it within the context of the existing academic literature. The methods discussion that follows describes how an author has chosen to answer the research question. Yet usually, there is very little discussion about *why* one question was chosen over another; nor is there a discussion of all the mistakes, uncertainties, wrong turns, and obstacles that were encountered along the way to formulating a particular research question, and an appropriate research design to answer that question. Instead, the professional norm is to cast aside all of the rejected research questions and the corresponding research designs, anomalous results, and messy findings that do not fit neatly into the story being told.

I make a contrasting claim: that the detritus of our efforts to construct a research question—and a corresponding research design—can provide insights that more accurately reflect how research is actually conducted. If choosing an appropriate research question lays the foundation for a compelling scholarly study, then it seems important to open up the black box of how research questions are constructed.

For example, those who use quantitative methods often generate many more models than are used in the final, published study. These are typically discarded because they do not add new information to the results, or in some cases, the findings may contradict the final result or lead to non-findings. But sometimes, these findings lead to a reframing of the original research question, creating a new iteration of the original research question. In this type of situation, knowing which variables were considered and rejected is useful information in itself for understanding how the author derived the final model. Some scholars helpfully provide online access to their dataset as well as links to these rejected models. This chapter suggests that a similarly open approach to our discarded frameworks and hypotheses may also prove useful.

THE RATIONALE FOR SHOWING YOUR WORK

The same principle for showing your work in an algebra problem should also apply to social science research: there is much to be learned from understanding how a particular research design is constructed, and how it came to be designed the way it was. This becomes even more important if the particular research terrain is not well defined or is in its infancy. The less we know about a given research space, the more important it becomes to clearly signpost the underlying logic of the study and how it was constructed.

In the analogy for learning algebra, the rationale for showing your work was to demonstrate your ability to provide the "right" answer to a defined problem. For research questions that are not clearly specified, with many alternative ways of approaching the problem and many ways of gathering data, unveiling that scaffolding is helpful for understanding how the author derived the final research design. Making explicit the twists and turns of research is particularly useful for readers who are less experienced.

Sharing the "crossed out" parts can be quite useful to the scholarly community in three ways. First, being honest about how a project and its central research question evolved over time is important because it forces the author to explain many of the key ideas that are internalized over the course of a project. At the start of a project, there are concepts and frameworks that are new and exciting that researchers will adopt to make sense of the problem. Over time though, these ideas are gradually absorbed and taken for granted. For the author, concepts that once seemed shiny and new eventually become so ingrained that it is difficult to remember that they were not always part of one's repertoire. Discussing the research scaffolding is about making these internalized ideas explicit, so that others can understand the intellectual journey that was taken to complete the project.

Second, wrong answers are often quite revealing (and interesting) in themselves. These "crossed out" parts uncover the different decision pathways of a project. These can be obscured in the final product. Understanding why a scholar chose one path over another allows the reader to learn from the author's choices, and encourages the reader to imagine alternative ways of answering the same research question, even if the author ultimately reject these other methods.

Third, laying out these discarded tangents and diversions improves the transparency of research findings. This is particularly helpful for scholars-in-training. In theory, a discussion of research design and methods exists in order to facilitate replication of the research. The concept of replication, taken from the sciences, implies that an independent person should be able to conduct the same experiment and generate similar results.[16] Yet it is clear that even in the sciences, where replication should be more straightforward, there are serious problems with reproducing research findings.[17]

---

[16] Roger Peng (2011).

[17] An essay entitled "Why Most Published Research Findings Are False" has provoked much soul searching in the scientific community since it was published by John P. A. Ioannidis (2005). Even in medical research, where the stakes are highest and lives are literally at stake, research replication problems have been endemic and persistent over time. See the influential editorial on the biases inherent in medical research by D. G. Altman (1994).

These concerns about the validity of research findings also extend to the social sciences. In recent years, teams of psychologists have sought to replicate the findings of one hundred of the most influential psychology studies from the discipline's three leading journals. They found that:

> 39% of effects were subjectively rated to have replicated the original result ... A large portion of replications produced weaker evidence for the original findings despite using materials provided by the original authors, review in advance for methodological fidelity, and high statistical power to detect the original effect sizes.[18]

Even with statistical studies where authors post their data publicly, it is important to note that the *raw data* used in the models are often not generated from scratch and are subject to a variety of problems.[19] In light of these problems across disciplines with data, evidence, and interpretation, there is no reason to think that the study of politics is immune to these vulnerabilities. For statistical analyses, aiming for a standard of reproducibility—such that an independent person who analyzes the same data is able to derive similar findings—offers one way to tackle this problem. However, reproducibility and replicability are not always possible or desirable, and depend on compatibility with a methodological approach. Making one's interviews publicly available has very different implications from posting one's dataset.[20]

Consequently, adopting transparency and a reflexive approach as guiding principles to research design is more pragmatic. The aim should be to provide the reader with enough guidance so that they can make sense of the methods used and the decisions taken to arrive at the findings.[21] Not only will a "Show Your Work" approach increase transparency and reflexivity, but it should also prompt more careful consideration of the ethics and responsibilities that come with making expert claims derived from the findings.

EXTRALEGAL GROUPS: UNVEILING THE SCAFFOLDING

To illustrate these ideas, I will use this project on extralegal groups to show the evolution of this project. To provide a focal point, I will discuss how the research question changed from one iteration of the project to the next based on earlier versions of research proposals which I will cite from directly. I will

---

[18] Open Science Collaboration (2015).
[19] This stands in contrast to the hard sciences, where raw data are repeatedly generated with each set of experimental results.
[20] Sarah Elizabeth Parkinson and Elisabeth Jean Wood (2015).
[21] P. Dunleavy (2014).

proceed chronologically, revealing how the project evolved over time (and not always in a linear fashion).

Iteration 1: Criminal Warfare

When this study was originally conceived,[22] the intention was to study "criminal warfare." I was interested in the analytical framing of "war" as compared to "crime." I wanted to understand: Why does the world pay so much more attention to the civilians who die in a civil war than those who die in a criminal setting, for example, in turf battles between drug traffickers? What makes one set of innocent civilian lives more worthy of attention than another set of innocent civilian lives?

From a human security perspective, the circumstances under which both sets of innocent civilians lost their lives had much in common. In both types of cases, thousands of people were being killed in battle zones; civilians were often caught in the crossfire; and the foot soldiers were mostly young men coming from environments with limited options for employment. I was struck that the battles that were taking place in the favelas of Rio de Janeiro, in the townships of South Africa, in areas of Dagestan, and in the borderlands of Mexico all resembled civil war zones. Yet these were countries that were considered "at peace." Despite the thousands of people being killed annually, these places received little international attention because there was no existential threat to the sitting government or to the state itself.

In the first version of my Ph.D. research proposal, I wanted to make sense of how these distinct settings were hybridizing:

> Since the end of the Cold War, a symbiotic relationship has developed between crime and conflict: criminals are recruited to fight wars, war is prolonged for criminal purposes, and violent crime is so prevalent in some areas that there is virtually a state of war. Furthermore, in many regions of conflict, civil war has become synonymous with high rates of violent crime and atrocities.
>
> Traditionally, conflict has been of international concern and crime has always been treated as an issue of domestic jurisdiction. These distinctions are no longer as clear or as valid. What is more prevalent now is what could be termed "criminal warfare": where criminals are recruited to fight wars; when war is prolonged for criminal purposes; when crime becomes an instrument of war; or where violent crime is so prevalent that there is virtually a state of civil war. This hybridization of crime and conflict into criminal warfare has become a significant threat to international peace and security.

---

[22] This was taken from my Ph.D. application.

In probing the crime-conflict link, the first version of my research question was: *In weak states, are high levels of violent crime a precursor to civil war?*

Re-reading these paragraphs from the first draft of the research proposal, I can identify several problems in the proposal, including a tendency to generalize when there is no evidential basis upon which to do so; conflating processes that are distinct; and an oversimplified understanding of state sovereignty. Nonetheless, looking back on this first version of my research proposal, I can still see a nugget of my current conception of extralegal groups: the blurred line between the functions, actions, and motivations of criminal groups and fighting groups.

Iteration 2: The Legacy of the War Economy

Building on the original proposal which focused on criminal warfare, the second iteration of the project examined the idea that vested interests develop around a war economy, and that these economic interests would impact the nature of the post-conflict state itself.[23] Consequently, the research question was modified to: *How does the illicit and illegal part of a war economy affect a country's transition to peace?* My intuition was that the pathologies of a war economy would pose serious challenges for the stability of the state. However, it was not clear how the beneficiaries of the war economy would behave and how they would adapt and react to the threat of peace.

I anticipated substantial challenges in trying to answer this question. Developing a convincing answer would require, at a minimum, an accurate portrait of how the informal and formal wartime economies functioned (and concomitantly, a reasonable estimation of the pre-existing peacetime economy). Yet gathering this data on the war economy would be extremely difficult, if not impossible, given the security challenges of a conflict zone, as well as the sensitive and illegal nature of the topic. Moreover, if my intuition was correct, then there would be people who would be motivated to actively shut down my study.[24] Given the difficulties of collecting good data, I opted to change the research question and to shift away from studying conflict environments directly.

---

[23] David Keen (1998); Mats R. Berdal and David Malone (2000).

[24] At this point, I should mention that I had originally intended to write my doctoral dissertation on Côte d'Ivoire, and that I was thinking about Liberia and Sierra Leone as additional comparative cases. However, when the conflict flared up in Abidjan, I decided that I did not want to conduct research in an active warzone.

Iteration 3: Local Political Authority

The third iteration of this project examined the same set of issues, but opened up the range of inquiry beyond control over the war economy to the assertion of local political authority. Having decided not to travel to active conflict zones, I shifted my focus to studying "post-conflict" environments:

> A common assumption about post-conflict environments is that there is a political authority vacuum.[25] Western conceptions of political authority lead us to this conclusion: since we are accustomed to political power being exercised through the state, there is a tendency to assume that the collapse of official state institutions during and after war inevitably leads to the collapse of political authority. Yet empirical evidence shows that there is no such collapse: politics continues on at the local level in one form or another.[26]
>
> However, it remains unclear who controls political authority when state institutions have decayed or have been destroyed by civil war. The possibilities include the UN,[27] local elites,[28] civil society,[29] traditional and religious elders,[30] warlords,[31] organized crime,[32] political criminal networks,[33] or local militias.[34] How this authority is regulated is also unclear: through self-enforcing governance mechanisms that are maintained through coalitions;[35] service-for-fee institutions such as vigilante gangs[36] or mafias;[37] personal relationships;[38] or patron-client relationships.[39] While we know that political life continues in the absence of effective state institutions, it remains unclear how political authority survives, in what form it survives, and under what circumstances.

To this end, this iteration of my research question asked: *How is local political authority asserted after civil war?*

On the surface, this version of the question sounds quite different from the first version, but in fact, I was still keen to understand how the dynamics of war economies affected the political sphere.

Hypothesis 1: Assuming a minimum level of physical security, local political authority is asserted through the control of economic resources.

---

[25] I. William Zartman (1995); Robert I. Rotberg (2004). Zartman makes a distinction between national political authority and local political authority. Collapsed states are defined by the vacuum of national political authority but not necessarily local political authority.

[26] Sofi Ospina and Tanja Hohe (2001); Jarat Chopra and Tanja Hohe (2004); Simon Chesterman, Michael Ignatieff and Ramesh Chandra Thakur (2005).

[27] Richard D. Caplan (2005).   [28] Timothy Donais (2003).

[29] Daniel Posner (2004).   [30] Hussein Adam (1995).

[31] William Reno (1998).   [32] R. T. Naylor (2001); Vadim Volkov (2002).

[33] Roy Godson (2003).   [34] B.R. Rubin (2002).

[35] Avner Greif (1993).   [36] D. M. Anderson (2002).

[37] Diego Gambetta (1993); Federico Varese (2001); Vadim Volkov (2002).

[38] Janet MacGaffey and Rémy Bazenguissa-Ganga (2000).

[39] Jean-François Bayart (1993); Patrick Chabal and Jean-Pascal Daloz (1999).

Hypothesis 2: Assuming a minimum level of physical security, local political authority is asserted through basic legal functions such as contract enforcement and dispute resolution.

In these hypotheses lay the foundations of my ideas about extralegal groups and how I believed they functioned. There was, however, a practical problem: I could not be sure that I would find the kinds of governance structures that I had predicted without first conducting fieldwork which would be difficult, time-consuming, and expensive. Social media, in the form we know it, did not yet exist, and it was near impossible to communicate with anyone who could tell me whether anything like an extralegal group had emerged. Without being able to confirm the existence of these networks, it seemed pragmatic to expand the scope of the research question to incorporate what I was interested in, while ensuring that there was still an interesting backup research project in case my hypotheses were wrong. I had a contingency plan: if I there were no extralegal groups, then I would turn to the issue of how local political authority is negotiated in a postwar community and why certain types of leaders (chiefs, politicians, ex-combatants, UNMIL officers, UNMIL peacekeepers, local police, business leaders) exerted authority in some localities but not others.

Iteration 4: Extralegal Groups

Having chosen Liberia as my case study (with the possibility of comparing it to Sierra Leone and Côte d'Ivoire), I arrived in Liberia in August 2005—a time when the country was still considered unstable. Almost immediately after I arrived, I realized that the original version of my research design which examined "criminal" groups fighting in wars would be viable. The hybrid criminal warfare groups that other scholars had previously written about had indeed resurfaced during the post-2003 transition period.[40] Once I was able to confirm their existence, my research design shifted decisively to studying the phenomenon that I refer to as extralegal groups.

> During a post-conflict transition, an equilibrium situation is possible where the state ends up sharing power with extralegal groups such as gangs, disgruntled ex-combatants, and organized crime. Initially, these groups represent a low-level security threat. Since their goals are economic, not political, they are unlikely to employ violence against the state. They are primarily involved in illicit, but not necessarily violent, economic activities (smuggling, illegal control of a resource, providing protection). The post-conflict transition provides them with a window of opportunity to take advantage of weakened security structures and judicial systems. At the same time, the breakdown in security also creates a demand for

---

[40] William Reno (1998); Stephen Ellis (1999).

protection by civilians and business interests (legal and illegal). Both resource capture and the creation of non-state protection networks are likely to result in physical control over a limited territory. If left unchecked, these extralegal groups develop powerful local bases and gradually expand, eventually posing a real threat to the state itself.

Usually, peacekeepers will not have the mandate to deal with these groups and a newly constituted (or severely weakened) government will not have the capacity or the desire to confront them. In the absence of any effective checks on their power, extralegal groups become embedded in society and remain there, outlasting the tenure of any international peacekeeping mission.

In short, the rise of extralegal groups in a post-conflict environment implies that a state will be embarking on a much less desirable equilibrium pathway. The outcome can end up compromising the state, as with the powerful influence of organized crime and gangs in post-conflict environments as varied as Bosnia, Kosovo, El Salvador and South Africa.

When the project began, my interest in these groups was focused on the threat that they posed to the peace process. As the project progressed though, I viewed the threat of these groups differently: it was no longer just their short-term potential for violence that was worrisome but also that these groups were consolidating their long-term power. The research question thus became: *After war, what are the processes by which extralegal groups emerge and how do they affect the statebuilding process?*

Iteration 5: Extralegal Groups—A Sectoral Approach

In analyzing the phenomenon that I had witnessed in Liberia, I was grasping for a vocabulary to describe these groups. They did not fit the description of warlords, mafias, or organized crime groups. What made them distinct? My first attempt at characterizing them led to three defining properties: "they control a material resource, they are profit-driven, and they pose a clear threat to the state." Having fit a basic description to them, I attempted a definition:

> An extralegal group is a set of individuals working together to control a specific territory primarily for profit and who are capable of using violence to maintain that control. I use the term "extralegal" to underscore the informal nature of these groups and their existence outside the law.

Having established that extralegal groups were important for understanding post-conflict transitions but also neglected by the existing literature, the research question shifted to: *Why do extralegal groups develop in some sectors of the economy but not others?* To answer this question, my research design focused on the subnational level, looking at extralegal groups by economic sector. It would have also been possible to compare these groups by geographical region or by the dominant military faction of its membership.

I examine the emergence (or lack of emergence) of extralegal groups in each of Liberia's four major economic sectors: timber, rubber, diamonds and iron ore. Which groups strengthen over time and what is the impact on the long-term trajectory of the statebuilding process?

In trying to understand the variation between the groups, three additional hypotheses were added:

1. If left undisturbed, extralegal groups lead to long-term institutionalized corruption and state capture.

2. The longer the period of extraction, the stronger and more organized the extralegal group will become.

3. The lower the start-up capital costs (relative to income levels) for a given economic sector, the more likely that extralegal groups will emerge in that sector.

In addition to the type of extralegal group that had originally motivated this study (as described earlier), I had also intended to discuss governance on corporate enclaves. For example, Firestone's corporate enclave would have met the three criteria for extralegal groups (controlling a material resource, profit-driven, threat to the state).

> In contrast to the state's efforts to rebuild its institutions, foreign corporations like Firestone have developed "state-within-a-state" structures of control. I argue that these parallel systems of governance prove to be as much of a threat to the state as extralegal groups.

In this iteration of the research design, I wanted to incorporate a discussion of the corporate enclaves that had previously dominated the resource extraction economy in Liberia. These enclaves functioned as an alternative governance system to the state, and to extralegal groups. If anything, it was this kind of governance that extralegal groups aspired to achieve: profitable, predictable, long-term control over territory. These groups were trying to become more like Firestone. Further, leaving out Firestone and its competing governance system made the study feel incomplete when the company's presence hovered over Liberia's political economy. Ultimately though, it became clear that this discussion of corporate enclaves would have taken me away from the original phenomenon that I was trying to understand. Even though corporate enclaves like Firestone sometimes behaved in extralegal ways, their relationship with the state was fundamentally different from the ex-combatant groups that were the focus of the study.

In contrast, if I had continued with the local political authority version of the thesis in iteration 3, I would have been able to study corporate enclaves as one of several forms of local governance. This version of the project would have compared institutions of traditional governance by village chiefs, informal governance by secret societies, formal governance by the state, extralegal group governance, and governance within corporate enclaves by the likes of Firestone.

Iteration 6: A Three-Stage Model—Emergence, Development, Entrenchment

Eventually, the core of the dissertation came to focus on how extralegal groups developed. This took me back to Iteration 4 of the research question: *How do extralegal groups emerge and develop after the end of the Liberian civil war?* At the time, the initial formation of these groups seemed to hinge on dozens of factors and it was difficult to distill which factors mattered and how they worked in combination with one another. What were the key causal mechanisms? How to separate out the general from the specific? How to edit out the less critical and idiosyncratic factors to pare down the model? Understanding the dynamics of these groups was only the beginning of the challenge—the next step was to distill these dynamics down to their simplest form, stripping bare the framework without losing the essence of the groups themselves. Building on the core logic of the framework, I could then add contextual factors to examine the specifics of each extralegal group, and the environment in which they operated.

I came to settle on a few core elements in my model of extralegal groups: sectoral barriers to entry, contract enforcement, the role of taxation, and local institutional capture. I began to cluster their activities into two stages: emergence and development. Emergence was related to low sectoral barriers to entry and contract enforcement, while organizational development was explained through taxation and local institutional capture. However, the term "development" implied that the groups were still evolving and did not accurately reflect the stability of the final equilibrium.

> The leaders running the group use some of the proceeds from taxation to enrich themselves, but they also set aside enough to pay off local and national authority structures like the police, the politicians, and the courts. At this point, the danger is that the extralegal group will have established a strong enough power base to bribe and coerce government officials on a regular basis, thus creating or reinforcing a system of entrenched corruption that will ultimately undermine the state. If the government decides to confront the group directly, there is the potential for organized violence, possibly leading to a return to civil war. In effect, if extralegal groups are left to their own devices, they have the potential to create substantial networks of influence that could undermine state institutions in the long run.
>
> On the other hand, the state can respond by co-opting the group. If this is done successfully, it is theoretically possible for an extralegal group to harness its influence to help stabilize the country and build state capacity.

The basic framework stayed the same, but I opted to separate out the entrenchment process because it had its own distinct dynamic. Consequently, the research question was modified slightly to: *How do extralegal groups emerge, develop, and become locally entrenched after the end of civil war?*

EXPLORING ALTERNATIVE EXPLANATIONS

For the development stage of the framework, there are at least two competing explanations for the increased organizational capacity of the extralegal group. First, the group may be building up its capacity in anticipation of a future confrontation with the state (or another armed group). To test this explanation, one could look for surges in recruitment and capacity when the state makes open threats to take over. If recruitment and capacity are not linked to the state's threats, then this explanation seems less plausible.

A second possibility for explaining extralegal group development is that taxation plays a minimal part in the development of the group as compared to the structures of resource extraction. This explanation suggests that it is not building the capacity to tax that strengthens the extralegal group, but rather, it is building the capacity of primary extraction—building the business—that explains the increase in organizational capacity. A logic of taxation and a logic of primary extraction are similar: constructing an organizational hierarchy and maintaining lines of control improves loyalty and lines of communication; in turn, these improvements facilitate collective action. To test this possibility, one would first need to confirm that the group was participating in the primary extraction business; then, it would be necessary to differentiate between the structures that served a tax purpose versus those involved in extraction. A basic comparison could measure the relative size and strength of these structures.

The problem is that both alternative explanations are difficult to test because very intimate knowledge of an extralegal group is needed. And while it is theoretically possible to obtain this information, it is not practical to do so. For example, it would be necessary to know: how an extralegal group's structure has evolved over time; the group's perceptions of the likelihood of state intervention over time; and the group's financial and coercive capabilities over time. Accessing this kind of information and measuring these perceptions and capabilities would have required inside information from the group's leaders.

For the third stage of entrenchment, a persuasive argument could be made that the corruption of government officials was an inevitable result because corruption of government officials is a local norm. Hence, corruption via extralegal groups is not special; they can be thought of as yet another mechanism through which corruption takes place. This interpretation suggests that the causality of Hypothesis 3 may be reversed: it is *not* the extralegal groups who are doing the corrupting, but in fact, it is the government authorities who are corrupting the extralegal groups. In practical terms, this means that government officials are asking for bribes in exchange for allowing the group to retain local control; this is qualitatively different from having extralegal groups neutralize local authorities by buying them out.

Ideally, this alternative hypothesis could be tested through controlled comparison. Each of the extralegal group case study areas could be paired with a similar area that is nearby. For each pairing, the local cultures of corruption are carefully studied, keeping track of information such as how long local authorities have been corrupted, who is bribing whom, how much is being paid, and which party solicited/offered. With this information, it is possible to determine whether areas with extralegal groups are different from paired areas without extralegal groups. Of course, accurate corruption data of this sort is not available.[41] There are also more feasible ways to test this alternative hypothesis. For example, we can qualitatively compare corrupt relationships in extralegal group areas with similar relationships in other parts of the country. If the depth, reach, and scope of corruption were qualitatively different,[42] then it is possible to conclude that corruption via extralegal groups is different.

UNCOVERING BIASES AND ASSUMPTIONS

After settling on the research question, I came to realize that my extralegal groups framework had embedded within it four implicit biases and mistaken assumptions. These included: stereotyping ex-combatants, conflating peace with order, overemphasizing the rationality of actors, and underestimating the malleability of the law and the legal system. These biases and assumptions had subtly affected the ways in which I understood and assessed extralegal groups, and the environment they inhabited.

The Good/Bad Paradigm

This project started with the simplistic notion that the members of extralegal groups were "bad." This labelling was not a conscious choice; initially, I was not even aware that I held such an assumption. This "good" vs "bad" framing only became apparent as the study progressed. As I continued to revise the theoretical framework, I also began to explore what "bad" actually meant. This normative judgment was underpinned by something very basic: I considered those who had committed human rights abuses to be "bad." Because a subset of Liberia's ex-combatants had clearly committed horrendous acts, I had subconsciously concluded that all ex-combatants were "bad." This was my

---

[41] Even if the data were available to conduct an accurate comparison, there are confounding variable problems.
[42] Mark Philp (2008).

first mistaken assumption: I had generalized from the specific. This led to a second mistaken assumption: bad people do bad things.

I had fallen prey to what Tversky and Kahneman termed the "availability heuristic."[43] In the same way that the average person significantly overestimates the likelihood of dying in a plane crash because of the prominence given to these stories by the media, my own availability bias had affected my perception of ex-combatants. Horrific acts of war had been committed by fighters from all major factions and these images remained prominent in my mind's eye. Studies in social psychology show that vividness significantly improves our ability to remember. We also know that memorability and disproportionate exposure both affect how likely we are to misjudge how likely something is to occur.[44] Humans are particularly poor at judging the probability of infrequent events. Even when we are made aware of our biases, it remains difficult to correct for them.[45] These violent images affected my perception of all ex-combatants. Even though I had deliberately set up the extralegal groups framework to be neutral, focusing primarily on what the groups did *after the war*, the ways in which these behaviors were framed were still affected by the availability heuristic and vividness bias.

As the study progressed, I realized that I was subconsciously grouping ex-combatants into a single monolithic category: I believed them to be destructive actors. One consequence of this framing was that I viewed their motivations more cynically than if I were an otherwise neutral observer: these were quasi-criminal groups rather than informal businesses; peace spoilers rather than guarantors of local security. Because so much of what I had read about the Liberian civil war had focused on the atrocities that had been committed, I had constructed a stereotype of an ex-combatant that was incompatible with furthering the public interest. Further, I had no sense of how many fighters had been forcibly recruited and forced to fight, how many had fought under the influence of drugs, and how many felt remorse for what they had done. Even among those who committed atrocities willingly and without remorse, I had no evidence to suggest that this group would be more or less likely to contribute to local public goods provision as compared to the rest of the population.

Peace as the Ultimate "Good"

The first iteration of this study focused on peace disruptors—specifically, those individuals who were willing to intentionally jeopardize a hard-won peace if it was in their material interest to do so. In this sense, the core of the study was

---

[43] A. Tversky and D. Kahneman (1973).
[44] S. Lichtenstein, P. Slovic, B. Fischhoff, M. Layman, et al. (1978).   [45] Ibid.

about those who were willing to prolong armed conflict for private economic gain—this was the premise that had initially motivated me to study civil war.[46] I viewed "peace" as the ultimate public good. Consequently, I saw noncombatants as "peaceful" while "armed" actors were potential disruptors of peace. Of course, the reality was much more complex, and privileging peace above all else masks other issues. Nordstrom's experience of the 1983 Sinhalese-Tamil riots in Sri Lanka illustrates the messiness of behavior during conflict:

> Under cover of the "truth" shouted from media headlines that 'the Sinhalese were rioting against the Tamils,' businesspeople burned out competitors' stores, neighbors set fire to the house of a person against whom they held a grudge, and countless thousands of people looted goods anywhere they found the chance. These were acts of acquisition and antipathy that had little, if anything, to do with ethnicity. Old scores were revisited and settled, and considerable fortunes were lost and made under cover of rioting.[47]

A closer examination of transition dynamics further complicated the neat categories of war and peace: more often than not, extralegal groups who threatened to disrupt "peace" had mixed motivations and were bound up in an ecosystem of local and national relationships that were difficult to fully untangle. Peace itself hinged on a common understanding of *whose* peace was being threatened (elites, the international community, a particular community); what "peace" looked like on the ground; and the relationship between extralegal groups and the communities they lived in. In practice, "peace" as a public good, was in fact, being traded off in side deals between powerful actors. Not everyone in the country agreed on what was "good" and what was "bad."

My own Western state-centered perspective has shaped how I think about peace. In Western democracies, peace takes a very specific form: that of a functioning liberal democracy. Even though peace, personal safety, and order were intertwined and inseparable in my own mental model of a peaceful society, it soon became clear that these three elements need not be bundled together in all cases.

Critically, from the perspective of states emerging from war, being at peace fundamentally implies order, but order is not necessarily accompanied by a sense of personal safety nor an absence of violence for its citizens. Consequently, in a framework that implicitly privileges "peace" without fully appreciating that states interpret "peace" in different ways, what ends up being implicitly condoned is actually the restoration of order. Peace and order are easily conflated—intentionally or unintentionally. In the theoretical framework, this unintended emphasis on order highlights two concerns: that *the way* in which order is restored is less important than ensuring its restoration,

---

[46] David Keen (1998); Mary Kaldor (1999); Mats R. Berdal and David Malone (2000).
[47] C. Nordstrom (2004), p. 31.

and that national peace matters more than local peace.[48] Privileging peace without being explicit about what peace *is* could give license to governments to restore order using whatever means are necessary, provided that the country is not considered to be "at war" by the rest of the world.

Rationality

When the Liberian civil war is evoked, images of brutality come to mind. It is hard to appreciate or understand the full impact of this viciousness from the safety of a television screen thousands of miles away. It is much easier to label a place or a people as barbaric when those doing the labelling have had little actual exposure to the country in question. Consequently, these acts appear to be both atrocious *and* irrational when they lack context. While some ex-combatants did commit atrocities during war, the general tendency in the West has been to dismiss these acts as barbaric, exotic, and irrational. Yet some acts, may in fact, be calculated to terrorize, to socialize, or to send a message to other factions. Scholars have made the point time and again that what some consider to be barbaric is not necessarily irrational.[49] For example, the amputation of hands[50] or the mass rape of women[51] have both served as deliberate, calculated strategies of war. In the Liberian context, the eating of human hearts was equally a symbolic and religious act as much as it was meant to be brutal and terrorizing.

Reflecting on this project, I am conscious that one hoped-for outcome of my research was to inspire people to think differently about the Liberian civil war, and about African civil wars more generally. The fieldwork confirmed that those who participated in extralegal networks were largely rational actors responding to perceived incentives. Consequently it seemed important to highlight this point, to provide a counter-narrative to common Western perceptions by demonstrating that these actors were more rational than Western media outlets had given them credit for. As a result, there is an assumption of careful rationality built into the framework—a desire to over-compensate. The framework casts the decisions of individual agents as deliberate calculations, when in fact, there was much greater fluidity in how these

---

[48] This is linked to Autesserre's argument that the international community's unwillingness to take community-level conflicts seriously ultimately prolonged Congo's civil war. See Séverine Autesserre (2010).

[49] For example, on the brutal recruitment practices of the Lord's Resistance Army, see: L. Falkenburg (2013). On the torture of women during the American Civil War: G. B. McKinney and J. C. Inscoe (2014) p. 195. In Peru, the Shining Path amputated the fingers of voters: Nelson Mandrique (1998), p. 205.

[50] P. Richards (1996).

[51] International Criminal Tribunal for the former Yugoslavia Appeals Chamber (2002).

decisions were made. We also know that rational decision-making is bounded and constrained in many different ways, from Tversky and Kahneman's experiments on loss aversion[52] right through to Mullainathan and Shafir's research on how scarcity affects our ability to make rational decisions.[53] My own overreliance on a rational actor model limits the accuracy of the extralegal groups framework.

"Extralegal," the Law, and the State

When this project began, my understanding of what it meant to be "extralegal" relied upon a particular conception of the rule of law. The law served as a reference point, implying that legal status—as determined by the state—was the defining feature of these groups and networks. Being "extralegal" provided a foil for a powerful, functioning state where the rule of law is robust and legitimate. Implicit in this understanding is the sense that laws are fair and just and equally applied. To be "extralegal" then was to exist outside this framework of a fair and orderly state. The problem was that this framing did not apply in Liberia, or for that matter, in most weak states. As soon as these assumptions about the legal framework were probed more deeply in the Liberian context, the foundations quickly crumbled.

Having watched the legal process operate in Liberia, interacted with lawyers and victims and defendants, observed how laws are made, and then studied how laws were actually enforced by agents of the state, my interpretation of the term "extralegal" shifted dramatically over the course of this study. My original, Western-influenced understanding of the law was that it existed as a common standard to which all citizens are subject. In reality, the Liberian law assumed a malleable quality at every stage, from its introduction as a piece of legislation through to its enforcement on the streets. The human element of the legal process was brought to the foreground—the discretion of law enforcement agents, the subjectivity of judicial interpretation, the ability of legislators to advocate for one agenda over another. Laws were created and enforced in a social context by individuals who each had their own incentives, their own biases, and their own loyalties. In the Liberian context, the law was used to punish and persuade, and formal legal recourse was an expensive and complicated tool that was only accessible to the wealthy. By themselves, laws no longer seemed inherently good nor fair; and this extended to the people who had created them, enforced them, or made official judgments about their validity. In hindsight, my original assumptions look naïve, but they were

---

[52] A. Tversky and D. Kahneman (1991).   [53] S. Mullainathan and E. Shafir (2013).

difficult notions to disabuse myself of, until they were thoroughly disproven while conducting fieldwork.

As my views on the rule of law and the legal system changed, so too did my concept of extralegal. Conceptually, the term "extralegal" had become distinct from "criminal" and "illegal." As the dysfunctionalities of the formal state and legal system became more apparent, I began to see how "extralegal" governance could be preferred by local populations over a formal, but predatory, state system. Extralegal now suggested an alternative system—one where local outcomes took precedent over national objectives. To be "extralegal" then, was not just about breaking the law; where laws and law enforcement are utterly malleable, extralegal was about an existence *outside* the formal and legal systems.

CONCLUSION

The goal of this chapter was to disrupt the fiction of tidy research. It began by arguing that the scaffolding that supports the research design process can provide important insights into the research process, even though scholars normally discard it in presenting the final study. The way in which research questions and methodologies are usually presented in scholarly works imply that they are conceived fully formed. Choosing a research question is not a singular, definitive act—rather, a question tends to develop through an iterative process. Outlining the research design scaffolding helps the reader to understand an author's thought process, and why she chose to answer this research question rather than some other question; why a study was conducted using one set of tools rather than a different set.

To illustrate how research scaffolding might be done, I returned to earlier iterations of this study: starting from the idea of criminal warfare, moving on to the illegal war economy, and then to local political authority, before refining the extralegal groups concept. It is important to note that these transitions did not always show linear progress and that some exploratory detours were taken that did not contribute to the core of the project. The chapter ends with a discussion of how different sets of biases and assumptions shaped the arc of the study.

Make no mistake: the process of doing research *shapes the researcher* in turn. Discussions of research design and methodology should acknowledge this more honestly. The point here is that social science research is rarely *a one-way process*. This may sound self-evident, but the ways in which politics scholars currently explain and justify research design and methodologies suggest that this is actually a contested idea.

In the discipline of politics, the researcher is expected to remain distant and separated from the data, and inert to its charms while the analysis is being conducted. This kind of distance is reflected in how social scientists write up their projects: a researcher's hypotheses and mental models are expected to remain static through the duration of the study while the study is ongoing—even though a given study might take years to complete. There is little acknowledgment of how a scholar's thinking might evolve over time and that these shifts in thinking are worth sharing.

In fact, the *reality* of conducting research is more fluid. As data is gathered to answer a given research question, information is absorbed and the researcher updates her mental models to accommodate the new information. Sometimes, the formulation of the question shifts, which in turn leads to new kinds of information being gathered, and the research question to change again. The researcher is iterating and updating all the time.[54] This chapter focused on why this iterative process was important and showed what this looks like in practice, using this extralegal groups project as an example. It is hoped that this chapter on research design scaffolding will encourage other researchers to adopt a similarly open and reflective role in writing up their own studies.

---

[54] This is different from changing the research question to suit the data. Instead, the researcher thinks about the topic differently as a result of the research process. This leads to a change in the research question.

APPENDIX A

Statistics on Killings

When the first stage of Liberia's civil war ended (1989–97), many sources cited 200,000 as the number of people that were killed.[1] Stephen Ellis argued that this figure was too high and extensively discussed how 200,000 came to be commonly cited.[2] Initially, the UN Secretary-General's Report in March 1993 referred to "150,000 casualties"—this figure likely included the wounded and those who had been killed indirectly through illness. This figure of 150,000 was referred to again in the UN Secretary-General's September 1993 report. By 1997, NGOs had updated it to 200,000.

In an effort to provide a more accurate estimate of the number of people killed during the first stage of fighting, Ellis reviewed estimates from a variety of sources including: ECOMOG (300,000),[3] the Catholic Church (75,000–100,000 as of November 1990),[4] the NPFL (13,000 as of September 1990),[5] journalist Bill Berkeley (20,000–25,000 as of December 1990),[6] journalist Cindy Shiner (20,000 as of January 1992),[7] and Charles Taylor himself (30,000–50,000,[8] and then 20,000 as of 1998[9]). Analyzing these figures along with the sources that produced them, Ellis argued that a more accurate estimate of battle deaths for the first stage of the war would be 40,000–50,000 for 1989–92 and 20,000–30,000 for 1993–97. In total, Ellis estimated that 60,000–80,000 people were killed during the entire 1989–97 period.[10]

However, Ellis' estimate does not cover the second stage of fighting from 1999–2003. Currently, there is no accurate estimate of the number of people who were killed during *both* periods of fighting. The most commonly cited figure remains 200,000,[11] which was based on the UN Secretary-General's 1993 report, which also included deaths from illness.

Deriving an accurate estimate without a random sample of the population (e.g., from household surveys or sibling surveys)[12] is fraught with problems. Debates over

---

[1] For example, see K. L. Cain (1999); Adekeye Adebajo (2002); U.S. Agency for International Development (2003). The Polynational War Memorial page on Liberia's civil war exemplifies the schizophrenic approach to conflict data, citing both the 200,000 figure and the more conservative numbers from the Uppsala Conflict Data Program. See Jon Brunberg (2016); Erik Melander, Thérése Pettersson and Lotta Themnér (2016).

[2] Stephen Ellis (1999), pp. 312–16.

[3] Nkem Agetua (1992) as cited in Stephen Ellis (1999), p. 313.

[4] Justice and Peace Commission (1994), p. 26 cited in Stephen Ellis (1999), p. 313.

[5] The Patriot (1991), p. 9 as cited in Stephen Ellis (1999), p. 313.

[6] Bill Berkeley (2001), p. 129 as cited in Stephen Ellis (1999), p. 313.

[7] Cindy Shiner (1992) as cited in Stephen Ellis (1999), p. 313.

[8] Aad van den Heuvel (1998) as cited in Stephen Ellis (1999), p. 316.

[9] Jon Lee Anderson (1998) as cited in Stephen Ellis (1999), p. 316.

[10] This does not include those who died of starvation or disease, nor does it include deaths that were unrelated to the war.

[11] For example, CNN (2003); Sarah Left (2003).

[12] Ziad Obermeyer, Christopher J. L. Murray and Emmanuela Gakidou (2008).

body count numbers have grown heated, even acrimonious, in recent years[13] Nevertheless, ignoring the inaccuracy of such a key statistic in Liberia's civil war also feels irresponsible. Starting with Ellis' estimate of 60,000–80,000 for 1989–1997, my aim is to construct a more plausible estimate than the misleading figure of 200,000 that is currently being cited. I conclude that a more accurate estimate of the number of people killed during Liberia's civil war is 100,000.

What Do We Know?

We know that the Uppsala Conflict Data Program tracked 3051 battle deaths between the government of Liberia and the NPFL (1989–2003), another 3057 battle deaths between nonstate armed groups, and one-sided violence against civilians that resulted in 17,141 deaths.[14] For the entire 1989–2003 Liberian civil war, UCDP was able to confirm that 23,249 people were killed by an armed actor. This is a conservative estimate because it relies on battle deaths that were reported by five international news agencies (including BBC Monitoring which provided local news sources) and supplemented by expert reports from human rights and advocacy organizations like Amnesty International and the International Crisis Group.[15] However, such a methodology means that killings, disappearances, and battles that were not reported or covered in the media are unlikely to have been counted.

Separately, we also know that Liberia's Truth and Reconciliation Commission (TRC) documented 28,042 killings from 1989 to 2003. This figure was arrived at by taking statements from over 17,000 witnesses throughout Liberia's fifteen counties in order to create a database of human rights violations; this was one of the most extensive TRC statement-taking exercises that has ever been conducted.[16] Like the UCDP database, the TRC dataset also presents a conservative figure because it only includes battle deaths that have been reported by witnesses. Despite the scale of the exercise, this dataset does not offer an accurate estimate on the number of people that were killed during the war. This data should be treated in a similar fashion to the UCDP data: 28,042 is the lower bound estimate for the number of people that were killed in the Liberian civil war from 1989 to 2003.

Unfortunately, we also know that TRC witness statements are not representative of the population at large due to selective sampling,[17] so it is not possible to obtain an accurate body count estimate only by extrapolating from this dataset. With that caveat, the TRC data remains the most accurate and extensive dataset of Liberia's civil war killings, so I have used it to construct a more accurate estimate.

Violations and Killings over Time

The charts tracking all reported violations (Figure A.1) and reported killings (Figure A.2) follow roughly the same trend lines, with a sharp peak in 1990, followed

---

[13] For vigorous debate on estimating the number of people that died in the Congo war, see *Science* (2010). Also see Taylor B. Seybolt, Jay D. Aronson and Baruch Fischhoff (2013).

[14] Erik Melander, Therése Pettersson and Lotta Themnér (2016).

[15] Kristine Eck and Lisa Hultman (2007).

[16] Kristen Cibelli, Amelia Hoover and Jule Kruger (2009). For a detailed discussion of their methodology, see pp. 52–65.

[17] Todd Landman and Anita Gohdes (2013).

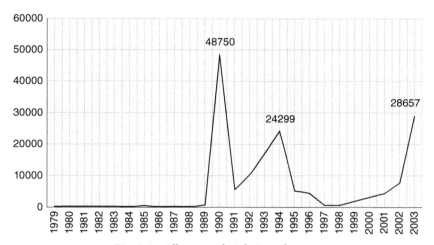

Fig. A.1. All reported violations, by year

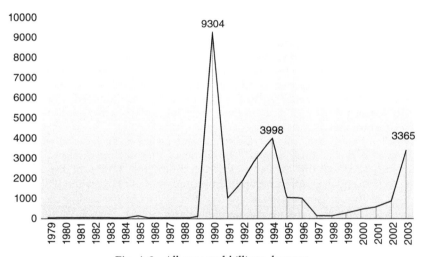

Fig. A.2. All reported killings, by year

by two smaller peaks in 1994 and 2003. Collectively, the evidence taken from news sources, journalistic accounts, academic scholarship, UN briefings, and NGO reports broadly confirm these trends in violence and killings with a peak in 1990, and smaller surges again in violence in 1994 and 2003.

To estimate the number of killings that occurred between 1997 and 2003, I make two assumptions:

(1) The ratio of unreported killings is roughly the same during the 1993–7 period and the 1998–2003 period; and

(2) Ellis's estimate of 20,000–30,000 civil war killings from 1994–7 is correct.

Returning to Figure A.2, we can see that there are two areas under the graph (representing the number of killings) that are roughly the same size: from 1994 to 1997, and from 1998 to 2003. Bearing in mind the two assumptions listed above, we can estimate that 20,000–30,000 deaths also occurred during the 1998–2003 period.

We can now add together the three estimates: 40,000–50,000 (1989–93), 20,000–30,000 (1994–7), and 20,000–30,000 (1998–2003). Taken together, the estimated number of people who were killed during the Liberian civil war is 80,000–110,000. For simplicity, I recommend using the figure of 100,000. Splitting the difference and using 95,000 would suggest a degree of accuracy for this estimate that does not exist.

Statistics on Displacement

There is similar variation for displacement figures—this includes refugees and internally displaced persons (IDPs). Figures from UNHCR show that there were two peaks in the total number of displaced Liberians: in 2003, there were 565,000, and in 1995 and 1996, there were 440,000 (see UN High Commission for Refugees (2004, 2007; Table A.1).

However, these figures only encompass those who have passed through the UNHCR system. Many of those who flee integrate directly into a new country or community and never receive any international assistance—these people elude the displacement statistics. Accurate statistics are even more difficult to obtain given that people usually try to flee without drawing attention to themselves.[18]

Another problem in determining the total number of displaced people throughout the war is that there were two waves of fighting in Liberia: 1989–97 and 1999–2003. After the first wave of fighting ended, hundreds of thousands of people returned home. But many of them were forced to flee again after the war resumed. Unfortunately, UNHCR data provide no indication about the number of times that people were forced to flee their homes.

Finally, there is the problem of displacement figures being recycled without any reference to the original sources. The figure of one million displaced people is frequently cited, but this number was derived from those who were displaced from 1989 to 1996 and does not incorporate the second wave of refugees and IDPs.[19] Other

Table A.1. UNHCR figures for displaced Liberians, 1993–7

	1993	1994	1995	1996	1997	1998	1999
Refugees	150,153	120,163	120,080	120,061	126,886	96,317	96,317
IDPs	–	220,000	320,000	320,000	166,000	128,292	90,584
Total		340,163	440,080	440,061	292,886	224,609	186,901

	2000	2001	2002	2003	2004	2005
Refugees	69,315	54,760	64,956	33,997	15,172	10,168
IDPs	110,686	196,116	304,115	531,616	498,566	237,822
Total	180,001	250,876	369,071	565,613	513,738	247,990

[18] Christine Cheng and Johannes Chudoba (2003), p. 4.
[19] U.S. Department of State (2009).

refugee specialists put the number of displaced Liberians during 1989–96 closer to 1.2–1.5 million;[20] one estimate is as high as 1.86 million.[21]

Given the displacement estimates leading up to 1997, it is safe to say that the lower bound of displaced people is one million. Unfortunately, it is impossible to say whether the second wave of fighting produced newly displaced people—this is why the displacement figure is characterized as "at least one million."

[20] U.S. Agency for International Development (1997); Joel Frushone (2004).
[21] Mark Cutts and UNHCR (2000), p. 261.

References

Aboagye, Festus and Alhaji M.S. Bah (2005). *A Torturous Road to Peace: The Dynamics of Regional, UN and International Humanitarian Interventions in Liberia*. Cape Town, Institute of Security Studies.

Acemoglu, Daron and James A. Robinson (2012). *Why Nations Fail: The origins of power, prosperity, and poverty*. London, Profile.

Achebe, Chinua (1958). *Things Fall Apart*. London, Heinemann.

Adam, Hussein (1995). Somalia: A Terrible Beauty Being Born, in *Collapsed states: the disintegration and restoration of legitimate authority*, I. W. Zartman (ed). Boulder, Colorado, Lynne Rienner.

Adebajo, Adekeye (2002). *Liberia's Civil War: Nigeria, ECOMOG, and regional security in West Africa*. Boulder, Colorado, Lynne Rienner.

Agetua, Nkem (1992). *Operation Liberty: the story of Major General Joshua Nimyel Dogonyaro*. Lagos, Hona Communications.

Ahmad, Aisha (2015). "The Security Bazaar: Business Interests and Islamist Power in Civil War Somalia." *International Security* 39(3): 89–117.

Ahmed, Mohamed (2009). *Somali Sea Gangs Lure Investors at Pirate Lair*. Reuters. Haradheere, Somalia, Reuters.

Alao, Abiodun (2007). *Natural Resources and Conflict in Africa*. Rochester, New York, University of Rochester Press.

Albaladejo, Angelika (2015). USIP Panel Discussion: "Colombia Peace Forum: Paths to Reintegration". https://angelikaalbaladejo.com/2015/02/01/usip-panel-discussion-colombia-peace-forum-paths-to-reintegration/

Alesina, Alberto, Paola Giuliano and Nathan Nunn (2010). On the Origins of Gender Roles: Women and the Plough. NBER Working Papers. Cambridge, Massachusetts, National Bureau of Economic Research.

AllAfrica.com (2009). "Liberia: Pit sawing illegal, but economical—FDA boss states." AllAfrica.com.

al-Tamimi, Aymenn (2015). "The Evolution in Islamic State Administration: The Documentary Evidence." *Perspectives on Terrorism* 9(4).

Altman, D. G. (1994). "The scandal of poor medical research." *BMJ* 308: 283.

Amnesty International (2006). *Dead on Time—Arms transportation, brokering and the threat to human rights*. London.

Anderson, Ben (2015). "Notes from Afghanistan's Most Dangerous Province." Vice.com.

Anderson, Benedict (1983). *Imagined Communities: Reflections on the origin and spread of nationalism*. London, Verso.

Anderson, David (2002). "Vigilantes, violence and the politics of public order in Kenya." *African Affairs* 101(405): 531–55.

Anderson, David (2009). Somali Piracy: Historical context and political contingency. European Security Forum.

Anderson, Jon Lee (1998). "The Devil They Know." *The New Yorker*. New York: 34–43.

Andreas, Peter. (2004). "Criminalized legacies of war—The clandestine political economy of the western Balkans." *Problems of Post-Communism* 51(3): 3–9.

Anten, Louise, Ivan Briscoe, and Marco Mezzera (2015). *The Political Economy of State-building in Situations of Fragility and Conflict: from Analysis to Strategy.* The Hague, Clingendael Institute.

Arias, Enrique Desmond and Corinne Davis Rodrigues (2006). "The Myth of Personal Security: Criminal Gangs, Dispute Resolution, and Identity in Rio de Janeiro's Favelas." *Latin American Politics and Society* 48(4).

Arjona, Ana, Nelson Kasfir and Zachariah Mampilly, Eds. (2015). *Rebel Governance in Civil War.* Cambridge, Cambridge University Press.

Ashforth, Blake E. and Fred Mael (1989). "Social Identity Theory and the Organization." *The Academy of Management Review* 14(1): 20–39.

Associated Press (1992). 38 Die in Attack on U.S.-Owned Rubber Plantation in Liberia. November 4. *New York Times.* Monrovia, Liberia.

Atkinson, Philippa (1997). *The war economy in Liberia: a political analysis. Relief and Rehabilitation Network.* London, Overseas Development Institute.

Autesserre, Séverine (2008). "The trouble with Congo—How local disputes fuel regional conflict." *Foreign Affairs* 87(3): 94–110.

Autesserre, Séverine (2009). "Hobbes and the Congo: Frames, Local Violence, and International Intervention." *International Organization* 63(2): 249–80.

Autesserre, Séverine (2010). *The Trouble with the Congo.* Cambridge, Cambridge University Press.

Autesserre, Séverine (2014). *Peaceland: conflict resolution and the everyday politics of international intervention.* Cambridge, Cambridge University Press.

Auty, Richard M. (1993). *Sustaining development in mineral economies: the resource curse thesis.* London; New York, Routledge.

Auty, Richard M. (2001). *Resource abundance and economic development.* Oxford; New York, Oxford University Press.

Bah, M. D. (2014). "Mining for peace: diamonds, bauxite, iron ore and political stability in Guinea." *Review of African Political Economy* 41(142): 500–15.

Bailey, John (2014). *The politics of crime in Mexico: Democratic governance in a security trap.* Boulder, Colorado, Lynne Rienner.

Baker, Bruce (2005). "Who Do People Turn to for Policing in Sierra Leone?" *Journal of Contemporary African Studies* 23(3): 19.

Ballah, Henryatta (2003). "Ethnicity, Politics and Social Conflict: The Quest for Peace in Liberia." *Pennsylvania State University McNair Scholars Journal* 10: 52–69.

Ballah, Zeze Evans (2008). "Citizens Want Probe On SRP Corruption Allegation." April 2. Monrovia, *Public Agenda.*

Ballentine, Karen and Jake Sherman (2003). *The political economy of armed conflict: beyond greed and grievance.* Boulder, Colorado, Lynne Rienner.

Bannon, Ian and Paul Collier (2003). *Natural resources and violent conflict: options and actions.* Washington, DC, World Bank.

Barak, Gregg (2003). *Violence and nonviolence: pathways to understanding.* London, Sage.

Barash, David P. and Charles Webel (2002). *Peace and conflict studies.* London, Sage Publications.

Bar-Yam, Yaneer and Jeff Schechtman (2016). "How Wars Will Be Fought in the 21st Century: Interview with Yaneer Bar-Yam." WhoWhatWhy, May 9, 2016.

Bates, Robert H. (2008). *When things fell apart: state failure in late-century Africa.* New York, Cambridge University Press.

Bateson, Regina (2011). Order and Violence in Postwar Guatemala. Ph.D., Yale.

Bateson, Regina (2012). "Crime Victimization and Political Participation." *American Political Science Review* 106(3): 570–87.

Bayart, Jean-François (1993). *The state in Africa: the politics of the belly.* London, Longman.

Bayart, Jean-Francois, Stephen Ellis, and Béatrice Hibou. (1999). *The criminalization of the state in Africa.* Oxford, James Currey.

Beevers, M. D. (2015). "Governing Natural Resources for Peace: Lessons from Liberia and Sierra Leone." *Global Governance* 21(2): 227–46.

Bekoe, Dorina Akosua Oduraa (2008). *Implementing peace agreements: lessons from Mozambique, Angola, and Liberia.* New York, Palgrave Macmillan.

Belge, Ceren (2011). "State building and the limits of legibility: kinship networks and Kurdish resistance in Turkey." *International Journal of Middle East Studies* 43(1): 95–114.

Berdal, Mats and Domink Zaum, Eds. (2012). *The Political Economy of Post-Conflict Statebuilding.* Abingdon, Routledge.

Berdal, Mats R. and David H. Ucko (2009). *Reintegrating armed groups after conflict: politics, violence and transition.* Abingdon, Routledge.

Berdal, Mats R. and David Malone, Eds. (2000). *Greed & grievance: economic agendas in civil wars.* Boulder, Colorado, Lynne Rienner.

Berkeley, Bill (2001). *The graves are not yet full: race, tribe, and power in the heart of Africa.* New York, Basic Books.

Berman, Bruce (1998). "Ethnicity, Patronage and the African State: The Politics of Uncivil Nationalism." *African Affairs* 97(388): 305–41.

Bermeo, Nancy (2003). "What the democratization literature says—or doesn't say—about postwar democratization." *Global Governance* 9(2): 159–77.

Beyerle, Shaazka (2014). *Curtailing Corruption: people power for accountability and justice.* Boulder, Colorado, Lynne Rienner.

Blair, Rob, Chris Blattman, and Alexandra Hartman. (2015). "Predicting Local-Level Violence." https://ssrn.com/abstract=2497153

Blattman, C. (2009). "From Violence to Voting: War and Political Participation in Uganda." *American Political Science Review* 103(2): 231–47.

Blattman, Christopher and Edward Miguel (2010). "Civil War." *Journal of Economic Literature* 48(1): 3–57.

Blattman, Christopher and Jeannie Annan (2011). *Evidence from Randomized Evaluations of Peacebuilding in Liberia Policy Report.* New Haven, US, Innovations for Poverty Action.

Bliesemann de Guevara, Berit (2012). *Statebuilding and state-formation: the political sociology of intervention.* London, Routledge.

Blore, Shawn (2007). *Land Grabbing and Land Reform: Diamonds, Rubber and Forests in the New Liberia.* The Diamonds and Human Security Project. I. Smillie and A. Brownell (eds). Ottawa and Monrovia, Partnership Africa Canada and Green Advocates.

Bøås, Morten (2003). "The Liberian Civil War: The crisis of neopatrimonialism and the West African state system." *Internasjonal Politikk* 61(4): 425–48.

Bøås, Morten (2005). *Power-sharing and positions in the National Transitional Government of Liberia; or no die, no rest—General Iron Jacket vs Sekou Conneh.* International Studies Association. Honolulu, Hawaii.

Bøås, Morten (2014). *The Politics of Conflict Economies: Miners, merchants and warriors in the African borderland.* Abingdon, Routledge.

Bøås, M. and K. C. Dunn, Eds. (2007). *African guerrillas: raging against the machine.* Boulder, Colorado, Lynne Rienner.

Bøås, M, and Utas, M. (2014). "The Political Landscape of Postwar Liberia: Reflections on National Reconciliation and Elections." *Africa Today* 60(4): 47–65.

Boege, Volker, Anne Brown, Kevin Clements, and Anna Nolan (2009). On Hybrid Political Orders and Emerging States: What is Failing—States in the Global South or Research and Politics in the West? in *Berghof Handbook for Conflict Transformation.* Berlin, Berghof Research Center for Constructive Conflict Management: 15–35.

Boersch-Supan, Johanna (2009). *What the communities say. The crossroads between integration and reconciliation: What can be learned from the Sierra Leonean experience?* Oxford, Centre for Research on Inequality, Human Security and Ethnicity (CRISE).

Boersch-Supan, Johanna (2012). "The generational contract in flux: intergenerational tensions in post-conflict Sierra Leone." *The Journal of Modern African Studies* 50(1): 25–51.

Bonaparte, T. H. (1979). "Multinational-Corporations and Culture in Liberia." *American Journal of Economics and Sociology* 38(3): 237–51.

Boone, Catherine (2003). *Political topographies of the African state: territorial authority and institutional choice.* Cambridge, Cambridge University Press.

BOPC Diggers' Focus Group (2005). October 18, 2005. Shampe, Sinoe County, Liberia.

Boschini, A. D., J. Pettersson, and J. Roine (2007). "Resource curse or not: A question of appropriability." *Scandinavian Journal of Economics* 109(3): 593–617.

Boulden, Jane, Ed. (2013). *Responding to Conflict in Africa: The United Nations and Regional Organizations.* Basingstoke, Palgrave Macmillan.

Bourdieu, Pierre (1985). The forms of capital, in *Handbook of theory and research for the sociology of education*, J. G. Richardson (ed). New York, Greenwood.

Boutros-Ghali, Boutros (1992). *An Agenda for Peace.* New York, United Nations.

Bowd, Richard and Alpaslan Özerdem (2013). "How to Assess Social Reintegration of Ex-Combatants." *International Peacekeeping* 7(4).

Brabazon, James and Jonathan Stack (2004). *Liberia: An Uncivil War.* 102 min.

Bratton, Michael and Nicolas van de Walle (1994). "Neopatrimonial Regimes and Political Transitions in Africa." *World Politics* 46(04): 453–89.

Braudel, Fernand (1958). "Histoire et sciences sociales: La longue durée." *Annales. Histoire, Sciences Sociales* 13(4): 725–53.

Brettle, Alison (2014). Social Networks, Informal Mechanisms and the Reintegration of Ex-Combatants. King's College London. Ph.D. Research Conference. Cumberland Lodge, UK.

Brettle, Alison (2017). Conflict and the Congo—Getting In and Staying In. Unpublished manuscript.

Brownell, Alfred (2005). A series of personal interviews with Alfred Brownell, Head of Green Advocates. October to December, 2005. Monrovia, Liberia.

Brownell, Alfred (2007a). *The Dirty Dozen*. Monrovia, Liberia, Green Advocates.

Brownell, Alfred (2007b). A series of personal interviews with Alfred Brownell, Head of Green Advocates. May and June 2007, Monrovia, Liberia.

Brownell, Alfred (2010). Personal email correspondence with Alfred Brownell, Head of Green Advocates. March 5. Monrovia, Liberia.

Bruch, Carl, David Jensen, Mikiyasu Nakayama, and Jon Unruh, Eds. (2011). *Peacebuilding and Natural Resources*, Six Volume Series Set. London, Earthscan.

Bruch, Carl, Carroll Muffett, and Sandra Nichols, Eds. (2015). *Governance, Natural Resources, and Post-conflict Peacebuilding*. London, Earthscan.

Brunberg, Jon (2016). Liberia Civil War. The Polynational War Memorial. http://www.war-memorial.net/Liberia-Civil-War-3.209

Buell, Raymond Leslie (1928a). "Mr Firestone's Liberia." *The Nation*.

Buell, Raymond Leslie (1928b). *The native problem in Africa*. New York, The Macmillan Company.

Buhaug, H. and J. K. Rød (2006). "Local determinants of African civil wars, 1970–2001." *Political Geography* 25(3): 315–35.

Buka, Stephen L., Theresa L. Stichick, Isolde Birdthistle, and Felton J. Earls (2001). "Youth exposure to violence: Prevalence, risks, and consequences." *American Journal of Orthopsychiatry* 71(3): 298.

Bunker, Robert (2010). "Strategic threat: narcos and narcotics overview." *Small Wars & Insurgencies* 21(1): 8–29.

Burke, Edmund (1790). *Reflections on the Revolution in France: And on the Proceedings in Certain Societies in London Relative to that Event. In a Letter Intended to Have Been Sent to a Gentleman in Paris*. London, James Dodsley.

Burrowes, Carl P. (1995). "Democracy or Disarmament: some second thoughts on Amos Sawyer and contemporary "politicians". XX. 1. 1995." *Liberian Studies Journal* 20(1).

Burrowes, Carl P. (2005). Liberia: Firestone's Rubber Plantations—Economic Development or Modern Day Slavery? U.S. Congressional Human Rights Caucus. Washington, D.C.

Buxton, Julia (2006). *The Political Economy of Narcotics: Production, Consumption and Global Markets*. London, Zed Books.

Büthe, Tim and Alan M. Jacobs, Eds. (2015). "Symposium: Transparency in Qualitative and Multi-Method Research." *Qualitative and Multi-Method Research* 13(1).

Cain, K. L. (1999). "The Rape of Dinah: Human Rights, Civil War in Liberia, and Evil Triumphant." *Human Rights Quarterly* 21(2): 265–307.

Calhoun, Lawrence G. and Richard G. Tedeschi (2006). *Handbook of posttraumatic growth: research and practice*. Mahwah, NJ, Lawrence Erlbaum Associates.

Call, Charles T. (2008). "The Fallacy of the 'Failed State'." *Third World Quarterly* 29(8): 1491–507.

Call, Charles T. (2011). "Beyond the 'failed state': Toward conceptual alternatives." *European Journal of International Relations* 17(2): 303–26.

Campbell, Susanna, David Chandler, and Sabaratnam, Meera (2011). *A liberal peace? The problems and practices of peacebuilding*. London, Zed Books.

Caplan, G. (2012). "Peacekeepers gone wild: How much more abuse will the UN ignore in Congo?" *The Globe and Mail*. Toronto.

Caplan, Richard D. (2005). *International Governance of War-Torn Territories: Rule and Reconstruction*. Oxford, Oxford University Press.

Carothers, T. (1998). "The rule of law revival." *Foreign Affairs* 77(2).

Carranza, Ruben (2017). "Dutch Court Convicts Arms Dealer for Role in Liberian Atrocities. What Does It Say About Justice for Economic Crime?". May 4, International Center for Transitional Justice.

Chabal, Patrick and Jean-Pascal Daloz (1999). *Africa works: disorder as political instrument*. Oxford, James Currey.

Chandler, David (2006). *Empire in denial: the politics of state-building*. London, Pluto.

Chandler, David (2009). *Statebuilding and intervention: policies, practices and paradigms*. London, Routledge.

Cheng, Christine (2010). "Field work in Liberia and a Review of The Vice Guide." https://christinescottcheng.wordpress.com/2010/02/06/field-work-in-liberia-and-a -review-of-the-vice-guide/

Cheng, Christine (2012). Private and Public Interests—Informal Actors, Informal Influence, and Economic Order after War, in *The Political Economy of Post-Conflict Statebuilding*, M. Berdal and D. Zaum (eds). Abingdon, Routledge.

Cheng, Christine (2013). Conflict Capital. Paper presented at the Annual Meeting of the International Studies Association, San Francisco.

Cheng, Christine and Dominik Zaum, Eds. (2011). *Corruption and Post-Conflict Peacebuilding. Cass Series on Peacekeeping*. Abingdon, Routledge.

Cheng, Christine and Dominik Zaum (2016). Corruption and the Role of Natural Resources in Post-Conflict Transitions, in *Governance, natural resources and post-conflict peacebuilding*, C. Bruch, C. Muffett and S. Nichols (eds). Abingdon, Earthscan, Routledge.

Cheng, Christine and Johannes Chudoba (2003). Moving Beyond Long-Term Refugee Situations: the Case of Guatemala. New Issues in Refugee Research. Geneva, Switzerland, UNHCR: 33.

Cheng, Christine and Jorge Delgado (2017). A criminalized peace in Colombia: Entrenchment of the Urabeños. International Studies Association Annual Meeting, Baltimore, Maryland.

Cheng, Christine, Jonathan Goodhand, and Patrick Meehan (2018). *Securing and Sustaining Elite Bargains that Reduce Violent Conflict*. London, Stabilisation Unit.

Chesterman, Simon, Michael Ignatieff, and Ramesh Thakur, Eds. (2005). *Making states work: state failure and the crisis of governance*. New York, United Nations University Press.

Chesterman, Simon (2004). *You, The People: The United Nations, Transitional Administration, and State-Building*. Oxford, Oxford University Press.

Chetty, R., N. Hendren, and L.F. Katz (2015). "The Effects of Exposure to Better Neighborhoods on Children: New Evidence from the Moving to Opportunity Experiment." NBER Working Paper No. 21156. Boston, National Bureau of Economic Research.

Cibelli, Kristen, Amelia Hoover, and Jule Krüger (2009). Descriptive Statistics from Statements to the Liberian Truth and Reconciliation Commission, Benetech.

Cikara, M., E. Bruneau, J.J. Van Bavel and R. Saxe (2014). "Their pain gives us pleasure: How intergroup dynamics shape empathic failures and counter-empathic responses." *Journal of Experimental Psychology* 55: 110–25.

Ciment, James (2013). *Another America: the story of Liberia and the former slaves who ruled it.* New York, Hill and Wang.

Clague, Christopher, Philip Keefer, Stephen Knack, and Mancur Olson (1996). "Property and contract rights in autocracies and democracies." *Journal of Economic Growth* 1(2): 243–76.

Clan Chief (2005). Palava Hut meeting with Clan Chief at BOPC. October 18. Shampe, Sinoe County, Liberia.

Clapham, Christopher (1978). Liberia, in *West African states: failure and promise—A study in comparative politics*, J. Dunn (ed). Cambridge, Cambridge University Press.

Clark, Philip (2010). *The Gacaca Courts and Post-Genocide Justice and Reconciliation in Rwanda: Justice without Lawyers.* Cambridge, Cambridge University Press.

Clements, Kevin (2004). Towards Conflict Transformation and a Just Peace, in *Transforming ethnopolitical conflict*, A. Austin, M. Fisher and N. Ropers (eds). Wiesbaden, VS Verlag für Sozialwissenschaften: 441–61.

Clunan, Anne L. and Harold A. Trinkunas (2010). *Ungoverned spaces: alternatives to state authority in an era of softened sovereignty.* Stanford, CA, Stanford Security Studies.

CNN (2003). "Liberia torn by long civil war." April 30.

Coate, Kelly and Camille Kandiko Howson (2013). "Indicators of Esteem: gender and prestige in academic work." Gender and Education Biennial Conference. London South Bank University.

Cockayne, James and Adam Lupel (2009). "Introduction: Rethinking the Relationship Between Peace Operations and Organized Crime." *International Peacekeeping* 16(1): 4–19.

Cohen, Ronald (1984). Warfare and State Formation: Wars Make States and States Make Wars, in *Warfare, Culture, and Environment*, R. B. Ferguson (ed). Academic Press Inc.: 329–358.

Cole, Henry B. (1956). *The Liberian year book.* London, The Diplomatic Press and Pub. Co.

Colee, Francis (2008). Preliminary Report on Pit-Sawing in River Cess County: An Assessment of the Socio-Economic Impacts of this Enterprise. RRI/FWG Civil Society Workshop on Alternative Tenure and Enterprise Case Studies from Africa. Accra, Ghana, Green Advocates.

Colee, Francis (2009). *Pit-Sawing Operations in River Cess County, Liberia: Promising Models for Small-Scale Forest Enterprises.* Rights and Resources Initiative. Washington, DC, Green Advocates.

Colee, Francis (2015). Interview with Francis Colee, Green Advocates' Program Coordinator. September 5, 2015. London.

Coleman, J. S. (1988). "Social Capital in the Creation of Human-Capital." *American Journal of Sociology* 94: S95–S120.

Colgan, Jeff (2013). *Petro-aggression: when oil causes war.* Cambridge, Cambridge University Press.

Colgan, Jeff, and Robert Keohane. (2017). "The Liberal Order Is Rigged." *Foreign Affairs*. December 3, 2017.

Colletta, Nat J., Markus Kostner, and Ingo Wiederhofer. (1996). Case studies in war-to-peace transition: the demobilization and reintegration of ex-combatants in Ethiopia, Namibia, and Uganda. World Bank discussion papers. Washington, DC, World Bank.

Colletta, Nat J. and Michelle Cullen (2000). *Violent Conflict and the Transformation of Social Capital: Lessons from Cambodia, Rwanda, Guatemala and Somalia.* Washington, DC, World Bank.

Collier, Paul, Anke Hoeffler, and Soderbom, Mats (2004). "On the duration of civil war." *Journal of Peace Research* 41(3): 253–73.

Collier, Paul (2007). *The bottom billion: why the poorest countries are failing and what can be done about it.* Oxford, Oxford University Press.

Collier, Paul (2011). *Conflict, political accountability, and aid.* New York, NY, Routledge.

Collier, Paul and Anke Hoeffler (1998). "On economic causes of civil war." *Oxford Economic Papers—New Series* 50(4): 563–73.

Connah, Graham (2001). *African civilizations: an archaeological perspective.* Cambridge, Cambridge University Press.

Connah, Graham (2012). "Early States and State Formation in Africa." African Studies, Oxford Bibliographies. 25 October. http://dx.doi.org/10.1093/obo/9780199846733-0047

Cooper, Helene (2008). *The house at Sugar Beach: in search of a lost African childhood.* New York, Simon & Schuster.

Cooper, Peter (1992). FDA Chides Loggers. *Patriot*, February 19. Gbarnga, Liberia.

Cooper, Robert and Mats Berdal (1993). "Outside intervention in ethnic conflicts." *Survival* 35(1): 118–42.

County Development Committee (2007). River Cess County Development Agenda, Republic of Liberia.

Cramer, Christopher (2006). *Civil war is not a stupid thing: accounting for violence in developing countries.* London, Hurst and Co.

Cramer, Katherine (2015). "Transparent Explanations, Yes. Public Transcripts and Fieldnotes, No: Ethnographic Research on Public Opinion." *Qualitative & Multi-Method Research* 13(1): 17–20.

Cutts, Mark and UNHCR (2000). *The state of the world's refugees, 2000: fifty years of humanitarian action.* Geneva and New York, Oxford University Press.

Daems, Maggie (2004). Ecosec evaluation mission in River Gee, Maryland and Grand Kru Zwedru, International Committee of the Red Cross: 6.

Daffah, Matthias (2010). Sime Darby Company in Western Liberia Accused. Star Radio. Monronvia, Global News Network.

Dandeker, Christopher and James Gow (1997). "The Future of Peace Support Operations: Strategic Peacekeeping and Success." *Armed Forces & Society* 23(3): 327–47.

Darden, Keith and Harris Mylonas (2012). "The Promethean Dilemma: Third-party State-building in Occupied Territories." *Ethnopolitics* 11(1): 85–93.

Davis, Diane E. and Anthony W. Pereira (2003). *Irregular armed forces and their role in politics and state formation.* Cambridge, Cambridge University Press.

de Boer, John and Louise Bosetti (2015). "The Crime-Conflict "Nexus": State of the Evidence." Occasional Paper 5. Tokyo, United Nations University Centre for Policy Research.

de Groot, Jasper H. B., Gün R. Semin, and Smeets, Monique A. M. (2014). "I Can See, Hear, and Smell Your Fear: Comparing Olfactory and Audiovisual Media in Fear Communication." *Journal of Experimental Psychology: General* 143(2): 825–34.

de Heredia, Marta Iñiguez (2012). "Escaping Statebuilding: Resistance and Civil Society in the Democratic Republic of Congo." *Journal of Intervention and State-building* 6(1): 75–89.

de Montclos, M. (1996). Liberia: des predateurs aux ramasseurs de miettes, in *Economie des Guerres Civiles*, F. Jean and J.-C. Rufin (eds). Paris, Hachette.

de Tocqueville, Alexis (1835). *Democracy in America*. London, Saunders and Otley.

de Vries, Hugo and Nikkie Wiegink (2011). "Breaking up and Going Home? Contesting Two Assumptions in the Demobilization and Reintegration of Former Combatants." *International Peacekeeping* 18(1): 38–51.

Deibert, Michael (2015). Could the gangs of Port-au-Prince form a pact to revitalise Haiti's capital? July 14. *The Guardian*.

Delesgues, L. and Y. Torabi (2010). *Afghan Perceptions and Experiences of Corruption: A National Survey 2010*. Kabul, Integrity Watch Afghanistan.

Denyer Willis, Graham (2015). The Killing Consensus: Police, Organized Crime, and the Regulation of Life and Death in Urban Brazil. Berkeley, University of California Press.

Diamond Company Manager (2009). Email Correspondence with Diamond Company Manager working in Liberia. May 10. Monrovia, Liberia.

Diggs, Bill E. (2009). As 'Redundant Workers' Cry out for Pay. *Daily Observer*. Monrovia.

Dodge, Toby (2006). "Iraq: The contradictions of exogenous state-building in historical perspective." *Third World Quarterly* 27(1): 187–200.

Doe, James W. (2005). Draft Issue Paper of Thematic Working Group IV on Forest Information, Training Institutions and Legislations. Strengthen the Forestry Development Authority and Developing the National Forest Program. Monrovia, Liberia, Food and Agriculture Organization of the United Nations.

Donais, Timothy (2003). "The political economy of stalemate: organised crime, corruption and economic deformation in post-Dayton Bosnia." *Conflict, Security & Development* 3(3): 359–82.

Donais, Timothy (2012). *Peacebuilding and local ownership: post-conflict and consensus-building*. New York, Routledge.

Dosso, Zoom (2006). "Government reclaims rubber plantation from rebels." Business in Africa Online.

Downes, Alexander B. (2008). *Targeting civilians in war*. Ithaca, Cornell University Press.

Doyle, Michael W. and Nicholas Sambanis (2000). "International peacebuilding: A theoretical and quantitative analysis." *American Political Science Review* 94(4): 779–801.

Doyle, Michael W. and Nicholas Sambanis (2006). *Making war and building peace: United Nations peace operations*. Princeton, Princeton University Press.

Dube, Oeindrilla and Juan Vargas (2013). "Commodity Price Shocks and Civil Conflict: Evidence from Colombia." *Review of Economic Studies* 80(4): 1384–421.

Duffield, Mark R. (2001). *Global governance and the new wars: the merging of development and security.* London, Zed Books.

Dufka, Corinne (2005). *Youth, Poverty and Blood: The Lethal Legacy of West Africa's Regional Warriors.* New York, Human Rights Watch.

Dugard, Jackie (2001). "From Low Intensity War to Mafia War: Taxi violence in South Africa (1987–2000)." *Violence and Transition Series,* Vol. 4.

Dunleavy, P. (2014). "In a PhD or academic book, do you really need a Methodology chapter early on?" Medium.com. https://medium.com/advice-and-help-in-authoring-a-phd-or-non-fiction/in-a-phd-or-academic-book-do-you-really-need-a-methodology-chapter-early-on-e596ac518f75

Dunn, D. Elwood (1995). *Liberia.* World Bibliographical Series, no. 157. Oxford, Clio Press.

Dwan, Renata and Laura Bailey (2006). *Liberia's Governance and Economic Management Assistance Program.* New York and Washington, DC, UN Department of Peacekeeping Operations and Fragile States Group and the World Bank.

Dziedzic, Michael and Robert M. Perito (2008). *Haiti: Confronting the Gangs of Port-au-Prince.* Washington, US Institute of Peace.

Eck, Kristine and Lisa Hultman (2007). "One-Sided Violence Against Civilians in War." *Journal of Peace Research* 44(2): 233–46.

Elias, Norbert (1982). *The civilizing process: State formation and civilization.* Oxford, Blackwell.

Ellis, Stephen (1999). *The Mask of Anarchy.* London, Hurst and Co.

Elster, Jon (2004). *Closing the books: transitional justice in historical perspective.* Cambridge, Cambridge University Press.

Engels, Friedrich and Ernest Untermann (1884). *The origin of the family, private property and the state.* Chicago, C.H. Kerr & company.

European Commission Official (2005). Interview with European Commission Official. September 26 and October 20. Monrovia, Liberia.

Evans, Peter B. (1995). *Embedded autonomy: states and industrial transformation.* Princeton, Princeton University Press.

Expedition (2008). "Somali Pirate Attacks." Google Earth Community Forum. https://productforums.google.com/forum/#!topic/gec-travel-information-moderated/3tXTwjwhujE;context-place=forum/gec-travel-information-moderated

Fahngon, Jimmey C. (2006). Ex-Combatants Remain Defiant. *The News.* Guthrie.

Faiola, Anthony and Souad Mekhennet (2015). The Islamic State creates a new type of jihadist: Part terrorist, part gangster. *The Washington Post.*

Falkenburg, L. (2013). "Youth Lost: Ugandan Child Soldiers in the Lord's Resistance Army." *Small Wars Journal,* March 15. http://smallwarsjournal.com/jrnl/art/youth-lost-ugandan-child-soldiers-in-the-lord%E2%80%99s-resistance-army

Fallah, Jennie K. (2006). UNMIL Takes Over Guthrie, But. *The Inquirer.* Monrovia.

Farah, Douglas (2004). *Blood from stones: the secret financial network of terror.* New York, Broadway Books.

Fearon, James D. (2004). "Why do some civil wars last so much longer than others?" *Journal of Peace Research* 41(3): 275–301.

Fearon, James D. and David D. Laitin (2003). "Ethnicity, insurgency, and civil war." *American Political Science Review* 97(1): 75–90.

Fearon, James D. and David D. Laitin (2004). "Neotrusteeship and the problem of weak states." *International Security* 28(4): 5–43.

Firchow, Pamina and Roger MacGinty (2014). "Everyday Peace Indicators: Capturing local voices through surveys." *Shared Space.* Belfast, Northern Ireland Community Relations Council and World Leadership Alliance—Club de Madrid. Issue 18: 33–40.

Fithen, Caspar (2005). Interview with Caspar Fithen, Member of UN Panel of Experts for Liberia. September 4, 2005. Monrovia, Liberia.

Ford, Martin (1992). Indirect rule and the emergence of the "Big Chief" in Liberia's Central Province, 1918–1944. Liberia Working Group Papers. Bremen: 88.

Forest Concession Review Committee Phase III (2005). Report of the Forest Concession Review Committee—Phase III. Monrovia.

Forest Development Authority (2007). FDA Info Sheet: Regulation Nr.28: Pitsawing Permit Procedures. Monrovia, Forest Development Authority, Government of Liberia.

Forests Monitor (2008). Strengthening forest management in post-conflict Liberia. Monrovia, Forests Monitor.

Former County Superintendent (2005). Interview with Former County Superintendent. September 17, 2005. Zwedru, Liberia.

Forrester, Skye (2016). "Inside South Africa's brutal prisons: 'If I didn't join a gang I'd have been raped'." *International Business Times*, April 13. Retrieved from http://www.ibtimes.co.uk/inside-south-africas-brutal-prisons-if-i-didnt-join-gang-id-have-been-raped-1554475

Fortna, Virginia P. (2004a). "Does peacekeeping keep peace? International intervention and the duration of peace after civil war." *International Studies Quarterly* 48(2): 269–92.

Fortna, Virginia P. (2004b). "Interstate peacekeeping: Causal mechanisms and empirical effects." *World Politics* 56(4): 481–519.

Fortna, Virginia P. (2004c). *Peace time: cease-fire agreements and the durability of peace.* Princeton, Princeton University Press.

Fortna, Virginia P. (2008). *Does peacekeeping work? Shaping belligerents' choices after civil war.* Princeton, Princeton University Press.

Fraenkel, Merran (1964). *Tribe and class in Monrovia.* London, Oxford University Press.

Freeman, Laura (2015). "The African warlord revisited." *Small Wars & Insurgencies* 26(5): 790–810.

Friedman, George (2010). "Mexico and the Failed State Revisited." April 6. Retrieved from http://www.stratfor.com

Friends of Liberia (1997). Liberia's Special Elections Preliminary Statement of Findings. Monrovia.

Frushone, Joel (2004). World Refugee Survey 2004. Arlington, U.S. Committee for Refugees and Immigrants. Retrieved from http://www.refugees.org/article.aspx?id=1158

Fund for Peace and Foreign Policy Magazine (2013). "The Failed States Index." *Foreign Policy.* Retrieved from http://foreignpolicy.com/2013/06/24/the-2013-failed-states-index-interactive-map-and-rankings/

Galtung, Johan (1969). "Violence, peace, and peace research." *Journal of Peace Research* 6(3): 167–191.

Gambetta, Diego (1993). *The Sicilian Mafia: The Business of Private Protection.* Cambridge, Massachusetts, Harvard University Press.

Garmany, Jeff (2009). "The embodied state: governmentality in a Brazilian favela." *Social & Cultural Geography* 10(7).

Gault, Mike (2015). Forget Bitcoin: What Is the Blockchain and Why Should You Care? July 5. *Re/code.*

Gaye, Solomon (2006). Armed Men Attack Plantation in Nimba. *The Inquirer.* Nimba.

Gbarpodolu, Moses (2007). Interview with Moses Gbarpodolu, Manager of Chain of Custody, Forest Development Authority. May 1, 2007. Monrovia, Liberia.

Gberie, Lansana (2004). Diamonds without Maps—Liberia, the UN, Sanctions, and the Kimberley Process. Partnership Africa Canada, Ottawa.

Gear, Sasha (2002). *Now that the War is Over.* Centre for the Study of Violence and Reconciliation. Cape Town, Centre for the Study of Violence and Reconciliation.

Gellner, Ernest (1983). *Nations and nationalism.* Oxford, Basil Blackwell.

General Resources Corporation (2006). The Management of the General Resources Corporation (GRC) vs. The Government of Liberia by and thru the Ministries of Agriculture and Justice. Appellant's Brief. Monrovia, Supreme Court of Liberia.

George, Alexander and Timothy McKeown (1984). Case Studies and Theories of Organizational Decision Making, in *Advances in information processing in organizations,* R. Coulam and R. Smith (eds). Greenwich, CT, JAI Press: 43–68.

George, Alexander L. and Andrew Bennett (2005). *Case studies and theory development in the social sciences.* Cambridge, MA, MIT Press.

Gettleman, Jeffrey (2009). For Somali Pirates, Worst Enemy May Be on Shore. May 8. *New York Times.*

Ghani, Ashraf and Clare Lockhart (2008). *Fixing failed states: a framework for rebuilding a fractured world.* Oxford, Oxford University Press.

Gillies, Alexandra and Page Dykstra (2011). International campaigns for extractive industry transparency in post-conflict settings, in *Corruption and Post-Conflict Peacebuilding,* in C. Cheng and D. Zaum (eds). Abingdon, Routledge.

Glenny, Misha (2015). *Nemesis: one man and the battle for Rio.* London, Bodley Head.

Global Witness (2002). *Logging Off.* London, Global Witness.

Global Witness (2004a). *Liberia: Back to the Future.* London, Global Witness.

Global Witness (2004b). *Resource Curse or Cure? Reforming Liberia's governance and logging industry.* London, Global Witness.

Global Witness (2005a). *An Architecture of Instability.* London, Global Witness.

Global Witness (2005b). *Briefing.* London, Global Witness.

Global Witness (2005c). *Timber, Taylor, Soldier, Spy.* London, Global Witness.

Global Witness (2006). *Cautiously Optimistic: The Case for Maintaining Sanctions in Liberia.* London, Global Witness.

Godson, Roy (2003). *Menace to society: political-criminal collaboration around the world.* New Brunswick, New Jersey, Transaction Publishers.

Goffman, Alice (2015). *On the run: fugitive life in an American city.* New York, NY, Picador.

Goldstone, Jack A., Ted Robert Gurr, Barbara Harff, et al. (2000). *State Failure Task Force Report: Phase III Findings*. McLean, VA, Science Applications International Corporation.

Gongora, Thierry (1997). "War Making and State Power in the Contemporary Middle East." International Journal of Middle East Studies 29(3): 323–40.

Goodhand, Jonathan (2004). Afghanistan in Central Asia, in *War Economies in a Regional Context*, M. Pugh, N. Cooper and J. Goodhand. London, Lynne Rienner.

Goodhand, Jonathan (2011). Corrupting or Consolidating the Peace? The Drugs Economy and Post-conflict Peacebuilding in Afghanistan, in *Corruption and Peacebuilding: Selling the Peace?*, C. Cheng and D. Zaum (eds). Abingdon, Routledge.

Government of Liberia (1957). *Liberian code of laws of 1956*. Ithaca, NY, Cornell University Press.

Government of Liberia (2004). *Millennium Development Goals Report*. Monrovia, Ministry of Planning and Economic Affairs and UNDP.

Government of Liberia, Liberians United for Reconciliation and Democracy, and Movement for Democracy in Liberia (2003). Comprehensive Peace Agreement Between the Government of Liberia and the Liberians United for Reconciliation and Democracy (LURD) and the Movement for Democracy in Liberia (MODEL) and Political Parties. August 18. Accra, Ghana.

Gray, Josephus Moses (2005). Fifty George Weah CDC Partisans Arrested Following Rioting. *The Perspective*.

Grayson, George W. (2010). *Mexico: narco-violence and a failed state?* New Brunswick, NJ, Transaction Publishers.

Green Advocates (2006). *Final Report on the Natural Resource Extraction Project*. Monrovia, Green Advocates.

Greene, Graham (1936). *Journey without maps*. Garden City, NY, Doubleday, Doran & Company, Inc.

Greif, Avner (1993). "Contract enforceability and economic institutions in early trade: The Maghribi traders' coalition." *The American economic review*: 83(3): 525–48.

Greif, Avner (2006). *Institutions and the path to the modern economy: lessons from medieval trade*. Cambridge, Cambridge University Press.

Grillo, Ioan (2011). *El Narco: inside Mexico's criminal insurgency*. New York, Bloomsbury Press.

Gros, Jean-Germain (1996). "Towards a taxonomy of failed states in the new world order: Decay in Somalia, Liberia, Rwanda and Haiti." *Third World Quarterly* 17(3): 455–71.

Gurr, Ted Robert (1970). *Why men rebel*. Princeton, Center of International Studies and Princeton University Press.

Hallgren, Mauritz A. (1933). Liberia in Shackles. *The Nation*.

Hamill, Heather (2011). *The hoods: crime and punishment in Belfast*. Princeton, Princeton University Press.

Hardgrove, Abigail (2012). Life After Guns: The Life Chances and Trajectories of Ex-combatant and War-Affected Youth in Monrovia, Liberia. D.Phil., University of Oxford.

Harris, David. (1999). "From 'warlord' to 'democratic' president: how Charles Taylor won the 1997 Liberian elections." *Journal of Modern African Studies* 37(3): 431–55.

Harris, David. (2006). "Liberia 2005: an unusual African post-conflict election." *Journal of Modern African Studies* 44(3): 375–95.

Hartill, Lane (2005). Liberians Protest Soccer Star's Defeat—In Presidential Runoff, Monitors Say Apparent Victory by Economist Was Largely Fair. November 12. *The Washington Post.*

Hartzell, Caroline, Matthew Hoddie, and Donald Rothchild (2001). "Stabilizing the Peace After Civil War: An Investigation of Some Key Variables." *International Organization* 55(01): 183–208.

Hayner, Priscilla B. (2001). *Unspeakable Truths: Confronting State Terror and Atrocity.* Abingdon, Routledge.

Hazen, Jennifer (2010). "Understanding gangs as armed groups." *International Review of the Red Cross* 92(878).

Hazen, Jennifer M. (2005). Social Integration of Ex-Combatants after Civil War. Expert Group Meeting on Dialogue in the Social Integration Process: Building Peaceful Social Relations by, for and with People. New York, United Nations Division for Social Policy and Development.

Hegre, H., G. Ostby, and Raleigh, C. (2009). "Poverty and Civil War Events A Disaggregated Study of Liberia." *Journal of Conflict Resolution* 53(4): 598–623.

Hegre, Havard (2004). "The Duration and Termination of Civil War." *Journal of Peace Research* 41(3): 243–252.

Hellman, Joel, Geraint Jones, Daniel Kaufmann, and Mark Schankerman (2000). Measuring Governance, Corruption, and State Capture: How Firms and Bureaucrats Shape the Business Environment in Transition Economies. World Bank Policy Research Working Paper. Washington, DC, World Bank.

Hellman, Joel, Geraint Jones, and Daniel Kaufmann (2000). *Seize the State, Seize the Day: State Capture, Corruption and Influence in Transition.* Washington, DC, World Bank.

Helman, Gerland B. and Stephen R. Ratner (1992). "Saving Failed States." *Foreign Policy* Winter (89): 3–20.

Helmke, G. and S. Levitsky (2004). "Informal institutions and comparative politics: A research agenda." *Perspectives on Politics* 2(4): 725–40.

Hendrickson, Dylan (1999). Key issues in security sector reform. The Conflict, Security & Development Group, Working Papers. King's College London.

Herbst, Jeffrey I. (1997). "Responding to state failure in Africa." *International Security* 21(3): 120–44.

Herbst, Jeffrey Ira (2000). *States and power in Africa: comparative lessons in authority and control.* Princeton, Princeton University Press.

Hilson, Gavin M. (2006). *Small-scale mining, rural subsistence and poverty in West Africa.* Rugby, Warwickshire, Practical Action Publishing.

Hirsch, John L. (2001). *Sierra Leone: diamonds and the struggle for democracy.* Boulder, Colorado, Lynne Rienner.

Hirschman, Albert (1984). "Against Parsimony: Three Easy Ways of Complicating Some Categories of Economic Discourse." *American Economic Association Papers and Proceedings* 74(2): 89–96.

Hirschmann, Nancy, Mala Htun, Jane Mansbridge, Kathleen Thelen, Lisa Wedeen and Elisabeth Wood (2015). "Dialogue on DA-RT." https://dialogueondart.org/

Hobbes, Thomas (1651). *Leviathan, or, The matter, forme, & power of a common-wealth ecclesiasticall and civill.* London, printed for Andrew Crooke, at the Green Dragon in St. Pauls Church-yard.

Hodges, Tony (2001). *Angola: from Afro-Stalinism to Petro-diamond capitalism.* Bloomington, Indiana University Press.

Hoffman, Danny (2011). *The war machines: young men and violence in Sierra Leone and Liberia.* Durham, North Carolina, Duke University Press.

Holsoe, Svend (1974). "The Manipulation of Traditional Political Structures among Coastal Peoples in Western Liberian during the Nineteenth Century." *Ethnohistory* 21(2): 158–67.

Holt, K. and S. Hughes (2004). Sex and death in the heart of Africa. May 24. *The Independent.*

Hozic, Aida A. (2006). "The Balkan Merchants: Changing Borders and Informal Transnationalization." *Ethnopolitics* 5(3): 243–56.

HPCR International (2007). "Introduction: Economic Recovery Strategies: Definitions & Conceptual Issues." New York, The Peacebuilding Initiative. Retrieved from http://www.peacebuildinginitiative.org/index7604.html?pageId=1769

Huang, Reyko. (2016). *The Wartime Origins of Democratization: Civil War, Rebel Governance, and Political Regimes.* Cambridge, Cambridge University Press.

Huband, Mark (1998). *The Liberian Civil War.* London, Frank Cass.

Hui, Victoria Tin-bor (2005). *War and state formation in ancient China and early modern Europe.* Cambridge, Cambridge University Press.

Human Rights Watch (2005). "Côte d'Ivoire: Government Recruits Child Soldiers in Liberia." New York, Human Rights Watch. Retrieved from https://www.hrw.org/news/2005/10/28/cote-divoire-government-recruits-child-soldiers-liberia

Humphreys, Macartan (2005). "Natural resources, conflict, and conflict resolution Uncovering the mechanisms." *Journal of Conflict Resolution* 49(4): 508–37.

Humphreys, Macartan and Jeremy Weinstein (2007). "Demobilization and reintegration." *Journal of Conflict Resolution* 51(4): 531–67.

Humphreys, Macartan, Jeffery D. Sachs, and Joseph E. Stiglitz, Eds. (2007). *Escaping the Resource Curse.* New York, Columbia University Press.

Huntington, Samuel (1993). "The Clash of Civilizations." *Foreign Affairs* 72(3).

Idler, Annette (2012). "Exploring Arrangements of Convenience among Violent Non-state Actors." *Perspectives on Terrorism* 6(4–5).

Interlandi, Jeneen (2015). The Brain's Empathy Gap. March 19. *New York Times.*

International Commercial Crime Services (2014). Somali pirate clampdown caused drop in global piracy, IMB reveals. January 15. International Chamber of Commerce. Retrieved from https://www.icc-ccs.org/news/904-somali-pirate-clampdown-caused-drop-in-global-piracy-imb-reveals

International Commission of Inquiry into the Existence of Slavery and Forced Labor in the Republic of Liberia (1931). Report of the International Commission of Inquiry into the Existence of Slavery and Forced Labor in the Republic of Liberia. Monrovia, Liberia, September 8, 1930. Washington, U.S. Government.

International Committee of the Red Cross (1949). *Geneva Conventions. Rule 3: Definition of Combatants.* I. C. o. t. R. Cross. Geneva, International Committee of the Red Cross.

International Criminal Tribunal for the former Yugoslavia Appeals Chamber (2002). Sentencing Judgement in the Kunarac, Kovac and Vukovic (Foca) Case. ICTY. The Hague. CVO/P.I.S./679-E.

International Crisis Group (2009). Liberia: Uneven Progress in Security Sector Reform, International Crisis Group.

International Dialogue on Peacebuilding and Statebuilding (2011). New Deal for Engagement in Fragile States. 4th High Level Forum on Aid Effectiveness, Busan, South Korea, International Dialogue on Peacebuilding and Statebuilding.

International Labor Rights Fund (2005). Class Action Complaint For Injunctive Relief and Damages. Filed November 17, 2005, United States District Court, Central District of California.

Ioannidis, John P. A. (2005). "Why Most Published Research Findings Are False." *PLOS Medicine*. PLoS Med 2(8): e124. https://doi.org/10.1371/journal.pmed.0020124

IRIN (2006a). Civilians want ex-fighters out of rubber plantation. March 13. *IRIN News*.

IRIN (2006b). "Gov't reclaims rubber plantation from former fighters." August 16. *IRIN News*.

IRIN (2006c). Rubber plantations "lawless", says UN. May 11. *IRIN News*.

IRIN (2006d). "Liberia: End of Diamond and Timber Sanctions Closer." April 10. *IRIN News*.

Jackson, Paul (2003). "Warlords as alternative forms of Governance." *Small Wars & Insurgencies* 14(2): 131–50.

Jackson, Stephen (2002). "Making a Killing: criminality and coping in the Kivu war economy." *Review of African Political Economy* 29(93/94): 517–36.

Jarat Chopra and Tanja Hohe (2004). "Participatory Intervention." *Global Governance: A Review of Multilateralism and International Organizations* 10(3): 289–305.

Jensen, David and Stephen Lonergan, Eds. (2012). *Assessing and Restoring Natural Resources in Post-Conflict Peacebuilding*. Abingdon, Routledge.

Jerue, Gibson W. (2006). GoL's Plan To Repossess Rubber Farms in The Offing. May 22. *The Analyst.*

Jerven, Morten (2013). *Poor numbers: How we are misled by African development statistics and what to do about it*. Ithaca, Cornell University Press.

Jesperson, Sasha (2013). "Addressing Organised Crime in Sierra Leone: The Role of the Security-Development Nexus." *Journal of Sierra Leone Studies* 2(1): 22–33.

Jesperson, Sasha (2014). Tensions in the Security-Development Nexus: Addressing Organised Crime After Conflict in Sierra Leone and Bosnia-Herzegovina. Ph.D., London School of Economics.

Johnson, Charles Spurgeon (1987). *Bitter Canaan: the story of the Negro republic*. New Brunswick, NJ, Transaction Books.

Johnson, Phillip James (2004). Seasons in hell: Charles S. Johnson and the 1930 Liberian labor crisis. Ph.D., Louisiana State University and Agricultural & Mechanical College.

Jones, Lee (2010). "(Post-)Colonial state-building and state failure in East Timor: bringing social conflict back in." *Conflict, Security & Development* 10(4): 547–75.

Jones, Lee (2015). *Societies Under Siege: Exploring how International Economic Sanctions (do Not) Work*. Oxford, Oxford University Press.

Jones, Seth G., Jeremy Wilson, Andrew Rathmell, and K. Jack Riley (2005). *Establishing law and order after conflict*. Santa Monica, California, RAND.

Jung, Dietrich (2008). State Formation and State-Building: Is there a lesson to learn from Sociology? Fragile Situations, Background Papers. Copenhagen, Danish Institute for International Studies.

Justice and Peace Commission (1994). *The Liberian Crisis*. Monrovia, National Catholic Secretariat.

Kahneman, Daniel and Amos Tversky (1979). "Prospect Theory: An Analysis of Decision under Risk." *Econometrica* 47(2): 263–291.

Kahneman, Daniel, Paul Slovic, and Tversky, Amos (1982). *Judgment Under Uncertainty: Heuristics and biases*. Cambridge, Cambridge University Press.

Kaldor, Mary (1999). *New and Old Wars: Organized violence in a global era*. Cambridge, Polity Press.

Kalyvas, Stathis N. (2006). *The Logic of Violence in Civil War*. Cambridge; New York, Cambridge University Press.

Kamara, Jangar, Edward Kamara, Letla Mosenene, and Francis Odoom. (2010). Chainsaw milling and national forest policy in Liberia, in *Chainsaw milling: supplier to local markets*, Mareike Wit and Jinke van Dam (eds). Wageningen, Netherlands, European Tropical Forest Research Network. 52: 174–80.

Kantor, Ana and Mariam Persson (2010). *Understanding Vigilantism: Informal security providers and security sector reform in Liberia*. Stockhom, Folke Bernadotte Academy.

Kaplan, Robert (1994). The Coming Anarchy: How scarcity, crime, overpopulation, tribalism, and disease are rapidly destroying the social fabric of our planet. *The Atlantic Monthly* 273(2): 44–77.

Kaplan, Robert (1993). *Balkan Ghosts: A journey through history*. New York, St. Martin's Press.

Karl, Terry Lynn (1997). *The paradox of plenty: oil booms and petro-states*. Berkeley, University of California Press.

Karnga, Mensiegar Jr (2005). Cocopa Rubber Farm Under Siege. April 27. *The Analyst*.

Kauffman, Stuart A. (1993). *The origins of order: self-organization and selection in evolution*. New York, Oxford University Press.

Keen, David (1994). *The benefits of famine: a political economy of famine and relief in southwestern Sudan, 1983–1989*. Princeton, Princeton University Press.

Keen, David (1997). "A rational kind of madness." *Oxford Development Studies* 25(1): 67.

Keen, David (1998). The Economic Functions of Violence in Civil Wars. Adelphi Paper 320. London, International Institute of Strategic Studies.

Keen, David (2005). *Conflict and Collusion in Sierra Leone*. Oxford, James Currey.

Keister, Jennifer and Branislav Slantchev (2014). Statebreakers to Statemakers: Strategies of Rebel Governance. Unpublished manuscript. Retrieved from http://slantchev.ucsd.edu/wp/pdf/RebelGovern-W079.pdf

Keister, Jennifer. (2015). "Rebel Rule." Retrieved from http://jennifer-keister.com/research/

Kelsky, K. (2011). "My Top Five Tips for Turning Your Dissertation Into a Book." Retrieved from https://theprofessorisin.com/2016/02/26/how-to-turn-your-dissertation-into-a-book-a-special-request-post/

Kerr, Michael (2011). *The destructors: the story of Northern Ireland's lost peace process.* Dublin, Irish Academic Press.

Kerr, R. and E. Mobekk (2007). *Peace and Justice.* Cambridge, Polity Press.

Kieh, George Klay Jr (2011). "Peace agreements and the termination of civil wars: Lessons from Liberia." *African Journal on Conflict Resolution* 11(3): 53–86.

Kilroy, Walt (2015). *Reintegration of Ex-Combatants After Conflict: Participatory Approaches in Sierra Leone and Liberia.* London, Palgrave Macmillan.

Kimberley Process (2015). 2007–15 Annual Rough Diamond Summary: Liberia, Kimberley Process.

King, Gary, Robert O. Keohane, and Verba, Sidney (1994). *Designing social inquiry: scientific inference in qualitative research.* Princeton, Princeton University Press.

Klein, Jacques Paul (2006). Interview with Jacques Paul Klein, former Special Representative of the Secretary-General and Coordinator of United Nations Operations in Liberia. April 19, 2006. Washington, DC.

Korkollie, Folo-Glogba (2002). Bassonians Decry OTC operations . . . Veep Blah Promises to Transmit grievances to Pres. Taylor. *The Inquirer.* Monrovia.

Kpagbor, Joseph (2008). *TRC Public Hearings in Buchanan, Grand Bassa County. Truth and Reconciliation Commission.* Buchanan City, Grand Bass County, Liberia.

Kpayili, Michael (2006). Cocopa Rubber Plantation Turns Bandit Ground. *The Liberian Times.* Monrovia.

Krasner, Stephen D. (2004). "Sharing sovereignty: New institutions for collapsed and failing states." *International Security* 29(2): 85–120.

Krause, Jana (2013). Resilient Communities: Explaining nonviolence during ethno-religious conflict in Indonesia (Ambon) and Nigeria (Jos). Ph.D., Graduate Institute of International and Development Studies.

Krause, Jana (2017). "Non-Violence and Civilian Agency in Communal War: Evidence from Jos, Nigeria." *African Affairs* 116(463): 261–83.

Krugman, Paul (2017). The Biggest Tax Scam in History. November 27. *New York Times.*

Lacey, Marc (2009). Mexican drug trafficking. October 16. *New York Times.*

Lacher, Wolfram (2012). Organized crime and conflict in the Sahel-Sahara region. The Carnegie Papers. Washington, Carnegie Endowment for International Peace.

Landman, Todd and Anita Gohdes (2013). A matter of convenience: challenges of non-random data in analyzing human rights violations during conflicts in Peru and Sierra Leone, in *Counting civilian casualties: an introduction to recording and estimating nonmilitary deaths in conflict,* T. B. Seybolt, J. D. Aronson and B. Fischhoff (eds). Oxford, Oxford University Press.

Landmine Action UK (2006). Impact and Feasibility Study on the Guthrie Rubber Plantation. Monrovia, Landmine Action UK, Community Habitat Finance (CHF), and Foundation for International Dignity (FIND).

Laudati, Ann (2011). "Victims of Discourse: Mobilizing Narratives of Fear and Insecurity in Post-Conflict South Sudan—The Case of Jonglei State." *African Geographical Review* 30(1): 15–32.

Le Billon, Philippe (2001a). "Angola's political economy of war: The role of oil and diamonds, 1975–2000." *African Affairs* 100(398): 55–80.

Le Billon, Philippe (2001b). "The political ecology of war: natural resources and armed conflicts." *Political Geography* 20(5): 561–84.

Le Billon, Philippe (2003). "Buying Peace or Fuelling War: the Role of Corruption in Armed Conflicts." *Journal of International Development* 15(4): 413–26.

Le Billon, Philippe (2006). "Fatal transactions: Conflict diamonds and the (anti) terrorist consumer." *Antipode* 38(4): 778–801.

Le Billon, Philippe (2008). "Diamond wars? Conflict diamonds and geographies of resource wars." *Annals of the Association of American Geographers* 98(2): 345–72.

Leander, Anna (2004). Wars and the Un-Making of States: Taking Tilly Seriously in the Contemporary World, in *Conceptual Innovations and Contemporary Security Analysis*, S. Guzzini and D. Jung (eds). London, Routledge: 69–80.

Lee, Daniel E. and Elizabeth J. Lee (2010). *Human rights and the ethics of globalization.* Cambridge, Cambridge University Press.

Leebaw, Bronwyn Anne (2008). "The Irreconcilable Goals of Transitional Justice." *Human Rights Quarterly* 30(1): 95–118.

Left, Sarah (2003). War in Liberia. August 4. *The Guardian.*

Levitt, Jeremy I. (2005). *The evolution of deadly conflict in Liberia: from 'paternaltarianism' to state collapse.* Durham, Carolina Academic Press.

Lew, Josh (2014). "A few unclaimed lands still there for the taking." September 4. Mother Nature Network. Retrieved from http://www.mnn.com/lifestyle/eco-tourism/stories/a-few-unclaimed-lands-still-there-for-the-taking

Lewis, Heather Parker (2006). *God's gangsters? The history, language, rituals, secrets, and myths of South Africa's prison gangs.* Cape Town, South Africa, Ihilihili Press.

Liberian Truth and Reconciliation Commission and Benetech Human Rights Program (2010). Descriptive Datafiles. March 25. Retrieved from https://hrdag.org/liberia-data-dictionary/

Lichtenstein, S., P. Slovic, B. Fischhoff, M. Layman and B. Combs (1978). "Judged frequency of lethal events." *Journal of Experimental Psychology: Human Learning and Memory* 4(6): 551.

Lidow, N.H. (2016). *Violent Order: Understanding Rebel Governance through Liberia's Civil War.* Cambridge, Cambridge University Press.

Liebenow, J. Gus (1987). *Liberia: the quest for democracy.* Bloomington, Indiana University Press.

Linde, Olya, Aleksey Martynov, Ari Epstein, and Stéphane Fischler (2016). The Global Diamond Industry 2016: The Enduring Allure of Timeless Gems, Bain & Company and Antwerp Diamond Centre.

Lindegaard, Marie Rosenkrantz and Sasha Gear (2014). "Violence makes safe in South African prisons: Prison gangs, violent acts, and victimization among inmates." *Focaal* 2014(68): 35–54.

Locke, John (1690). *Second treatise of government.* London.

Lujala, Päivi (2009). "Deadly Combat over Natural Resources Gems, Petroleum, Drugs, and the Severity of Armed Civil Conflict." *Journal of Conflict Resolution* 53(1): 50–71.

Lujala, Päivi, Nils P. Gleditsch, and Elisabeth Gilmore. (2005). "A diamond curse? Civil war and a lootable resource." *Journal of Conflict Resolution* 49(4): 538–62.

Lujala, Päivi and Siri Aas Rustad, Eds. (2011). *High-Value Natural Resources and Post-Conflict Peacebuilding.* Abingdon, Routledge.

Lyons, Terrence (1999). *Voting for peace: postconflict elections in Liberia*. Washington, DC, Brookings Institution Press.

MacGaffey, Janet and Rémy Bazenguissa-Ganga (2000). *Congo-Paris: transnational traders on the margins of the law*. London, James Currey.

MacGinty, Roger (2010). "Hybrid Peace: The Interaction Between Top-Down and Bottom-Up Peace." *Security Dialogue* 41(4): 391–412.

MacGinty, Roger and Oliver Richmond (2016). "The fallacy of constructing hybrid political orders: a reappraisal of the hybrid turn in peacebuilding." *International Peacekeeping* 23(2): 219–39.

MacGinty, Roger (2014). The "dirty little secret" of "field" research? March 5. Retrieved from https://rogermacginty.com/2014/03/05/the-dirty-little-secret-of-field-research/

MacGinty, Roger (2011). *International Peacebuilding and Local Resistance*. Basingstoke, Palgrave Macmillan.

MacGinty, Roger (2013). "Indicators +: A proposal for everyday peace indicators." *Evaluation and Program Planning* 36(1): 56–63.

MacKinlay, John (2000). "Defining warlords." *International Peacekeeping* 7(1): 48–62.

Maconachie, R. and T. Binns (2007). "Beyond the resource curse? Diamond mining, development and post-conflict reconstruction in Sierra Leone." *Resources Policy* 32(3): 104–15.

Malayea, Marcus (2006). Gunmen Seize Cocopa. August 18. *The Analyst*.

Malgas, Christopher Glen (2003). A series of personal interviews with Pollsmoor prison guard, Christopher Glen Malgas. November 17–28, Cape Town, South Africa.

Mallaby, Sebastian (2002). "The Reluctant Imperialist—Terrorism, Failed States, and the Case for American Empire." *Foreign Affairs* 81(2): 2–7.

Mamdani, Mahmood (1996). *Citizen and subject: contemporary Africa and the legacy of late Colonialism*. Princeton, Princeton University Press.

Mampilly, Zachariah C. (2011). *Rebel rulers: insurgent governance and civilian life during war*. Ithaca, NY, Cornell University Press.

Management Systems International (2004). *Institutional Assessment of Movement of Concerned Kono Youth (MOCKY)*. Washington, DC, Management Systems International.

Mandrique, Nelson (1998). The War for the Central Sierra, in *Shining and Other Paths: War and Society in Peru, 1980–1995*, S. J. Stern (ed). Durham, North Carolina, Duke University Press: 193–223.

Marinelli, Lawrence A. (1964). *The new Liberia; a historical and political survey*. New York, Africa Service Institute of New York and F. A. Praeger.

Marques, Rafael and Rui Falcão de Campos (2005). Lundas: as pedras da morte—relatório sobre os direitos humanos. Luanda. Retrieved from https://www.wilsoncenter.org/sites/default/files/LPMMarq.pdf

Marshall, McCarey (2006). Ex-Combatants Set Conditions To Leave Guthrie. August 16. *The Analyst*.

Marten, Kimberly Z. (2006). "Warlordism in comparative perspective." *International Security* 31(3).

Marten, Kimberly Zisk (2012). *Warlords: strong-arm brokers in weak states*. Ithaca, Cornell University Press.

Martin, Mike (2018). *Why We Fight*. London, Hurst and Co.

Martínez, Óscar (2016). Living Within the Boundaries of El Salvador's Gang "War." January 7. *Insight Crme*. Retrieved from https://www.insightcrime.org/news/an alysis/living-within-the-boundaries-of-el-salvador-gang-war/

Martínez, Oscar, Efren Lemus, Carlos Martínez, and Deborah Sontag (2016). Killers on a Shoestring: Inside the Gangs of El Salvador. November 16. *New York Times*.

Maryland County News. (2007). Cavalla Rubber Plantation in Maryland County Turns into an Elephant Meat. Dec 14. Retrieved June 26, 2008.

Matthews, Dylan (2013). The black/white marijuana arrest gap, in nine charts. June 4. *Washington Post*.

Maugham, R. C. F. (1920). *The republic of Liberia, being a general description of the negro republic, with its history, commerce, agriculture, flora, fauna, and present methods of administration*. London, G. Allen & Unwin Ltd.

Mayall, James and Ricardo Soares de Oliveira (2011). *The new protectorates: international tutelage and the making of liberal states*. New York, Columbia University Press.

McArdle, Megan (2014). Why writers are the worst procrastinators. February 12. *The Atlantic*. Retrieved from https://www.theatlantic.com/business/archive/2014/02/why-writers-are-the-worst-procrastinators/283773/

McCandless, Erin (2010). *Second Generation Disarmament, Demobilization, and Reintegration (DDR) Practices in Peace Operations*. New York, Disarmament, Demobilization and Reintegration Section of the Office of Rule of Law and Security Institutions.

McDoom, Omar Shahabudin (2014). "Antisocial Capital." *Journal of Conflict Resolution* 58(5): 865–93.

McFate, Sean (2013). *Building Better Armies: An Insider's Account of Liberia*. Carlisle, Pennsylvania, US, US Army War College Press.

McIntosh, Susan Keech (1999). *Beyond chiefdoms: pathways to complexity in Africa*. Cambridge, Cambridge University Press.

McKinney, G. B. and J. C. Inscoe (2014). *The Heart of Confederate Appalachia: Western North Carolina in the Civil War*, Carolina, University of North Carolina Press.

McMullin, Jaremey (2013). *Ex-Combatants and the Post-Conflict State*. Basingstoke, Palgrave Macmillan.

Meagher, K. (2007). "Hijacking civil society: the inside story of the Bakassi Boys vigilante group of south-eastern Nigeria." *Journal of Modern African Studies* 45(1): 89–115.

Meagher, K. (2010). *Identity Economics: Social Networks & the Informal Economy in Nigeria*. Oxford, James Currey.

Meagher, Kate (2012). "The strength of weak states? Non-state security forces and hybrid governance in Africa." *Development and Change* 43(5): 1074–101.

Meehan, Patrick (2011). "Drugs, insurgency and state-building in Burma: Why the drugs trade is central to Burma's changing political order." *Journal of Southeast Asian Studies* 42(03): 376–404.

Melander, Erik, Thérése Pettersson, and Lotta Themnér (2016). "Organized violence, 1989–2015." *Journal of Peace Research* 53(5).

Menkor, Ishmael F. (2006). As Armed Men Continue to Terrorize Farmers: Cocopa Rubber Closed. *The Daily Observer*. Monrovia.

Miklaucic, Michael and Jacqueline Brewer (2013). *Convergence: illicit networks and national security in the age of globalization*. Washington, DC, Center for Complex Operations, Institute for National Strategic Studies, National Defense University Press.

Miller, R. E. and P. R. Carter (1972). "Modern Dual Economy—Cost Benefit Analysis of Liberia." *Journal of Modern African Studies* 10(1): 113–21.

Milliken, Jennifer and Keith Krause (2002). "State Failure, State Collapse, and State Reconstruction: Concepts, Lessons and Strategies." *Development and Change* 33(5): 753–74.

Ministry of Lands Mines and Energy (2000). *Map of Gold and Diamond Areas*. M. *Ministry of Lands, and Energy*. Monrovia, Government of Liberia: Mineral Resources Development Portfolio.

Mitton, Kieran (2012). "Irrational Actors and the Process of Brutalisation: Understanding Atrocity in the Sierra Leonean Conflict." Civil Wars 14(1).

Mitton, Kieran (2015). *Rebels in a rotten state: understanding atrocity in the Sierra Leone Civil War*. London, Hurst and Co.

Mongrue, Jesse N. (2011). *Liberia: America's Footprint in Africa: Making the Cultural, Social, and Political Connections*. Bloomington, Indiana, iUniverse.

Moran, Mary (2006). *Liberia: The Violence of Democracy*. Pennsylvania, University of Pennsylvania Press.

Moyn, Samuel (2010). *The last utopia: human rights in history*. Cambridge, MA, Belknap Press of Harvard University Press.

Mueller, John E. (2003). "Policing the remnants of war." *Journal of Peace Research* 40(5): 507–18.

Mueller, John E. (2004). *The remnants of war*. Ithaca, Cornell University Press.

Muggah, Robert and Albert Souza Mulli (2012). "Rio Tries Counterinsurgency." *Current History* 111(742).

Mukhopadhyay, Dipali (2009). "Disguised warlordism and combatanthood in Balkh: the persistence of informal power in the formal Afghan state." *Conflict, Security & Development* 9(4).

Mukhopadhyay, Dipali (2014). *Warlords, strongman governors, and the state in Afghanistan*. Cambridge, Cambridge University Press.

Mullainathan, Sendhil and Eldar Shafir (2013). *Scarcity: Why Having Too Little Means So Much*. London, Allen Lane.

Munck, Gerardo L. and Richard Snyder (2007). *Passion, Craft, and Method in Comparative Politics*. Johns Hopkins University Press.

Munive, J. (2011). "A Political Economic History of the Liberian State, Forced Labour and Armed Mobilization." *Journal of Agrarian Change* 11(3): 357–76.

Murphy, Helen and Luis Jaime Acosta (2013). FARC controls 60 percent of drug trade - Colombia's police chief. April 22. *Reuters*.

Murray, Rebecca (2009). Wild West—the Sinoe Rubber Plantation. April 8. *Inter Press Service*. Retrieved from http://www.ipsnews.net/2009/04/liberia-wild-west-the-sinoe-rubber-plantation/

Murtazashvili, Jennifer Brick (2010). The microfoundations of state building: Informal institutions and local public goods in rural Afghanistan. Ph.D., University of Wisconsin-Madison.

Naím, M. (2012). "Mafia States." *Foreign Affairs* 91(3): 100–11.

Nathan, Laurie (2005). The frightful inadequacy of most of the statistics': a critique of Collier and Hoeffler on causes of civil war. Crisis States Research Centre Discussion Papers.

National Elections Commission (2005). 2005 Election Results. National Elections Commission. Monrovia, Liberia.

Naylor, R. T. (2001). *Economic warfare: sanctions, embargo busting, and their human cost.* Boston, Massachusetts, Northeastern University Press.

Neudorfer, Kelly (2015). *Sexual exploitation and abuse in UN peacekeeping: an analysis of risk and prevention factors.* Plymouth, UK, Lexington Books.

Nevin, Timothy D. (2011). "The Uncontrollable Force: A Brief History of the Liberian Frontier Force, 1908–1944." *The International Journal of African Historical Studies* 44(2): 275–97.

Newman, Edward and Oliver P. Richmond (2006). *Challenges to peacebuilding: managing spoilers during conflict resolution.* New York, United Nations University Press.

Nillesen, E. and E. Bulte (2014). "Natural Resources and Violent Conflict." *Annual Review of Resource Economics* 6: 69–83.

Nordstrom, Carolyn and Antonius Robben (1995). *Fieldwork under fire: contemporary studies of violence and survival.* Berkeley, University of California Press.

Nordstrom, Carolyn (2004). *Shadows of war: violence, power, and international profiteering in the twenty-first century.* Berkeley, University of California Press.

Nordstrom, Carolyn (2007). *Global outlaws: crime, money, and power in the contemporary world.* Berkeley, University of California Press.

North, Douglass C. and Robert P. Thomas (1973). *The rise of the Western world: a new economic history.* Cambridge, Cambridge University Press.

North, Douglass C., John Joseph Wallis, and Barry R. Weingast (2009). *Violence and social orders: a conceptual framework for interpreting recorded human history.* Cambridge, Cambridge University Press.

North, Douglass Cecil (1990). *Institutions, institutional change, and economic performance.* Cambridge, Cambridge University Press.

Nozick, Robert (1974). *Anarchy, state, and utopia.* New York, Basic Books.

Nunnally, Shayla (2012). *Trust in Black America.* New York University Press.

Nussio, Enzo and Ben Oppenheim (2014). "Anti-Social Capital in Former Members of Non-State Armed Groups: A Case Study of Colombia." *Studies in Conflict & Terrorism* 37(12): 999–1023.

Nyame, Frank K., J. Andrew Grant, and Natalia Yakovleva (2009). "Perspectives on migration patterns in Ghana's mining industry." *Resources Policy* 34(1–2): 6–11.

Obermeyer, Ziad, Christopher J. L. Murray, and Emmanuela Gakidou (2008). "Fifty years of violent war deaths from Vietnam to Bosnia: analysis of data from the world health survey programme." *BMJ* 336(7659): 1482–6.

O'Boyle, Maeve (2014). Firestone and the Warlord. November 18. *PBS Frontline.* Retrieved from https://www.pbs.org/wgbh/frontline/film/firestone-and-the-warlord/

OCR Compliance (2004). Denied Person Update. Regulatory Compliance Newsletter. O. J. 23. Washington, DC 0903–2004.

Odell, John S. (2000). *Case Study Methods in International Political Economy.* Los Angeles, CA, International Studies Association.

Olson, Mancur (1993). "Dictatorship, Democracy, and Development." *American Political Science Review* 87(03): 567–76.

Olson, Mancur (2000). *Power and prosperity: outgrowing communist and capitalist dictatorships*. New York, Basic Books.

Onishi, Norimitsu (2015). Empty Ebola Clinics in Liberia Are Seen as Misstep in U.S. Relief Effort. April 11. *New York Times*.

Open Science Collaboration (2015). "Estimating the reproducibility of psychological science." *Science* 349(6251).

Open Society Justice, Initiative (2013). *The Trial of Charles Taylor before the Special Court for Sierra Leone: the Appeal Judgment*. The Hague, Open Society Foundations.

Oppenheimer, Franz (1922). *The state: its history and development viewed sociologically, translated by John M. Gitterman*. New York, B.W. Huebsch.

Organisation for Economic Co-operation and Development (OECD) (2007). *Enhancing the Delivery of Justice and Security*. Paris, OECD.

Ospina, Sofi and Tanja Hohe (2001). *Traditional Power Structures and Local Governance in East Timor: A Case Study of the Community Empowerment Project (CEP). Etudes courtes*. Geneva, Graduate Institute of Development Studies.

Pachirat, Timothy (2015). "The Tyranny of Light." *Qualitative & Multi-Method Research* 13(1): 27–31.

Panel of Experts on Liberia (2001). *Report of the Panel of Experts: 17 October 2001*. New York, United Nations.

Panel of Experts on Liberia (2002). *Report of the Panel of Experts: 19 April 2002*. New York, United Nations.

Panel of Experts on Liberia (2004). *Report of the Panel of Experts: 17 May 2004*. New York, United Nations.

Panel of Experts on Liberia (2005a). *Report of the Panel of Experts: 7 June 2005*. New York, United Nations.

Panel of Experts on Liberia (2005b). *Report of the Panel of Experts: 25 November 2005*. New York, United Nations.

Panel of Experts on Liberia (2006). *Report of the Panel of Experts: 15 December 2006*. New York, United Nations.

Panel of Experts on Liberia (2007). *Report of the Panel of Experts: 24 May 2007*. New York, United Nations.

Panel of Experts on Liberia (2008a). *Report of the Panel of Experts: 12 June 2008*. New York, United Nations.

Panel of Experts on Liberia (2008b). *Report of the Panel of Experts: 30 November 2008*. New York, United Nations.

Panel of Experts on Sierra Leone (2000). *Report of the Panel of Experts: 19 December 2000*. New York, UN.

Paris, Roland (2004). *At War's End*. Cambridge, Cambridge University Press.

Paris, Roland (2010). "Saving liberal peacebuilding." *Review of International Studies* 36(2): 337–365.

Paris, Roland and Timothy D. Sisk (2009). *The dilemmas of statebuilding: confronting the contradictions of postwar peace operations*. London, Routledge.

Parkinson, Sarah Elizabeth and Elisabeth Jean Wood (2015). "Transparency in Intensive Research on Violence: Ethical Dilemmas and Unforeseen Consequences." *Qualitative & Multi-Method Research* 13(1): 22–26.

Patel, Seema, Steven Ross, Frederick Barton, and Karin von Hippel (2007). *Breaking Point- Measuring progress in Afghanistan. Post-Conflict Reconstruction Project.* Washington, DC, Center for Strategic and International Studies.

Patrick, Stewart (2010). Are "Ungoverned Spaces" a Threat? January 11. Washington, DC, Council on Foreign Relations.

Peace Building Resource Center (2005). *Rapid Conflict Assessment Report: Guthrie Rubber Plantation.* Monrovia, Peace Building Resource Center.

Peng, Roger (2011). "Reproducible Research in Computational Science." *Simply Statistics.* Retrieved from https://simplystatistics.org/2011/12/02/reproducible-research-in-computational-science/

Penglase, Ben (2009). "States of Insecurity: Everyday Emergencies, Public Secrets, and Drug Trafficker Power in a Brazilian Favela." *PoLAR: Political and Legal Anthropology Review* 32(1): 47–63.

Persson, Mariam (2012). "The logic of staying mobilised—Liberian ex-combatants and the 2011 elections." Retrieved from https://matsutas.wordpress.com/2012/09/10/the-logic-of-staying-mobilised-liberian-ex-combatants-and-the-2011-elections-guest-post-by-mariam-persson/

Pham, John-Peter (2004). *Liberia: Portrait of a Failed State.* New York, Reed Press.

Phillipson, D. W. (2012). *Foundations of an African civilisation: Aksum and the northern Horn, 1000 BC–AD 1300.* Woodbridge, James Currey.

Philp, Mark (2008). "Peacebuilding and Corruption." *International Peacekeeping* 15(3).

Piketty, Thomas (2013). *Capital in the twenty-first century.* Cambridge, Harvard University Press.

Pincus, Steven and James Robinson (2016). "Wars and State-Making Reconsidered— The Rise of the Developmental State." *Annales (English ed.)* 71(1): 9–34.

Podder, Sukanya (2013). "Bridging the 'Conceptual–Contextual' Divide: Security Sector Reform in Liberia and UNMIL Transition." *Journal of Intervention and Statebuilding* 7(3).

Political Science Journal Editors (2014). "Journal Editors' Transparency Statement (JETS)."

Ponzio, Richard (2011). *Democratic peacebuilding: aiding Afghanistan and other fragile states.* Oxford, Oxford University Press.

Portes, Alejandro (1998). "Social Capital: its origins and applications in modern sociology." *Annual Review of Sociology* 24: 1–24.

Posner, Daniel (2004). Civil Society and the Reconstruction of Failed States, in *When states fail: causes and consequences,* R. I. Rotberg, (ed). Princeton, Princeton University Press.

Powell, Robert and Mohamed Yahya (2006). *Survival Diamonds: The current state of diamond mining in West Africa and ideas for using diamonds as a tool for future development.* London, International Alert.

Prinsloo, Gerhard, Yury Spectorov, and Olya Linde. (2011). *Lifting the Veil of Mystery.* Bain & Company and Antwerp World Diamond Centre.

Public Agenda (2008). More Corruption Exposed . . . at Sinoe Rubber Plantation. March 28. *Public Agenda.* Monrovia.

Public Agenda. (2006). Cocopa- A Liberian Plantation Turning into Death Camp." December 9. *Public Agenda.* Monrovia.

Public Prosecutor (2006). *Guus van Kouwenhoven trial transcript: witness testimony. Public Prosecutor's Office number 09/750001–05.* The Hague, Government of The Netherlands.

Pugh, M. (2004). "Rubbing salt into war wounds - Shadow economies and peace-building in Bosnia and Kosovo." *Problems of Post-Communism* 51(3): 53–60.

Pugh, Michael and Boris Divjak (2011). The Political Economy of Corruption in Bosnia and Herzegovina, in *Corruption and Post-Conflict Peacebuilding,* C. Cheng and D. Zaum (eds). Abingdon, Routledge.

Pugh, Michael, Neil Cooper, and Jonathan Goodhand (2004). *War Economies in a Regional Context.* London, Lynne Rienner.

Putnam, Robert D., Robert Leonardi, and Rafaella Nanetti (1993). *Making democracy work: civic traditions in modern Italy.* Princeton, Princeton University Press.

Putzel, James (2010). *Do no harm: International Support for Statebuilding.* Development Assistance Committee (DAC) Fragile States Group, OECD.

Quinones, Sam (2009). "State of War." *Foreign Policy,* March/April. Retrieved from http://foreignpolicy.com/2009/09/30/state-of-war/

Radiolab, Alex Goldmark, and Manoush Zomorodi (2015). *Eye in the Sky.* New York, WNYC.

Rawls, John (1971). *A theory of justice.* Cambridge, Massachusetts, Harvard University Press.

Reeve, Richard and Jackson Speare (2012). "Human security in Liberia: Local perspectives on formal and informal security sectors." *Accord* 23: 40–3.

Reno, William (1995). *Corruption and state politics in Sierra Leone.* Cambridge, Cambridge University Press.

Reno, William (1995b). "Reinvention of an African Patrimonial State: Charles Taylor's Liberia." *Third World Quarterly* 16(1): 109–20.

Reno, William (1997). "War, markets, and the reconfiguration of West Africa's weak states." *Comparative Politics* 29(4).

Reno, William (1998). *Warlord Politics and African States.* Boulder, Colorado, Lynne Rienner.

Reno, William (2000). "Clandestine economies, violence and states in Africa." *Journal of International Affairs* 53(2): 433–59.

Reno, William (2008). "Anti-Corruption Efforts in Liberia: Are they aimed at the right targets?" *International Peacekeeping* 15(2).

Reno, William (2010). "Transforming West African Militia Networks for Postwar Recovery." *Comparative Social Research* 27: 127–49.

Ribot, Jesse C., Arun Agrawal, and Anne M. Larson (2015). "Recentralizing while decentralizing: How national governments reappropriate forest resources." *World Development* 34(11).

Richards, Paul (1996). *Fighting for the rain forest: war, youth & resources in Sierra Leone.* Oxford, James Currey.

Richards, Paul, Ed. (2004). *No Peace No War: Anthropology of Contemporary Armed Conflicts.* Athens, Ohio, Ohio University Press.

Richmond, Oliver P. (2010). *Palgrave advances in peacebuilding: critical developments and approaches.* Basingstoke, Palgrave Macmillan.

Richmond, Oliver P. and Audra Mitchell (2012). *Hybrid forms of peace: from everyday agency to post-liberalism.* Basingstoke, Palgrave Macmillan.

Riddell, James (1979). The Gbannah Ma (Mano) in Two Economies: dynamics of finite-labour economics, in *Essays on the economic anthropology of Liberia and Sierra Leone*, V. R. Dorjahn and B. L. Isaac (eds). Philadelphia, Institute for Liberian Studies.

Risse, T., Ed. (2011). *Governance Without a State? Policies and Politics in Areas of Limited Statehood*. New York, Columbia University Press.

Rivercess County Residents (2010). Focus Group with local residents of Rivercess County. October 15. River Cess, Liberia.

Robinson, James A., Daron Acemoglu, Simon Johnson. (2003). An African Success Story: Botswana, in *Search of Prosperity: Analytic Narratives on Economic Growth*, D. Rodrik (ed). Princeton, Princeton University Press: 80–119.

Rosner, R. and S. Poswell (2006). Posttraumatic growth after war, in *Handbook of posttraumatic growth: research and practice*, L. G. Calhoun and R. G. Tedeschi (eds). Mahwah, New Jersey, Lawrence Erlbaum Associates.

Ross, Michael L. (2004a). "How do natural resources influence civil war? Evidence from thirteen cases." *International Organization* 58(1): 35–67.

Ross, Michael L. (2004b). "What Do We Know About Natural Resources and Civil War?" *Journal of Peace Research* 41(3): 337–356.

Rossler, Andrew (2006). The Political Economy of the Resource Curse: A Literature Survey. IDS Working Paper. Brighton, Institute of Development Studies.

Rotberg, Robert I., Ed. (2004). *When states fail: causes and consequences*. Princeton, Princeton University Press.

Rousseau, Jean-Jacques (1762). *Du contrat social; ou Principes du droit politiques*. Amsterdam, Marc Michel Rey.

Rubber Plantations Task Force (2006). Final Report. Monrovia, Government of Liberia and UNMIL.

Rubber Sector Expert (2007). Interview with Liberian Civil Society Rubber Sector Expert. May 16. Monrovia, Liberia.

Rubin, Barnett R. (2002). *The Fragmentation of Afghanistan: State Formation and Collapse in the International System*. New Haven, Yale University Press.

Sabaratnam, Meera (2013). History Repeating? Colonial, socialist, and liberal state-building in Mozambique, in *Routledge Handbook of International Statebuilding*, D. Chandler and T. Sisk (eds). Abingdon, Routledge.

Sachs, Jeffrey D. and Andrew Warner (2001). "The curse of natural resources." *European Economic Review* 45(4–6): 827–38.

Sartori, G. (1970). "Concept Misformation in Comparative Politics." *American Political Science Review* 64(4): 1033–53.

Saul, John Ralston (1995). *The unconscious civilization*. Concord, Ont., House of Anansi Press.

Sawyer, A. (1992). *The Emergence of Autocracy in Liberia: Tragedy and Challenge*. California, Institute of Contemporary Studies Press.

Sawyer, A. (2004). "Violent conflicts and governance challenges in West Africa: the case of the Mano River basin area." *Journal of Modern African Studies* 42(3): 437–63.

Schade, E. (1995). *Report on experiences with regard to the United Nations peace-keeping forces in Mozambique*. Norway, Redd Barna.

Schelling, Thomas C. (1971). " What is the Business of Organized Crime?" *Journal of Public Law* 20(1): 71–84.

Schulhofer-Wohl, Jonah and Nicholas Sambanis (2010). *Disarmament, Demobilization, and Reintegration Programs: An Assessment.* B. Heldt, Folke Bernadotte Academy.

Schwidrowski, Arnim, Jiro Honda, et al. (2005). IMF Country Report—Liberia: Selected Issues and Statistical Appendix. IMF Country Report No. 05/167. IMF. Washington, DC, IMF: 58.

Science (2010). "How Many Have Died Due to Congo's Fighting? Scientists Battle Over How to Estimate War-Related Deaths." January 21. *Science.* Retrieved from https://www.sciencemag.org/news/2010/01/how-many-have-died-due-congos-fighting-scientists-battle-over-how-estimate-war-related

Scott, James C. (1985). *Weapons of the weak: everyday forms of peasant resistance.* New Haven, Yale University Press.

Scott, James C. (2009). *The art of not being governed: an anarchist history of upland Southeast Asia.* New Haven, Yale University Press.

Seay, Laura (2009). Authority at Twilight: Civil Society, Social Services, and the State in the Eastern Democratic Republic of Congo. Ph.D., University of Texas at Austin.

Sedra, Mark (2006). "Security sector reform in Afghanistan: The slide towards expediency." *International Peacekeeping* 13(1): 94–110.

Senior FDA Director (2005). Interview with Senior Director, Forest Development Authority. October 20. Monrovia, Liberia.

Sesay, M. A. (1996). "Politics and society in post-war Liberia." *Journal of Modern African Studies* 34(3): 395–420.

Seybolt, Taylor B., Jay D. Aronson, Baruch Fischhoff, Eds. (2013). *Counting civilian casualties: an introduction to recording and estimating nonmilitary deaths in conflict.* Oxford, Oxford University Press.

Shafer, D. Michael (1994). *Winners and losers: how sectors shape the developmental prospects of states.* Ithaca, Cornell University Press.

Shearman, P.L. (2009). An Assessment of Liberian Forest Area, Dynamics, FDA Concessions Plans, and their Relevance to Revenue Projections, Green Advocates.

Sheehan, Helena and Sheamus Sweeney (2009). "The Wire and the world: narrative and metanarrative." *Jump Cut* 51 (Spring).

Shewfelt, Steven D. (2009). Legacies of War: Social and Political Life after Wartime Trauma. Ph.D., Yale University.

Shih, Victor (2015). "Research in Authoritarian Regimes: Transparency Tradeoffs and Solutions." *Qualitative & Multi-Method Research* 13(1): 20–2.

Shiner, Cindy (1992). Report. January 9–22. *Africa News.*

Shonkoff, Jack P., Andrew S. Garner, The Committee on Psychosocial Aspects of Child and Family Health, Committee on Early Childhood, Adoption and Dependent Care, and Section on Developmental and Behavioral Pediatrics (2012). "The Lifelong Effects of Early Childhood Adversity and Toxic Stress." *Pediatrics* 129(1): 232–46.

Shortland, Anja (2012). *Treasure mapped: using satellite imagery to track the developmental effects of Somali Piracy.* London, Chatham House.

Siakor, Silas (2002). *Plunder: The Silent Destruction of Liberia's Rainforest.* Monrovia, Save My Future Foundation.

Skaperdas, S. (2002). "Warlord competition." *Journal of Peace Research* 39(4): 435–46.

Skarbek, David (2014). *The social order of the underworld: how prison gangs govern the American penal system.* Oxford, Oxford University Press.

Smilie, Ian, Lansana Gberie, and Ralph Hazelton (2000). *The Heart of the Matter: Sierra Lone, Diamonds and Human Security.* Ottawa, Partnership Africa Canada.

Smith, Daniel Jordan (2007). *A culture of corruption: everyday deception and popular discontent in Nigeria.* Princeton, Princeton University Press.

Smyth, Marie (2004). "The process of demilitarization and the reversibility of the peace process in Northern Ireland." *Terrorism and Political Violence* 16(3): 544–66.

Snyder, R. and R. Bhavnani (2005). "Diamonds, blood, and taxes: A revenue-centered framework for explaining political order." *Journal of Conflict Resolution* 49(4): 563–97.

Snyder, Richard (2001). "Scaling down: The subnational comparative method." *Studies in Comparative International Development* 36(1): 93–110.

Söderström, Johanna (2015). *Peacebuilding and Ex-Combatants: Political Reintegration in Liberia.* Abingdon, Routledge.

Söderström, Johanna (2013). "Second time around: Ex-combatants at the polls in Liberia." *The Journal of Modern African Studies* 51(3): 409–33.

Spears, Ian S. (2000). "Understanding inclusive peace agreements in Africa: The problems of sharing power." *Third World Quarterly* 21(1): 105–18.

Special Court of Sierra Leone (2009). Charles Taylor judgment. Special Court of Sierra Leone. Freetown.

Spectorov, Yury, Olya Linde, Wetli, Pierre-Laurent, Ari Epstein, and Stephane Fischler (2012). The Global Diamond Industry: Portrait of Growth, Bain & Company.

Spiegel, S. J. (2015). "Contested diamond certification: Reconfiguring global and national interests in Zimbabwe's Marange fields." *Geoforum* 59: 258–67.

Spruyt, Hendrik (2005). *Ending empire: contested sovereignty and territorial partition.* Ithaca, NY, Cornell University Press.

Spruyt, Hendrik (2011). War, Trade, and State Formation, in *The Oxford handbook of political science.* R. E. Goodin (ed). Oxford, Oxford University Press.

Staniland, Paul (2012). "States, Insurgents, and Wartime Political Orders." *Perspectives on Politics* 10(2): 243–64.

Stanski, K. (2009). "'So These Folks are Aggressive': An Orientalist Reading of 'Afghan Warlords'." *Security Dialogue* 40(1): 73–94.

Statista (2017a). Diamond jewelry market value worldwide from 2013 to 2015.

Statista (2017b). Global diamond jewelry retail sales and value of diamond content from 2005 to 2013.

Stedman, Stephen J. (1997). "Spoiler problems in peace processes." *International Security* 22(2): 5–53.

Stedman, Stephen J., Donald S. Rothchild, and Elizabeth M. Cousens (2002). *Ending civil wars: the implementation of peace agreements.* Boulder, Colorado, Lynne Rienner.

Steenkamp, Chrissie (2005). "The Legacy of War: Conceptualizing a 'Culture of Violence' to Explain Violence after Peace Accords." *The Round Table* 94(379): 253–67.

Steenkamp, Christina (2009). *Violence and post-war reconstruction: managing insecurity in the aftermath of peace accords.* London, I.B. Tauris.

Steinberg, Jonny (2005). *The number: one man's search for identity in the Cape underworld and prison gangs.* Johannesburg, Jonathan Ball Publishers.

Strayer, Joseph R. (1965). *Feudalism*. Princeton, Van Nostrand.

Strazzari, Francesco (2003). Between ethnic collision and mafia collusion: The "Balkan route" to state-making, in *Shadow globalization, ethnic conflicts and new wars: a political economy of intra-state war*, D. Jung (ed). London, Routledge.

Sugden, Robert (1989). "Spontaneous Order." *Journal of Economic Perspectives* 3(4): 85–97.

Sumner, William G. (1906). *Folkways: A Study of Mores, Manners, Customs and Morals*. Boston, Ginn.

Sundiata, I. K. (1974). "Prelude to Scandal—Liberia and Fernando Po, 1880–1930." *Journal of African History* 15(1): 97–112.

Sundiata, I. K. (1996). *From slaving to neoslavery: the bight of Biafra and Fernando Po in the era of abolition, 1827–1930*. Madison, WI, University of Wisconsin Press.

Tajfel, Henri (1981). *Human groups and social categories: studies in social psychology*. Cambridge, Cambridge University Press.

Tansey, Oisín (2009). *Regime-building: democratization and international administration*. Oxford, Oxford University Press.

Taylor, Brian D. and Roxana Botea (2015). "Tilly Tally: War-Making and State-Making in the Contemporary Third World." *International Studies Review* 10(1): 27–56.

Taylor, Charles (2009a). SCSL Testimony: Charles Taylor on July 21, 2009 Special Court of Sierra Leone. The Hague. http://www.rscsl.org/Documents/Transcripts/Taylor/21July2009.pdf

Taylor, Charles (2009b). SCSL Testimony: Firestone on July 16, 2009. Special Court of Sierra Leone. The Hague. http://www.rscsl.org/Documents/Transcripts/Taylor/16July2009.pdf

The Analyst (2005). Stop the Imminent Rubber War. *The Analyst*, February 22, Monrovia.

The Analyst (2006a). Rubber War Ends Soon. *The Analyst*, May 22. Monrovia.

The Analyst (2006b). UNMIL Lapsing Security! *The Analyst*, June 26. Monrovia.

The Analyst (2006c). UNMIL, Gov't Takes Guthrie Today. *The Analyst*, August 15. Monrovia.

The Analyst (2008). Theft or Misapplication, Sinoe Superintendent on Hook. *The Analyst*, October 30. Monrovia.

The Hague Justice Portal (2010). Dutch Supreme Court quashes Court of Appeal decision in Guus K. case.

The Patriot (1991). Monrovia, National Patriotic Front of Liberia. May–June.

Themnér, Anders (2012). Intermediaries of peace or agents of war: the role of ex-midlevel commanders in Big Man networks, in *African Conflicts and Informal Power: Big Men and Networks*, M. Utas (ed). London, Zed Books.

Themnér, Anders (2014). *Violence in Post-Conflict Societies: Remarginalization, Remobilizers and Relationships*. London, Routledge.

Themnér, Anders (2015). "Former Military Networks and the Micro-Politics of Violence and Statebuilding in Liberia." *Comparative Politics* 47(3): 334–53.

Thies, Cameron G. (2007). "The Political Economy of State Building in Sub-Saharan Africa." *Journal of Politics* 69(3): 716–31.

Thiessen, Chuck (2013). *Local ownership of peacebuilding in Afghanistan: shouldering responsibility for sustainable peace and development*. Plymouth, UK, Lexington Books.

Tilly, Charles (1975). *The Formation of National States in Western Europe*. Princeton, Princeton University Press.

Tilly, Charles (1985). War Making and State Making as Organized Crime, in *Bringing the State Back In*, P. Evans, D. Rueschemeyer and T. Skocpol (eds). Cambridge, Cambridge University Press: 169–191.

Tilly, Charles (1992). *Coercion, capital, and European states, AD 990–1992*. Oxford, Blackwell.

Toft, Monica Duffy (2010a). "Ending Civil Wars: A Case for Rebel Victory?" *International Security* 34(4): 7–36.

Toft, Monica Duffy (2010b). *Securing the peace: the durable settlement of civil wars.* Princeton, Princeton University Press.

Torjesen, Stina (2013). "Towards a theory of ex-combatant reintegration." *Stability: International Journal of Security and Development* 2(3). doi.org/10.5334/sta.cx.

Traunmüller, Richard, David Born, and Markus Freitag (2015). "How Civil War Experience Affects Dimensions of Social Trust in a Cross-National Comparison." Available at SSRN: https://ssrn.com/abstract=2545816.

Trigger, Bruce G. (2003). *Understanding Early Civilizations: A Comparative Study.* Cambridge, Cambridge University Press.

Trut, Lyudmila (1999). "Early Canid Domestication- The Farm-Fox Experiment." *American Scientist* 87(2): 160–9.

Truth and Reconciliation Commission of Liberia (2008a). TRC Public Hearings: Testimony of James Kabah. Truth and Reconciliation Commission of Liberia. Monrovia, Liberia.

Truth and Reconciliation Commission of Liberia (2008b). TRC Public Hearings: Testimony of Mannah Massalay. Truth and Reconciliation Commission of Liberia. Monrovia, Liberia.

Truth and Reconciliation Commission of Liberia (2009). Final Report. Monrovia, Truth and Reconciliation Commission II.

Tull, Denis M. and Andreas Mehler (2005). "The hidden costs of power-sharing: Reproducing insurgent violence in Africa." *African Affairs* 104(416): 375–98.

Tusalem, R. F. and M. K. C. Morrison (2014). "The impact of diamonds on economic growth, adverse regime change, and democratic state-building in Africa." *International Political Science Review* 35(2): 153–72.

Tversky, Amos and Daniel Kahneman (1973). "Availability: A heuristic for judging frequency and probability." *Cognitive Psychology* 5(2): 207–32.

Tversky, Amos and Daniel Kahneman (1991). "Loss Aversion in Riskless Choice: A Reference-Dependent Model." *The Quarterly Journal of Economics* 106(4): 1039–61.

Tversky, Amos and Daniel Kahneman (1974). "Judgment under Uncertainty: Heuristics and Biases." *Science* 185(4157): 1124–31.

Twaddell, William (1996). Hearing on Liberia. House International Relations Committee. Washington, DC.

Twadell, William (1996). Bloody Hands: Foreign Support for Liberian Warlords. Committee on International Relations: Subcommittee on Africa. Washington, DC.

U.S. Agency for International Development (2003). Liberia: Complex Emergency, Situation Report #5, August 8, 2003. Centre Bureau for Democracy, and Humanitarian Assistance (DCHA) and Office of U.S. Foreign Disaster Assistance (OFDA). Washington, DC.

UK Stabilisation Unit (2014). The UK Government's Approach to Stabilisation. Ministry of Defence, Foreign and Commonwealth Office, and Department for International Development. London, UK Government.

UN Dag Hammarskjöld Library (2017). DAG Repository. New York, United Nations.

UN DDR Resource Centre. (2008). "Liberia." United Nations Inter-Agency Working Group on Disarmament, Demobilization, and Reintegration. Retrieved June 19, 2008, from http://www.unddr.org/countryprogrammes.php?c=5

UN Humanitarian Information Centre for Liberia (2005). *Counties of Preferred Resettlement for Ex-combatants: September 2005.* Monrovia, UN HIC.

UN Joint Mission Analysis Cell (2005a). UN JMAC Daily Sitrep: 21 Dec 2005. Monrovia.

UN Joint Mission Analysis Cell (2005b). UN JMAC Weekly Information Summary 9–16 July 2005, UNMIL.

UN Joint Mission Analysis Cell (2005c). UN JMAC Weekly Information Summary 9–16 Sept 2005. Freetown.

UN Joint Mission Analysis Cell (2005d). UN JMAC Weekly Information Summary 16–23 July 2005. Freetown.

UN Joint Mission Analysis Cell (2005e). UN JMAC Weekly Information Summary 23–30 July 2005. Freetown.

UN Joint Mission Analysis Cell (2005f). UN JMAC Weekly Information Summary 25 Jun–2 Jul 2005. Freetown.

UN Joint Mission Analysis Cell (2005g). UN JMAC Weekly Information Summary 26 August–2 Sept 2005. Freetown.

UN Joint Mission Analysis Cell (2005h). UN JMAC Weekly Information Summary 31 July – 6 Aug 2005. Freetown.

UN Joint Mission Analysis Cell (2005i). Weekly Security Report: 16–22 January 2005. Monrovia, UNMIL.

UN Joint Mission Analysis Cell (2005j). Weekly Security Report: 16–23 July 2005. Monrovia, UNMIL.

UN Joint Mission Analysis Cell (2005k). Weekly Security Report: 5–12 February 2005. Monrovia, UNMIL.

UN Joint Mission Analysis Cell (2005m). Weekly Assessment 9–16 September. Monrovia, UN.

UN Mediation Support Unit (2015). UN Peacemaker Database. UN Department of Political Affairs. New York.

UN Panel of Experts on Liberia (2001). *Report of the Panel of Experts: 17 October 2001.* New York, United Nations.

UN Panel of Experts on Liberia (2006). *Report of the Panel of Experts on Liberia submitted pursuant to resolution 1689 (2006).* New York, United Nations.

UN Security Council (2001a). *Report of the Secretary-General in pursuance of paragraph 13 (a) of resolution 1343 (2001) concerning Liberia. 5 October*, New York, UN Security Council.

UN Security Council (2001b). UN Security Council Resolution 1343. March 7, New York, UN Security Council.

UN Security Council (2003a). UN Security Council Resolution 1509. September 19, New York, UN Security Council.

UN Security Council (2003b). UN Security Council Resolution 1521. December 22, New York, UN Security Council.

UN Security Council (2004). Security Council Committee on Liberia Updates Travel Ban List. October 6, New York, United Nations.

UNDP (2005). West and Central Africa Newsletter. Vol. 2, No. 3. July 25, Dakar, UNDP Sub-Regional Resource Facility for West and Central Africa.

UNDP Liberia (2005). *Diamonds for Development Programme Framework*. Monrovia, UNDP Liberia.

UNHCR and Save the Children UK (2002). Sexual Violence and Exploitation: The Experience of Refugee Children in Guinea, Liberia and Sierra Leone.

UN High Commission for Refugees (2004). *2002 UNHCR Statistical Yearbook Country Data Sheet: Liberia*. Geneva, UNHCR.

UN High Commission for Refugees (2007). *2005 UNHCR Statistical Yearbook Country Data Sheet: Liberia*. Geneva, UNHCR.

UNHCR (2015). "An Introduction to Statelessness." Geneva, UNHCR. Retrieved from http://www.unhcr.org/stateless-people.html

UNMIL (2005a). *Report on the Occupation of the Guthrie Rubber Plantation. June 22.* Monrovia, UNMIL.

UNMIL (2005b). *Sinoe Rubber Plantation. May*, Greenville, Liberia, UNMIL.

UNMIL (2005c). *UNMIL Briefing Notes. August 16 2005*. Monrovia, UNMIL.

UNMIL (2005d). *UNMIL Briefing Notes. July 15 2005*. Monrovia, UNMIL.

UNMIL (2005e). *UNMIL Briefing Notes. July 18 2005*. Monrovia, UNMIL.

UNMIL (2005f). *UNMIL Briefing Notes. September 27 2005*. Monrovia, UNMIL.

UNMIL and World Health Organization (2005). InterAgency Assessment re: Cholera in BOPC Aug 12–17, 2005. Sinoe County.

UNMIL Civil Affairs (2005a). Analysis of SRP MOU Process. April 17, UNMIL.

UNMIL Civil Affairs (2005b). UNMIL meeting with Wedjah District Citizens at the Sinoe Rubber Plantation. July 11, Greenville, UNMIL.

UNMIL Civil Affairs (2005c). Sinoe Rubber Plantation Strategizing. May 11, Greenville, UNMIL Civil Affairs, Sinoe County.

UNMIL Civil Affairs (2005d). SRP Conflict Resolution Paper. July 6, Greenville, UNMIL Civil Affairs, Sinoe County.

UNMIL Civil Affairs (2005e). Profile of River Cess County. July 20, River Cess County, Liberia, UNMIL.

UNMIL Civil Affairs Officer (2007). Interview with UNMIL Civil Affairs Officer, with former responsibilities for Maryland County. November 12. Monrovia, Liberia.

UNMIL Civil Affairs Officer for Grand Bassa County (2005). Interview with UNMIL Civil Affairs Officer for Grand Bassa County, September 29. Buchanan, Liberia.

UNMIL Civil Affairs Officer for Sinoe County (2005). Interviews with UNMIL Civil Affairs Officer for Sinoe County. November 7–14. Greenville, Liberia.

UNMIL Civil Affairs Officer, Ministry Liaison (2005). Interview with UNMIL Civil Affairs Officer, Ministry Liaison. October 10, 2005. Monrovia, Liberia.

UNMIL Human Rights (2006). Human Rights in Liberia's Rubber Plantations: Tapping into the Future. Monrovia, UNMIL.

UNMIL Human Rights Officer (2005). Interviews with UNMIL Human Rights Officer for Sinoe County. November 7–14. Greenville.

UNMIL Regional Officer (2005). Interview with UNMIL Regional Officer. September 23. Zwedru, Liberia.

UNMIL Security Officer for Sinoe County (2005). Interviews with UNMIL Security Officer, November 7–14. Greenville, Liberia.

U.S. Agency for International Development (1997). USAID Congressional Presentation FY 1997. Washington, DC.

U.S. Agency for International Development (2003). Liberia: Complex Emergency Situation Report #5, August 8, 2003. Conflict, and Humanitarian Assistance (DCHA) and Office of U.S. Foreign Disaster Assistance (OFDA). Washington, DC.

U.S. Department of State (2009). Liberia: Rubber Sector Overview. US Department of State. Liberia, Monrovia.

U.S. Department of State. (2006). "Background Note: Liberia." Retrieved Jul 14, 2006, 2006. Washington, DC. Retrieved from https://2001-2009.state.gov/r/pa/ei/bgn/6618.htm

U.S. Department of State (2009). Background Note: Liberia. Bureau of African Affairs. Washington, DC.

Uslaner, E. M. (2008). "Where You Stand Depends Upon Where Your Grandparents Sat." *Public Opinion Quarterly* 72(4): 725–40.

Utas, Mats (2013). "Generals for good? Do-good generals and the structural endurance of wartime networks." Retrieved from https://matsutas.wordpress.com/2013/05/29/generals-for-good-do-good-generals-and-the-structural-endurance-of-wartime-networks/

Utas, Mats, Anders Themnér and Emy Lindberg (2014). "Commanders for good and bad: alternative post-war reconstruction and ex-commanders in Liberia." Nordic Africa Institute Policy Note. http://www.diva-portal.org/smash/get/diva2:762411/FULLTEXT01.pdf

Utas, Mats, Ed. (2012). *African conflicts and informal power: Big men and networks.* London, Zed Books.

van den Heuvel, Aad (1998). President in Africa. Interview with Charles Taylor. July 29. Nederland 1 TV.

van der Kraaij, Fred P.M. (1983). The Open Door Policy of Liberia: An Economic History of Modern Liberia. Ph.D., Tilburg University.

van der Kraaij, Fred P.M. (2017). "Convicted war criminal Guus Kouwenhoven on the run!" May 7, *Liberian Perspectives.*

Varese, Federico (2001). *The Russian Mafia: private protection in a new market economy.* Oxford, Oxford University Press.

Venkatesh, Sudhir Alladi (2008). *Gang leader for a day: a rogue sociologist takes to the streets.* New York, Penguin Press.

Vinci, Anthony (2005). "The Strategic Use of Fear by the Lord's Resistance Army." *Small Wars & Insurgencies* 16(3): 360–81.

Vinjamuri, Leslie and Jack Snyder (2004). "Advocacy and scholarship in the study of international war crime tribunals and transitional justice." *Annual Review of Political Science* 7(1): 345–62.

Vogt, Heidi (2007). Rubber production illustrates challenges in Liberia. March 21, *Associated Press.*

Volkov, Vadim (2002). *Violent entrepreneurs: the use of force in the making of Russian capitalism.* Ithaca, Cornell University Press.

von Billerbeck, Sarah (2015). "Local Ownership and UN Peacebuilding: Discourse Versus Operationalization." *Global Governance: A Review of Multilateralism and International Organizations* 21(2): 299–315.

von Billerbeck, Sarah (2017). *Whose peace? Local ownership and UN peacekeeping.* Oxford, Oxford University Press.

von Lampe, Klaus. (2017). "Organized Crime Research." www.organized-crime.de

Wainwright, Tom (2016). *Narconomics: how to run a drug cartel.* London, Ebury Press.

Waltz, Kenneth N. (1979). *Theory of international politics.* Boston, McGraw-Hill.

Wantchekon, Leonard (2004). "The Paradox of 'Warlord' Democracy: A Theoretical Investigation." *American Political Science Review* 98(1): 17–34.

Waugh, Colin M. (2011). *Charles Taylor and Liberia.* London, Zed Books.

Weber, Max (1919). *Politics as a vocation.* Free Students Union of Bavaria, Munich.

Webersik, Christian (2005). Reinterpreting environmental scarcity and conflict: evidence from Somalia. D.Phil., University of Oxford.

Weinstein, Jeremy M. (2007). *Inside rebellion: the politics of insurgent violence.* Cambridge, Cambridge University Press.

Wenar, Leif (2008). "Property Rights and the Resource Curse." *Philosophy & Public Affairs* 36(1): 2–32.

Wenar, Leif (2016). *Blood oil: tyrants, violence, and the rules that run the world.* Oxford, Oxford University Press.

Wesseh, Emannuel S. (2008). Institutional/Thematic Hearings. Truth and Reconciliation Commission of Liberia. Greenville City, Sinoe County.

Whalan, Jeni (2010). "The power of friends: The Regional Assistance Mission to Solomon Islands." *Journal of Peace Research* 47(5): 627–37.

Whitwer, Tod (2009). "An interesting Liberian." January 4, *Spirit Liberia.* Retrieved from https://spiritliberia.blogspot.co.uk/2009/01/interesting-liberian.html

Wildavsky, Aaron (1994). "Why Self-Interest Means Less Outside of a Social Context: Cultural Contributions to a Theory of Rational Choices." *Journal of Theoretical Politics* 6(2): 131–59.

Williams, Phil (1994). "Transnational criminal organisations and international security." *Survival* 36(1): 96–113.

Willie, Horatio Bobby (2010). Sime Darby speaks out…dismisses report that it is employing more foreigners Monrovia. Star Radio.

Wilson, S. A. (2013). "Company-Community Conflicts Over Diamond Resources in Kono District, Sierra Leone." *Society & Natural Resources* 26(3): 254–69.

Wood, Elisabeth J. (2006). "The Ethical Challenges of Field Research in Conflict Zones." *Qualitative Sociology* 29(3): 373–86.

Woodrow Wilson Center (2006). Liberia in Transition: A Discussion With the UN Panel on Liberia. Washington, DC.

Woodward, Susan L. (2017). *The Ideology of Failed States: Why Intervention Fails.* Cambridge, Cambridge University Press.

World Bank (2011). World Development Report: Conflict, Security, and Development. Washington, DC, World Bank.

World Bank (2017). World Bank Commodity Price Data (The Pink Sheet). World Bank. Washington, DC.

World Federation of Diamond Bourses (2017). "Bourse Listing." www.wfdb.com/wfdb-bourses

World Food Programme (2006). "World Food Programme Emergency Report. Report No. 11 / 2006–Date 17 March 2006." Rome, UN World Food Programme.

World Health Organization (2016). Ebola Situation Reports: 30 March 2016. Geneva, World Health Organization. Retrieved from http://apps.who.int/ebola/current-situation/ebola-situation-report-30-march-2016

World Justice Project (2015). *WJP Rule of Law Index*. Washington, World Justice Project.

Yahya, Mohamed (2007). Interviews with Mohamed Yahya. April 24, 2007 and May 9, 2007. Monrovia, Liberia.

Yawanarajah, Nita (2014). The Comparative Advantage of Regional Organisations and the UN in Conflict Prevention and Peacemaking. Seminar, November 11, King's College London.

Yoder, John C. (2003). *Popular political culture, civil society, and state crisis in Liberia*. Lewiston, New York, Edward Mellen Press.

Yoffee, Norman (2005). *Myths of the Archaic State: Evolution of the Earliest Cities, States and Civilizations*. Cambridge, Cambridge University Press.

Young, Helen and Lisa Goldman, Eds. (2015). *Livelihoods, Natural Resources, and Post-Conflict Peacebuilding. Post-Conflict Peacebuilding and Natural Resource Management*. Abingdon, Routledge.

Zack-Williams, Alfred (1995). *Tributors, supporters, and merchant capital: mining and underdevelopment in Sierra Leone*. Aldershot, U.K., Avebury.

Zartman, I. William (1995). *Collapsed states: the disintegration and restoration of legitimate authority*. Boulder, Colorado, Lynne Rienner.

Zaum, D. (2012). "Beyond the 'Liberal Peace'." *Global Governance: A Review of Multilateralism and International Organizations* 18(1): 121–32.

Zaum, Dominik (2007). *The sovereignty paradox: the norms and politics of international statebuilding*. Oxford, Oxford University Press.

Zukerman-Daly, Sarah (2009). *Bankruptcy, Guns or Campaigns: Explaining Armed Organizations' Post-War Trajectories*. Centre for International Security and Co-operation, Stanford University.

Index